W9-BNF-149

Fruit of an Impulse

FORTY-FIVE YEARS
OF THE CARNEGIE FOUNDATION
1905-1950

Howard J. Savage

BRIAR CLIFF COLLEGE
LIBRARY
SIOUX CITY, IOWA

NEW YORK · HARCOURT, BRACE AND COMPANY

COPYRIGHT, 1953, BY
HARCOURT, BRACE AND COMPANY, INC.

*All rights reserved, including
the right to reproduce this book
or portions thereof in any form.*

first edition

Permission to quote granted by owners of copyrights is gratefully acknowledged as follows: Appleton-Century-Crofts, Inc., from Wilson Gee, *Research Barriers in the South,* 1932; Harvard University Press, from D. B. Updike, *Notes on the Merrymount Press and Its Work,* 1934; Robert M. Lester for Carnegie Corporation of New York, present holder of the copyrights on B. J. Hendrick, *Life of Andrew Carnegie,* two volumes, Doubleday, Doran, 1932, and on Robert M. Lester, *Forty Years of Carnegie Giving,* Charles Scribner's Sons, 1941.

Material on Mr. Carnegie's sailing, April 1905, and his "latest benefaction" is used by kind permission of the New York *Herald Tribune,* and of the *New York Times* in so far as it originated with that newspaper.

LC
243
.C35
S3

LIBRARY OF CONGRESS CATALOG CARD NUMBER: 53-5657

PRINTED IN THE UNITED STATES OF AMERICA

An institution is the lengthened shadow of one man.

—EMERSON, "Self Reliance"

Preface

"NEVER forget," said Dr. George Hutcheson Denny when he heard that the present work was to be undertaken, "that the Carnegie Foundation is an American institution. It could have come into being only in America."

The activating suggestion that the history of the Carnegie Foundation for the Advancement of Teaching should be written as a record of experience and possibly as a sort of guidebook for one area of American philanthropy was broached by President Carmichael in the spring of 1948. Laid before the Foundation's Executive Committee and Board of Trustees, it found favor, and ways and means for the task were at once authorized.

Throughout the work I have had not only the friendly and sympathetic encouragement of the Foundation's officers, but—at least equally important—full access to all records and data of every description. The Foundation's tradition of finding a man for the job and then according him full co-operation and every facility has never been better exemplified. The only concern has been that the truth be told. For the conclusions and inferences set forth in these pages, the author is alone responsible.

One of the pleasures of the work has flowed from the help freely accorded when I have asked for it. For this aid and much comfort I thank Mr. Peter C. Devine, landing agent, Cunard Steamship Co., Ltd., who furnished facts for Chapter 1; Mrs. Eva McAllister Pritchett, whose keen memory and "Log Book" yielded much more of interest than could be used; Miss Edythe W. Maslen, who as

25208

computer and assistant had a part in most of the events these pages sketch, made preliminary soundings in the material, and verified many data; Dr. Ben D. Wood and certain officials of the International Business Machines Corporation, whose assistance with Chapter 13 was most welcome; officials of the Manuscripts Division of the Library of Congress; and Mr. C. Herbert Lee, treasurer of Carnegie Corporation of New York and latterly of the Carnegie Foundation, whose preliminary suggestions, reading of typescript, and pertinent comments concerning Chapter 14 were invaluable.

 Miss Dorothy A. Maddox, my co-worker for many years, I thank especially for her diligence, loyalty, and criticism, to which every page of this volume testifies.

HOWARD J. SAVAGE

June 30, 1951

Contents

PART ONE: 1905-1918

1. Fons et Origo   3
2. Backgrounds   23
3. "For the Advancement of Teaching"   41
4. Friends and Others   71
5. Upholding the Cause   98

PART TWO: 1918-1930

6. Relationships   123
7. Apogee   143
8. Gathering Clouds   167

PART THREE: 1930-1945

9. Another Day   193
10. Harvest   212
11. Workaday Decade   236

PART FOUR: 1945-1950

12. Giving Place to New   263

13. Experiment in Graduate Testing   283

14. Notes on Investment and Finance   305

15. Of Men and Measures   326

16. Impulse and Fruits   344

APPENDIXES   361

INDEX   399

Part One ~ 1905-1918

~ 1 ~

Fons et Origo

ANTECEDENTS · A HASTY STEP · FINDING THE MEN · BREAKING THE NEWS · HOW THE NEWS WAS TAKEN · LETTER OF GIFT—FIRST DRAFT; SECOND THOUGHTS; THIRD DRAFT · TWENTY QUESTIONS · A DOZEN NAMES · EASTER WEEK, 1905

ON WEDNESDAY, April 26, 1905, the steamship *Baltic*, 20,000 tons, Commander E. J. Smith, R.N.R., sailed from Pier 48, North River, for Liverpool. At that time she was the largest ship of the White Star fleet on any sea and, having made her maiden voyage about nine months previously, she was new, comfortable, and steady, a craft to be favored by knowledgeable travelers.

For this crossing her first-class passenger list of 371 persons included many names which have survived the erosion of the years: E. J. DeCoppet, banker; Mr. and Mrs. Julian Gerard; Colonel George Harvey; Lord Hedley, who had landed a six-foot tarpon off the coast of Texas after a two-hour struggle; the Viscountess Maitland; J. P. Morgan, Jr., and his family, on one of his annual European jaunts. Mr. and Mrs. Andrew Carnegie and their eight-year-old daughter, Margaret, occupied a suite beginning with Stateroom 82. They were en route to Skibo Castle, Dornoch, Scotland, for their usual summer sojourn.

The day they sailed was sunny and clear. On deck before departure the ship news reporters soon found Mr. Carnegie, who was almost always good copy and was seldom averse to helping out newspapermen. A group of them surrounded him. One wanted to know about his plans for the summer. Mr. Carnegie replied that he was to address the St. Andrew's Society of Edinburgh in October and asked the reporters to choose a subject for him. Before

3

any could reply he went on, "I might speak about life insurance." With a twinkle he added, "That is a very interesting subject at this time"—an allusion to the current internal difficulties of one of the great life insurance companies. Then more seriously, "I think every young man should get his life insured." The reporter reverted to the newspaper statement by Mrs. Carnegie on April 16, giving reasons why she and her husband would not contribute to the Japanese Red Cross and setting forth their belief in going to war only for the holiest cause. What would Mr. Carnegie consider a holy cause for war? "Well," Mr. Carnegie replied, "if a man hits you, why, hit him back. If your country is invaded, why, fight the invader."

A reporter asked him to say something about tainted money. Mr. Carnegie laughed: "I'm hardly in a position to discuss the subject." "But," someone interrupted, "you did not get your money in a tainted way."

"No, I didn't, and I never give money where I think it will not be accepted. I believe that money given in any good cause will do good and bring about good results, even though the source may be considered 'tainted' by some. Besides, I don't contemplate giving any money out at this time."

The interview closed with all participants seemingly in good spirits. A day later a writer in the *Times* recalled that when Mr. Carnegie sailed he seemed "so lively and talkative that he was almost suspected of having something to conceal." This was a shrewd speculation; on the following day, April 27, a formal statement for release on April 28 disclosed that for several months Mr. Carnegie had been occupied with a project to give the then princely sum of ten million dollars for pensioning college teachers. Mr. Carnegie had not wished to announce his gift until he was well on his way to Scotland. Hence the statement to the reporters that he did not "contemplate giving any money out at this time" was the literal truth; the ten million had already been "given out." His carefully planned announcement succeeded perfectly. Small wonder that Mr. Carnegie enjoyed his interview.

The city Mr. Carnegie was leaving was in its eighth year as Greater New York; the population of its five boroughs numbered about four million. It—and the country at large—was getting somewhat accustomed to Mr. Carnegie's surprise gifts; he had already endowed the Carnegie Institute, of Pittsburgh, 1896; his

Trust for the Universities of Scotland, 1901; the Carnegie Institution of Washington, 1902; and the Carnegie Hero Fund Commission, 1904. At the moment, the nation was mourning the death of Joseph Jefferson, and the Players planned to hold a service in his memory at "The Little Church Around the Corner." President Theodore Roosevelt was successfully bear-hunting in Colorado. Cigarettes had just been prohibited in Indiana. J. P. Morgan, Sr., had a new granddaughter. H. C. Frick, in the midst of his activities as head of an insurance company commission (the forerunner of the Armstrong inquiry), was remodeling the Vanderbilt mansion at Fifty-first Street and Fifth Avenue preparatory to an early autumn move. The week before, William Winter, dean of the dramatic critics, had contributed to the *Tribune* a poem on "The Passing Bell at Stratford" as a memorial to the Bard. Miss Marie Tempest had just arrived with her company to play "The 'Freedom' of Suzanne."

There was other news aplenty, local, national, and international. George Gould was resigning from the directorship of the Union Pacific Railroad to facilitate construction of the Western Pacific from Great Salt Lake to the coast. The crusade against the destruction of the aigrette was making excellent progress at Albany. Dr. D. K. Pearsons was giving $135,000 to five southern colleges. Paderewski was ill in London, but John Hay, Secretary of State, was improved in health at Bad Nauheim. Senator Orville H. Platt had just died at Washington, Connecticut. France and Germany were engaged in direct negotiation of the Morocco dispute. The Japanese felt confident of victory over the Russians. The whereabouts of Admiral Togo and his fleet was unknown. St. Petersburg was not a comfortable place to be because of peasant disorders and threats of disorders there and in other Russian capitals. Dean Wickliffe Rose announced that the Peabody Education Fund was giving a million dollars to Peabody College, Nashville, to assure the establishment of the Teachers College in that city. The outlook for the 1905 baseball season was unusually good. And ten million dollars was still a gigantic sum.

ANTECEDENTS

Mr. Carnegie had founded the Carnegie Institution of Washington, a District of Columbia corporation, with a ten-million-dollar endowment in 1902. Daniel Coit Gilman, formerly of The Johns

Hopkins University, was its president. Certain details of the act of incorporation soon required adjustment, and accordingly Congress passed, April 28, 1904, a second act. Evidently it was drawn or most of its essential provisions devised by John L. Cadwalader, a leader of the New York Bar.

On May 18, 1904, the reorganization meeting of the Institution took place. Although the founder was not present, it is probable that it was at about this time that he first met at a White House luncheon Henry S. Pritchett, member of the Theodore Roosevelt "tennis cabinet" and of the Lighthouse Board, and president since 1900 of the Massachusetts Institute of Technology. Afterwards Mr. and Mrs. Carnegie and Pritchett, en route to Boston, rode back to New York together in adjoining seats. Mrs. Carnegie had been given Pritchett's brochure "What is Religion" which had stirred her interest in its author. Mr. Carnegie and Pritchett discussed the financial problems Pritchett was dealing with as president of M.I.T.

At any rate, the train journey had important results. The two men subsequently talked together and corresponded upon a number of topics. On August 2 the Pritchetts sailed from Boston on the Cunarder *Ivernia* for a holiday in the British Isles; Pritchett on July 18 had sent a note to Mr. Carnegie at Skibo as to the intended trip. On landing the Pritchetts were greeted by an invitation from Mr. Carnegie to visit Skibo. This they did. Their stay was timed to coincide with a four-day visit of the four principals of the Scottish universities and their wives. During August walks on the Highland moors, in conversations between host and guests, the Carnegie Foundation had its inception.

One afternoon, on a long tramp with some of the guests, the Laird asked about Pritchett's present work. The matter chiefly troubling Pritchett at the time was Benjamin Franklin's Boston bequest, then maturing, which a committee of citizens of whom Pritchett was one had determined under the terms of Franklin's hundred-year-old will should be used to build a trade school. The funds were insufficient. On hearing this, Mr. Carnegie's generosity took flame. "Why," he exclaimed, "I'll match Ben Franklin any time!" The gift was announced that evening at dinner.

Before Mr. Carnegie and Pritchett met at the White House the older man knew of the younger. About May 12, 1902, when the Institution of Washington was being organized, Colonel Henry L. Higginson, of Boston, a trustee, inquired of Pritchett whether he would "care for the place of director under this plan of organization." Pritchett replied gently in the negative; his views, as he had outlined them to Gilman nearly two years before, were not sympathetic to a plan which appeared to him to limit seriously "the service of the Institution to science and to the nation." Nevertheless, on January 14, 1904, W. N. Frew, of Pittsburgh, in a personal note to Mr. Carnegie recommended Pritchett for the presidency of the Institution of Washington.

Then, with the Institution of Washington reconstituted, Mr. Carnegie set off in full cry on another trail, the pensioning of college teachers. Of this matter he continued discussion with Pritchett during the autumn and early winter of 1904, in correspondence and especially in person. On December 12 Pritchett wrote to him in part:

> I was interested to see your appreciation of the fact that we must offer better inducements, either by the payment of better salaries or, preferably, by provision for retired pay in our institutions of learning, or else the quality of teachers is going to seriously deteriorate. Few men appreciate how pressing that question is today, although you may have noted a word of warning sounded by Sir William Ramsay, the eminent English chemist, in his speech in New York, very much to the point. Now I have the impression that you do not intend to give money to the larger institutions of learning for the reason that you have other things in mind, . . . The cause I mention is . . . one that few appreciate. . . . Nothing would go so far to dignify the teacher's profession or to attract strong men to it. . . .

At this time it was Pritchett's notion that a million dollars would endow a retirement plan—a Carnegie Foundation, as he puts it—in a large higher institution. This suggestion Mr. Carnegie did not accept. He was moving towards larger things.

What these things were became evident in the ensuing late winter or early spring. About the first of February 1905, Mr. Carnegie asked Pritchett's opinion about a retirement plan for college teachers on a national scale. It was to deal both with "retired pay," that is, noncontributory retiring allowances, and also with insurance. He needed basal information, he knew. Pritchett thought the matter over long and hard. He was a mathematician and not an actuary, but he knew that actuarial study underlies both pensions and insurance and that the fuel for the actuarial engine is statistical. On February 6 he wrote to Mr. Carnegie that he was sure

Frank A. Vanderlip, "a very interesting and high-minded man," had "just the information" Mr. Carnegie wanted. After Vanderlip had called upon Mr. Carnegie matters moved with typical Carnegie celerity.

Pritchett and Vanderlip divided roughly between them the task of assembling the data. Resident in Boston and crowded with routine and other duties of a college president, Pritchett worked at long range, with not infrequent personal talks with Mr. Carnegie. For his share of the task he associated with himself Walter Humphreys, an M.I.T. graduate, class of '97, in 1905 registrar of the institute and much later president of the American Association of Collegiate Registrars. Mr. Humphreys was also a notary public. He and Pritchett set to work immediately and intensively. By March 5, 1905, Pritchett was able to report to Mr. Carnegie that there were approximately 100 higher institutions not under control of a state or a religious denomination. He thought also that he had "a feasible scheme of combining an insurance arrangement with the [retirement] plan . . ." The life insurance feature Mr. Carnegie had broached to Pritchett in conversation some time previously. Their data, collected from college catalogues and other literature, they sent to Vanderlip on March 21, together with "a carefully prepared statement of a plan of retired pay for colleges," and tables compiled by Mr. Humphreys. Pritchett asked Vanderlip to examine and pass to Mr. Carnegie these data and the statement, with such comments as Vanderlip cared to make. When Mr. Carnegie had had a chance to look them over Pritchett hoped that he might have some talk with him regarding the matter.

Meanwhile, in New York City, Vanderlip had enlisted the assistance of Mr. G. E. Gregory, who had been with the National City Bank since 1890. Gregory lived in Nyack, where he was registered as a Rockland County notary. Mr. W. Randolph Burgess has characterized Gregory as "an able and intelligent person who held for many years a responsible position in this bank." In 1914 he was "loaned to the [newly established] Federal Reserve Bank for some months to help get it organized. Mr. Gregory does not appear to have had any formal education in the actuarial or statistical field," although as National City Bank comptroller he dealt intimately with figures. Vanderlip and Gregory worked no less diligently than Pritchett and Mr. Humphreys. Government statistics were procured for them by M. E. Ailes, vice-president of the Riggs National Bank in Washington, and by W. T. Harris, Commissioner of Education. By March 15 the four men between them had assembled data and drafted an inclusive report, which Pritchett and Vanderlip presented to Mr. Carnegie on April 10.

They had sought, within the limitations imposed by Mr. Carnegie's intentions, to ascertain the number of colleges, universities, and technical schools which could be regarded as possible recipients or channels of transmission of Mr. Carnegie's beneficence. They counted ninety-two such institutions, with an aggregate faculty membership of 3,100, and annual salaries amounting to $6,200,000. They based their computations on replies from forty-eight such institutions, which employed about 60 per cent of the professors. Salaries, teaching and administrative, averaged from $800 to $2,900 a year, with an approximate median figure of $2,000. They concluded that an annual income of $500,000 would enable the new foundation to support a system of pensions available at the recipients' age sixty-five after thirty years of service, limited to half of the average annual salary received during the last five years of activity. A similar benefit was proposed in case of physical disability. Pensions were to be paid to widows but should cease upon death or remarriage. There was a tentative provision for orphans up to their majority. The administration of the fund was to be lodged with a board of trustees operating through an executive committee. Title to the properties of the foundation should vest in the board; operations should be supervised and directed by the executive committee.

In addition to the retirement provision just outlined it was suggested that consideration be given to a supplementary plan to be operated under an arrangement with an insurance company for life insurance in the amount of $10,000 issued at cost on a nonparticipating basis without commissions. After age sixty-five this might provide an annual pension of $1,200, payable in quarterly amounts. Before age sixty-five, after five years protection, the policy might be surrendered for the amount of the reserve held against it. It was computed that to maintain some such system as this for 3,000 persons on an interest basis of 4 per cent would require capital of $15,000,000. The insurance features were labeled as Plan B, the pension features as Plan A. After due consideration Mr. Carnegie decided to adhere to Plan A. Plan B was discarded altogether and finally. It is noteworthy, however, that the general purposes of these two plans were ultimately to be embodied in the Teachers Insurance and Annuity Association of America, inaugurated in 1918 with Mr. Carnegie's blessing.

Into the pattern Vanderlip had been weaving another strand. In personal talks he appears to have urged upon Mr. Carnegie that the new foundation should be incorporated. Evidence is lacking that Pritchett was consulted in detail about this matter, or that he was able to give timely or careful consideration to it. Towards the end of his life, indeed, he once intimated that in 1905 he considered the steps taken towards the first incorporation of Mr. Carnegie's foundation as precipitate. It seems in retrospect that events of the year 1905-06 justified some such view. At any rate, on Vanderlip's initiative, a firm of lawyers, Philbin, Beekman & Menken, 52 Wall Street, was engaged to handle legal matters, which were placed in the hands of Mr. Joseph E. Freeman. On April 14, 1905, Mr. Freeman was able to send Vanderlip a draft of articles of incorporation for the new foundation, to be submitted to a justice of the Supreme Court of the State of New York, and a version of bylaws consonant with it.

Concurrently Mr. Carnegie was considering three problems fundamental to his project: questions of taxation, the terms under which he would make his great gift, and the composition of the group whom he would choose to hold it. As for taxation, he found that an Act of Congress, July 1, 1902, specifically exempted from tax certain charitable and educational corporations having headquarters in the District of Columbia. Mr. Robert A. Franks, his financial secretary, consulted counsel about the New Jersey Tax Act of 1903, which seemed to exempt from taxation only such endowments or funds as were held and administered exclusively for charitable purposes within that state. Any notion that may have existed that the new foundation should have its principal office connected with Mr. Carnegie's Home Trust Company at Hoboken was thereby terminated. Upon Mr. Carnegie's receipt of the draft of the proposed charter and bylaws and the legal observations pertaining to them, the choice lay between incorporation by the Congress of the United States, such as the General Education Board enjoyed, or incorporation under the New York State membership corporation law. The second alternative was elected.

Mr. Carnegie then proceeded to the drafting of his Letter of Gift.

A HASTY STEP

At the risk of confusion, before carrying the story further, it will be well to glance briefly at the New York State charter of "The Carnegie Foundation." The corporators in the order of their signatures were Nicholas Murray Butler, Alex. C. Humphreys, Henry S. Pritchett, Robert A. Franks, and Frank A. Vanderlip. The territory for operations was the United States of America, the Dominion of Canada, and Newfoundland. It was proposed that the corporation, to be known as the Carnegie Foundation "provide retiring pensions without regard to race, sex, creed, or color, for the teachers of universities, colleges, and technical schools" within those confines "who, by reason of long and meritorious service, . . . shall be deemed by the board of directors to be entitled to the assistance and aid of this corporation, or who, by reason of old age or disability, may be prevented from continuing in the active work of their profession; to provide for the care and maintenance of the widows and families of the said teachers; to make benefactions to charitable and educational institutions, and generally to promote the cause of science and education. . . ." Retiring pensions were to be paid only in such institutions as were not under the control of a sect and did not impose a theological test for membership in governing boards, administrative posts, teaching positions, or student bodies. The principal office of the Foundation was to be located in the Borough of Manhattan, City and State of New York, and the directors of the corporation were to number twenty-five. Vanderlip acknowledged his signature before Mr. Gregory on April 28, 1905, the day the news of the new foundation was released. Pritchett's signature was acknowledged before Mr. Humphreys in Boston on May 1. The certificate of incorporation was approved and its filing consented to by Justice H. A. Gildersleeve, of the New York Supreme Court, May 8, 1905. The draft of the bylaws was reserved for later action by the new board when it should be duly constituted and assembled.

FINDING THE MEN

All this is somewhat ahead of the story. The lawyers had completed their preliminary work and turned over the results to Vanderlip. As soon as Vanderlip received the lawyers' drafts of the early charter and bylaws he brought or sent them to Mr. Carnegie. It

was then high time to enlist the interest and the services of the men
who were to become trustees. On April 14, the day Mr. Carnegie
received the Pritchett-Vanderlip preliminary report and the lawyers' draft, he sent to each of his trustees-to-be the following letter,
adapted in each case to individual circumstances:

Dear Sir,

I propose handing over $10,000,000 in 5% bonds to a commis-
sion, as I did to the Research Commission in Washington, and to
the Commission for Scotch Universities, the revenue to provide retiring pensions for the teaching staff of universities, colleges, and
technical schools under such conditions as the Trustees may from
time to time adopt. I am able now to say expert calculation proves
that the revenue will be sufficient for the purpose.

I hope you will do me the favor to act as one of the first trustees,
who will be (with few exceptions) like yourself, the Presidents of
educational institutions. A prompt reply by wire or mail will
greatly oblige.

Very truly yours,   (*Signed*) Andrew Carnegie

Acceptances were prompt and complete; by Monday, April 24,
all but one were in hand—Charles W. Eliot was in Europe. Mr.
Carnegie acknowledged each in part as follows:

Dear Sir,

Thanks for your kind acceptance of the Trusteeship.

I have instructed my Financial Secretary, Mr. R. A. Franks,
President of the Home Trust Company, Hoboken, N. J., to transfer Ten Millions of Dollars of Bonds to the Trustees when organized.

Messrs. Vanderlip and Pritchett will proceed to obtain data
from all institutions concerned for use at the meeting of the
Trustees . . . (at my house, Wednesday, November 15th—two
o'clock). The gift will be announced after I sail for Europe next
Wednesday [April 26, 1905] and the whole subject . . . will no
doubt be fully discussed during the coming summer months, especially by the Trustees as they happen to meet each other or others
interested. In the meantime a corporation will be organized. . . .

Much will depend upon finding the right man for permanent
Secretary to organize the office and working plans for disbursing
the funds. It is hoped the Trustees will be on the lookout for the
indispensable man.

Very truly yours,   (*Signed*) Andrew Carnegie

The decision to announce the new philanthropy only after sailing for Europe Mr. Carnegie had taken perhaps a fortnight or more previously. It met with complete success.

BREAKING THE NEWS

Thus far not a word of the new philanthropy had leaked. Now, since Vanderlip was a former newspaperman, he was naturally, being, so to speak, on the ground, the associate to whom Mr. Carnegie entrusted the preparation and release of the public announcement. On Thursday, April 27, 1905, Vanderlip, acting upon an autograph memorandum of Mr. Carnegie, sent to the newspapers a press release which internal evidence indicates Vanderlip wrote or revised himself. The announcement stressed particularly the fact that "the gift will be of distinct value to the cause of education in offering an opportunity to the Trustees of a college to retire the members of the Faculty who have faithfully served the institution for many years, and to replace such men with young, vigorous and effective professors." A copy of the Letter of Gift, dated April 18, 1905, and a list of trustees were enclosed. Vanderlip noted, rather casually but none the less pointedly, that Mr. Carnegie's ten-million-dollar gift had a market value of $11,500,000, and would produce an annual income of half a million. In concluding his statement he wrote: "The corporation which is now being formed will be styled 'The Carnegie Foundation.'"

The *Times* story characterized Vanderlip as "a banker as to business, but a statistician and a publicist on Economics . . . an authority on the subject of old-age pensions," and continued: "He and Prof. Pritchett . . . [tentatively set] the years of superannuation at sixty-five, and the rate of pension at half-pay, with a limit of full pay of $5,000 per annum." The *Tribune* gave the limit of the pension as $2,400, and cited further figures furnished by Vanderlip from the Vanderlip-Pritchett report.

HOW THE NEWS WAS TAKEN

New York City papers of the day gave the news an equal prominence. The *Tribune* ran, banner-like across its first page, half-tones of twelve of the trustees flanking Mr. Carnegie. There were congratulatory editorials galore, some viewing possible results in detail, most of them *dégagé*, as if reflecting a growing public inurement to

Mr. Carnegie's sudden benefactions, and a determination not to be astonished by any of his philanthropic surprises; the *Times* captioned its editorial "Mr. Carnegie's Latest."

Many of the budding trustees issued statements on request. Among them Butler of Columbia University called the new foundation "the most far-reaching and important of Mr. Carnegie's benefactions." Pritchett of M.I.T. independently agreed with him. Harrison of Pennsylvania seemed much pleased with the founder's generosity. Harper of Chicago called it "one of the most significant steps in the interest of higher education in the last twenty-five years." Hadley of Yale termed it "an exceedingly valuable gift." Eliot of Harvard, just back from Europe, found it unquestionably "a very valuable gift to the cause of education." McCormick of Western Pennsylvania thought Mr. Carnegie had done "a very wise thing," while Seelye of Smith believed that "no gift has been made to colleges in general which will prove of such great value." Plantz of Lawrence University was more concretely appreciative. Schurman of Cornell thought that "nothing better, nothing else so good, could have been done . . . with $10,000,000 for the cause of higher education in America."

There were, of course, cautious, lukewarm, or dissident comments. Faunce of Brown University, which was not eligible on sectarian grounds, rather hoped the trustees would distribute the principal of the gift among individual institutions. Ira L. Remsen of The Hopkins, who was not included among the trustees, confessed himself "rather surprised" that the university was not to be represented on the board. Woodrow Wilson of Princeton, asked for his views on the gift, telegraphed: "Regret circumstances prevent my expressing an opinion," and a professor in an eastern university said: "I don't like it. . . . I don't like Mr. Carnegie's methods. . . . I do not believe in pension systems in general; . . . it could not help but lower the profession." With such views as these, the professor seemed to Mr. Carnegie "to be left in solitary grandeur." Ultimately the gentleman was granted a Carnegie retiring allowance of $3,000 a year in 1920, which he received until his death some twelve years later. The total cost to the Foundation approximated $36,000.

It is of interest to trace the evolution of the basal document in which Mr. Carnegie made his benefaction.

LETTER OF GIFT

It is not possible to reconstruct definitively Mr. Carnegie's development of his concept, but there exist in his own handwriting many notes which contributed to the final form of his Letter of Gift. Almost all of these memoranda are undated. Although entertaining, conjecture about their chronological order would contribute little to understanding and add less of value to the knowledge of how the Letter of Gift evolved. Suffice it to say that probably these memoranda were made between January 15 and April 23, 1905. At any rate, it is certain that Mr. Carnegie worked personally over their details and the phrasing. It is certain also that he had assistance and advice in the task. Yet when the Letter reached its final form on Easter morning, April 23, 1905, it represented less the help of others than Mr. Carnegie's own purposes and ideas, wherever acquired, however assimilated.

First Draft

The earliest draft extant is in Mr. Carnegie's penciled script. It runs—

That Professors in our Educational Institutions are the poorest paid of any class may safely be affirmed. While New York City generously and wisely provides retiring pensions for every teacher in her public schools and for her policemen only a few universities are able to do this for a life time of faithful service.

From calculations made for me it is seen that an annual revenue of from 350 to [$]400,000 would provide pensions to Professors who had served say thirty years & also for cases of total disability as these occurred.

I have decided therefore to place in your hands as Trustees serving for five years and eligible for re-election from term to term Ten Millions of five per cent bonds yielding [$]500,000 per year, to be applied to the purpose indicated under such conditions as you may deem proper.

All Universities, Colleges & Technical Schools in the United States, Canada & Newfoundland——

Second Thoughts

The next draft is typewritten, probably from stenographic dictation, on stationery of 2 East 91st Street. It begins—

It may be taken for granted that professors in our educational institutions are the worst paid branch in the community, hence the growing indisposition of young men to enter one of the highest of all callings . . .

Mr. Carnegie proceeded:

I have had statistics gathered bearing upon the subject and am assured that Three hundred and fifty to Four Hundred thousand dollars per annum would meet the demand [of a pensioning scheme] including expenses of administration.

He intends the new foundation to "embrace all higher institutions which may elect to participate" but instructs his trustees-to-be not to include state institutions unless they apply. He would exclude "sectarian institutions" because he feels that "in the pursuit of knowledge men should be left free to accept the truth as revealed to them from year to year." Mr. Carnegie was anxious that "in naming the first board some attention . . . be given to residences"—the geographical distribution ultimately imposed by the Charter—but the stenographer transcribed *residences* as "circumstances," a not unnatural error which Mr. Carnegie himself corrected. The reason for this stricture was his desire that a quorum be readily obtainable "for the numerous meetings which may be necessary in starting the work."

Third Draft

The third draft displays many changes, not so much in purposes as in sharpness of phrase. His opening words become "It may be taken for granted." "The worst paid branch in the community," is now "the worst paid class . . ." "Cases of total disability in early years" are to be provided for, in addition to "professors who had served say thirty years at the age of perhaps sixty or sixty-five" who "had better be retired." Here also the donor again reverts to "the United States, Canada & New Foundland" as comprising the area to be served. In the preceding draft he had noted that many institutions by 1905 had "become practically non-sectarian; that is to say, men of all creeds or of none being welcome." Such "are not to be considered sectarian." This he lets stand in the third draft almost as written, but he simplifies and points another paragraph dealing with ineligibility of institutions of a sectarian nature to read as follows:

No man's creed honestly entertained should be a barrier to his admission [to higher education] or his appointment [as a teacher].

And he adds:

Such institutions as are established to propagate some particular religious creed or dogma and shall require a majority of Trustees or all of their officers or students to belong to any particular sect shall not be eligible.

Representation on the new foundation's board of trustees he now believes should be on the basis of constituent institutions, and he apparently intends to name the initial trustees as institutional representatives rather than as individuals.

TWENTY QUESTIONS

At this point, Mr. Carnegie apparently asked Pritchett to furnish him a list of higher institutions which might be eligible to the benefits of the foundation-to-be and the presiding officers of which would make suitable trustees. Pritchett responded with a list of twenty universities, colleges, and technical schools, all in the United States, which he thought would be worthy, probably with a cautionary statement as to the possible ineligibility of some on sectarian grounds. Pritchett listed the following:

Harvard University, Cambridge, Massachusetts
Massachusetts Institute of Technology, Boston, Massachusetts
College of William and Mary, Williamsburg, Virginia
Williams College, Williamstown, Massachusetts
Columbia University, New York City
Stevens Institute of Technology, Hoboken, New Jersey
Oberlin College, Oberlin, Ohio
Cornell University, Ithaca, New York
The Tulane University of Louisiana, New Orleans, Louisiana
W[ester]n. Reserve University, Cleveland, Ohio
Bryn M[awr] College, Bryn Mawr, Pennsylvania
Armour Institute of Technology, Chicago, Illinois
The Johns Hopkins University, Baltimore, Maryland
Leland Stanford, Jr., University, California
Princeton University, Princeton, New Jersey
Washington [and] Lee University, Lexington, Virginia

Yale University, New Haven, Connecticut
Western University [of] Pennsylvania, Allegheny, Pennsylvania
[B]erea College, Berea, Kentucky
[The Citadel,] Charleston, South Carolina
Colorado [College,] Colorado Springs, Colorado

This list Mr. Carnegie studied. His memoranda show that he reached two very definite conclusions: First, that Vanderlip and Pritchett should be members of the board in any event, and, secondly, that trustees should have expenses paid in attending board meetings, together with provision for a wife or sister to accompany each. Evidently he also inclined to the view that the president of Harvard, Charles W. Eliot, might make the kind of chairman he would like to see the board itself elect.

A DOZEN NAMES

The list of institutions was soon translated into a list of men, set down in Mr. Carnegie's own handwriting evidently as a memorandum of a conversation with Pritchett. The group included the following persons, all or almost all of whom Mr. Carnegie knew personally or through previous correspondence:

Frank A. Vanderlip
Robert A. Franks
Alexander Crombie Humphreys
Henry S. Pritchett
Nicholas Murray Butler
Arthur Twining Hadley

Charles W. Eliot
David Starr Jordan
Henry Churchill King
Charles F. Thwing
Woodrow Wilson
William Henry Crawford

Apparently Mr. Carnegie did not catch the name of the president of Allegheny College. Four names Mr. Carnegie included twice, and three other names he included here but did not retain in his final selection.

The penciled list bears three other pertinent notations: First, "State Institutions," a topic which was soon to demand much time and attention; second, "No theological tests for Trustees, Officers, Professors or Students"; third, the words "Professors Fund," a phrase significant in devising a name for the new foundation, which was to give considerable trouble in the months to come.

With the draft of the Letter of Gift now approaching a final form and with a working list of men to be invited as trustees and, of course, to receive individually the Letter of Gift, when at last it should be whipped into shape, the course seemed clearer.

EASTER WEEK, 1905

The fourth and semifinal form came into being on Palm Sunday, April 16, 1905. Another draft was apparently made two days later. Some of the provisions of the April 18 version were rephrased by Mr. Carnegie personally for the final form, after discussion with Pritchett on Easter morning, April 23—the references to the state universities and to sectarian institutions—but the intent of the document was not altered.

The Letter of Gift as dispatched to the Founder-selected trustees was printed in the First Annual Report of the new Foundation (1906), but under date of April 16. It was considerably longer than any of the working drafts, but it embodied the most discerning provisions of all of them. As between the final form of the Letter of Gift and the Foundation's District of Columbia Charter the only important change concerned the selection of the board of trustees. The Letter stipulated that—

> Trustees shall hold office for five years and be eligible for re-election. The first Trustees shall draw lots for one, two, three, four, or five year terms, so that one-fifth shall retire each year. Each institution participating in the Foundation shall cast one vote for Trustees.

The charter or act of incorporation of the Carnegie Foundation for the Advancement of Teaching made the original trustees a self-perpetuating body to serve without limit of term, with power to select their successors. For this it had the advice and consent of Mr. Carnegie. The official text of the Letter of Gift is as follows:

New York, April 18, 1905.

Gentlemen:

I have reached the conclusion that the least rewarded of all the professions is that of the teacher in our higher educational institutions. New York City generously, and very wisely, provides retiring pensions for teachers in her public schools and also for her policemen. Very few indeed of our colleges are able to do so. The consequences are grievous. Able men hesitate to adopt teaching as a career, and many old professors whose places should be occupied by younger men, cannot be retired.

I have, therefore, transferred to you and your successors, as Trustees, $10,000,000, 5% First Mortgage Bonds of the United States Steel Corporation, the revenue from which is to provide retiring pensions for the teachers of Universities, Colleges, and Technical Schools in our country, Canada and Newfoundland under such conditions as you may adopt from time to time. Expert calculation shows that the revenue will be ample for the purpose.

The fund applies to the three classes of institutions named, without regard to race, sex, creed or color. We have, however, to recognize that State and Colonial Governments which have established or mainly supported Universities, Colleges or Schools may prefer that their relations shall remain exclusively with the State. I cannot, therefore presume to include them.

There is another class which states do not aid, their constitution in some cases even forbidding it, viz., Sectarian Institutions. Many of these established long ago, were truly sectarian, but to-day are free to all men of all creeds or of none—such are not to be considered sectarian now. Only such as are under the control of a sect or require Trustees (or a majority thereof), Officers, Faculty or Students, to belong to any specified sect, or which impose any theological tests, are to be excluded.

Trustees shall hold office for five years and be eligible for re-election. The first Trustees shall draw lots for one, two, three, four, or five year terms, so that one-fifth shall retire each year. Each institution participating in the Fund shall cast one vote for Trustees.

The Trustees are hereby given full powers to manage the Trust in every respect, to fill vacancies of non-ex-officio members; appoint executive committees; employ agents; change securities, and, generally speaking, to do all things necessary, in their judgment, to secure the most beneficial administration of the Funds.

By a two-thirds vote they may from time to time apply the revenue in a different manner and for a different, though similar purpose to that specified, should coming days bring such changes as to render this necessary in their judgment to produce the best results possible for the teachers and for education.

No Trustee shall incur any legal liability flowing from his Trusteeship. All travelling and hotel expenses incurred by Trustees in the performance of their duties shall be paid from the Fund. The expenses of a wife or daughter accompanying the Trustees to the Annual meeting are included.

I hope this Fund may do much for the cause of higher education and to remove a source of deep and constant anxiety to the
poorest paid and yet one of the highest of all professions.

Gratefully yours,

(*Signed*) Andrew Carnegie

The trustees finally named by Mr. Carnegie all accepted their
appointments. They were:

Founder's Trustees

Hill McClelland Bell, Drake University, Des Moines, Iowa

Nicholas Murray Butler, Columbia University, New York City

T. Morrison Carnegie, 542 Fifth Avenue, New York City

Edwin B. Craighead, Tulane University, New Orleans, Louisiana

William H. Crawford, Allegheny College, Meadville, Pennsylvania

George H. Denny, Washington & Lee University, Lexington,
Virginia

Charles William Eliot, Harvard University, Cambridge, Massachusetts

Robert A. Franks, Home Trust Company, Hoboken, New Jersey

Arthur T. Hadley, Yale University, New Haven, Connecticut

William Rainey Harper, University of Chicago, Chicago, Illinois

Charles C. Harrison, University of Pennsylvania, Philadelphia,
Pennsylvania

Alexander C. Humphreys, Stevens Institute of Technology, Hoboken, New Jersey

Edwin H. Hughes, DePauw University, Greencastle, Indiana

David Starr Jordan, Leland Stanford, Jr., University, Stanford
University, California

Henry C. King, Oberlin College, Oberlin, Ohio

Thomas McClelland, Knox College, Galesburg, Illinois

Samuel B. McCormick, Western University of Pennsylvania,
Allegheny, Pennsylvania

William Peterson, McGill University, Montreal, Canada

Samuel Plantz, Lawrence University, Appleton, Wisconsin

Henry S. Pritchett, Massachusetts Institute of Technology, Boston, Massachusetts

Jacob Gould Schurman, Cornell University, Ithaca, New York

L. Clark Seelye, Smith College, Northampton, Massachusetts

Charles F. Thwing, Western Reserve University, Cleveland, Ohio

Frank A. Vanderlip, National City Bank, New York City

Woodrow Wilson, Princeton University, Princeton, New Jersey.

Of these twenty-five original trustees chosen and appointed by Mr. Carnegie, the oldest was President Eliot, of Harvard, seventy-one years of age, and the youngest Mr. T. Morrison Carnegie, aged thirty-one years. The average age of the group was forty-five years. Mr. Carnegie himself was in his seventieth year. Thus was youth served.

~~ 2 ~~

Backgrounds

"THE GOSPEL OF WEALTH" · THE DISGRACE OF DYING RICH · PREACH-
MENT PRACTICED · PATTERN OF GIVING—CARNEGIE CORPORATION OF
NEW YORK; OTHER ENDOWMENTS; IN PERPETUITY · FOUNDING THE
FOUNDATION—ITS OFFICERS; MECHANISM; BENEFITS AND RULES;
STUDIES IN PENSIONS; STUDIES IN EDUCATION; AN OPERATING BODY;
PUBLICATIONS; CONSULTATION; FUNDS · RECAPITULATION

ANDREW CARNEGIE during his lifetime gave away or directed the giving of about one-third of a billion dollars. In the days when ten million was, in his own words, an enormous sum, three hundred and thirty million and more was a fantastic figure. It still is. How did he get started on this road to fame?

The outline of his life is familiar; the course of his earlier benefactions and the reasoning which lay behind them are less well known. Brought a poor boy by his parents from his native Dunfermline to the United States, Carnegie by the time he was forty-six years of age had become a wealthy man. To the town of his birth he presented in 1881 his first public library building, a gift that marked his entry into the career of public benefactor. That career had a background of philosophy. Commonly it is taken for granted that that philosophy took shape when, in June and December 1889, the *North American Review* printed a paper of his under the title "Wealth," changed upon reprinting in the *Pall Mall Gazette* to "The Gospel of Wealth" at the suggestion of W. E. Gladstone or W. T. Stead, or both. This is not the case.

"THE GOSPEL OF WEALTH"

That paper embodied a mature statement of a principle which, as B. J. Hendrick showed, Carnegie had worked over in his mind as early as 1868, when on a single sheet of hotel stationery he had sketched "a life program which involved devoting his surplus each year to benevolent purposes." In the years succeeding, as great American fortunes grew greater, there sprang up apprehension not only as to their size but also as to their ultimate use and influence. Of this feeling Mr. Carnegie seems to have become increasingly conscious. "The Gospel of Wealth" summarized his answer to the growing fears and provided reassurance. The millionaire, he insisted, could honestly claim as his right only a reasonable provision for himself and his dependents. His fortune was the creation of society as a whole, and honesty demanded that it be returned to society in ways and for purposes that should alleviate the common lot. Thus, by 1889, Hendrick remarks, Carnegie's conception of wealth and the responsibilities which it imposes was no "improvised inspiration"; it had been his fixed goal for a third of a century: "He pursued wealth chiefly with the plan of giving it away." A year after publication, "The Gospel of Wealth" was followed in the gift of a public library building and hall to Allegheny, Pennsylvania, where the Carnegie family had first settled when they came to the United States. An earlier offer (1881), renewed, enlarged, and accepted in 1895, grew ultimately into the Carnegie Institute, Pittsburgh, with related benefactions in terms of a library and a library school. Meanwhile, Mr. Carnegie had made other gifts for Dunfermline. By the end of the century his career as a philanthropist was well launched. His name was associated with magnificent giving, and his fortune, which had amounted to about thirty million dollars in 1889, had multiplied many times. Mr. Carnegie was practicing to the letter what he had preached. "Perhaps," Pritchett said in an address (1931) at the dinner in celebration of the founding of Carnegie Corporation of New York, "the greatest thing he ever did was to live up to his Gospel of Wealth."

THE DISGRACE OF DYING RICH

In 1887 Mr. Carnegie told Gladstone, who entered the fact in his diary, that "he should consider it disgraceful to die a rich man."

During the ensuing decade and more Mr. Carnegie increasingly looked forward to withdrawal from the Carnegie Company, his principal business enterprise; Hendrick, in the *Life*, quotes him to the effect that his "resolve was made in youth to retire before old age." In March of 1901 the opportunity came. During a fifteen-minute interview he and J. Pierpont Morgan agreed upon a price for the Carnegie Company and the buyer was able to grasp the seller's hand with: "I want to congratulate you upon being the richest man in the world." Whether he was or not, on March 11, 1901, his fortune amounted to about three hundred million dollars, mostly in five per cent bonds of the newly formed United States Steel Corporation. The "disgrace of dying rich" was thus made harder than ever to avoid.

Hendrick relates an episode that occurred not long afterward. Mr. Carnegie and Morgan were fellow-passengers in a transatlantic voyage.

> One day in deck conversation Carnegie said:
> "I made one mistake, Pierpont, when I sold out to you."
> "What was that?"
> "I should have asked you $100,000,000 more than I did."
> "Well," replied Morgan with a grin, "you would have got it if you had."

And if he had, Mr. Carnegie would have had just that much more trouble in eluding the disgrace of dying a rich man.

PREACHMENT PRACTICED

Almost at once he set about the development of a sort of home-made science of giving. He created a Trust for the Universities of Scotland in 1901 with a Royal Charter and resources of $5,000,000 for student scholarships, subsequently increased to $10,000,000 so that the Trust might undertake wider benefactions. A year later he acquired for the public Pittencrief Glen and set up in 1903 the Carnegie Dunfermline Trust with $2,500,000 to maintain the Glen and other work for the benefit of the people of the countryside. Then his philanthropic course turned once more westward.

It was also in 1901 that in Scotland Mr. Carnegie seriously considered a proposal to found a great university at Washington in honor and memory of the man for whom the city was named. This purpose he relinquished when he reached the view that such a university appropriately financed might tend to weaken existing higher institutions. Various proposals that endowments should be given to American universities and colleges, although they emanated from friends, were one by one examined and dropped. Ultimately, perhaps acting partly upon advice given him by Arthur J. Balfour in the matter of the Scottish Universities Trust, and partly upon the counsel of certain Americans, including his friend, Elihu Root, Mr. Carnegie decided to endow an agency for scientific research at the national capitol with $10,000,000. In 1902 the Carnegie Institution of Washington was incorporated under District of Columbia laws. Two years later it was incorporated by an act of Congress. In 1903 John D. Rockefeller, Sr., had established the General Education Board with a Congressional charter; this fact may have had a certain influence upon the form of the Institution's revised incorporation.

Andrew Carnegie did not invent the American philanthropic endowment. Its origin goes back to the Middle Ages, and perhaps even further. As for the United States, Mr. Carnegie was anticipated by, for example, the Slater Fund 1882, the John Edgar Thompson Foundation 1882, the Baron de Hirsch Fund 1891, and the Thompson Fund 1899. But he was the first American to establish a congeries of philanthropies under preconceived patterns and motives.

PATTERN OF GIVING

The extent to which he was capable of following a course of giving is illustrated in the Hero Funds. In 1904 he established the Carnegie Hero Fund Commission, Pittsburgh, with $5,000,000 of endowment, to recognize those heroes of peace who had tried, successfully or unsuccessfully, to save human life. It bodied forth an impulse of his that few others might have experienced, let alone acted upon. Satisfied with the results, he proceeded to organize (1909-11) similar funds in France, Germany, Norway, Switzerland, the Netherlands, Sweden, Denmark, Belgium, and Italy.

It has been said that in establishing endowments Mr. Carnegie thought in units of $10,000,000. If so, he did not follow this thought invariably. Two motives he adhered to in his philanthropic giving: One is reflected in the fact that all his trusts were designed to be perpetual. This characteristic is so basal to Mr. Carnegie's concept of philanthropy, and indeed to much American giving other than his own, that it will be considered in more detail on a subsequent page. The other pertains to his choice of trustees. In the main, he selected for trusteeship men he knew personally or by reputation, men of success or occasionally of great promise, whose achievement and work he knew or respected. His range of friendship was wide— indeed, its breadth was almost a unique characteristic of his life. It included distinguished men in many callings and of many sorts. In his benefactions it provided him with a human treasury upon which he could draw to accomplish his beneficent purposes.

Matters usually went somewhat like this: The human problem and the human need and the course of action having been defined or established to Mr. Carnegie's satisfaction, and the size of the sum to be initially devoted to the purpose determined, he thought the business through in terms of men. "Find the man" became a guiding maxim in his philanthropic life, as it had been in his career as steelmaster. Beginning with his selection of Daniel Coit Gilman to preside over the Carnegie Institution of Washington, he acted upon it.

Carnegie Corporation of New York

For one endowment, Carnegie Corporation of New York (1911), of which he himself became the first president, he probably would have denied having followed it, but the Corporation more than once has been called "Andrew Carnegie, Incorporated," and so for some years it was indeed. To it he gave an initial endowment "for the advancement and diffusion of knowledge and understanding among the people of the United States," totaling some $125,000,000, later increased by his will to $135,000,000. At first Mr. Carnegie intended to create the Corporation by bequest. Fortunately, upon the advice of Senator Root, he changed his mind, and Carnegie Corporation became a fact during the donor's lifetime, with the broadest charter purposes of any of his philanthropies.

One of these charter purposes is the source of considerable public misapprehension. Carnegie Corporation of New York is not uncommonly regarded as a sort of holding company or parent corporation for other Carnegie trusts. This notion is in error. True, the Corporation is chartered in part to aid "technical schools, institutions of higher learning, scientific research, hero funds, useful publications. . . ." True also, that Mr. Carnegie himself had personally established funds within these fields, and that the presiding officers of the resulting independent philanthropic foundations served until recent years as trustees, ex officio, of the Corporation.

But Mr. Carnegie's mode of giving led to his establishing each of his philanthropies as a separate entity complete in itself, whether incorporated or not. There resulted a sort of democracy of philanthropies bearing the Carnegie name, in which the Corporation by reason of its princely endowment of more than $135,300,000 and Mr. Carnegie's presidency became *primus inter pares*. While the purposes of most of the Carnegie endowments—that for Pittsburgh, for research in science, for the heroes of everyday life, for college professors and higher education, and for peace on earth—were, comparatively speaking, restricted to specified areas of thought or human endeavor, the purposes of the Corporation were so broad as to include the aims of all the other American Carnegie philanthropies. A large proportion of the total grants of the Corporation have been made to or through the other philanthropic creations of Mr. Carnegie. It is perhaps only natural that the Corporation should have been frequently referred to as "the uncle with the deep pocket."

Other Endowments

Of the other foundations established by Mr. Carnegie during his lifetime and titled with his own name there remain to be accounted for only the Carnegie Foundation (1905), the Carnegie Endowment for International Peace (1910), and the Carnegie United Kingdom Trust (1913), each originally endowed with $10,000,000. The peace endowment, to which Mr. Carnegie devoted much time during his later years, and the United Kingdom Trust enter the present account not at all. To the seven American trusts Mr. Carnegie contributed endowments totaling $195,336,867; to the four British trusts about $25,000,000; to the continental Hero Funds $4,290,000. These gifts took some $224,626,867, which with $9,-003,842 for other purposes, makes a grand total of about $333,-295,460 (Lester, *Forty Years of Carnegie Giving*, pp. 72-73). At the self-appointed task of giving, no man ever worked harder or more constantly than Andrew Carnegie. He enjoyed it; a word of sincere appreciation yielded him the greatest pleasure and satisfaction. Elihu Root was amply justified in his remark to Mr. Carnegie: "You have had the best run for your money I have ever known."

In Perpetuity

Reference has already been made to the fact that Mr. Carnegie's foundations are of the perpetual nature. Ever since the eighteenth century of Adam Smith in Scotland and Baron Turgot in France there has been difference of opinion about the advisability, even the ethics, of establishing perpetual trusts, only the income, never the principal, of which can be spent for designated purposes. Andrew Carnegie, Charles Hayden, John Simon Guggenheim, and the incorporators of the Ford Foundation stand among those ranged on the side of perpetuity. The Buhl Foundation, the Maurice and Laura Falk Foundation, the Rockefeller Foundation, the Field Foundation, and many others exemplify the terminable type. In this matter, Mr. Carnegie's actions speak louder than his words. His views, however, are stated by one who worked and often discussed them with him:

How desirable it may be to establish foundations which are perpetual, whose trustees are authorized to expend only the income of their endowments, has been a much discussed matter in recent years on both sides of the Atlantic. This question did not escape Mr. Carnegie's keen vision. He frequently discussed with those who were associated with him in the development of his plans, whether such perpetual endowments as he proposed might in time become either useless or even injurious. He had an answer which is worth repeating. "No man of vision," he said, "will seek to tie the endowment which he gives to a fixed cause. He will leave to the judgment of his trustees, as time goes on the question of modifying or altogether changing the nature of the trust so as to meet the requirements of the time." As to the second objection, his reply was even more interesting. "Any board of trustees," he was wont to say, "is likely to become indifferent or careless or to make wrong decisions. In the perpetual trust, as in all human institutions, there will be fruitful seasons and slack seasons. No doubt a foundation left to the care of a board of trustees will at times fall upon mediocre days. But as long as it exists there will come, from time to time, men into its control and management who will have vision and energy and wisdom, and the perpetual Foundation will have a new birth of usefulness and of service. I am optimistic," he was wont to say, "in my estimate of my fellowmen and I am willing to risk some slack periods in the fruitfulness of the foundations I have established in the confident belief that the service they will render in the fruitful years under able men will far counterbalance the mediocrity into which they may fall in other periods." Mr. Carnegie's optimism was based on a wide experience of human nature. The centuries alone can judge as to its essential soundness. The trustees who have the responsibility for the conduct of the great agencies for human improvement that he set going will do most to realize his faith when, in accordance with his direction they adapt these institutions, in the light of the best knowledge they can gather, to the changing circumstances of the country and of the age. (Henry S. Pritchett, Twenty-second Annual Report, 1927, pp. 22-23.)

On November 24, 1915, in an address at the Carnegie Institute of Technology, Pittsburgh, Pritchett appraised these philanthropic endowments:

These constructive agencies which Mr. Carnegie has conceived and set in motion are today in their infancy, but they are to have immortal lives. Decade after decade, century after century, they will make their contribution to the progress of their age and of their generation. They are immortal agencies in the forward march of humanity. To have conceived and to have set in motion such immortal forces for human upbuilding is to become oneself a partaker of immortality.

FOUNDING THE FOUNDATION

Respect for learning has long characterized the Scot. When in 1890 Mr. Carnegie became a trustee of Cornell University he was shocked, as Lester shows, to discover the meagerness of the salaries paid to American college teachers; of all professions he found the least rewarded was that of the teacher in our colleges and universities. Now, he had come to see clearly some of the problems that flow from incapacitation and old age in industry. These he tried to meet by giving, in 1901, $4,000,000 to the Carnegie Relief Fund of his steel companies and subsidiaries. One of the functions of the fund was, and still is, to pay pensions to employees. Meanwhile his impulse to do something for the forgotten men and women of American higher education gathered force and conviction. It was Pritchett who furnished the spark which turned that impulse into the Carnegie Foundation.

As of April 18, 1905, Mr. Carnegie by Letter of Gift transferred to twenty-five trustees, most of whom were presidents of universities or colleges in the United States and Canada, $10,000,000, the revenue from which was "to provide retiring pensions for the teachers of Universities, Colleges, and Technical Schools in our

Country, Canada and Newfoundland . . . without regard to race, sex, creed, or color."

Its Officers

Pritchett, of course, became the Foundation's president. He guided it in its earlier and its more mature years, until his retirement in 1930. His successor was Henry Suzzallo, formerly president of the University of Washington, who presided over the Foundation until his death September 25, 1933. Walter A. Jessup, president of the State University of Iowa, took office as president of the Foundation May 1, 1934. He died in service July 5, 1944. Oliver C. Carmichael, chancellor of Vanderbilt University, assumed his duties as the Foundation's fourth president February 1, 1946. The history of the Foundation reflects the influence of each of these men.

The first treasurer of the Foundation was the Founder's nephew, T. Morrison Carnegie. Upon his resignation Robert A. Franks, formerly the Donor's financial associate, became treasurer, November 16, 1910, to hold office till his death October 1, 1935. He was succeeded by Frank A. Vanderlip, an original incorporator and trustee of the Foundation, a member of the first and subsequent executive committees, who became acting treasurer October 4, 1935, and treasurer November 18, 1936. Upon his death June 29, 1937, Howard J. Savage became treasurer of the Foundation. He was succeeded on February 1, 1949, by C. Herbert Lee, treasurer of Carnegie Corporation of New York.

The Foundation has had five secretaries: Albert LeForest Derby, who came from Boston with Pritchett to be "assistant secretary" until a month or two before his death in 1907; John Gabbert Bowman, January 23, 1907–August 1, 1911, whose title was first "assistant secretary" and later "secretary of the executive committee"; Clyde Furst, August 1, 1911–March 6, 1931; Howard J. Savage, acting secretary February 6–May 1, 1931, and thereafter secretary until February 1, 1949; and Robert M. Lester, February 1, 1949–. The following have been members of the Foundation's staff: Monell Sayre, 1905-13; I. L. Kandel, 1914-23; William S. Learned, 1913-46; Alfred Z. Reed, 1913-40; Howard J. Savage, 1923-31, 1949-. At no time have active staff members exceeded three in number. Walter M. Gilbert, assistant secretary, 1906-47, was in charge of the Washington office; he was succeeded by Paul A. Scherer. R. L. Mattocks, associate actuary of the Teachers Insurance and Annuity Association, has had the title of the Foundation's actuarial consultant since 1931.

Mechanism

The organization of the Foundation has more closely resembled that of an American university or college than a business enterprise. Broadly speaking, the membership of its board of trustees has shown unusual stability. The terms of its first three presidents averaged nearly thirteen years. Its treasurers and secretaries have had comparatively long service, and so too have most of its staff members. The resulting stability of personnel and the overlapping of service have brought a degree of continuity in administrative policy and procedure.

The Carnegie Foundation's activities might be grouped in four interrelated categories: those involved with its retiring allowances and widows' pensions, the work of the Division of Educational Enquiry, publication, and advisory and consultative services in higher education. These activities, together with those operations conjunctive with Carnegie Corporation of New York, have been carried on in fulfillment of two of the Foundation's charter purposes: the first, specifically to provide retiring pensions under certain conditions; and the second, "in general to do and perform all things necessary to encourage, uphold, and dignify the profession of the teacher and the cause of higher education within the United States, the Dominion of Canada, and Newfoundland. . . ."

Benefits and Rules

The benefits which the Foundation has provided since 1906, in retiring allowances on the basis of both age and disability for teachers and pensions for their widows, are disbursed under the Rules for the Granting of Retiring Allowances. Eligibility for Foundation benefits is restricted in two ways: First, the teacher or administrative officer must have attained a certain age and completed a certain length of service at higher institutions specified by the board of trustees, and, secondly, his name must appear in the Closed List of Pensionables adopted by the executive committee May 1, 1931. For those teachers who retire for age Carnegie Corporation provides contractual retiring annuities which are paid quite independently of the disbursements of the Carnegie Foundation. The rules also make possible arrangements for disability annuity allowances. The Foundation's annual payments on account of allowances and pensions, having reached their peak in 1939, are now gradually subsiding.

On November 18, 1939, at a special term, Part I, of the Supreme Court of the State of New York, Justice William T. Collins issued a court order which, seen in the light of today's conditions, enables the Carnegie Foundation for the Advancement of Teaching to meet payments on account of retiring allowances and widows' pensions over a term of years when its income is insufficient. The court authorized and directed the Foundation to accept supplementary funds to be advanced by Carnegie Corporation of New York and to use about a third of the Foundation's principal for the purpose. The plan is ultimately to repay the borrowings from the Foundation's General Endowment Fund and the Corporation, without interest, out of income. An amendment to this court order August 2, 1945, facilitates its practical operation.

Studies in Pensions

The Foundation, in connection with its own pension problems, studied actively for a quarter of a century retirement systems in the United States, Canada, Europe, South America, Australia, and Africa. The results of these studies were presented in four special publications of the Foundation and regular Annual Reports. These inquiries were pursued not only in furtherance of Mr. Carnegie's expressed interest in the field, but also as a means of acquiring for American higher education the best information available about pension theory and practice, sound and unsound. From them were learned many of the principles which underlay the founding in 1918 of the Teachers Insurance and Annuity Association of America, which is in effect an endowed insurance company providing life insurance and annuity protection for college teachers. It was to the Association that in 1931 the Foundation's pension studies were turned over.

Studies in Education

Side by side with these studies of retirement and pensions the Foundation conducted inquiries into various aspects of education at home and abroad. In its early days difficulty was experienced in determining its scope and significance. The detached position of the newly organized foundation afforded it opportunity for the study of educational problems. Moreover, when application was received by the executive committee from a university to be "ac-

25208

BRIAR CLIFF COLLEGE
LIBRARY

SIOUX CITY, IOWA

cepted" one of the matters considered was its "standards of professional education." The Foundation's more general educational
studies had their origin in a combination of these and other facts.

The earlier educational studies of the Foundation were supported
through income from the General Endowment Fund not currently
needed for payment of benefits. Later Mr. Carnegie decided to endow them separately. On February 11, 1913, the executive committee, the trustees approving, accepted an additional sum for purposes of research in education. Following Mr. Carnegie's decision
to relinquish all of his philanthropic giving to the new Carnegie
Corporation of New York, the Corporation turned over to the
Foundation the promised $1,250,000 face value of bonds and the
Division of Educational Enquiry came into being.

Work of the division has lain principally in three fields: studies
or inquiries made by persons temporarily associated with the
Foundation for the purpose; studies or inquiries made by members of the staff; co-operation with Carnegie Corporation of New
York both as to studies and to some of the grants made by the
Corporation within the field of education. Studies by associates spe-
cially engaged dealt with medical education in the United States,
Canada, and Europe by Abraham Flexner, and the teaching of
physics by M. Llewellyn Cooke. These first three inquiries resulted
in Bulletins Number 4 (1910), 5 (1910), and 6 (1912) of the
Foundation.

After the opening of the Division of Educational Enquiry in
1913 results of the studies by staff members, who then began to
be appointed, usually appeared in Bulletins and Annual Reports in
the regular series of Foundation publications. In a number of instances inquiries were undertaken which did not result in publication. The Bulletins of the Foundation bodied forth the work of
Josef Redlich on *The Common Law and the Case Method in
American Law Schools* (Number 8, 1914), Charles Riborg Mann's
Engineering Education (Number 11, 1918), *Dental Education in
the United States and Canada* (Number 19, 1926) by William J.
Gies, *The Literature of American School and College Athletics* by
W. Carson Ryan, Jr. (Number 24, 1929), and *Examinations and
Their Substitutes in the United States* by I. L. Kandel (Number
28, 1936). Strictly speaking, Reginald Heber Smith's *Justice and
the Poor* (Number 13, 1919) concerned not the teaching of law
but its administration for all. The studies in this group were con-

ducted by men temporarily associated with the Foundation for these specific purposes.

The Foundation has also published, besides *Justice and the Poor*, inquiries financed by Carnegie Corporation of New York and made by persons not associated at all with the Foundation. These documents are usually classified as supplementary publications.

Work of the Division of Educational Enquiry began with a study of education in Vermont (Bulletin Number 7, *Education in Vermont*, 1914). Simultaneously Alfred Z. Reed was pursuing inquiries into legal education, and Kandel was studying on the one hand the social and educational relationships of pensions, and on the other a variety of educational problems, including *Federal Aid for Vocational Education* (Bulletin Number 10, 1917). Many of the thirty-one Bulletins of the Foundation present the results of educational inquiries by staff members appointed to work without term and for the most part in more than one field of inquiry. They have been concerned, for example, with legal education, the training of teachers, American college athletics, the relation of secondary and higher education in Pennsylvania, and educational testing in a variety of forms.

An Operating Body

The Carnegie Foundation for the Advancement of Teaching has been what is known in foundation parlance as an operating organization; that is, with funds derived from its own income or from outside grants it conducts educational research or directs the progress of undertakings associated with its charter purposes. On the other hand, Carnegie Corporation of New York has not been an operating body. From time to time the trustees of the Corporation receive requests for assistance the merits of which lie outside the Corporation's knowledge or experience. To the president of the Foundation, who has been a trustee and special adviser of the Corporation since its inception, the Corporation refers many of the requests relating to higher education for recommendation or report, or both. If in such cases grants are made they often are voted to the Foundation for specified purposes external but usually related to its work and carried on by other agencies or institutions. Thus, these grants the Foundation administers for the Corporation; it transmits funds when and as received from the Corporation's treasurer, and compiles reports of progress and results. Examples of the outcome of this relationship are to be seen in the Learned studies of *Education in the Maritime Provinces of Canada* (Bulletin Number 16, 1922), and the European examination project headed by Dr. Paul Monroe for the International Institute of Education. Moreover, Carnegie Corporation has financially supported the pursuit or publication of other studies by staff members of the Foundation and for others temporarily associated with the Foundation's staff. It should be noted that the Carnegie Foundation awards no fellowships or scholarships of any kind, nor does it make a practice of publishing results of researches with the direction and progress of which it has not been in close touch.

Publications

Records of the Foundation's activities and results of its studies have been published in four series of documents. These have been sent regularly to universities and colleges of the United States, Canada, and Newfoundland, to a selected list of libraries, both institutional and public, and to scholars and educators throughout the world. The Foundation's publications consist of Annual Reports, Bulletins, supplementary brochures, and miscellaneous documents.

Each Annual Report has had four main parts: results of inquiry into educational problems that affect the advancement of teaching, particularly at the higher level; records of the business of the year and administration of funds; up to 1948 brief biographical sketches of recipients of retiring allowances who had died during the year; and the report of the treasurer, which embodies the results of the annual audit by public accountants and lists and classifies the investments of the Foundation.

Excepting the first three (1907-10) the Bulletins of the Foundation have generally been in the nature of signed reports dealing with various phases of education and its relationships. Of the thirty-one Bulletins nine (Numbers 4, 1910; 6, 1912; 8, 1918; 10, 1917; 11, 1918; 13, 1919; 15, 1921; 19, 1926-27; 21, 1928) deal with aspects of professional or vocational education; four (Numbers 7, 1914; 14, 1920; 16, 1922; 27, 1932) with state or provincial provisions for education; four (Numbers 18, 1927; 23, 1929; 24, 1929-30; and 26, 1931) with college sport and its place in education; five (Numbers 9, 1915-16; 12, 1918; 17, 1926; 22, 1928; 25, 1930) with pensions and retirement for teachers; and six (Numbers 5, 1910; 20, 1927; 28, 1936; 29, 1938; 30, 1939; and 31, 1940) with more general problems of teaching, new-type testing and cog-

nate matters, as well as with graduate education. Twenty-one of
the thirty-one Bulletins have been prepared by members of the staff
individually or in collaboration with others.

The supplementary publications of the Foundation include more
extensive studies not on an annual basis. Among them two have
been issued in collaboration with the United States Office of Education, five with Purdue University, and two independently. Funds
for ten of these publications have come from Carnegie Corporation
of New York.

All of the Foundation's publications here classed as miscellaneous
have been prepared in the offices of the Foundation: reprints of
portions of Bulletins and Annual Reports, the eight Annual Reviews
of Legal Education (1928-35), the Program (1928) and the four
Progress Reports (1929-31) of the Pennsylvania Study, and fifteen documents connected with the framing and use of the Graduate Record Examination. In addition, other brochures containing
descriptive and expository matter concerning the Foundation have
issued.

Consultation

In retrospect it is quickly apparent that the advisory and consultative functions which officers and staff members have carried out
from the beginnings of the Foundation have had an important place
in the development of American higher education, whether or not
directly related to bulletins and organized studies. Administrative
officers and teachers have consulted freely and confidentially with
members of the Foundation concerning all manner of college and
university problems, less frequently with reference to matters be-
longing primarily to the secondary schools. In recent years consultation as to projects and researches connected with Corporation
grants to and through the Foundation has bulked increasingly large
in its work.

Funds

Funds of the Foundation have been five in number: the General
Endowment Fund, the endowment of the Division of Educational
Enquiry, Reserve Fund Number One, Reserve Fund Number Two,
now Contingency Fund, and the Emergency Reserve Fund, now
known more simply as the Reserve Fund. Of these five funds the
first- and second-named constitute endowments under the terms of
gift or establishment; the other three may be spent principal and

interest for their respective purposes. Under the Foundation's by-laws an investment committee determines investment policies and to a degree the individual securities in which investments may be made.

The General Endowment Fund and the endowment of the Division of Educational Enquiry were given by Mr. Carnegie, or at his behest. He provided the General Endowment Fund in two gifts, 1905 and 1908, totaling $15,000,000. The endowment of the Division of Educational Enquiry, as actually paid by Carnegie Corporation of New York, amounted, 1913, to $1,250,000, face value of bonds. At the end of the fiscal year 1949-50, the allocated assets of the General Endowment Fund totaled $12,276,833; of the Division of Educational Enquiry $555,374. Through the Division of Educational Enquiry have been paid research and project grants made by the Corporation for which the Foundation assumes responsibility in payment and oversight. They have amounted all told to more than $3,360,000, by 1950.

The reserve funds of the Foundation, now two, formerly three in number, differ in nature from the two endowment funds in that they may be spent both principal and interest for the specific purposes for which they were created.

Reserve Fund Number One was set up by vote of the Foundation's Board of Trustees November 21, 1917, for "the liquidation of pension obligations to accrue from teachers in the associated institutions," the accumulations, principal and interest, to become available for this purpose as of January 1, 1928. To this Reserve Carnegie Corporation of New York contributed $10,733,831; in addition, the Foundation was able to transfer to it considerable sums from unexpended income of the General Endowment Fund. Reserve Fund Number One was largest in 1928, when it amounted to some $12,905,000. It terminated April 19, 1944, and its accounts were closed.

In accordance with board action November 21, 1917, the executive committee of the Foundation on December 21, 1917, established Reserve Fund Number Two "to provide assistance to institutions hereafter admitted to association with the Foundation either in the form of retiring allowances to old and distinguished teachers or in assisting such colleges to inaugurate the contributory plan" of contractual retiring annuities offered by the Teachers Insurance and Annuity Association of America. It was specifically provided that "the reserve fund thus established shall not be deemed a trust fund. . . ." The principal of Reserve Fund Number Two was given by

Carnegie Corporation of New York in the amount of $1,000,000. Appropriations for grants reduced it between 1920 and 1944 by about $402,800. In 1948 the name of the Reserve Fund was changed to Contingency Fund. It has been subject to actuarial scrutiny.

"In order to prepare a reservoir from which other demands upon the Foundation . . . may be met" the executive committee, also on December 21, 1917, established "an Emergency Reserve available for such purposes as the Trustees and the Executive Committee may direct." To it the committee authorized the transfer of $100,000 of the "cash surplus now in the treasury of the Foundation." Following advice of the actuarial consultant the executive committee, May 6, 1932, earmarked a part of the Emergency Reserve to sustain the disability annuity provisions of the Rules for the Granting of Retiring Allowances. As of June 30, 1950, to the fund was allocated a little more than $300,000. In 1948 the Emergency Reserve was retitled simply the Reserve Fund.

The investments of the Foundation are held in two portfolios, in accordance with executive committee decision June 30, 1945. The Composite Portfolio as of June 30, 1950, contained bonds and common and preferred stocks having a book value of $11,297,539. In addition, the expendable portion of the General Endowment Fund consisted of bonds having a book value of $2,049,459. Income from the Composite Portfolio is allocated to various purposes of the Foundation on a basis of percentages established at the time the funds were amalgamated, which may, however, be altered at the direction of the executive committee.

RECAPITULATION

All told, since 1905 the Carnegie Foundation for the Advancement of Teaching has disbursed more than $57,492,000 for retiring allowances, disability allowances, and widows' pensions, in 168 universities, colleges, and technical schools in the United States, Canada, and Newfoundland, for more than 4,797 beneficiaries, of whom 2,089 were living at June 30, 1950. It has conducted numerous educational inquiries, the results of which have been published in thirty-one Bulletins, forty-five Annual Reports, and more than forty other documents, comprising altogether more than 16,000 printed pages. It has engaged also in a variety and a considerable number of other studies, large and small, the results of which it has not published but which have been of use in advisory services and in its own administration. It is not too much to say that the Foundation has indeed played a part in the shaping of American education, especially at the higher level, over the past forty-five years. Some account of the ways and means, the successes and failures, and the relationships which have entered into the Foundation's growth and development is set forth in the pages that follow.

~~ 3 ~~

"For the Advancement of Teaching"

GETTING UNDER WAY—EXPLORATION; A BROADER GLIMPSE · "THE CARNEGIE FOUNDATION"—NEW YORK STATE INCORPORATION; FIRST ANNUAL MEETING · AFTERMATH—VIEWS OF THE BOARD: CHARLES W. ELIOT, ARTHUR T. HADLEY, JACOB GOULD SCHURMAN, SAMUEL PLANTZ, OTHER DIRECTORS; A DINNER MEETING · MORE SECOND THOUGHTS · MOVING FORWARD—THE QUESTION OF STATE INSTITUTIONS; THE NONDENOMINATIONAL TEST · CRITICISM · THE NAME · WASHINGTON—BILL INTO ACT OF CONGRESS; BRIDGING THE GAP · PROGRESS—BYLAWS; PENSION RULES · FIRST MEETINGS—THE BOARD, APRIL 9, 1906; EXECUTIVE COMMITTEE, MAY 9, 1906; EXECUTIVE COMMITTEE, JUNE 7, 1906; EXECUTIVE COMMITTEE, JUNE 21, 1906 · FOURTEEN MONTHS OF WORK: RESULTS

A NDREW CARNEGIE was not one who having started something would let it lag for lack of prodding. For his latest foundation he had promised sensational resources for pensioning college teachers. He had enlisted in the cause an eminent galaxy of trustees, principally from the academic world, and especially two energetic men, one with educational background, the other with financial and what then passed for sociological interests: Henry Smith Pritchett of Boston, and Frank A. Vanderlip of New York City. Thoroughly satisfied with these steps, enjoying in anticipation the acclaim which the new adventure would bring from press and public, Mr. Carnegie had sailed for a summer at Skibo.

There is no evidence that he had cogitated very deeply over his new endowment and its implications. Indeed, all remaining signs indicate that he had simply and directly followed his own intuitions and then left to others the nurture and development of an

41

extraordinary impulse. This course was wise in the best sense of the term.

GETTING UNDER WAY

Having made preliminary approaches to the problem, Pritchett and Vanderlip more than doubled their efforts after Mr. Carnegie's April sailing. They conferred frequently in person and in numerous letters. They asked advice from their fellow-trustees about "the Carnegie pensions business," as one referred to it, and sought questions suitable to be asked of North American universities and colleges which might be included in it.

Pritchett's imagination began to take fire. "I am persuaded," he wrote, May 10, 1905, to the Founder at Skibo, "that nothing you could have done would in the end be so far-reaching in educational matters; and I am beginning to see one fruit of it I had not before thought of, and that is that the educational institutions themselves and those who conduct them will by means of this [gift to the teachers] be brought together to consider common needs and common opportunities. . . ."

Letters and questionnaires were dispatched June 30, to 627 colleges from Vanderlip's Wall Street office, and replies and correspondence multiplied during the summer months. There were laggards among the colleges and ultimately only 331 replied. One of the promptest respondents was the young Columbia dean, Frederick P. Keppel, who sent his answer to Vanderlip on August 12th. By contrast, the acting-president of the University of Missouri dated his response February 5, 1906, too late by nearly three months for practical use. Freeman and Mr. Gregory worked through the answers and the returned questionnaires. Pritchett and Vanderlip scanned results and reported progress to Mr. Carnegie.

Exploration

All through the summer and autumn of 1905, before and after Mr. Carnegie returned to the United States, Vanderlip and Pritchett, Freeman and Gregory, and their associates plowed steadily ahead through the maze which the questionnaires and resulting correspondence had opened to them. Having provided the endowment, Mr. Carnegie was eager that it should be put to use for pension purposes at once; "it was the union of happiness and usefulness in old age which [he] had in mind when he made his gift. . . ."

He had summoned his trustees to meet in New York City on November 15. Late in October Pritchett staked out for Vanderlip the areas he thought their report should cover. He suggested seven topics, six of which, of the "how-many" variety, bore directly upon the pensions; the seventh trenched upon more obviously educational matters: "One of the first duties of the Trustees, and particularly of the executive officers, will be to undertake certain educational definitions, as for example, what grades of work should be expected of institutions which shall be eligible to be called colleges, universities, and technical schools in the sense intended" by Mr. Carnegie in his Letter of Gift.

A Broader Glimpse

Now the matter of pensions was dual in content and nature. It pertained, of course, to the immediate results flowing from the questionnaire, but it also had broader implications. The provost of McGill University, Sir William Peterson, on receipt of the questionnaire and circular letter sent much information about pensions in Canadian and Scottish universities to Pritchett and Vanderlip, who studied them thoroughly and fruitfully. Thus began probably the first American attempt to examine in bulk the principles underlying pensions and retirement. On November 8, 1905, Pritchett wrote in part to Mr. Carnegie:

> . . . the more I have seen of the work the more clearly I understand that this Foundation is to become one of the great educational influences in our country, because it is going to deal, necessarily, not alone with the payment of retired pensions to deserving teachers, but as well with the most far-reaching educational questions and with the most important problems of educational policy. . . .

"THE CARNEGIE FOUNDATION"

During the spring of 1905, Pritchett, living in Boston, saw Mr. Carnegie rather infrequently. Vanderlip, however, was often conferring with the Founder, and it was probably Vanderlip who persuaded Mr. Carnegie that his foundation should be incorporated. Pritchett appears never to have favored this early step; he regarded it as premature and hence as motion lost.

New York State Incorporation

Vanderlip engaged Philbin, Beekman and Menken, of 52 Wall Street, New York City, for the legal work. A certificate of incorporation was drawn up, signed by five corporators (Butler, Humphreys, Pritchett, Franks, and Vanderlip) as of April 28, and approved May 8, 1905, by the Hon. H. A. Gildersleeve, Justice of the Supreme Court of the State of New York. It legally created "The Carnegie Foundation" for the purpose of "providing funds to establish retiring pensions for the teachers of universities, colleges and technical schools, in the United States, Canada and Newfoundland, and . . . aiding the cause of higher education and removing a source of deep and constant anxiety to the poorest paid and yet one of the highest of all professions . . ." The third section set forth the "particular objectives" of the corporation, all of which pertained to the payment of retiring pensions, except that benefactions might be made to charitable and educational institutions "generally to promote the cause of science and education." Sectarian institutions were not eligible. The instrument named the twenty-five directors to hold office until the first annual meeting, and made New York City the Foundation's headquarters.

For the shortcomings of the New York State charter Mr. Carnegie's desire to see matters started was in part responsible, but Vanderlip and the other corporators, Pritchett included, were not beyond responsibility. The Pritchett of 1905 lacked the experience, persuasiveness, and propinquity which at a later date would have prompted a firm stand. All of the corporators realized that Mr. Carnegie, abroad, was eager for a beginning. And it was made.

Although Pritchett joined in signing the necessary papers, he had already envisioned for the new organization a wider field of usefulness than its charter contemplated or even implied, and had written of the matter to Mr. Carnegie. As late spring became summer and summer advanced, he seems to have grown increasingly conscious of the charter's limitations—perhaps of a lack of dignity in it. This consciousness he communicated to Mr. Carnegie and Vanderlip, and he won both to his broader point of view; namely, that while the pensioning of teachers was the primary purpose of the new endowment, there were other, perhaps more enduring ends to be served than the New York State Certificate of Incorporation took into account.

First Annual Meeting

The corporators, upon due notice, met November 15, 1905, at ten in the morning at Mr. Carnegie's house. All five were present. The preliminary legal work had been attended to, and the formalities were soon completed. Probably Mr. Carnegie attended this organization meeting, but direct evidence is lacking.

Vanderlip presented the proposed bylaws, which had been drawn principally by the lawyers, and they were adopted. One or two sections are worth emphasis. Article V provided for an executive committee of seven members, including the president. In Section 2 of this article is contained one of the most useful of provisions: "During the intervals between the meetings of the Board the Executive Committee shall exercise all the powers of the Board of Directors in the management and direction of the business and conduct of the affairs of the Foundation. . . ." The twenty-five directors were to be elected annually, and so, too, the six directors to be members of the executive committee. Article VII prescribed only the pensioning function; there was no provision permitting the board of directors to vary the purposes of the new Foundation to sort with changing times. Upon vote to accept the $10,000,000 fund formal organization concluded.

The first meeting of the board assembled at four-fifteen in the afternoon. Its principal scheduled business was the election of officers, but other matters turned out to have equal importance.

There was only one absentee, William Rainey Harper, president of the University of Chicago, who was ill. Charles W. Eliot was chosen temporary chairman for the meeting, and Charles F. Thwing temporary secretary. Mr. Carnegie was present, at his best in geniality and graciousness.

Plans for filling the offices had been some weeks in the making. At one time an executive committee of thirteen directors had been contemplated, probably as a safeguard to provide for membership in the committee a majority of the board. There is extant in Mr. Carnegie's hand an early penciled notation of his preferences for this committee. He himself expected to be on it. The others he favored were (in his own order) Hadley, Wilson, Schurman, Butler, Humphreys, Franks, Vanderlip, the director or president, Harrison, Pritchett, King, Peterson. Apparently he had not approached Pritchett directly at that time about the presidency, but there is evidence that all along he had been the Donor's first choice. When the matter had been threshed out and Pritchett had indicated his willingness to serve he set about persuading Mr. Carnegie not to undertake a directorship. This must have required patience.

Officers of the board were chosen first: Eliot as chairman, Harper vice-chairman, Thwing secretary. They began their duties immediately.

Under the newly adopted bylaws the chairman appointed Eliot, Crawford, and Thwing to act as nominators for the executive committee. The bylaws had cut membership in the committee to seven. Those unanimously chosen were Harrison, Butler, Wilson, Vanderlip, Humphreys, and Franks. These directors then withdrew to discuss filling the presidency and the treasurership. Probably Mr. Carnegie accompanied them to another room.

This work completed, Butler read the executive committee's report, which nominated Pritchett to be president and the Founder's nephew, T. Morrison Carnegie, treasurer. Their election was unanimous upon a single ballot cast by the secretary. Although these choices fulfilled Mr. Carnegie's principal wishes, he was not himself to be a member of the board.

The Pritchett-Vanderlip report was then presented. It counted 389 colleges as possibly acceptable for benefits of the Foundation. These institutions had 6,969 professors whose annual salaries averaged $1,376, with a maximum of $1,783, and a minimum of $726. The incumbents' service averaged eight years. Unquestionably acceptable institutions numbered 112. The cost of pensioning at half-salary 300 men for age and 60 men for disability, while paying at the same time into a reserve fund 5 per cent, or $25,000, out of a total income of $500,000, and using a similar proportion for administration, would amount to an annual load of $410,000. Pritchett and Vanderlip made two recommendations: First, that the new Foundation confine itself within these limits, and secondly, that attempt should be made to induce colleges to raise their own standards. The report was accepted.

Discussion continued and questions arose thick and fast. The board adopted a resolution conferring upon the executive committee power, "if in their judgment such action be expedient," to approach the Congress of the United States or the New York State legislature, with the object of securing a legislative charter. In this resolution the hand of Pritchett is plainly discernible. Mr. Carnegie thoroughly approved.

It was furthermore "Resolved that the president and the Executive Committee be . . . requested to report at a subsequent meeting of the Directors, with respect to the various questions brought up for discussion at the meeting." The results of this action will soon be apparent.

Dr. George Hutcheson Denny has the unique distinction of being the only member of the original board of directors now alive. He recalls "the high spots" of the first board meeting clearly:

1. The personnel of the group, consisting as it did of the foremost presidents of the privately-endowed colleges and universities of the country. 2. The skilful handling of the meeting by President Eliot and Dr. Pritchett. 3. The presence and manifest interest and gratification of Mr. Carnegie, who was not only a gracious host, but also a helpful influence in the discussion. Apparently the only thing he failed to grasp was the fact that the amount of money he had provided was quite inadequate to serve the purposes for which it had been donated. 4. The impression made on many of the trustees was that Mr. Carnegie felt very deeply that the Foundation was destined to take high rank among his benefactions in the service of the country. 5. Mr. Carnegie showed no disposition to dominate the meeting. He evidently had the utmost faith in Dr. Pritchett's leadership. 6. Mr. Vanderlip took little part in the meeting. He deferred to the college presidents. 7. Woodrow Wilson rarely had a word to say either at the first meeting or at any subsequent meeting of the Board. The most voluminous talker of this early period was President David Starr Jordan. His closest competitor was President Schurman of Cornell.

AFTERMATH

The public's reception of the new foundation and reports of its first meeting must have gratified even Mr. Carnegie, accustomed though he was to publicity. Vanderlip, still handling press relations, played his part well, and interest was nationwide. Although approval was not unanimous the dissidents were comparatively few, though vociferous. The new officers and the executive committee began their task at once, Pritchett still resident in Boston, Vanderlip and T. Morrison Carnegie in New York.

Views of the Board

First fruits of the sessions at Mr. Carnegie's house included lively correspondence between Pritchett and his fellow-trustees. Of these letters those from four directors deserve separate consideration; others may be grouped together. All of this correspondence deals with subjects considered at the meetings.

CHARLES W. ELIOT

On the way back to Boston Eliot had noted down certain provisions which he considered fundamental to administration of the benefits which the great gift would provide. His memorandum was derived in the main from the system of retiring allowances in use at Harvard, which, he pointed out, was an adaptation of the "British Civil Service Pension Plan." He was the first to use the term "retiring allowance" in Foundation correspondence. As for detail, Eliot would have applications come through institutions. Denominational questions should be decided under the Foundation's charter or certificate of incorporation, on the basis of the statutory control or nominating powers resident in the denomination. He looked forward to the framing of certain rules for the granting of the Foundation's allowances. The retiring age, he thought, should be sixty years after twenty years' service in college, university, or technical school. The allowance should be $2\%_0$ of the average salary over the last five service years, plus $\frac{1}{60}$ of the average for each year over twenty, up to a limit of $4\%_0$ of the final salary. Sabbatical leave should be counted as active service. The Foundation should retain the prerogative of altering its rules and abridging rights as necessary.

ARTHUR T. HADLEY

A fortnight after the meeting Hadley of Yale wrote about the quality desirable in the academic requirement and the nature of the professional work to be looked for in order to assure the eligibility of both institutions and their teachers to Foundation benefits. He discussed standards of college work to be required and the kind of work the professors would be doing. Pensions, he noted, should be paid to the treasurers of institutions and by them distributed to beneficiaries. The Foundation should not pay pensions to professors who still retained regular classes; "if this were once admitted it would give a loophole for all kinds of abuse." He pointed out the danger to standards that arose from preparatory schools affiliated with higher institutions.

Jacob Gould Schurman

As for denominational institutions, Schurman of Cornell believed that the Foundation should enforce their exclusion "just as strictly or as leniently as the terms of the act of incorporation provide." He was opposed to making exceptions. As for academic requirements, he appears to have based most of his views upon the regulations of the Regents of the University of the State of New York, with which, of course, he was familiar. Under certain restrictions a professor reaching age 65, he held, should have his pension as a matter of course as soon as his institution applied for it. For all practical purposes he was disposed to make thirty years' service the maximum condition. A disability pension should be determined by circumstances, and the scale of pensions should bear some proportionate relation to the salary for each of the final five or ten service years. This provision was later to wreak havoc with the Foundation, but not so the pension limit of $2,500 which Schurman proposed. He felt "very strongly" that widows should be provided for, a stretching of generosity not apparently contemplated by Mr. Carnegie or Pritchett up to this date but, of course, a measure that appealed strongly to every married man.

Samuel Plantz

Plantz of Lawrence University, Wisconsin, wished to base the pension upon years of service; this and not age should determine the importance of the service rendered. "I presume," he adds, "that what Mr. Carnegie intends is not to reward men, but to care for them." In a subsequent letter Plantz called Pritchett's attention to the joint contributory retirement plan in operation for German universities, an almost prophetic notation. If something similar were adopted, Plantz felt that "the best way for the trustees to proceed would be to subsidize institutions which would establish a pension system" for themselves. Apparently Plantz was thinking not of distributing the Foundation's capital but of subsidizing out of income year by year.

Other Directors

Other members of the board—among them Hughes, King, Peterson, McClelland, and Bell—presented their views. Hughes, stressing the fact that the denominational requirement would shut out "several of the broadest universities in [his] own church," went on to deal with academic standards in terms of church-related universities, in particular those under the University Senate of the Methodist Episcopal Church. This whole matter was already occasioning wide discussion, and Hughes only repeated some of what was being said in denominational circles. King wanted to insist upon "the N.E.A. standard of fifteen units" for admission to college, but proposed a loose enforcement of the nonsectarian test. Peterson would start a reserve fund to deal with worthy but exceptional applications. He hoped that nothing "would make the Founder . . . doubt the wisdom of his stand on the denominational question," and that the plan would enable eligible teachers "to look forward confidently, on certain conditions of service, to a pension. This is the case . . . with the Scottish universities." McClelland, Bell, and others contributed earnestly, but scarcely to the enlargement of the new endowment's horizon.

A majority of the directors saw the retirement problem as a real issue in American colleges and not as a fantasy, but they naturally tended to approach it in terms of their own experience and loyalties. A few foresaw dangers but apparently no financial pitfalls. This aspect, however, Pritchett had stressed in sending Vanderlip, probably in October 1905, a draft of an introduction for their report to the first directors' meeting: "You must confine it to a limited number of institutions. A $10,000,000 bequest spread out over the whole United States will be too thin to have any effect." In this statement Pritchett appears to have been the first director to approach the question of financial resources.

A Dinner Meeting

Correspondence among the board was well enough, as far as it went, but it soon became apparent that a face-to-face discussion of some of the questions raised on November 15 was essential. Accordingly, Pritchett assembled in New York a group of the directors, probably early in December 1905 for dinner and discussion. The precise date and place cannot be now determined. The company included Butler, Hadley, Humphreys, Harper, and Pritchett, and probably others. Butler, Humphreys, and Pritchett were members of the executive committee.

Although no record of proceedings was kept some of the topics discussed can be inferred. Pritchett probably pointed out that while

Mr. Carnegie had given funds primarily for pensions there would be involved a scrutiny of education, even down to such basal questions as, What is a college? The group canvassed various possibilities as regards organization of offices, where they should be located, and what kind of personnel should be employed. Pritchett stressed simplicity and feeling out the way, rather than plunging into full equipment. Most important of all the topics dealt with stood the inadequacy of the charter of "The Carnegie Foundation," its limits as a working document, and the means of repairing its defects. The board had empowered the executive committee to seek a legislative charter, either in Albany or in Washington. Pritchett, having in mind experience in connection with the reincorporation of Carnegie Institution of Washington, and being acquainted with the man who had handled the legal steps for the Institution, brought to the group's attention John L. Cadwalader, one of the leaders of the American Bar. Probably he had already approached Cadwalader. In any event, the proposal to seek Congressional action through Cadwalader's efforts commended itself to all present.

One more matter of discussion deserves a passing word. Those were the days of distrust of "tainted money." Mr. Carnegie had maintained to ship reporters who besieged him on the pier in April that his money was not tainted. Already two directors had dealt with the matter, the presidents of Yale and of Harvard. At New Haven, Hadley had laughed at the tainted money stigma: "Bring on your tainted money," he is reported to have said before a college gathering. "We will purify it with the Yale spirit" and use it well. On December 7, 1905, at the dedication of Harvard Hall in the new building of the Harvard Club of New York City, Eliot delivered an address in which he said: "We have no objection at Cambridge to riches and the good use of riches. We have every objection to the bad use of riches, to the demoralizing use of riches. . . ." Thus the ghost was laid.

MORE SECOND THOUGHTS

The directors, probably spurred somewhat by Pritchett and certainly by Mr. Carnegie's known views about starting the work, continued correspondence among themselves and with their elected president. Butler had taken a prominent part in the meetings of November 15 and the dinner discussion, but he appears not to have put his views in writing until, probably at Pritchett's request, he set down some of them in a letter dated February 13, 1906.

In connection with rules of procedure for "normal cases" upon which Pritchett was already at work, Butler wrote in part: "I should be sorry to have persons get the notion that they acquired *rights* from the Foundation rather than *privileges*." In this he was at one with Cadwalader. "Had we not better treat the beneficiaries as recipients of a privilege, which privilege is granted and may, in case of necessity, be amended or wholly withdrawn by the Trustees, rather than grantees of a right which might, on occasion, be legally defended?" This was wise foresight.

As to educational standards, Butler, as Schurman had done, called attention to the definition of a college in use by the Regents of the University of the State of New York, which he quoted at length. This definition, he wrote, "was the product of the activity of Mr. Melvil Dewey who was very much given to a quantitative method of determining matters essentially qualitative." Mr. Dewey, of course, was the leading proponent of simplified spelling which was greatly interesting Mr. Carnegie, who, after all, was not an accomplished speller, probably because his ideas always outran his pen.

Butler's letter reached Pritchett in time to be considered during the framing of a "Memorandum to the Executive Committee" which Pritchett submitted to Mr. Carnegie on February 19th. That ten-page draft presented Pritchett's recommendations as to rules for the granting of benefits but it touched other matters as well. Mr. Carnegie went over it with careful attention, penciling his comments on the sheets. Aside from the question, what name should be chosen for the proposed Congressional incorporation which was to succeed the New York State body, Mr. Carnegie's comments stressed first and foremost the pensioning functions of the Foundation; he even changed one important phrase so as to emphasize "pensioning the teachers."

Beside a section on "pensions of widows and orphans," he jotted: "Questionable this. Would submit trustees to innumerable claims. The gift was not intended to be retroactive—but widows of professors hereafter who receive pensions get the pension during life. I am disposed to think orphans going too far. Widows certainly, and *these only if needy*. Children of parents older than 65 will be self-supporting before both parents die." The widow's pension was certainly a second thought.

As to "pensions for meritorious service," he asked: "Does this mean that years may be added to render him eligible to the usual pension, or does it add to the pension itself?" For disability pensions, "the disability must be absolute." He changed "ten years service in an office of a grade not less than that of assistant professor" to "ten years service in an office of a grade not less than that of professor, and fifteen as assistant professor . . ." He balked a little at the Harvard phrase "retiring allowance," which he changed to "pension," and he shied at the implications of the word "right" as applied to benefits.

At the end of the memorandum he wrote: "I like this report. Have noted a few points suggestively only. A.C."

MOVING FORWARD

The "scrutiny of education" which the directors had requested of the Foundation's officers at the first meeting was already well under way. Pritchett and Vanderlip had been at work upon it for at least six months before the directors had met, and following their more or less formal request Pritchett pursued it with extraordinary energy. As of January 1, 1906, he began part-time duty in New York City.

Now it was all very well to lay out policy in general; its details proved much more difficult. The devising of operating procedure, requirements for accepting institutions and for granting allowances, selection of office space and personnel, the choosing out of 700-odd widely varying institutions those which merited eligibility, to hew to the line marked by the Letter of Gift and the Certificate of Incorporation regarding denominational and state control, to plan to take the steps necessary in procuring a new charter—all this took devastating care and attention. Even to make a start in all these matters early in the new year was a tremendous task.

By March 2, 1906, when Pritchett reported by letter to Mr. Carnegie at San Fernandina, Florida, the executive committee had accepted by letter the recommendations Pritchett and Vanderlip had framed on the results of their scrutiny. Pritchett wrote:

> We are trying to develop the plan in such a way as to confer these pensions, while at the same time paying due regard to the somewhat shy and proud attitude of the teacher, and I trust we may succeed in this effort. I am sure you would feel many times

repaid, if you could see some of the expressions of appreciation which these men have given.

The machinery is now all ready to set the work going, and this will be done as soon as the whole Board has come together and accepted the work of the Executive Committee.

The best pleasure which I have had in all this matter, is your approval.

Two further topics demanded what perhaps seemed at the time an inordinate amount of care.

The Question of State Institutions

Even when the Letter of Gift was being framed the eligibility of publicly controlled institutions to participate in Foundation benefits had been canvassed. Mr. Carnegie was opposed. So also was Pritchett, who pointed out to Vanderlip that the states would never do for themselves what a "private citizen steps in to do . . . for them."

The problem persisted through the first meetings. Hadley, whose opinion Pritchett often sought and much respected, believed that "we certainly should not raise the question whether we could include state universities . . . until . . . we have seen whether the fund is fully adequate to meet the needs of the institutions more directly contemplated." "On the subject of state institutions," Schurman wrote, "we should be governed entirely by Mr. Carnegie's wishes." Others were definitely opposed to admitting state institutions. Peterson, however, would "be glad to see them included." On the whole, the directors inclined to defer to Mr. Carnegie's wishes.

Discussion was not confined to the board. There was much newspaper and some magazine comment for and against. On December 12, 1905, President H. C. White of the University of Georgia, chairman of the executive committee of the Association of American Agricultural Colleges and Experiment Stations, asked permission to appear before the Foundation directors and present an account of the character and services of the land-grant colleges making up his association. Beyond acknowledgment, no immediate result ensued, although the question was kept alive in numerous public discussions and meetings.

The Nondenominational Test

Among church bodies only the American Unitarian Association seems to have been well disposed towards the nondenominational criterion for institutions' eligibility. On October 22, 1905, Pritchett wrote to Mr. Carnegie: "I feel quite sure that [this association] is right in saying that your action in helping nonsectarian education is farreaching and wise." Wishes certainly were parents of a notion which spread widely in 1906 to the effect that Mr. Carnegie had added "five million more to his gift and that he had withdrawn his limitation barring . . . denominational schools," as Jordan wrote from California. This T. M. Carnegie called "entirely without foundation." Crawford of Allegheny and others had seen similar newspaper statements, some of which revealed a touchy or questioning attitude.

CRITICISM

Correspondence with directors showed that not all of the opinions expressed concerning the new endowment were favorable. The most brilliant critic of the Foundation, and all it stood for or might become, was a well-known psychologist of the University of Wisconsin, Professor Joseph Jastrow. His principal objections derived from his view that the income of the Foundation should be applied to the raising of professors' salaries. He circularized members of the board on the subject of salaries rather than pensions, and Pritchett sent parts of one of his memorandums to all board members.

Jastrow claimed to have canvassed the opinions of some forty to fifty men "in many faculties," and turned up much opposition to Mr. Carnegie's gift. He even suggested instead "cheap insurance on the annuity plan" as a substitute. He disliked the name of the Foundation and wanted it called "The Foundation for the Advancement of Academic Welfare" without reference to the donor.

There were objections to Jastrow's objections and many directors posed them. Bell thought Jastrow's method hardly "calculated to get the best opinion of those with whom he consulted." Others took issue with his argument at a number of points. Schurman probably represented a minority view in the board when he wrote Pritchett: "I have no doubt that it would have been better for the colleges and universities if Mr. Carnegie had given $30,000,000 to raise professorial salaries instead of $10,000,000 for professorial pensions. But the two objects are not incompatible and both are highly important." Jastrow early won his place in the van of opposition to the new philanthropy and his recruits multiplied over succeeding years.

THE NAME

Although the New York State incorporation had given the new endowment a name that has persisted ever since, many felt that the designation lacked meaning. As possibilities of useful service became increasingly apparent, first to Pritchett, and then to others as he won them to his views, "The Carnegie Foundation" as a title seemed colorless and inadequate. Mr. Carnegie continued strong in his wish to emphasize the pensioning functions; Pritchett foresaw a time when these might subside and bring the need of a broader designation for a broader function. By mid-December 1905 the whole matter of a new incorporation, legislative or Congressional, was under discussion, and first steps towards Washington had already been taken.

Pritchett raised the question with Mr. Carnegie on December 9. He asked "whether it might not be wise to call the foundation 'The Carnegie Foundation for Education.' . . . While the primary purpose . . . is the formulation of a pension system our charter enables us to undertake any sort of educational work for colleges and universities. . . . It may well happen in the future that our activities may cover a far greater range with respect to education."

Mr. Carnegie dissented: " 'The Carnegie Foundation for Education' does not strike me favorably. 'Foundation' seems superfluous. 'Carnegie Professorial Pension Fund' or 'Carnegie Educational Pension Fund' seems to me better. It might be well, I think, for you to ask suggestions for the name from the [directors]. . . . I don't think that you should disguise the fact that it is first and foremost a pension fund. The closer union it may bring about is incidental though important."

Pritchett tossed the ball back the next day: "I think the words 'Carnegie Foundation for the Betterment of the Teachers' Profession' carry out the thought. . . . The word 'Foundation' I like very much. . . ."

Then the executive committee took a hand in the give-and-take. In transmitting its collective views to the Founder, Pritchett referred to "our correspondence with teachers throughout the country who are taking the greatest interest in the development of this Foundation. [The executive committee's] theory . . . is to follow as closely as possible the language and the ideas of your original letter. . . . The idea back of that letter is 'the Advancement of the Profession of the Teachers'—the establishment of the system of pensions . . . [and] the advancement of education by dignifying and improving the calling of the teacher. . . ."

"We have . . . suggested a sort of sub-title, to be written in smaller letters underneath the main title:

THE CARNEGIE FOUNDATION
For the Advancement of Teaching

[or]

THE CARNEGIE FOUNDATION
For the Advancement of the Profession of Teaching

or

THE CARNEGIE FOUNDATION
Established to Advance the Profession of Teaching.

. . . The term 'Pension Fund' . . . has a rather narrow significance, and . . . correspondence shows that this would be an unhappy term to use."

While Franks liked "The Carnegie Foundation to Advance the Profession of Teaching," Butler, master of phrase that he was, preferred "The Carnegie Foundation for the Advancement of Teaching," and Eliot, equally skilled in words, leaned to "The Carnegie Foundation for the Promotion of Higher Education." For another month Mr. Carnegie clung to emphasis on his original purpose through the title "The Carnegie Foundation for the Pensioning of Teachers," but at last he yielded. Long afterwards Butler recalled that it was Pritchett's advice that kept the word "pensions" out of the name and brought about the final adoption of the designation "The Carnegie Foundation for the Advancement of Teaching"; "this was a wise and fortunate suggestion." Upon it the negotiations that looked towards national incorporation were predicated.

WASHINGTON

One of the most fortunate choices Pritchett ever made was his selection of John L. Cadwalader, member of the firm of Strong & Cadwalader, New York attorneys, as pilot through the storms and shoals of Congressional action. Not only had Cadwalader guided Carnegie Institution of Washington to national incorporation, but he had served as trustee of the Institution since 1903, and he was destined so to serve until 1914. Among the first persons he consulted about Foundation affairs was the Secretary of State, Elihu Root, who particularly urged incorporation on a national rather than a state basis. The Speaker of the House, "Uncle Joe" Cannon (Joseph Gurney Cannon, Illinois), "agreed . . . to undertake the obtaining of a national charter from Congress." Members of the executive committee, consulted individually, had approved, and so had Mr. Carnegie. Thus the course was set, and the voyage began.

By January 2, 1906, Cadwalader had drafted and put in print for submitting to the Congress a charter, under which a new foundation should succeed the New York State "Carnegie Foundation," although the name it was to bear was still not finally determined. Now Congress, he noted, had "no particular affection for Carnegie," and so he purposed to say nothing concerning the United States Steel Corporation bonds as an investment of the new Foundation's funds lest "some Southern members might 'shy off' at the idea of a trust." He was omitting state residences after the names of trustees "because if [a] committee began to dicker with the subject everybody would consider that there ought to be a trustee from his particular State." And he inserted in his draft a clause as to purpose with intent similar to that devised for Carnegie Institution of Washington, which will give "some freedom hereafter in varying the purposes of the gift." On the legal side there were other stopgaps and reassurances as well. At a number of points the charter draft reflected in phrase the influence of both Mr. Carnegie and Pritchett, and both thought well of it.

So too did the executive committee, when at last they received individual copies by mail. Delivery of those copies was seriously held up because the printer's messenger carrying them to Pritchett at the Foundation's new offices, 542 Fifth Avenue, under instructions to hurry, on the contrary dawdled and, panic-stricken by the delay he thus had caused, threw them all away. More were at last procured but the boy never went back to his job.

Bill into Act of Congress

A bill to incorporate was introduced into the House on January 29, 1906. By that time the name of the new organization had crystallized into "The Carnegie Foundation for the Advancement of Teaching." The bill, backed by Congressman James T. McCleary of Minnesota, and Congressman Charles R. Thomas of North Carolina, readily passed the House on January 31. But in the Senate a bill sponsored by Senator William P. Dillingham of Vermont, was referred to the Committee on the Judiciary, "a very large commit-tee, which takes things seriously," Pritchett reported to the execu-tive committee; "a few Southern Democrats have objected to it on the ground that it involves a recognition of the Steel Trust." Both a Senate and a House committee went to work on the proposed measure. Probably the House committee considered it at a hearing January 29 or 30; the Senate committee on the Judiciary, February 16. Pritchett appeared at both hearings.

The possible objections centered upon mention and "recognition" of the Steel Corporation bonds in the old Certificate of Incorpora-tion, locating the principal office in New York City, and making that city a meeting place for a corporation legislated into existence by Congress. To all these and other objections Cadwalader found answers. He also briefed Pritchett for his appearance before the committees, on which the principal opponents of the bill were Sen-ator Charles A. Culberson of Texas, and Congressman John Sharp Williams of Mississippi—formidable opponents both. The hearings concluded, correspondence ensued between Culberson and Pritchett. At Pritchett's request numerous trustees-to-be wrote personally to their senators and congressmen, and Pritchett enlisted the good offices of his brother-in-law, Senator Frank G. Newlands of Nevada. Cadwalader's skill and devotion enabled the proponents of the bill to carry the day, and the act to incorporate the Carnegie Founda-tion for the Advancement of Teaching became law on March 10, 1906, over the signature of President Theodore Roosevelt, friend of both Mr. Carnegie and Pritchett. Another good and famous friend, Secretary Root, sealed and certified the act as of April 6, and the new Foundation became a fact under its District of Colum-bia Charter.

All but one of those who had been intimately involved in the legislation were relieved, pleased, and gratified; Congressman Mc-Cleary wrote Pritchett: "I am sorry that the Senate amended certain sections of the bill as it did but perhaps it will be just as effective, even though not quite so complimentary to the founder."

Bridging the Gap

All along Cadwalader and Pritchett had seen that New York State legislation would be essential to enable the directors of "The Car-negie Foundation" to convey its property, the $10,000,000 worth of U. S. Steel bonds, to the new Carnegie Foundation for the Ad-vancement of Teaching. The reason was that "the trustees of a corporation in the State of New York ought not, without legislative action, to convey their entire property to a foreign corporation," especially when the transfer was to be made by a single group of trustees, holding for the first body, to themselves as trustees of another body of separate legal origin.

At the end of February and early in March, Pritchett talked in Albany with New York State legislators about ways and means. He, Assemblyman Robert L. Cox of Buffalo, Senator Edgar T. Brackett of Saratoga Springs, and J. M. Wainwright of Westchester, agreed that the bill must be short—"under a hundred words in length." Timing gave trouble, but it was soon if not readily adjusted. The only opposition of record—perhaps it was merely routine questioning—developed in the office of the Counsel to the Governor. With Cadwalader again prompting, Pritchett disposed of the obstacle, and on April 5, 1906, the New York State Legislature passed the Act necessary to "permit the transfer of property of 'The Carnegie Foundation' to 'The Carnegie Foundation for the Advancement of Teaching.' "

A semifinal word about Cadwalader is in order. On Pritchett asking him for a bill for his work he replied, April 13, 1906: ". . . When I consider the purpose of the charity . . . I am unwilling to make a charge for my services or to decrease the funds of the Foundation."

PROGRESS

The spring of 1906 must have been one of the busiest of Pritchett's career. From January 1 he divided his time between the Massachusetts Institute of Technology in Boston, and "The Carnegie Foundation" in New York City. The enterprise was to have a new name; its local habitation was at 542 Fifth Avenue, near Forty-fifth Street, where much trouble had been taken, as Pritchett wrote to Mr. Carnegie, "to give these rooms the appearance, not of an office, but of a library and to make it a place to which . . . college people will come when they are in New York." That purpose held for more than a third of a century, but Pritchett's wish for a good portrait of the Founder to hang in the rooms was fulfilled only approximately.

In these restricted quarters several studies were under pursuit. Inquiries into pensions pressed forward on an expanding scale, not only in the educational field but in the areas of governmental pensions in the United States, Canada, Germany, Great Britain, and elsewhere. The work was social and statistical rather than actuarial, and it was pursued in relation only to the purposes of the new foundation. So also was the information about American universities and colleges, gathered, regathered, and churned over interminably. The questions which grew out of this process related to definitions and standards of higher institutions, especially the matter of admission to college. They pointed in the direction of decreasing the field to be served by the Foundation's distribution of benefits, but they also clearly showed directions in which the quality of higher education might improve and the stimulus that might be applied to that end. Even with the state universities out of the reckoning, restriction of the group of institutions seemed to Pritchett, and also to Vanderlip, a necessary step. Mr. Carnegie remained to be convinced; he "only accepted the plan . . . after much argument," Pritchett recalled some years later. "It was made clear to him that these pensions must be given in some other way than by a process of favoritism or of barter between contending institutions, and that no other objective means of choosing institutions could be devised better than some standard of educational effectiveness. . . . This plan not only afforded a sound method of discrimination but it also looked to the betterment of the standards of the high school and of the college." Clearly this matter impinged upon the question of accepting state institutions, which was growing with the increasing pertinacity and even vehemence of its proponents.

As early as February 24, Pritchett and Cadwalader had determined that the next and last meeting of "The Carnegie Foundation" should be held on April 9. Cadwalader thought that Pritchett "ought to accomplish all the purposes at one meeting; that is, organize the [new] corporation and pass the necessary resolutions for a transfer of the bonds."

Bylaws

Now, organizing the Carnegie Foundation for the Advancement of Teaching implied a new set of bylaws. In March, Pritchett submitted to Cadwalader a version which showed signs of familiarity, the lawyer noted, with the bylaws of the Institution of Washington, which Cadwalader and Secretary Root had drawn "after considerable examination of the necessities of the case." The lawyer believed that Pritchett needed "more checks than you have got," a finance committee, provision for financial administration, a budget to adhere to, a trust company as assistant treasurer, and a method of electing the president, the treasurer, and the executive committee by the board itself. He would not appear "to show a distrust of the general body and vest all the powers in the Executive Committee, because the Executive Committee itself is simply a creature of the Board for the convenience of doing business. . . ." All these suggestions Pritchett heeded. He did not, however, change the record-keeping duties of the secretary, who was to be an officer of the board; administration was concentrated in the hands of the president, with the financial work allotted to the treasurer. This emphasis obtained until in 1911 a secretary of the Foundation was appointed under a bylaw provision permitting employment of other officers than the treasurer and the president. It was not until 1938 that a secretary of the Foundation was recognized in the bylaws. "The reason for not putting into the hands of the secretary [of the board] the custody of the seal and the certification of legal instructions, was that the secretary was almost sure to live a thousand miles away from the office of the Board and it was decided to have such power in a resident officer."

Pension Rules

With the advice and consent of as many trustees as he could enlist, Pritchett set about formulating rules under which pensions might be granted. The sources of some of these provisions have already been indicated. It looks very much as if Pritchett had in mind a trial set of regulations containing a provision to the effect that they might be altered as circumstances and experience indicated.

FIRST MEETINGS

In any event, he asked Cadwalader to furnish him "an exact statement of the legal order in which the various steps should be taken, together with copies of the resolutions to be adopted by each board and the order in which they should be passed." Two calls to the meeting of "The Carnegie Foundation" were dispatched, one, March 10, 1906, signed by Eliot as chairman of the board, the other, March 13, by Thwing as its secretary. A call to the meeting of the Carnegie Foundation for the Advancement of Teaching was mailed, March 27, by Albert LeForest Derby, Pritchett's secretary and assistant at Tech, who had entered the employ of the Foundation on March 1, 1906.

The Board, April 9, 1906

Cadwalader had warned Pritchett that he should assemble all of the persons involved in the two foundations, one moribund, the other waiting to be born, without fail. Pritchett accomplished this by calling the meeting of the Foundation for ten o'clock in the morning of April 9. The first quarter-hour probably passed in chatter, explanation, and settling those present. At ten-fifteen the directors of "The Carnegie Foundation" went into session.

After rehearsing the enabling resolution of November 15, 1905, Pritchett called for a report by the treasurer. During the period in which "The Carnegie Foundation" had had no funds of its own Mr. Carnegie himself had advanced money for the payment of certain obligations, which included a bill for about $1,364 for legal assistance, $925 for compiling records, and other items of expense. The ten millions of endowment, of which $3,350,000 in 5 per cent Steel Corporation bonds had been received December 1, 1905, had now been accepted in full, and there was about $72,000 in bank. By formal vote these resources were made over to the Carnegie Foundation for the Advancement of Teaching, subject only to appropriate transfer and registry of the bonds. The meeting then adjourned and "The Carnegie Foundation" existed only in name.

Its directors, probably without leaving their seats, began at 10.45 A.M. their duties as trustees of the Carnegie Foundation for the Advancement of Teaching. The proceedings went smoothly. The same officers of the board and of the Foundation were elected, the new bylaws were adopted, the minutes of the last meeting of "The Carnegie Foundation" were spread upon the record, and Pritchett presented a report, already approved by the executive committee and sent to all trustees before the meeting, proposing "certain definitions and principles for the administration of the Foundation and rules for the granting of retiring allowances and pensions." The trustees took a hand in pointing up Pritchett's proposal. They referred the matter of widows' pensions to the executive committee, which withdrew and submitted an amendment giving the widow of a professor during her widowhood "one-half of the allowance to which he would have been entitled." The trustees further voted that no retiring allowance be granted anyone whose active service ceased before April 16, 1905, and applied an analogous limit to widows' pensions. Questions about service- and disability-provisions were recommitted to the executive committee.

The trustees fumbled toward definitions looking to eligibility of institutions, but postponed this matter and the question of the state universities until "the next meeting in November." By and large, the trustees must have congratulated themselves when they adjourned at seven that evening.

Of the meetings Pritchett wrote to Mr. Carnegie, at Hot Springs, Virginia, April 10, in part:

> The Trustees voted unanimously to sustain the denominational and educational standards which the Executive Committee had set up, notwithstanding the fact that the adoption of these will exclude, for a time at least, some of the institutions represented on the Board. For instance, it was a surprise to all of us, in making our study of these institutions, to find that not a single institution in the South maintained a standard of entrance requirement equal to the modest standard prescribed by the law of the State of New York.
>
> The temper and spirit of the Trustees was admirable, and I am sure that you would have been delighted to have heard the discussions that went on. All felt that we were launching what is to be a great influence in education, . . .

Mr. Carnegie saw another and an unexpected product of the new Foundation. "Perhaps not the least of the benefits to flow from the fund," he wrote to Thwing, "is to be the friendship sure to develop among the heads of our educational institutions."

Executive Committee, May 9, 1906

The trustees meeting of April 9 had left a number of matters to be dealt with by the executive committee at its first meeting a month later. So carefully had its work been planned that they consumed only half an hour of its seven members' time.

Financial affairs came first. The president and treasurer reported completion of the transfer of ten millions of 5 per cent Steel Corporation registered bonds from "The Carnegie Foundation" to the Carnegie Foundation for the Advancement of Teaching. T. Morrison Carnegie was named secretary to the executive committee, and as treasurer was bonded, with Mr. Andrew Carnegie as surety, for the amount of $250,000. Since April 1 current expenses had been about $21,000. Mr. Carnegie's advances up to December 1, 1905, which amounted to about $28,000, had been refunded to his bank. A finance committee was constituted to recommend bonds for the investment of any surplus receipts remaining over operating expenses: Franks, Vanderlip, and T. M. Carnegie. Mr. Carnegie's Home Trust Company of Hoboken, New Jersey, was designated assistant treasurer, as Pritchett and Cadwalader apparently had had in mind. Safe deposit space was rented elsewhere.

The committee then went forward to personnel. Pritchett was authorized to appoint as assistant secretary of the Foundation his former assistant at M.I.T., Albert LeForest Derby. Other assistance was approved. As for an office in Washington, the executive committee, accepting the offer of Carnegie Institution to provide a legal headquarters, put in charge Mr. Walter M. Gilbert, the Institution's assistant secretary, and made him assistant secretary of the Foundation as well. The salaries voted for appointees and officers seem today moderate to the point of parsimony, although Pritchett was allowed $3,000 to cover expenses of his removal to New York for full-time duties beginning June 1.

Next the committee discussed announcing a first provisional list of forty-five institutions accepted for retiring allowances. It authorized Pritchett to request from their administrative heads assurances of their nonsectarian status and nominations for benefits. Although this list contained at least one university that received state aid, it included no publicly-controlled university or college.

As for administrative details, the committee determined that payment of allowances should begin as of July 1, 1906—by inference in arrears not in advance—checks to be mailed on or about the twenty-fifth of each month to individuals or to institutions which should distribute their moneys to beneficiaries. Consideration of applications for allowances was postponed until the committee's next meeting, but "in view of the long service to education and to the advancement of learning in this country" the first retiring allowance of the Foundation was offered to Dr. William Torrey Harris, United States Commissioner of Education, then in his seventy-first year, in the maximum amount of $3,000.

Finally, the committee opened wide the whole question of accepting state institutions by authorizing the president to invite representatives of the Association of State Universities to present to the Foundation's trustees by October 1, 1906, "a statement of their reasons for believing it desirable that state institutions should be admitted to the benefits of the Foundation," and authorized Pritchett to invite a representative of that association to attend the annual meeting November 21, "to submit these reasons and to answer such questions as may be asked." From every point of view, then, the meeting was both expeditious and efficient.

Executive Committee, June 7, 1906

The executive committee's second meeting, June 7, was largely devoted to discussion and adoption of an accepted list composed of the forty-five institutions of the May meeting, to which two Canadian universities were added. Pritchett presented results of a study of entrance requirements which had been some months in the making. Following his recommendations the committee voted that "in determining the academic standards of institutions fourteen points or units shall be accepted as an equivalent of the high school," each unit to signify five recitations a week throughout the year in one subject. Of the forty-five American institutions listed, thirty demanded 15 or more points for admission, fourteen demanded 14 or 14.5 points. A flat requirement of at least 15 units would have excluded several prominent eastern institutions from the list.

That list was far from perfect. Consisting mostly of "prestige" institutions, it was heavily weighted in the New England and mid-Atlantic areas. Only one university was situated on the Pacific Coast, and the farthest south was Washington University, St. Louis. At the same meeting, on the basis of new entrance requirements in 1907, the Tulane University was accepted. The leaven was beginning to work.

The Harris retiring allowance was formally granted. The Commissioner had written to Pritchett and Pritchett had reported to Mr. Carnegie: "I accept the offer of the retiring allowance with the feelings of the profoundest gratitude for the delicate and honorable expressions of esteem and appreciation with which it is tendered. Permit me to say that I have never in my life been so completely taken by surprise, nor have I ever before received so high an honor —an honor which I feel to be completely beyond my deserts." He was to receive his allowance until his death in November 1909.

Forty-two other allowances and four widows' pensions were granted, whose recipients included Hiram Corson of Cornell, Henry P. Bowditch of Harvard, and Francis A. March of Lafayette. The Harris and March allowances were two of ten granted outside the accepted list. The executive committee had done a good day's work.

Executive Committee, June 21, 1906

The executive committee's third meeting before the end of the fiscal year and prior to the date on which its initial benefits were to become effective, assembled at two-thirty in the afternoon June 21, 1906. Only Pritchett, Vanderlip, Humphreys, and Franks attended. After approving the investment of $120,000 of surplus income in 3½ per cent and 4 per cent railroad bonds, as recommended by the finance committee, the executive committee considered applications and petitions for the granting of retiring allowances. The petitions presented somewhat irregular cases urged by faculty colleagues. Discussion of the predicament of Bowdoin College, which had an endowed professorship, retention of which depended upon a majority of its trustees being members of the Congregational Church or "in doctrinal sympathy with it," led to omitting Bowdoin's name from the first provisional list of accepted institutions, which was to issue under the date of July 9, 1906. To the accepted list Stevens Institute of Technology was added, on the basis of entrance requirements announced for 1907.

So closed the Foundation's first "fiscal year," June 30, 1906. Although the Carnegie Foundation for the Advancement of Teaching had existed less than four months, it had been more than fourteen since Mr. Carnegie had made his princely "gift to the teachers." Three or four developments during the period call for special emphasis, one in the words of the Foundation's first president.

FOURTEEN MONTHS OF WORK: RESULTS

In the fourteen months that intervened between the Letter of Gift and June 30, 1906, Pritchett, Vanderlip, and Cadwalader, not to mention their friends and associates, had brought to fulfillment Mr. Carnegie's dear wish. Six American and two Canadian higher institutions had pension schemes of their own, at least one of which had existed since 1890. Two others were either considering or beginning similar plans. The public and academic attention which had followed Mr. Carnegie's announcement, and Pritchett's and Vanderlip's efforts to collect facts about teachers retirement, had spread wide. By mid-July 1906 not only had forty-eight universities and colleges in North America, including five having pension schemes, entered upon a degree of pension protection, but many of them had actually received proof of this protection in the first of a long series of monthly checks for Foundation benefits. Thanks to the work of the officers, as exhibited in the First Annual Report, more information about pensions and retirement was available in the United States and had received closer scrutiny than ever before. Mr. Carnegie had good reason to be pleased with his new philanthropy.

A second development had taken place over the past two years and more in the relation between Mr. Carnegie and Pritchett. Pritchett's devotion to the task, the energy and care he expended in it, and the manner in which he handled immense amounts of detail had commended themselves to the Founder.

This was important, not only for the immediate future but for more distant days. During the last fourteen years of Mr. Carnegie's life Pritchett acted, not without misgivings and a degree of embarrassment, as an intermediary and a channel of communication between Mr. Carnegie and numbers of college presidents and others seeking gifts. The notion seemed to be that as soon as a college president received a request from the president of the Foundation for information about his institution he felt himself therein to possess an avenue of ready approach to "Carnegie money." After the first year or two Pritchett made it general practice not to introduce money-seekers to Mr. Carnegie directly, although once he had weighed their claims he sometimes advised them as to modes of written approach. Frequently he counseled them that they would be wasting time and effort if they went to Mr. Carnegie at all. There was, of course, in any case, the hazard of James Bertram, Mr. Carnegie's private secretary, to be passed. Possessing Mr. Carnegie's confidence to an unusual degree, Pritchett felt that in dealing with suitors for funds he could not allow personal relationships to cloud the integrity of his advice. When, after study of a request, he arrived at a negative view, he invariably took pains to inform the suitor of the grounds. Inevitably there was disappointment, but very little if any feeling of injustice appears in the correspondence. There are reasons for belief that Mr. Carnegie valued this relationship with Pritchett highly and trusted his judgment to an unusual extent.

Those who referred to Pritchett as "Carnegie's 'yes-man' "— or whatever was the parlance of the day—showed almost complete ignorance of this relationship. Far from being anyone's "yes-man," Pritchett was among the firmest honest critics of Mr. Carnegie's plans and projects. All who knew Pritchett, as he was, recognized him as highly tenacious and given to yielding, once his mind was made up, only under the keenest intellectual pressure. Thus Pritchett was rather Mr. Carnegie's "no-man" than an uncritical sycophant and follower.

In many ways the Board of Trustees of the Foundation was a remarkable group of men. When Mr. Carnegie dispatched his Letter of Gift he and Pritchett had no personal acquaintance with some of them, but Pritchett seems to have known them all by reputation. Among the strongest board members were Eliot, Hadley, Schurman, and Jordan; no member of the board was far behind these men except in years or academic experience. While Pritchett resided in Boston he talked frequently with Eliot and the intimacy continued after Pritchett removed to New York. He constantly consulted Hadley by letter and received much advice about matters educational, administrative, and statistical. Butler he was to meet increasingly at their clubs and on the golf course, and their interchange of views was both friendly and frank over more than a third of a century. With Schurman and Jordan correspondence grew. The second assistant secretary of the Foundation has written of all these relationships:

> Those early days, as it seems to me, were a contest of personalities. Mr. Carnegie and Dr. Pritchett were both strong personalities. On many things they did not agree. The fact that the policy of the Carnegie Foundation worked out as well as it did is under all circumstances, in my opinion, a far greater credit to Dr. Pritchett than has ever been told. In the issue also were other conflicting elements, notably from Woodrow Wilson, Nicholas Murray Butler, and Jacob Schurman. The balance wheel at the meetings was Charles William Eliot.

Finally, in an article which Pritchett contributed to *The Outlook* of May 19, 1906, probably prepared at least a month earlier, stands the following revealing passage:

> The annual income of the fund provided by Mr. Carnegie is a half-million dollars. It is evident that this sum will be inadequate for the maintenance of a fair system of retiring allowances in all these hundreds of institutions, and that, if the principle of the pension system is to be established, it can be done only by the devotion of this income, not to isolated individuals as a general charity, but by its use in the recognition of institutions and individuals along some definite and well-considered plan. . . . The

practical problem which the trustees have to face is the administration of this trust in such a way as to deal generously and fairly with the individual teacher, and at the same time establish the principle of the retiring allowance as a part of American academic administration.

Essentially the history of the Carnegie Foundation is a history of the interaction of personalities and their respective individual loyalties to men, institutions, and ideas.

~ 4 ~

Friends and Others

A PROMISING START · LIBERALIZING THE RULES—THE STATE UNI-
VERSITIES; THE DENOMINATIONAL BARRIER · FORCES AND COUNTER-
FORCES IN LIBERALIZATION—NEWLY ACCEPTED INSTITUTIONS;
GRANTS AT DISCRETION; TECHNICAL LIBERALIZATIONS; CAUTIONS AND
COUNTERMEASURES; VERDICTS OF THE ACTUARIES; PENSION-EXPERT
OPINION · THE CASE OF WOODROW WILSON · SLINGS AND ARROWS—
DENOMINATIONAL PROTESTS; INTERFERENCE: "STANDARDIZING";
THE "OUTS" VS. THE "INS" · EXCHANGE OF TEACHERS WITH PRUS-
SIA · FORMATIVE RESULTS—CARNEGIE CORPORATION OF NEW YORK;
PERSONS AND PROJECTS; REPUTE

O F THE development of the Carnegie Foundation for the
Advancement of Teaching the Annual Reports offer a
revealing conspectus, particularly of the early days. The First
carries the new Foundation from the Letter of Gift, April 18,
1905, up to October 15, 1906, three months and a half after the
scant beginning fiscal year had closed.

It evinces the extraordinary activity which Mr. Carnegie's benefaction and his eagerness for results had occasioned in the Foundation offices. Along with statistical and other data, it sets forth
the legislative instruments involved, speculates upon the possible
number of future allowances, discusses retired pay in the United
States Army 1890-97, professors' pensions in parts of Europe, and
the eight American and Canadian institutions that offer them.
There is included one of the first international bibliographies on
teachers' pensions, in which the dates of the twenty references range
between 1883 and 1902. The importance of the sections of the report
dealing with pensions lies, first, in evidence that the new enterprise
was not being undertaken without knowledge of other similar work

71

in the world, and, secondly, in its inauguration of the series of
pension studies that, over the next quarter century, was to present
a distillate of information unique for completeness and range in the
field.

The Second Annual Report (1907), somewhat more tranquil in
tone, deals in greater detail than the first with operating policies,
the work of the executive committee in carrying them out, and
certain considerations which they involved. Writing at length of
the American type of university, Pritchett drew distinctions which
still merit consideration after nearly fifty years. His stress upon
the "common understanding" which the seven-year-old Association
of American Universities is helping to engender brings into focus
the larger purposes the Foundation is to serve, while a "tabular
survey of the various methods of legal connection of colleges and
universities with religious organizations" exhibits some of the
results of the questionnaire studies of Pritchett and Vanderlip related to one of the most difficult problems besetting the new
Foundation.

These first two Reports set a high standard. They initiate a fresh
approach to American educational problems through their breadth
and precision of statement. Some of the discussions look far ahead
into the Foundation's future. The obituaries of beneficiaries in the
Second Annual Report inaugurate a continuing roll of honor which,
covering more than forty years, was to contain a large majority of
the most distinguished and respected names in American and
Canadian higher education. Viewed now in perspective, the early
Annual Reports appear almost prophetic in both subject matter
and quality.

A PROMISING START

By early 1907, within the limitations of the Letter of Gift and
the District of Columbia Charter, the new Foundation had acquired
form, substance, and repute. With Mr. Carnegie's acquiescence,
certain principles and policies had been shaped. Pritchett had begun
to emphasize two general purposes: the first, to bring to American
academic life "the principle of retiring pensions for the professor
and his widow" through the institution in which he works, not so
much as charity as of right; the second, closely related, to help
raise the quality of higher education. These two aims received wide
approval, partly because of their novelty. The dissents related less
to general principles than to details and administrative measures.

Activities of those formative years touched many fields. Led by Pritchett, assisted, beginning 1907, by John Gabbert Bowman, a young Columbia instructor who succeeded the fatally stricken Derby as assistant secretary, the executive committee dealt with internal administrative problems as they arose. Between 1907 and 1912, the officers, particularly Pritchett and increasingly Bowman, rendered consultative service in numerous matters: Jordan's Stanford attempt to eliminate the first two college years, low-cost life insurance in Massachusetts, the form and utility of college treasurers' reports, the Harvard "New Plan" of admissions, standards of true research, investigations proposed for the United States Bureau of Education by Commissioner P. P. Claxton looking to continuous classification of higher institutions, college admissions and the unit, the situation at the University of Montana, costs of teaching various college subjects, the work of Hamilton College. Some of these matters received attention in Annual Reports; others grew into more ambitious studies published in Foundation Bulletins. As the Foundation's utility and possibilities became recognized, its nationwide opportunities for service and the requests it received for counsel generated pressures to extend its scope for both educational study and distribution of benefits. All of these pressures, external and internal, bore heavily upon the officers.

LIBERALIZING THE RULES

The earlier versions of the Rules affecting eligibility for benefits gave in both form and substance an impression of rigidity, whether they concerned the acceptance of institutions or the age and service requirements for allowances. Although the Rules had been framed with extreme care, nevertheless, tried by later standards, they lacked statistical and actuarial groundwork and, of course, the superhuman clairvoyance needed to foresee the future growth of our higher education.

The Rules of 1906 restricted admission to the accepted list in three ways: by confining benefits to nondenominational institutions, according to both Letter of Gift and charter; by following the Letter of Gift in excluding state universities, colleges, and technical schools; and by imposing academic and financial requirements devised by the president and certain trustees. The nondenominational requirement endures. The second curb was shortly mitigated by new endowment. The third set of curbs was subject to censure, principally on a regional basis, but it was maintained and it resulted, directly and indirectly, in self-improvement of higher education, particularly in the South. Examination of these three curbs will reveal some of the pressures which in the early days bore upon the Foundation's officers and its Donor to liberalize the Rules.

The State Universities

The initial exclusion of state universities turned upon a point of public policy. For fifty years "the great universities in the Central West [had] labored to establish the principle that higher education in their respective states is to be maintained by the state itself." As Pritchett showed in the *Educational Review* for June 1906, this tenet had been finally recognized, but meanwhile, in December 1905 and January 1906, President H. C. White of the University of Georgia, for the Association of Land-Grant Colleges, and also the Executive Committee of the National Association of State Universities sent communications to Mr. Carnegie and the Foundation urging consideration of "including the State Universities in the list of institutions which may enjoy the benefits of the Pension Fund." The Founder forwarded these to Pritchett for answer, with the request that the executive committee consider the matter when Mr. Carnegie was present. James Burrill Angell of Michigan also wrote. Pritchett laid the subject before the April trustees' meeting, but it was put off until autumn. He argued for a year's delay and study, which the executive committee favored. This seemed to Mr. Carnegie "extremely wise" after all.

Much correspondence resulted, on May 9, 1906, in the executive committee inviting the State Universities committee to submit their reasons in writing and to send a representative to the Foundation's annual meeting November 21, 1906. Rallying, the institutions pressed the matter hard.

At the annual meeting, 1906, the trustees having resolved themselves into a committee of the whole, Presidents Van Hise of Wisconsin, with whom Mr. Carnegie had had previous dealings, and Fellows of Maine, with White of Georgia, spoke and answered questions. It was a long session. Ultimately the trustees voted to grant for ten years in state universities allowances up to one-half the amounts granted in nonstate institutions, the states to supply the rest and the recipient institutions to be selected by the executive committee. No action was taken looking to "accepting" state universities. This step appears to have been a stopgap to make possible further study. The executive committee discussed the subject on January 23, 1907, and decided, without formal vote, that it would be wise to confer no retiring allowances on state university professors at this time, "unless in the case of a man of unusual distinction," a proviso which amounted to a step toward liberalization.

Pressure and argument continued. Joseph Jastrow at Wisconsin, and James Rowland Angell at Chicago, pushed the matter, Jastrow suavely, but Angell accusing Pritchett and the Foundation of working "grievous wrong." The executive committee standing firm, Van Hise, Fellows, and Wheeler of California, appeared before the board on November 20, 1907, and emphasized somewhat the legal aspects. The only result was that the matter was again committed to the executive committee.

The fact was that the board was divided on the subject. Some members, including Butler, plumped for acceptance of state institutions which could meet the academic requirements, lest a division result in the academic field. Others, including Pritchett and Wilson, were opposed on diverse grounds. At Chicago on January 28, 1908, some twenty-six of the institutional heads met Pritchett and Eliot, chairman of the board, and applied heat for the ten-year plan of acceptance. Probably as a result of conversations on the return trip East, Pritchett proposed compromise measures, all tending to make the step less expensive if taken. Some of these the committeemen of the National Association of State Universities labeled discriminatory; Pritchett and Eliot between them tried to meet the charge. Countering, White appealed for "the influence of the Carnegie Foundation in elevating standards in *all* American collegiate institutions." Pritchett still inclined to a negative position, albeit somewhat modified.

Not so Mr. Carnegie. To Wilson, March 11, 1908, Pritchett wrote: "Mr. Carnegie has quite changed his attitude and now desires unrestricted admission of state universities" to the accepted list, although he was "particularly anxious that nothing should be done to give the slightest support to the idea that we *officiously* wish to render aid to State University Faculties. . . . I admire the State that says 'this is our duty' and performs it."

A talk with Mr. Carnegie led Pritchett to understand that the Founder wished the whole matter decided without regard to its financial bearings, and that the funds of the Foundation would be increased "whenever in the course of regular administration of the work it becomes necessary." Accordingly, Pritchett advised the executive committee that Mr. Carnegie was considering an important step and called the trustees to meet on March 31. Three days before, Mr. Carnegie and Pritchett talked again, and the latter left in the former's hands a memorandum on the current pension load and the probable "result of adding to our list the state universities." On March 31 Mr. Carnegie sent Pritchett his second Letter of Gift increasing by half the Foundation's funds.

Pritchett had set the figure, drafted the letter, and stipulated that application by the university should be approved by the legislature and governor of the state, in accordance with the procedure then in force in obtaining federal grants. The trustees gratefully accepted the gift.

This fresh benefaction, announced April 4, brought a shower of public notice in news columns and editorials, mostly favorable. The Omaha *Herald*, however, declared, April 5, that "Mr. Carnegie was right in the first place," a view which contributed to William Jennings Bryan's speech to the Nebraska legislature that resulted in no application for acceptance being made by the state university. University presidents congratulated the Donor in personal letters: Wheeler of California, MacLean, James, Drinker, Barrow, McClelland. Negative views were not many. Most of the trustees were, of course, pleased. On request, President James Burrill Angell of Michigan, tried his hand at defining a state university. Jastrow expressed his "great gratification" and his view that the Foundation was "easily the most important influence for academic welfare that we have." And Mr. Carnegie thoroughly enjoyed "the warm approval of the press and the public."

Naturally, members of the committee of the National Association of State Universities began to press for quick admission of state institutions. Pritchett was for adhering to the Foundation's academic requirements which these proposals had apparently failed to consider fully. The first formal application was transmitted April 28 by Angell, in accordance with action by the regents of the University of Michigan in February. The hurdles for the universities to clear still included academic and professional-school requirements, handling of special and conditioned students, organization, defects in agricultural training, and other matters. When the trustees next met they so amended the Rules as to admit state universities on the same basis as other institutions, but reserved the right to refuse acceptance when in their view political control or interference impaired academic efficiency. Mr. Carnegie planned to pay the fresh gift in installments as the additional pension load demanded increased income.

In spite of all sorts of rumors, local institutional difficulties in complying with the Rules, and immense care and correspondence, Pritchett was able to report to the executive committee, April 8, 1909, that twenty-four states and the Province of Ontario had passed the required resolutions and that in most cases application for acceptance had been filed. Others followed, and on June 4, 1909, the first admissions under the new requirements passed the executive committee: Wisconsin and Minnesota, except their agricultural departments, Michigan, and Toronto, except affiliated denominational colleges.

All this contributed to the process of liberalizing the Rules, through enlarging the Accepted List, and particularly through palliative grants to individual professors in nonaccepted state institutions. Ultimately, seventeen state universities were included. While it may be that the second gift of five millions helped appreciably in meeting the increase in the pension load which this phase of liberalization brought about, it is by no means certain that it covered the costs it ultimately entailed.

The National Association of State Universities at its meeting, November 16-17, 1908, formally elected Pritchett a special member "on the ground of distinguished service to education, past and present, but particularly for your service in behalf of State Universities and their relations to the Carnegie Foundation for the Advancement of Teaching."

The Denominational Barrier

The Foundation's charter limits payment of its benefits to "institutions not under control of a sect or which do not require their trustees, their officers, faculties, or students (or a majority thereof) to belong to any specified sect, and which do not impose any theological test as a condition of entrance therein or of connection therewith." A complete account of attempts to circumvent this provision, which merely echoes the first Letter of Gift, would scarcely make pleasant reading; it would only cast again the shadow of human weakness over actions motivated mainly by high institutional or denominational loyalties. The matter will therefore be reduced to the merest sketch.

For a great number of universities and colleges the sectarian issue, as raised through the questionnaires, was clear-cut. For others it was determined only after much correspondence and not a few campus visits by the Foundation's officers. Results from these inquiries entered heavily into the executive committee's deliberations. Undoubtedly, the motives involved seemed of the highest to those whom they actuated. The pity is that they led so often to accusations of unfair discrimination, to weaseling, and to special pleading in attempts to further what is now revealed as deliberate circumvention of both the Congressional Act and the Donor's terms of gift. Nor were these attempts confined to overloyal, overanxious college or church leaders; they touched even certain members of the Board of Trustees. A few cases were presented temperately for executive committee consideration and decided coolly. All too many roused bitterness and anger.

Ultimately some thirteen institutions were accepted: five after procuring new charters, two after passages in denominational handbooks had undergone amendment, two others after agreement to exclude from benefits teachers in certain departments, the rest after suitable action or clarification of existing church relationships. Out of the thirteen, three withdrew from the list between 1909 and 1921, but their current allowances and their pensions in force or in prospect at the time of separation were paid until natural termination. The curious will find this matter amply discussed in Annual Reports; but only between the lines, if at all, will the sharp dealings that darkened some of the cases be inferable. The final result was that the executive committee and the trustees, influenced in part by Pritchett, in part by Mr. Carnegie, ultimately stood upon the basal instruments, which after all reflected the Donor's right to give his money on his own terms. Nevertheless, in consequence of pressures, internal and external, for this phase of liberalization, whether through the accepting of institutions that changed their spots for financial reasons or through allowances granted as extenuating exceptions outside the Accepted List, at least $2,600,000 was added to the Foundation's long-term pension load.

FORCES AND COUNTERFORCES IN LIBERALIZATION

From the earliest days of the Foundation a majority of the executive committee have been college presidents, with interests and loyalties already fixed. In even greater proportion this has been true also of the Board of Trustees. Mr. Carnegie set the original pattern, and the years matured it. During the formative days especially, it must often have been very difficult for many individual members to differentiate between the interests of the great body of college teachers as a group, the interests of the particular institution employing the Foundation trustee as president, and just plain self-interest.

In the early nineteen hundreds, the pressure group was only beginning to burgeon at full strength in American life. Guided by Pritchett, the Foundation, its officers and trustees, were groping their way along an untraveled route beset by pitfalls, some unknown, others unrecognized for what they might become. However frequently the executive committee met, its members did not, like Pritchett, have to live with the Foundation's problems day and night. After two years, the Foundation was expending only about 35 per cent of its income and a reserve was accumulating. Among the trustees, participation in a new and unique enterprise, the favorable mortality the Foundation was enjoying, and the consciousness of being agents for good in the world all combined to generate and to foster a spirit of optimism. This spirit laid the board and in a measure the executive committee open to influences and pressure from state institutions, denominational colleges, and other entities which stood to gain by favorable change. Every liberalization of Rules or procedures added afresh to the cost of the Foundation's free benefits. That the burden was not only immediate but also cumulative over the future was a fact of starkest reality.

Newly Accepted Institutions

This, however, seemed to cause few misgivings. Between April 9 and June 30, 1906, the accepted institutions increased from forty-five to fifty-two. In 1907, there were five additions. By June 30, 1912, the Accepted List numbered seventy-six institutions, including eleven state universities. The burden of expense for allowances and pensions granted within the Rules increased proportionally, but two other practices forced the load even higher: the policy of making a few immediate regular grants at the time an institution achieved acceptance, and the tendency "to take care of" certain other teachers not always strictly eligible, as a sort of earnest of the Foundation's good intentions. These liberal procedures had future importance.

Grants at Discretion

Under pressure, the tendency to help nonaccepted institutions early acquired the status of a policy. For example, on June 21, 1906, out of sixteen allowances granted six were classified as "normal," although one of these was at a college under discussion but not yet actually "accepted," and the remaining ten were in institutions definitely outside the List. For perhaps three years the practice continued, with only an occasional pause for breath if not for stock-taking. The actuating motives were charitable and benevolent, but at the time the cost could not be counted except through estimates which amounted to mere guesses.

Technical Liberalizations

Meanwhile, those portions of the Rules and procedures which supposedly fixed the requirements for grants and governed the mechanisms of payment underwent almost constant tinkering. The process paralleled the voting of grants in exceptional circumstances. In September 1906 two allowances were granted within the Accepted List and fifteen outside it. On the grounds of "great service," one $1,500 allowance was voted to a man who had been a college teacher for only eight years and left the profession a year before "The Carnegie Foundation" had been created. Even at the 1906 annual meeting the board instructed the executive committee to "deal generously with pioneer educators in colleges not on the Accepted List who have rendered long and conspicuous service in the cause of education." Up to May 1907, more than seventy allowances had been granted in accepted institutions, as against fifty-seven in nonaccepted. Of all these, New England and the Atlantic seaboard received by far the largest share.

Pressures, within and outside of the board, to use more income gathered force. It was not unusual to increase allowances once granted, although none was decreased. Early in 1910 the executive committee ruled that an allowance should remain in force thirty days after the death of the beneficiary, instead of terminating at the end of the month of death. In the autumn of the same year the trustees formally voted to request the executive committee to extend the allowance posthumously for ninety days; the executive committee took no action. It looks very much as if Pritchett were more successful in showing the smaller group the paths of righteousness than Eliot, up to his resignation in 1909, and his successors Harrison of Pennsylvania and Peterson of McGill, among the larger group.

Nevertheless liberalization continued. Under Eliot's chairmanship widows' pensions, after being permissive were made mandatory, a change much appreciated by college professors and naturally by presidents also, although it was decided that remarriage should terminate a pension. The maximum allowance was raised from $3,000 to $4,000. At least one teacher who had accepted only part of his salary received an allowance (the maximum) based upon his full scheduled compensation. It had been intended that the 1910 Rules should base the allowance on final salary over the past five active years, but by error this provision was omitted from the printed version. Still it was followed in practice, and as if this were not sufficiently liberal the executive committee ruled that an eligible after sixty-five might work part-time on diminished salary while enjoying his allowance, the widow's pension to be computed on the basis of the last five years of full pay. Although the title of lecturer had generally been regarded as indicating temporary status, and therefore service under it not countable towards retirement, Canadian lecturers were made equally eligible with American instructors.

True, a few liberalizing proposals met defeat: For example, one that a retired "teacher might continue in his institution at reduced salary when engaged in teaching or research without accepting a diminished pension," and another that an eligible relinquishing active service before age sixty-five retain his eligibility until that age, and that his allowance be based on his last five years of active service. But the term "teacher" was interpreted with almost absurd liberality. As Pritchett wrote later: "Mr. Carnegie had not expected originally that presidents, deans, and, still less, the treasurers, registrars, librarians, and others . . . would receive retiring allowances through his foundation. He had in mind only the faithful and ill-paid teachers." When it was decided to admit this group of officers to benefits "he accepted this decision of the trustees with some misgivings. The most difficult times I have had . . . have been when some old teacher would write to Mr. Carnegie calling his attention to the fact that while a pension was denied him by the Foundation, much larger pensions were being paid to persons who did no teaching." Ultimately, it would appear, it was Nicholas Murray Butler who persuaded Mr. Carnegie to modify his view. It became fairly common practice among institutions to change titles in order to bring as many persons as possible within the Foundation

Rules. Thus the list of pensionables was heavily increased, by how many names cannot now be ascertained.

For the first three years representative allowances ran to some $1,500 each, during the next three to about $2,000. By 1912 the Foundation was paying 297 allowances in 72 accepted institutions, at a cost of $478,440 for the year. A number of temporary disability allowances were granted, most of which ultimately became permanent, many in larger amounts, and thus the endowment that was intended to furnish provision for retirement, was used in part after the manner of a relief fund. A proposal that annual physical examinations be instituted to check upon continuance of disability came to nothing.

The record indicates that alone of the board and the executive committee Pritchett foresaw the results of liberalization. His opposition to extending and increasing the Foundation's benefits was persuasive but only partly effectual. Perhaps his misgivings and warnings were regarded among his fellow-trustees as untimely trouble-borrowing. Probably they arose from large discrepancies in the 1906 and 1907 statistics and from the results of actuarial inquiries, however crude, made during the Foundation's first five or six years.

Cautions and Countermeasures

It really seems as if the early executive committees, when faced in interpreting the Rules with a choice between liberality and reasonable enforcement, decided usually in favor of liberality. Probably in every individual instance that liberality seemed to be justified, but the net result was to the Foundation's disadvantage and the disadvantage of the other pensionables. Among the prime movers towards liberality stood Lowell, Jordan, Peterson, Wilson, and Schurman, within the board. Outside it were Charles R. Van Hise, then teaching at the University of Chicago, Professor Jastrow of Wisconsin, Presidents Harry Pratt Judson of Chicago, A. W. Harris of Northwestern, and others. Jastrow desired that after twenty-five years of service a professor should be free to cease teaching and retain his eligibility at age sixty-five under formal certification. Harris of Northwestern was critical on denominational grounds, and Professor M. Anstice Harris of Elmira, with a number of other teachers, protested the sectarian restrictions and the seeming exclusion of smaller colleges. Some of the pressures thus generated reached even Mr. Carnegie. The trustees were sensitive to accusations of unfairness. In the spring of 1909, B. J. Hendrick stated in *McClure's* that the Foundation had received more than 500 applications for allowances from individual teachers alone; few, if any, could be granted. Pritchett's resistance to liberalization gathered vigor and force, but naturally his stand and his clarity of vision and statement did not increase his general popularity. He was fortified in his attitude by the results of certain actuarial studies as well as by the Foundation's own nonactuarial inquiries.

Verdicts of the Actuaries

Need for actuarial supervision in the Foundation's work was recognized as early as November 21, 1905, when a young but apparently qualified actuary wrote to Mr. Carnegie, asking "to be considered as a candidate for such a position." The Founder may or may not have consulted Pritchett, but, as Pritchett more than once stated in later years, "Mr. Carnegie had no use for actuaries," and the matter dropped.

The Pritchett-Vanderlip statistical inquiries were not in nature actuarial. Sayre's readings in the literature of pensions, which began almost as soon as he joined the Foundation in 1906, touched the work of the actuary only incidentally. It was in 1906 that Pritchett engaged his friend, S. S. Hall, Sr., of the Mutual Life Insurance Company of New York, to work over whatever data were available. Hall's 1906 results were apparently inconclusive, probably because the data were very defective.

The second inquiry followed in 1908-09. The firm that made it is not identifiable, but some of the conclusions appear in the Fourth Annual Report (1909) : " 'The problem is,' they said, 'only partly actuarial. No man can possibly predict what will happen under any assumed method of retirement. Frame your rules according to your judgment of what will best serve the interests of the teachers, within the general estimates indicated. Reserve carefully the power to amend your rules . . . as circumstances may require, and go forward to acquire such experience as may enable you to make permanent and final rules.' " The important kink came in the fact that more institutions than anticipated qualified for acceptance and thus the list of eligibles mounted, and the future load as well.

In the spring of 1909, the executive committee, on Pritchett's recommendation, authorized a study by a "competent actuary." The action was purely formal; Pritchett had already approached Gardner Ladd Plumley, F.A.S.A., a well known actuary, who had at once begun his task. It was practically completed by April 15.

His report, while cautious, appears not to have impressed the executive committee as particularly illuminating, and in June Pritchett again turned to Hall.

Hall's figures were ready August 4, 1909. For first calculations he used McClintock's 3½ per cent Tables, but on Pritchett pointing out that that rate of interest was much below the Foundation's current investment return, he repeated his work on a basis of 5 per cent. Now, the McClintock Male Tables, compiled in 1899 from "practically all the standard annuity tables in use," and characterized by their author as "abundantly safe," had been legally standard for the New York State Department of Insurance since January 1, 1907. As for a suggestion that the Foundation should purchase from commercial companies $1,000 annuities, with half stipend to widows, covering 3,357 pensionables then under sixty years of age, Hall, thinking it through, found it practicable if the colleges paid the handling charges.

His final conclusions were cautious. Although he advised continuing the present accumulation of surplus, he thought the $15,000,000 then in sight, or $20,000,000 at the outside, would probably carry the plan as then operating, but he asked that more accurate data be collected and recorded, and he foresaw that by 1914 the load of allowances alone would be very close to "$500,000 per annum." He thought the resources of the Foundation ought to be "very considerably larger."

This was a warning. Pritchett not only heeded it but persuaded the executive committee, and even a majority of the trustees, to heed it also. Almost immediately there developed changes in policy which, although unannounced, tended towards retrenchment. Admission to the Accepted List was reduced by stricter application of requirements, entrance, academic, and financial. The granting of allowances outside the list was moderated; 155 had been voted in no fewer than 76 nonaccepted institutions up to May 5, 1910, at an annual cost of $144,000 and more. This now seems pretty extravagant, however charitable it then appeared. College salaries had risen, and so, too, the amounts of retiring allowances to which they led; grants became more restricted. Temporary allowances ceased to be granted in October 1912. And the service retirement rule (Rule 2), which had undergone trustee liberalizing, was greatly modified. This modification operated in one much-publicized case.

In the past the nonactuarial studies of the Foundation had underlain every change of rule or requirement; after the cautionary

Hall report of 1909 actuarial inquiries assumed, somewhat gradually, a fundamental position in the administration of the Foundation. This was well, for the annual load by June 1911 approximated $505,000.

At that time, Professor W. F. Willcox of Cornell, having in correspondence almost forced himself into the situation, was engaged by Pritchett to study it. Pritchett supposed him to be an actuary; he was not—he was a statistical economist, and it turned out in 1913 that he had had the actuarial work done by a graduate student. Willcox completed his first draft in July 1912. It was not cheerful reading for Pritchett at Santa Barbara, who commented in part: "It is evident from your estimate that the ultimate load . . . will be much larger than our original estimates, based upon the American Mortality Tables, and a much smaller registration of teachers had indicated." Willcox suggested several means of retrenchment for the future. He found the McClintock Tables too liberal, although he somewhat hesitantly assumed an increase in the number of pensionables, and he stressed organizing and maintaining full records. The tone of his report was decidedly pessimistic.

Pension-expert Opinion

So, too, was a passage traditionally attributed to Sayre in the Seventh Annual Report (1912). Tracing the New South Wales civil service pension debacle of 1903-12, which Sayre is said to have discovered for himself, he wrote: "Any pension system administered from a fixed income and unprovided with a source from which its income may be increased, is bound to come to a point where the calls upon it under its own rules exceed its income." This was an ominous verdict.

All this evidence, laid by Pritchett before the executive committee and the trustees and much of it published, served to check effectively most of the liberalizing proclivities of the group, but not before much danger had developed. The root of the difficulty was that a course of action or procedure once liberalized persisted, and that it could be made temporary, mitigated, or rescinded only in new cases. Of this harvest the future was to see the reaping.

THE CASE OF WOODROW WILSON

Among the cases that abrogation of the service retirement rule affected, that of Woodrow Wilson acquired most notoriety. After

Wilson's seventeen years as teacher at Bryn Mawr and Princeton, and nearly eight as Princeton's president, controversy developed over the location of the Princeton Graduate School. This put Wilson in a thorny position. He was still one of the Foundation trustees Mr. Carnegie had selected.

The Foundation's rule permitting retirement after twenty-five years service, for university presidents as well as others, was promulgated in 1908. In the Fourth Annual Report sent confidentially to trustees in October 1909, Pritchett wrote, after twenty-eight service retirements: "It seems that this rule offers too large a temptation to certain qualities of universal human nature. . . . The object of the Foundation is not the encouragement of research (desirable as that may be), nor is it concerned with the transfer of men from the calling of the teacher to some other." This passage reflects not alone Pritchett's individual views but views of the executive committee during discussion of the working of Rule 2.

Commenting on the passage Wilson expressed doubts that the service rule had been in operation long enough to justify conclusions as to its influence: "I should hesitate to change it just yet. . . . Personally, I value the service rule as it now stands very highly. I think it very desirable both that men should have the opportunity of retiring before they have lost their full vigor and also that the institution should be permitted to correct occasional mistakes in appointment."

On November 15, 1909, Pritchett for the executive committee recommended to the trustees that the Rules should be revised according to his suggestion in the Fourth Annual Report: Rule 1 to set sixty-five years as the age requirement; Rule 2, which hitherto had dealt with service, to become in effect a provision for retirement based upon disability. Wilson was present at the annual meeting held two days later. On formal vote Pritchett's Fourth Annual Report was accepted. The report of the executive committee containing the revision of the Rules, including Rule 2, was amended and accepted; in addition, the executive committee was "instructed to safeguard the interests of . . . those whose twenty-five years of service includes service as a college president; and . . . those in whose mind a definite expectation has been created by official action that they will be accorded the benefits of the Foundation within the year 1910; and that . . . the Executive Committee be authorized to formulate regulations in accordance with these instructions." This motion was made by Wilson, but the form in which it passed differed considerably from the form in which he had originally offered it, as Pritchett later pointed out. The phrase "safeguard the interests" turned out to be ambiguous.

Nearly a year passed. On October 20, 1910, Wilson's resignation from the Princeton presidency became effective. His salary ended. According to his own statement, he had resources of only about $1,000 a year in book royalties, etc. On November 1 Dean Henry B. Fine made application for a retiring allowance for Wilson, who was fifty-three years and ten months old. His service totaled twenty-five years and about one month. His reasons for retirement were given as "to accept nomination for the governorship of New Jersey and devote myself to public life. I dare not do this without any independent resources." In forwarding the signed application Wilson wrote: "I would come to the meeting of the [Executive] Committee [where the application would be considered] on the tenth [of November 1910] were I not obliged to apply to it for a retiring allowance. . . . It is necessary that I should be a free man in my new life, and I do not think a beneficiary of the Foundation should serve upon the Board. . . ." On the same date Wilson also resigned from the Board of Trustees, stating that he had severed his "connection with Princeton University and given up teaching after twenty-five years of service to enter public life."

In replying to Pritchett's acknowledgment of both application and resignation, November 4, 1910, Wilson expressed the hope "that that Committee will see its way to granting me a retiring allowance. . . . Of course, the only ground upon which I can ask for an allowance since the recent alterations of the Rules, is that as President of Princeton I have rendered services out of the usual run of the teacher's work." On November 8 Wilson was elected governor of the State of New Jersey.

When, on November 10, Pritchett introduced Wilson's application at the Executive Committee meeting, he apparently encountered considerable difficulty because of doubts "whether the Foundation ought in any case to pay a retiring allowance to a man, however distinguished, who retires from educational service to undertake other work on salary." This doubt he put to Wilson December 3, 1910.

Wilson in a letter of December 6 stood fast: "I would never have gone into public life with all its risks and uncertainties had I not believed myself entitled . . . to a full retiring allowance" of

$4,000 under the rule he had helped amend. "It chagrins me very much," he added, "to feel that I have been asking a favor. . . . I do not feel that I can argue either for or against it. I can only state what my understanding was. . . ." That understanding now appears to have differed from that of all, or almost all, of the other Foundation trustees who took part in the annual meeting of 1909.

In hopes of making a proposal that would meet Wilson's difficulties Pritchett, by appointment, went to see him at Princeton on December 10, 1910. He found the governor-elect "firmly set on having a [retiring allowance]. He explained . . . that he was going into political life for very unselfish and disinterested reasons; he felt that the Foundation should be glad to assist him in this effort." "Before the interview ended," Pritchett once wrote, "he became irritated and I was not without some indignation on my part."

Years later Pritchett confirmed a view of Dean Fine's: "The real misunderstanding . . . was this. . . . In 1909 the trustees decided to end the 'service pension' for good and sufficient reasons. Mr. Wilson desired to retain this rule long enough to bring his own case under it. . . . Mr. Wilson thought his proposal had accomplished that result, but the trustees did not agree with him. . . ."

The executive committee on January 19, 1911, again sought ways of meeting the trustees' instructions as to "safeguarding the interests" of men with twenty-five years service that included "noteworthy presidential or other administrative service in a college or university." At last it was decided to refer the matter back to the Board of Trustees for instructions. The Wilson allowance was not granted. Pritchett on January 24, notified Wilson that the executive committee had turned again to the board for instructions about its "direction" to "safeguard the interests" of college presidents of conspicuous service, who desired retirement after twenty-five years.

This took Wilson aback, he replied February 13, 1911, and discouraged him: "I have evidently made a great blunder in entering a new career without private resources."

Pritchett addressed the board at its sixth annual meeting, November 15, 1911, on behalf of the executive committee, to the effect that attempts to administer the "safeguard" provision had not proved successful. Hence, "in order that apparent preference to the trustees in their own favor may be removed from the records," the executive committee recommended repeal of the instructions. This the board voted.

Meanwhile, Wilson's fame was growing to presidential size. On December 5, 1911, a New York newspaper printed a story about the Wilson application, purporting to quote a trustee of the Foundation on the reasons behind refusal of the allowance. The piece might have passed without much comment except for its references to the Foundation trustee and his views on Wilson's motives. Pritchett was ill at Santa Barbara. When a weekly magazine took up the matter editorially he was roused to write Wilson a sincere and cordial denial of the accusation that trustees had "given out this information to injure you and Vanderlip." Other writers and other newspapers took up the cudgels. The squabble raged for the better part of a year, and two decades later it had not abated. Wilson had the sense and taste not to comment upon the episode publicly, but had he received the allowance, the clamor might have been even louder than it was. He seems never again to have communicated in writing with Pritchett or other Foundation officers, or even trustees, but with Mr. Carnegie he carried on from the White House what was, for Wilson, an animated correspondence—which to be sure Mr. Carnegie initiated—in spite of the Founder's very substantial contribution to the Taft campaign.

Twice in outlining this drama Pritchett stipulated that the full facts should not be set forth until the principals had made their final exits. None is now living.

SLINGS AND ARROWS

The adverse publicity over the Wilson affair was only one wave in a tide of criticism of the Foundation and all its works that began to rise in the third year of operation. Most of it was written, either in correspondence or in newspapers and periodicals. Censure by word of mouth was extensive and at times bitter, but it was ephemeral and it lay outside the record although much of it found its way into print.

Printed criticism was both general and specific. General objection was voiced against the charter of the Foundation, its operation and administration, its allegedly indiscriminate liberality in distributing benefits, and its supposed arbitrary discrimination against groups as well as against individuals. This sort of censure was essentially local or regional. Censure of specific actions, being wider spread, attracted more public attention through clipping and reprinting among newspapers, often under a localized "lead." Examples are to be found among articles originating mainly in Chicago and in or near New York City, pertaining to changes in the Rules, denial of a retiring allowance to a particular person, reflections occasioned by local or state pride in matters and institutions reported upon adversely in educational inquiries, and especially by the time-worn notion that where there is smoke there must be fire.

The hottest attacks developed on three general fronts: the non-sectarian provisions of Letter of Gift and charter; the power inherent in the new Foundation and its alleged abuse in "standardizing" higher education; and discontent, mainly personal, with not a few acts and official pronouncements. Even with the way clear for accepting the state universities, there remained for protest and censure an abundance of other topics, some of which are traceable directly to the hidden retrenchment policies above outlined. The present discussion can convey only a faint notion of the virulence of some of these assaults, a modicum of which in their day filled at least one volume.

Denominational Protests

On the whole, the view of most newspapers of the day seemed to be that Mr. Carnegie had acted within his rights in restricting his gift to the teachers on sectarian grounds. Certain southern and religious publications showed a resentment that was perhaps not astonishing. A preacher branded the Foundation as "a breeder of agnosticism" in higher education. With Protestant laymen Pritchett carried on a very considerable correspondence in which he sought to define the Foundation's position. But a Roman Catholic scholar and churchman penned a vitriolic attack, and the Catholic Education Association in Chicago in 1911 passed condemnatory resolutions. The difficulty seemed to lie in the Foundation assumption that the American college ought to rest upon the rising public secondary school. When Pritchett brought the matter to Mr. Carnegie's attention the reply was, ". . . we are engaged in a good fight; push it."

Interference: "Standardizing"

One of the serious accusations brought against the Foundation, and especially against Pritchett, was the charge of trying to standardize higher education by imposing arbitrary requirements impossible for many worthy colleges to meet in order to attain acceptance and procure grants for retiring allowances. There are indications that this notion penetrated even into the Board of Trustees; President Jacob Gould Schurman of Cornell was quoted in an Ohio newspaper as voicing fear of the Foundation's influence: "The purse strings [in American higher education] are now controlled by an immortal power which makes it its business to investigate and supervise and which lays down conditions that the university must accept if it is to receive grants of money, an irresponsible, self-perpetuating board . . ."

This sort of stricture, fairly widespread but far from unanimous among those who commented, grew out of certain misconceptions. The first involved the failure to perceive or credit what Pritchett was driving at. His view was that the fifteen-unit entrance requirement was set by the colleges themselves, that while only quantitative in nature it came as near reflecting quality as was possible in that day, and that much chicanery was practiced in circumventing it. He and his colleagues gave chapter and verse, not only about requirements for admission but about undergraduate promotion, conditioned students, and "specials" as well. Finally, the Foundation's studies, beginning with Pritchett's and Vanderlip's, and progressing to those bearing upon medical education, college accounting, the teaching of physics, college efficiency, and the training of teachers, aimed at thoroughness in procedure and honesty in presentation. Most of them drew blood.

Pritchett and his colleagues, particularly Bowman and his successor Furst, worked long and patiently with the College Entrance Examination Board and the National Conference Committee on Standards of Colleges and Secondary Schools, which were concerned with improving college admission requirements. Here many institutions were more than merely vulnerable. The unit stipulations in the Rules entailed revising the requirements for entering perhaps as many as half of the colleges accepted. Resulting correspondence was prodigious, and while much good flowed from it, goodwill towards the Foundation did not perceptibly increase on numerous campuses. The story of the Foundation's connection with the entrance unit is reserved for a subsequent chapter.

Pritchett tried to make the term "standardizing" imply uniting for better academic quality; all too many saw it as meaning the imposition from without of requirements fantastically high. The resentment the term fanned was hottest in the South, but the results obtained there were more impressive than anywhere else in the land. Pritchett in 1911 wrote to John G. Hart of Harvard: "It is . . . perhaps a natural inference that we were in a measure seeking to standardize colleges, but our only effort has been to obtain some sort of agreement amongst the colleges and secondary schools as a first step toward unity and progress."

Passages in certain Annual Reports revealing and discussing political interference with state universities, exposing college advertising practices, and showing a tendency to make grants predominantly through institutions in the northern and especially the northeastern regions, occasioned no little criticism which was eagerly seized upon by certain individuals, whose machinations began early and persisted late in the Foundation's history.

The "Outs" vs. the "Ins"

The most acute leaders of opposition, 1906-12, were five men of agile minds, high pertinacity, and unfathomable motives: Jastrow of Wisconsin, James McKeen Cattell of Columbia, A. O. Lovejoy of the Johns Hopkins, W. W. Cook of Yale, and Otto Heller, Pritchett's former friend and colleague at Washington University. As has been shown, Jastrow opened his almost lifelong campaign early in the Foundation's history. Pressing his attacks—some of which he even submitted in typescript to Pritchett before printing, perhaps as an indirect way of "serving notice"—he drew the rest into his orbit. Cattell, who about 1909 resigned his post at Columbia, published several attacks in two periodicals which he owned. In 1910 Lovejoy took up the cudgels and Cook followed. Heller circulated for signature among professors documents protesting a number of the Foundation's policies and procedures. One chief complaint was that there were no professors on the Board of Trustees. Others touched modification of the rule permitting retirement on the basis of service, contended that the Foundation allowances kept professorial salaries low, that the board was precipitately changing its rules and retroactively curtailing benefits, and protested against the alleged notion that "colleges and universities should be conducted on machine-shop principles." The critics also seized upon insignificant details that offended them and inflated these to giant proportions. No point was too small for unfavorable attention.

The bill of complaint, including one return postcard vote on Rule 2 among teachers, came down ultimately and essentially to a personal indictment of Pritchett. The specifications, expressed or implied, included charges of incompetence, lack of good judgment, "unmitigated duplicity," autocratic behavior, willful disregard of facts and the wishes and rights of others, perpetration of injustices, and "officious shuffling" (Jastrow adapts the phrase)—that is, covering up the facts with intent to deceive. The bill of particulars ran to many pages and much printers' ink.

The astounding thing is the unruffled poise with which Pritchett endured these accusations. Urged by one teacher to reply, he wrote to the effect that he felt that an answer "from one connected with the [Foundation] would have little weight. . . ." To Hadley he commented in later years: "All this . . . is part of the price we are paying for getting on the right track, and since whatever mistake has been made in the past was mainly mine I hope that I am now expiating such sins by a highly deserving virtue." With incredible self-control, Pritchett only once or twice displayed even mild resentment. A few trustees replied in print, including Jordan of Stanford, but Pritchett silently went his ways. This alone must have exasperated his critics to fury. The winds it generated were to reach gale proportions by 1919.

EXCHANGE OF TEACHERS WITH PRUSSIA

In July 1907, Pritchett for the Foundation received from the Prussian Ministry of Education a request "to undertake on this side of the water an exchange of teachers" between *gymnasia* in Prussia and secondary schools in the United States. This proposal Pritchett considered mainly a tribute to Mr. Carnegie's stand for "the promotion of educational good feeling" on an international scale. He therefore communicated it to Mr. Carnegie in Scotland for approval or disapproval. Much pleased, as later events showed, the Founder cabled his reply in a single word, "Yes." While the monetary advantage, if any, in the plan, which was to be financed entirely through the teachers, their respective schools, and the Ministry, appeared to lie with the visiting Prussians, the proposal promised well for alert American teachers with whom they were to be exchanged. On Pritchett's recommendation the Foundation trustees approved the arrangement November 20, 1907, and the details for America were handled in the Foundation offices.

A committee on American applications was constituted: Dr. Calvin Thomas, Columbia University; Dr. Julius Sachs, Teachers College, Columbia; and James G. Croswell, Brearley School, New York City. Public announcement first appeared in newspapers of April 7, 1908. Comment was favorable, especially in the German-language press. But the American applications came mostly from the Midwest, with very few from New England and the Middle Atlantic states. Subsequently this situation corrected itself to a large degree but not entirely. The American teachers ultimately chosen represented twenty-three states and the Province of Ontario, while fifteen American secondary and higher institutions received Prussians. In the course of the school years 1908-09 to 1913-14 there was a total of fifty-three American appointees, with three repeats, and forty-seven German. Then the exchange was "temporarily interrupted by the European War." It was never resumed.

Each returning American prepared an account of his experiences in Prussia. These reports for the most part were rosy, and especially respectful as to German pedagogical procedures, student conduct and morals, the thoroughness of German schoolboy self-help, and even methods of conducting athletics. The influence of the exchange upon American and German education is obscure and cannot now be appraised. In one particular the Foundation itself was the principal gainer.

Second on the list of successful Americans, 1909-10, stood the name of William Setchell Learned, teacher of Greek and history in the Moses Brown School, Providence, who went to the *Hohenzollernschule*, Schöneberg, *bei* Berlin. Subsequently the Foundation issued his report under the title *An American Teacher's Year in a Prussian Gymnasium 1910-11*, and on Pritchett's appointing Learned, 1912, to the Foundation staff he took his place among the most brilliant and influential members the Foundation was to have.

FORMATIVE RESULTS

There is good reason to regard the fiscal year 1911-12 as terminating the formative period of the Carnegie Foundation. Since 1905 Mr. Carnegie had maintained his active interest, and Pritchett had kept him informed of developments in general policy, and to a certain extent of administrative details. To Mr. Carnegie he frequently referred letters of appreciation from beneficiaries, in which the older man took great pleasure: "Thanks," he penciled in the margin of one, "—such letters as these are the sweetest reward on earth. Yours, A C."

Although as Pritchett once pointed out to Eliot: "Mr. Carnegie has never had very much sympathy with that side of the Foundation which has had to do with . . . studies . . . and . . . discussion of educational problems," the Founder wrote to Eliot June 16, 1910, in part: "I believe that next to the relief afforded to teachers of mankind by the Foundation comes the good work it is doing in raising the standards of education."

Carnegie Corporation of New York

Mr. Carnegie had large plans for the future. On November 10, 1911, by Letter of Gift, he endowed a new philanthropy with $25,000,000 of United States Steel Corporation bonds, shortly increased to $125,000,000, "to promote the advancement and diffusion of knowledge and understanding among the people of the United States . . ."—Carnegie Corporation of New York. According to Pritchett, it was at the time "the largest philanthropic agency so far as resources are concerned that the world has ever seen." As trustees of the new philanthropy Mr. Carnegie chose his close associates and the presidents of the six other American endowments he had already founded. His notion may have been that the Corporation should serve in part as a reservoir upon which the six endowments might draw for their charter purposes, as if from himself. On March 24, 1912, he wrote to a "Dear Frend,"—perhaps John D. Rockefeller, Jr.—"I am transferring all to 'the New York Corporation' . . ." As his time of more active giving drew towards its close he became increasingly absorbed in the cause of peace and international amity, a dedication that in conjunction with World War I and its destruction of his own hopes brought into his life its only real tragedy.

Persons and Projects

By 1912 a personnel pattern for the Carnegie Foundation was taking form. The long-term staff appointees were few: Bowman, as assistant secretary and secretary of the Foundation, 1906-11; A. Monell Sayre, whose connection began in 1905 and who was first a general and statistical assistant, and subsequently did spade work on federal assistance to education and grants under the Morrill Act, the relations of colleges to secondary schools, which Pritchett discussed as "a disinterested observer" in the Fifth Annual Report, agricultural education 1911-12, repudiation of state bonds in the South, and especially the Foundation's general study of pensions and retirement. In 1911 Clyde Furst, secretary of Teachers College, Columbia University, succeeded Bowman as secretary of the Foundation, when Bowman became president of the State University of Iowa. Pritchett in 1911, suffering what Bowman called "a sharp and serious illness," received winter leave for recuperation, and Butler at the executive committee's behest "act[ed] as president in his absence, in such matters as . . . need[ed] to be passed upon promptly," which proved to be few indeed. Two men were "temporarily" associated with the Foundation in these days: Abraham Flexner, primarily for studies of medical education, and Morris Llewellyn Cooke for work on academic and industrial efficiency with special illustrations from the teaching of physics. The industry of Pritchett and his colleagues was remarkable, their intellectual integrity unquestionable—and every one of them wrote well.

Repute

With this personnel it is small wonder that the reputation of the Foundation increased. And yet this could not have come to pass without honest and direct revealing of facts and results. At first Vanderlip, subsequently Pritchett, conducted relations with press and public. Of the two, the former was perhaps the more successful with newspapers and journalists, the latter with periodicals and their editors. Very early the Foundation became good newspaper copy and American dailies were not long in discovering its usefulness pro and con educational questions. The first press summary was released February 28, 1910, in connection with the Fourth Annual Report (1909). To Pritchett it was, as he wrote to Mr. Carnegie in 1911, "a great encouragement to find the authorities in education admitting so generously as they do today that the Foundation has been the agent for bringing into our school system a wider co-operation. . . . None of us could foresee that the Foundation would make itself felt in this way so soon."

That the name and nature of the Foundation soon spread from the United States and Canada to the European continent and to England is shown both by reviews of its publications and by correspondence. This, too, pleased Mr. Carnegie. Primed by Pritchett, Dr. George R. Parkin, former Canadian teacher then in England, wrote for *The Times* (London) an appraisal of the Foundation's work, which, though much delayed, appeared in December 1911 and attracted considerable attention. *The Times, The Nation,* and *The Spectator* covered Annual Reports at some length. After much advisory assistance had been given to the British Rhodes Trust its secretary, F. J. Wiley, later Sir Francis Wiley, told Bowman, who reported his words to Pritchett, "that the Foundation was considered at Oxford the greatest single influence in American education."

From all evidence, favorable or unfavorable, it is clear that by 1912 the Carnegie Foundation for the Advancement of Teaching had acquired stature, usefulness, and reputation.

5

Upholding the Cause

INFORMAL INQUIRIES AND INTERESTS—ANNUAL REPORTS; STANDARDS
AND STANDARDIZERS; THE UNIT; STUDIES NEVER MADE · FORMAL
STUDIES: EARLY BULLETINS—MEDICAL EDUCATION IN NORTH AMER-
ICA AND EUROPE; ACADEMIC AND INDUSTRIAL EFFICIENCY · DIVISION
OF EDUCATIONAL ENQUIRY—EDUCATION IN VERMONT; THE COMMON
LAW AND THE CASE METHOD; FEDERAL AID FOR VOCATIONAL EDUCA-
TION · PENSION STUDIES AND PROBLEMS: A SOLUTION—ACTUARIAL
STUDIES; A VERY PRESENT HELP · OFFSPRING OF THE FOUNDATION,
T.I.A.A.—CARNEGIE CORPORATION, THE FOUNDATION, AND THE ASSO-
CIATION · THE WAR AND THE FOUNDATION

IT IS anomalous that the Carnegie Foundation for the
Advancement of Teaching acquired its chief reputation
through its studies and not through its professors' pensions. While
Pritchett from the beginning realized that study and educational
inquiry underlay the Foundation's pension activities, it was nearly
a decade before Mr. Carnegie became convinced that fulfillment of
the more general of the Foundation's charter purposes was worthy
of strong support. Of the two men, Pritchett, out of the detail
which he mastered, saw the situation the more clearly.

The attempt by Pritchett, Vanderlip, and others to answer the
question, What is a college, was basal in getting the new endowment under way. It quickly showed Pritchett, and then Eliot, Humphreys, and Butler, already a proponent, the importance of educational inquiry conducted by an independent, nongovernmental
agency which should neither fear to tell the truth nor favor special
interests. By November 1908, Pritchett had matured a notion of
investigating graduate, law, medical, and theological schools, to
take about two years and cost approximately $18,000. He broached

the matter in the Third Annual Report. Vanderlip stood aloof, but after Pritchett had had summer conferences with leading physicians and lawyers, he fell into line, probably not without misgivings. Agreeing that the Foundation's charter was "broad enough to include the study of education at every point where it may affect the higher institutions," the executive committee approved the enterprise and Pritchett, Bowman, Sayre, and later Furst not only continued study of pensions and retirement but went to work upon the broader program. The Foundation's series of educational inquiries originated solely with Pritchett.

The harvest from this sowing took the form of letters, consultations, magazine articles, committee proceedings, and other activities; brief discussions in Annual Reports; and between 1907 and 1918, no fewer than eleven formal studies published as separate Bulletins.

INFORMAL INQUIRIES AND INTERESTS

The less extended discussions, oral and written, touched a variety of topics and affairs. On request, advice and counsel were accorded numerous higher institutions and educational bodies: for example, Columbia, Harvard, Teachers College, Stevens Institute, various state universities and state departments, Canadian provincial universities, denominational colleges in all sorts of difficulties, the Association of American Universities, which was concerned with European recognition of universities in the United States, the Bureau of Education, the New England Association of Colleges and Preparatory Schools, and uncounted individuals. Pritchett also compiled a pamphlet, clear trace of which has now vanished, on Mr. Carnegie's various benefactions in the hope of dispelling confusion about them in the public mind. Only the confusion itself has survived.

Annual Reports

Besides pensions, some of the strictly educational topics under study found place in the Annual Reports: school and college standards, college entrance requirements, life insurance for professors, the influence of denominational boards of education, conditioned and special students, agricultural education, the relations between school, college, and university, politics and education in Montana, Iowa, Kansas, and other states, college catalogues, state educational reports. Certain of these discussions were by-products of more extended inquiries; most of those noted here were prepared *ad hoc.*

A glance at some of the Annual Reports will show their general nature. The material they contained dealing with pensions and retirement, the administration of the Foundation, and financial data does not enter present consideration.

The First Annual Report (1906) revealed Pritchett's astonishing sense of the directions in which the new foundation might move. The Second (1907) treated among other topics the place of the college in American education, the use of the term *university* in the United States, and the evolution of the American type of university. In the Third (1908) are reviewed the "acceptance" of the state institutions, statements on progress toward unity in college entrance requirements, the support and organization of higher education, professional and denominational education. Some of these discussions stand among the best the Foundation has published. The Fourth (1909) was not so successful. Indeed, it gives the impression, particularly in a section on educational administration, that the writers had taken on more than could be digested in the space available. The Fifth (1910) contained a notable discussion of the relations of colleges and secondary schools, which drew widespread editorial comment. The Sixth (1911) set forth opinion on the development of a college board of trustees which deserves rereading by every college president. In the Eighth (1913) some twenty pages related to politics and education in Iowa. For a discussion of the financial status of the college teacher, probably prepared by Furst, Professor Edward L. Thorndike of Teachers College collected data.

The Ninth Annual Report (1914) reveals Pritchett's concern with standards and standardizers: ". . . nobody in American education is in the standardizing business, and no educational agency is seeking to control education in the United States." In the Eleventh (1916) Furst, without by-line, reported on absurdities and the inutility of 145 college entrance certificate forms. The Thirteenth (1918) barely mentions the World War.

Standards and Standardizers, 1915

Those who sought a missile to cast at Pritchett or the Foundation —and they were many, as toes began to be stepped on—could always seize upon the matter of standards. Pritchett began his work for the Foundation with the notion that the Foundation might be made one means of bringing unity into the American educational chaos by improving the college requirements for entrance and for degrees. The questionnaire returns of 1905-07 from the colleges revealed confusion, paper requirements inconsistent with the higher level, readily evaded by both matriculants and matriculates as well as by institutions, and much that looked like dishonesty—at the very least it was laxity with a purpose—in administering them. All this shocked Pritchett. He was essentially a man of fierce integrity and of action, and he felt a necessity to do something about the situation. Seeing high quality in education as of first importance, he believed that a unity of high quality might be achieved through honest requirements honestly applied. The institutional requirements for Foundation "acceptance," borrowed from the State of New York, were certainly minimal even in 1906, but they were definite and they were comparatively administrable. They probably represented what he had in mind when he spoke of "standards" during the first four or five years of the Foundation's existence.

Indeed, at Knox College in 1910 he emphasized the influence of the Foundation "in unifying American colleges and universities and in extending higher standards." Morris Llewellyn Cooke's *Academic and Industrial Efficiency* (Bulletin Number 5) in the same year put forward, perhaps under Pritchett's prompting, a definition: "A standard under modern scientific management is simply a carefully thought out method of performing a function, or carefully drawn specifications covering an implement or some article of stores or of product. The idea of perfection is not involved. . . ." This was all very well, but the outcries against alleged academic interference, attempted dictation, and inhuman, machine-made education gathered force. They were not abated by some of the strictures Flexner—once labeled "Pritchett's handyman"—laid upon medical education and Learned upon education in Vermont. The ensuing screams of agony almost always echoed the charge of attempted standardization.

Pritchett hearkened. In the *North American Review*, April 1915, he emphasized part of his Ninth Annual Report (1914): "College standards are set by the college; not by the Foundation. . . . The Foundation has never attempted to dictate to any college what its standards of admission ought to be. . . . The only standards that the Foundation has urged . . . have been those of common honesty and sincerity." And he noted that the accusation of standardizing gave the Foundation trustees cold chills.

These charges taught Pritchett and his colleagues to abstain from even the appearance of arrogance that flows from sure knowledge, and to cultivate the arts of patience and persuasion in presenting the results of studies.

The Unit

The connection of the Carnegie Foundation with the unit as a "counter" in college admissions is already a twice-told tale. R. L. Duffus in *Democracy Enters College* (New York, 1936) discussed it clearly and conclusively. The Forty-third Annual Report (1948) goes into it more extensively and presents details from the Foundation's own records which completely corroborate Mr. Duffus's views. There is therefore no need for extended discussion here.

It is clear that the Foundation did not invent the unit or its definition. A Subcommittee on History as a College Entrance Requirement used the term when reporting to the National Education Association in 1899 and defined it arithmetically and precisely, much as the New York Board of Regents had used the word *count* in its "credit table" of 1895. The unit soon took its place as a quantitative device useful in appraising school instruction for college admission.

Now, from the Foundation's earliest days, Pritchett and his colleagues perceived that one point where educational quality, high or low, manifested itself clearly was the junction between school and college. In setting the "Educational Standards" which accompanied the Foundation's Rules of 1906, the executive committee adopted an academic requirement of fourteen units for admission to "acceptable" colleges, "a unit being a course of five periods weekly" throughout a school year.

In 1906, also, the National Conference Committee on Standards of Colleges and Secondary Schools was formed with nine regional components to consider educational problems on a nationwide rather than a sectional basis. With such working members as Dean Frederick C. Ferry of Williams and Wilson Farrand, headmaster of Newark Academy, the committee, acting in concert with the College Entrance Examination Board, founded in 1900, exerted influence towards unifying college requirements. Of the committee Pritchett was a corresponding member for a time, and afterwards Furst served in a similar capacity. The committee often met in the Foundation offices, once at least on invitation of the executive committee.

Entrance requirements were discussed in several Annual Reports of the Carnegie Foundation.

Though the Foundation's interest came naturally enough, it aroused widespread feeling that Pritchett was attempting to set up unreasonable and arbitrary standards for admission to the Accepted List. Institutions in the South, being the least stringent, were the hardest hit. The outcry was loud, but it did not drown the calmer voices of such southern leaders as James H. Kirkland of Vanderbilt, who rallied a movement to raise requirements, or President William A. Sledd of the University of Florida, who wrote to Pritchett: "*We need your standards* more than we need your classification or your recognition."

Men of their stamp pressed forward and won the day. Whereas in 1906 only five southern institutions required for entrance graduation from a four-year high school, and in 1908 the University of South Carolina was admitting on 7.2 units, by 1911 college entrance requirements had materially strengthened in 172 typical institutions and in thirteen states, and 160 southern institutions had announced a four-year high-school course as necessary for matriculation. "The better colleges of the South already required similar standards" to those in use in New York, the Midwest, and the Pacific area, with progress particularly notable in Virginia, North Carolina, West Virginia, and Georgia.

By 1912, Pritchett saw that the unit had served its main purpose. The most promising antidote to its abuse seemed to be the comprehensive type of entrance examination inaugurated at Harvard. He noted in 1914 that the accusation of dictation in matters of entrance had been so unreasonable that even "Mr. Andrew Carnegie has been attacked for inventing the 'Carnegie unit.' " These tides of controversy eddied round the Foundation until about 1919 when the new psychological test, widely used for the Adjutant General's Office in World War I, began to come into its own. Fifteen years later the unit as a device of academic measurement was giving ground on all sides to new-type comprehensive examining, but it is difficult to conceive what might have been the state of American entrance requirements without the patient understanding and effort of those who fought the battle for quality in college admissions during the first three decades of the century. One of the strongest forces in the action was the Carnegie Foundation—but it did not invent the unit. "We call the thing his in the long run who utters it clearest and best," even if the ascription be erroneous.

Studies Never Made

Growth of the Foundation's prestige is illustrated in the number and nature of the requests it received in its early years to conduct educational studies. These began almost at once, when Charles W. Eliot urged upon Pritchett the importance of trying to get American understanding of a true university, a task at which Eliot said he had long labored. During the next decade, not dissimilar requests poured into the Foundation's offices: to study correspondence schools, dental education, individual universities and colleges, college athletics (two requests: 1913, 1917), education in various states and localities, hospitals and their organization, particularly in their relation to medical schools, education in the Maritime Provinces of Canada, art education, schools for the deaf, business education, graduate work, drugless healing, college scholarships and loans, moral education, the utilization of university buildings, and many other matters. Some of these were inspired by the success of Flexner's studies and by the Vermont inquiry; others reflected perennial problems of academic life. All for good reasons were declined. Two topics, the training of teachers and engineering education, led in the immediate future to extended inquiries.

FORMAL STUDIES: EARLY BULLETINS

The Foundation's series of Bulletins embodying usually the results of inquiries into various phases of higher education opened in 1907 with a forty-five page pamphlet of information about the problems resident in the possible extension of the retiring allowances to state universities. Its interest was ephemeral; Mr. Carnegie was supposed to have solved the financial problems by his five-million-dollar gift. In less than a year after Bulletin Number 1 appeared in print, came Bulletin Number 2, *The Financial Status of the Professor in America and in Germany*, which had its roots in the Foundation's pension studies and data collected by questionnaire from 156 American colleges and universities. Pritchett, Bowman, and Sayre gave those roots a larger development. The third Bulletin reflects some of Pritchett's convictions about the unification of our higher education in its presentation of twenty-five practical blank forms for reporting college finances, based principally on the recommendations, after considerable travel and consultation, by a Boston firm of accountants. None of these three Bulletins had much interest for the general public in spite of Pritchett's cautions about superficial education in Bulletin Number 3. With Bulletin Number 4 the case was different.

Medical Education in North America and Europe, 1910, 1912

The story of Abraham Flexner's studies in medical education has been told by Flexner himself in both his autobiography, *I Remember* (1940) and his life of *Henry S. Pritchett* (1943). These accounts need no paraphrasing here.

After mulling over studies of professional training since 1907 or early 1908, Pritchett had pitched upon medical education, and, on Eliot's recommendation, but apparently with only nominal approval by some of the members of the executive committee, had selected Abraham Flexner, a brilliant young schoolmaster and writer, to do the job. Results were published in 1910 in *Medical Education in the United States and Canada*, Bulletin Number 4.

The volume presents the first full-length, one-man detailed study of a single phase of American education to be sponsored by the Foundation. Search reveals no comparable document preceding it in the American educational field.

Flexner's technique was relatively simple. Under Pritchett's instructions to get the facts and to appraise them without fear, he consulted such men of standing in the medical profession as Dr. William H. Welch of the Johns Hopkins University, Dr. Simon Flexner of the Rockefeller Institute for Medical Research, who was much later to become Welch's biographer, Dr. Arthur D. Bevan, chairman, and Dr. N. P. Colwell, secretary, of the Council on Medical Education of the American Medical Association; read widely in technical treatises, American, British, European; personally visited all of the 155 schools of medicine in the United States and Canada; and presented the facts he found and his own conclusions. The immediate results were sensational, and rightly.

Flexner's outstanding ability lay in his power to seize facts and ideas, to correlate them with a central pattern, and to present his results clearly for both technicians and laymen. The volume contains not alone some of his best writing but some of the best writing ever produced on American education.

Flexner recommended that the 155 medical schools be reduced to 31, capable of graduating 3,500 well-trained physicians a year until more were needed. This was scarcely so radical a stand as at first may appear, for of the 120 schools thus to be "wiped off the map" 37 were "already negligible," while under pressure of the American

Medical Association others closed their doors before the Flexner report could be published, and still others merged with established institutions. By 1913, the number had dropped to 115 schools, all of which had been classified by the American Medical Association's Council on Medical Education as A+ (24), A (39), B (23), C (29).

Flexner analyzed the schools individually and intensively, and he made his comments stick by boldness and sheer weight of fact. Few were the schools that were not found wanting.

Pritchett summarized the situation somewhat as follows: For twenty-five years there had been an enormous overproduction of uneducated and ill-trained medical practitioners. This situation had arisen from the very large number of commercial schools, "sustained in many cases by advertising methods." Until recently, conducting a medical school had been a profitable business because instruction was mainly didactic. Half of the schools had income below $10,000 a year and the quality of the work was as low as the resources. The poor-boy argument was really an argument in behalf of the poor medical school. A hospital under complete educational control is as necessary to a medical school as a laboratory of chemistry or pathology; the university, of which medical schools should be integral parts, should seek more teachers devoted to clinical science.

Perhaps no learned or scientific publication since Martin Luther's day has called forth more violent storms of protest, approbation, and argument than Flexner's initial Bulletin. Newspapers in most cities and all sections, popular and learned periodicals, speakers upon many topics, related or not, all took sides. Flexner was accused of having tailored his facts to fit a preconception not really his own. Downright abuse was not infrequent. Recalcitrants threatened suit, but had the good sense to stop at the threat. Flexner stood his ground and Pritchett stood by Flexner. Neither made any claim to infallibility.

Gradually the smoke lifted. As the volume came to be read, it was taken more and more at its face value. Out of the murk, as Pritchett had hoped, emerged a new national effort in which the intelligent citizen and the physician united to strengthen medical education and at the same time to relate it rightly to the university. Huge increases in private support of medical education followed. States like Iowa vied with Minnesota, and, together with individuals, rich and poor, more than doubled huge foundation benefactions. The full results of Flexner's work have not yet been reached in American education, but four decades of improvement have changed our concept of medical training and practice. Today the danger seems rather to be that medical training shall consume too much of a young man's life at a cost beyond private ability to meet.

Acting upon suggestions which followed the publication of the American study, the Foundation sent Flexner to inquire into medical education in Europe—that is, in Germany, Austria, France, England, and Scotland—during the year 1910-11. Bulletin Number 6, *Medical Education in Europe*, is therefore "to a large extent a supplement" of Bulletin Number 4. Its purpose was "to present a picture" not "a detailed account" of contemporary medical education abroad.

Pritchett's brilliant introduction is one of his longest. Although, in pointing a future for medical education in the western world, he, following Flexner's text, leans heavily upon Germany, he treats of the fundamental lessons to be drawn from the handling of the basic sciences, the medical curriculum, clinical opportunities, teaching, and support, and the relation of the medical school to the laboratory, to the hospital, and to the university.

The best of Flexner's historical summary of the growth of medical education deals with the development of the scientific point of view. Most of his statistical matter he drew from methodical German sources, largely because the German schools and universities exemplified the only systematic educational procedure for medicine to be found in Europe or elsewhere made possible by the high quality of teaching and equipment available, the secondary-school preparation of its students, and liberal government financial support. American private benefaction had not yet touched medical education with its golden wand.

Although French and British students were drilled in details, they acquired no method; in England only the branches—e.g. physiology —had "full academic recognition and protection." The English clinical tradition, however, Flexner found to be essentially sound; the relation of the hospital to instruction, he said, deserved to be copied everywhere. What was needed, he insisted, was a noncommercial relation between medical school, hospital, laboratory, and university. This was the pattern which the best medical education in the United States was destined to follow.

Not without justice has Flexner been called the Father of Modern Medical Education. First and last, he has probably exercised more influence upon the course of medical education all over the world than any other one man.

The two studies of medical education cost the Foundation $60,457.

The wide public attention that Flexner's Bulletins gained established a reputation for the Carnegie Foundation. Threats of legal reprisals from commercial medical schools soon faded. Even if the two reports "simply expressed and disseminated what enlightened medical educators have been working patiently to bring about," their vigor, completeness, and timeliness became fundamentals to great changes. The medical curriculum was remade. Schools that could not face the test of quality closed their doors, until in 1914 no fewer than 52 of the 155 that Flexner had visited had disappeared. Guided by Flexner's concepts the Rockefeller endowments, which Flexner joined in 1913, and Carnegie Corporation invested more than 130 millions in medical education, a sum which attracted as much again from other sources. For many years Pritchett was called upon to advise in the subject. The Flexner studies, plus Rockefeller and Carnegie money and other benefactions they spurred, wrought what was probably the greatest improvement that ever took place during four decades in professional education.

Academic and Industrial Efficiency, Bulletin Number 5, 1910

Meanwhile, at Pritchett's request, the executive committee had authorized a study of Academic and Industrial Efficiency by Morris Llewellyn Cooke, M.E., concentrated upon departments of physics in six institutions, all but one in the eastern United States. Appearing in 1910, the slender volume was not too favorably received. Some scientists saw it as showing little comprehension of what a university was all about. Many found it doctrinaire. In the preface Pritchett himself disavows its comments on research.

DIVISION OF EDUCATIONAL ENQUIRY, 1913

At the luncheon following the sixth annual meeting, 1911, Mr. Carnegie spoke to his trustees of his interest and pleasure in the Foundation's helping "to solve our problems of education from a national point of view. . . ." This Pritchett called "an outcome of the Pension Fund administration which has far exceeded all our expectations." By November 25, he was writing to Mr. Carnegie his hope "that at some time you will place in the hands of the Founda-

tion a moderate sum, the income of which shall be . . . available
. . . for . . . educational studies and publications." Discussion of
this matter between the two men continued at intervals until January
23, 1913, when Pritchett's persistence prevailed upon Mr. Carnegie
to give the Foundation an endowment for the study of education.

The Letter of Gift, January 31, 1913, to all trustees offered a
million and a quarter dollars in 4 per cent bonds under certain conditions: the organizing of a Division of Educational Enquiry (the
spelling was apparently due to Bertram's predilections) to use its
income for possible studies and publications within a broad educational range, separate from the endowment for professors' pensions.
Later Pritchett stated that "Mr. Carnegie was quite willing to make
a larger endowment if it were needed," and indicated that he
(Pritchett) thought an annual income of $50,000 was sufficient for
the purpose. Responses from the trustees were immediate and enthusiastic. None doubted the worth of the new benefaction: indeed,
Denny thought that "the service rendered by this new endowment
may be made of really greater value than a pension system," and
other trustees approximated his view. The executive committee, acting in their behalf, had no hesitation in accepting the gift on February 13 "with the highest appreciation." At last, Vanderlip pointed
out, Pritchett's "pet idea" was realized.

What caused this change in the Founder's attitude? The most
important reason was Pritchett's patient persistence. Secondly, the
success of Flexner's American Bulletin was undoubtedly persuasive.
Thirdly, proposals for a study of engineering education—preparation for a profession which Mr. Carnegie much respected—may have
been influential, and the newly received legislative request for an
inquiry into education in Vermont certainly helped. The president
was authorized to employ such additional hands as might be needed
to carry on studies already begun and to adjust salaries and other
costs between the income of the new Division and that from the general funds. Steps were taken to finance the new department until
interest from the bonds promised by Mr. Carnegie should be available.

A policy was at once devised "not to build up . . . with this
endowment a bureau, but to bring into its service temporarily those
believed to be best suited to deal with a particular problem, leaving
them to return at the end of their work to their permanent studies."
Yet William S. Learned and Alfred Z. Reed, the first new appointees (Sayre's salary was paid from the Division's income begin-

ning March 1913) served in the Division until their retirement some thirty years later.

Education in Vermont

Under joint resolution, November 19, 1912, the Vermont legislature provided for a commission of nine persons whom the governor was to appoint to inquire into education in the state and report recommendations for all levels. The commission, of which Lowell of Harvard was invited to be a member but declined, asked the Carnegie Foundation to make the underlying study, assistants to be determined by its president. Professor Edward C. Elliott of Wisconsin, experienced in similar work, was engaged early. Professor Milo B. Hillegas of Teachers College, Columbia, was named to examine into the elementary schools, and the secondary schools were assigned to Dr. William S. Learned, then Fellow for Research at the Harvard Graduate School of Education. Others engaged for their respective fields were Professor Edward H. Farrington, College of Agriculture, University of Wisconsin; Dr. N. B. Potter, assistant professor of internal medicine at Columbia; Dr. G. R. Olshausen, United States Bureau of Standards, for the three engineering schools; Miss L. E. Stearns, Wisconsin Free Library, for library provisions in the public schools; and Mr. William Leslie for school accounting and finances. The Foundation staff also worked on the data, although Pritchett's name does not appear in the text of the report.

The Vermont study, one of many state surveys made in the period, had four major characteristics: simplicity of the report as addressed to laymen; diplomatic temper; the number of its conclusions, four only; and recommendations, only fifty-two in contrast with the hundreds, even thousands, in other similar enterprises. The work was sympathetically done, but it was searching, detailed, and based upon much visiting and a wealth of data.

Bulletin Number 7 received considerable attention in Vermont. State newspapers generally approved it, especially as to the elementary and secondary schools, except in matters affecting their particular localities. There was little support for the sections on colleges and universities. Politics and attempted logrolling underlay most of the opposition, but by 1915 notable changes had been legislated into Vermont education. A new commissioner of education and a five-member state board with greatly increased powers began to function. Funds for the primary and secondary levels were much increased and vocational training for men inaugurated. Although all of the changes recommended by the commission were not carried out, enough resulted amply to justify the whole undertaking.

The Common Law and the Case Method, Bulletin Number 8, 1914

The spring of 1913 found Reed beginning his studies of legal education in fulfillment of Pritchett's hope as expressed in the Sixth Annual Report (1911) "to present a study of legal education . . . its present status, . . . supply of practitioners and . . . admission to practice in the several states." Meanwhile, the executive committee, February 11, 1913, had authorized Pritchett to invite Professor Josef Redlich of Vienna to undertake a study of "the comparative teaching of law and the Case System." This Pritchett did. Just about a year after Reed was appointed, Redlich submitted a manuscript in German and probably Reed, Pritchett, and others hammered it into shape. Of 130 American law schools, Redlich had visited 10 which used the case method. The result is not impressive today; even on publication, Pritchett's preface, which emphasized Redlich's scholarship, was lukewarm and dry. The German had produced a pleasant essay, but all of his recommendations were already in American use. Although the disquisition is said to have aroused much discussion, the press references now appear pretty perfunctory.

During World War I correspondence continued between Redlich and Pritchett, and also Reed, but none of the three yielded an inch as to his own nation's stand in world affairs. After the Allies' victory, Redlich's letters were pathetic but still patriotic and by 1925 he was hard pressed for money, a situation which Pritchett tried but found impossible to relieve.

Federal Aid for Vocational Education, Bulletin Number 10, 1917

When Sayre resigned as of December 13, 1913, to become head of the Church Pension Fund, Protestant Episcopal Church, Dr. I. L. Kandel of Teachers College, who had assisted Paul Monroe in preparing his *Cyclopedia of Education*, succeeded him in 1914 as a sort of general utility man. Kandel was probably the most accomplished scholar ever to work for the Foundation. Into Sayre's chaotic manuscript on agricultural education he succeeded in putting order and converted it into a bulletin with far wider bearings. As matters have since developed, the whole study was rather a waste of time, for while Kandel's discussion is painstaking and illuminating, federal aid in all sorts of higher education has assumed such proportions since 1945 as to make Pritchett's preface to the Bulletin resemble a lament for a lost cause.

PENSION STUDIES AND PROBLEMS: A SOLUTION

"We were pretty ignorant," Pritchett wrote in August 1915 to a correspondent, "when we began administering the Foundation's pension fund ten years ago." In another connection he went further: "The decade . . . has been rich in experience, . . . a period of unexampled activity in the creation of pension systems on the part of institutions of learning, of the great industries, and of the states themselves. Today, more than ever before, there is needed a clear exposition of the fundamental social and economic principles upon which a pension system ought to rest." Thus to Pritchett, by 1915, the defects in the Carnegie Foundation were becoming evident, although not as yet their seriousness. Upon these matters the Foundation's pension studies were casting light.

The work involved was the care of Pritchett, Bowman, later Furst, Sayre until his resignation, and Kandel. The Seventh Annual Report (1912), the first to present in one segregated section discussion of pensions and retirement, contained Sayre's unsigned analysis of the New South Wales pension debacle. To Pritchett this was handwriting on the wall for the Foundation. The result was the publication of Bulletin Number 9 (1915, 1916), *A Comprehensive Plan of Insurance and Annuities for College Teachers*, which set forth in detail the first sound set of pension principles for a contractual college retirement system in an annuity and insurance association for teachers. When the Teachers Insurance and Annuity Association was set up in 1918 some of the provisions were changed, but not the central concept or the validity of the principles that Pritchett had laid down.

In 1918, also, appeared the Foundation's Bulletin Number 12, *Pensions for Public School Teachers*, a report for the Committee on Salaries, Pensions, and Tenure of the National Education Association. Its authors were given as Furst and Kandel, but Kandel did the spade work and most of the writing. The first twelve pages set forth the Social Philosophy of Pensions, a title and a subject dear to Pritchett's heart. The Suggested System of Retiring Allowances for . . . the Public Schools of Vermont, the first of such Foundation studies to be based upon complete actuarial and personal data, is brief, clear, and nonlegalistic—an innovation in the field. Most of its provisions were enacted into law. As far as possible it avoided "basing pensions upon salaries at or near the age of retirement, since no one can predict what any teacher's salary will be 30 or 40 or 50 years hence." The author of that clause knew intimately the pension experience of the Carnegie Foundation.

These two Bulletins sprang from the Foundation's pension studies. In addition, each Annual Report of the day contained a section on pensions and retirement prepared earlier by Sayre, later by Kandel and Furst. These discussions set new standards and shed fresh light upon pension problems not alone in the United States, but in many other countries, whether for teachers, governmental employees, or workers in industry. By 1913, in an article for the *Independent*, Pritchett was advocating for public schools a joint contributory system, the amount of the pension determined by thorough actuarial investigation with moderate interest on accumulations, withdrawal and death benefits, and centralized administration on a statewide basis. Colleges such as Brown, Chicago, and Haverford were "rapidly establishing their own systems," and the Foundation was learning fast and none too pleasantly.

The continuous study of retirement and pension systems had affected the administering of the Foundation. Some of the executive committee rulings and decisions showed an increase of caution both in "accepting" institutions and in granting and promising pensions, although occasional bursts of liberalization recurred. A suggestion promulgated by Jastrow, which would have permitted academic teaching after retirement—rather "on the sly"—was denied. In 1915 the trustees changed the designation of the Accepted List to Associated List.

Actuarial Studies

In 1914 the executive committee authorized Pritchett to expend not more than $5,000 for the service of outside "actuarial and pensions experts." Gradually the function of the pension expert, as exemplified by Pritchett, Kandel, and Furst, and those of the actuary were differentiated. To the former's activities belonged the study of the Baltimore and Ohio Relief Association and Pension System made in 1916 by Professor George E. Barnett of the Johns Hopkins, and much of the work Professor W. F. Willcox began in 1913 and concluded two years later. Herbert D. Brown and especially a graduate student, C. J. West, did the actuarial work involved. The data for these inquiries were faulty, but the conclusions pointed in a valid direction. Deaths of beneficiaries, 1913-14, were only about 44 per cent of those expected; during the period 1905-15, about 82 per cent. The mortality of those retiring at over age sixty-six was only 60 per cent of that for those retiring at younger ages. While the lists showed 5,498 pensionables in 1914, there were 6,626 in 1915. S. S. Hall, Sr., had assumed in 1909 only 3,400 for 1914.

Even the institutions in many cases could not furnish exact figures. In 1915 Professor Charles S. Brooks of the University of California was engaged upon an actuarial study, the results of which were indicative and disturbing. Off and on, Hall himself worked at valuations, but neither he nor anyone else really comprehended how the growth of American colleges and their faculties was mounting. At length Pritchett convinced the board and the executive committee that the burden of the pension load for the future must be shifted from the free-pensioning shoulders of the Foundation to a joint contributory contractual agency. It became clear that the Rules had to be tightened and, among other measures, the age of retirement advanced.

Matters were even more serious than that. Pritchett had a plan for meeting the situation and the trustees served notice on all concerned that changes were inevitable.

In December 1917, at Pritchett's request, Hall calculated the Foundation's present load. For about 6,600 eligibles the cost of pensions up to about 1965 would approximate $69,000,000, of which the Foundation's income of $750,000 yearly would provide less than half. Obviously, the rest had to be sought elsewhere. The old free-riding days were nearly over.

A Very Present Help

Pritchett used most of Hall's conclusions in an appeal for the assistance of Carnegie Corporation of New York, which in January 1917 had granted the Church Pension Fund, at Pritchett's energetic recommendation, $324,744.87 and thereby evinced its interest in retirement problems even outside the immediate shadow of the Foundation's dangers.

OFFSPRING OF THE FOUNDATION, T.I.A.A.

Mr. Carnegie had been a great advocate of life insurance—witness the report of his interview when sailing for Europe in 1905.

His interest was lively in 1907. In the spring of that year he discussed with Pritchett the possibility of operating through the Foundation, under the New York State Insurance Law, with separate endowment, a "Carnegie Life Insurance Association," which should offer college and other teachers life insurance at cost plus a small loading. Who originated this notion cannot now be discovered, but Pritchett developed it at length into a project in which officers of the Foundation should double as officers of this association except for the hiring of an actuary who should serve also as "manager." The cost he computed at about $20,000 a year to be met from income on a $5,000,000 endowment. "At the time we talked of a pension system, you had the insurance plan much in mind," wrote Pritchett to Mr. Carnegie March 19, 1907. Perhaps this sentence accounts for Mr. Carnegie's remarks to the ship reporters on April 26, 1905.

Foundation trustees, especially Eliot and Hadley, believed "heartily" in the idea and some even favored the Foundation's itself writing the insurance. Cadwalader endorsed it, providing a separate corporation were set up; his opinion was to the effect that the Foundation could not issue insurance policies under its District of Columbia Charter. On hearing this, "Mr. Carnegie . . ." Pritchett found, "rather lost interest in the matter. . . ." By November 13, 1908, it was "not likely that anything will be done." Pritchett, however, in the Fourth Annual Report (1909), wrote of The Teacher's Obligations in Life Insurance.

The project did not entirely expire; it continued a sort of underground existence. S. S. Hall, Sr., whom Pritchett had consulted about it in 1907, recurred to it once or twice though not very definitely. In 1911 Willcox suggested that the Foundation require annual contributions from each prospective beneficiary towards his own pension. The Seventh Annual Report (1912) presented Pritchett's views on Contributory and Non-contributory Pensions, and most of the principles he set forth therein were later put to use. In the same year Hall produced figures on combined annuity and insurance benefits dovetailed together, based on an annual 5 per cent of salary, and the McClintock Tables, 4 per cent interest during the period of accumulation, and 3½ per cent during payment of the annuity. The immediate origin of the Teachers Insurance and Annuity Association was, however, in the Foundation's general pension inquiries and actuarial studies of its own situation.

It was in the Eleventh Annual Report (1916) that Pritchett,

after six months of very intensive work, set forth his Fundamental
Principles of a Pension System. "Until these underlying principles
are accepted," he wrote, "there is no occasion to discuss details."
This order of approach brought considerable adverse comment, because many felt that through it Pritchett cut off discussion until
he could get his own way. The Twelfth Annual Report (1917) returned to the attack. Pritchett, apparently assisted by Furst and
Kandel, pointed out that, Mr. Carnegie's vision of "free" pensions
not as a bounty but as a right having been effectuated, the results
had negative aspects sufficient to force the Foundation trustees to
conclude that they had two duties: first, to carry out as fairly as
they could their present commitments, and, secondly, "promptly to
establish a system of pensions open to all college teachers in English-speaking North America." Under long-standing reservations,
the terms on which future retiring allowances would be granted
should be much modified. The Foundation could proceed only by
cutting its cloth to fit the facts and by acting upon the results of
its investigations. It was "to be regretted that this knowledge was
not available" earlier.

Bulletin Number 9, *A Comprehensive Plan of Insurance and Annuities for College Teachers*, already in type by October 1915, was
distributed generally in April 1916. In November 1915 Pritchett
opened the matter with John Dewey, president of the American
Association of University Professors, asking co-operation over the
confidential version. Both Dewey and Dean John H. Wigmore, who
succeeded him as A.A.U.P. president, pleaded for delay and careful
consideration. Committee P of the association took up the matter.
As will be shown in Chapter VI, by composition and nature this
group was hostile to the plan, which on examination it found, in
December 1916, it could not approve. A committee of the National
Association of State Universities adopted a more favorable attitude
and contributed much to the discussion. Meanwhile the matter was
presented to the Associated institutions.

In lowest terms, the proposal was to establish an association to
provide insurance and joint contributory deferred retiring annuities to college teachers on a net-premium basis, assuming $4\frac{1}{2}$ per
cent interest and using for the annuities the McClintock Tables of
Mortality. Term insurance expiring at age sixty-five was to be the
staple policy. The annuity was to be contractual and to provide
(on option) for the wife and also for migration. On November 15,
1916, after hearing representatives of the Association of American

Universities, the National Association of State Universities, and the American Association of University Professors, the Foundation trustees appointed a commission of eleven persons to study the plan. Of these, six members were to be trustees of the Foundation, including the president, the other five to represent the various bodies just listed named by their respective presidents. The A.A.U.P. was to have two representatives on the commission.

The commission at its fifth sitting, April 17, 1917, adopted a report recommending Pritchett's fundamental principles of a pension system and the combining of the annuities and insurance in a nonprofit insurance and annuity association operating under New York State law as a stock company, the stock to be owned ultimately by the association trustees, who should be representative of the policyholders themselves. The underlying principle had been devised by Mr. Elihu Root, Jr., of Root, Clark, Buckner and Howland, and the Insurance Department of the State of New York. It outlined in general the Teachers Insurance and Annuity Association of America as it finally emerged in its own charter.

There were to be thirteen incorporators, of whom five (three named by the A.A.U.P., one by the Association of American Colleges, one by Canadian institutions) should, with the Carnegie Foundation, initially hold the stock. The Foundation apparently was to use a one-million-dollar unexpended balance to provide capital and surplus and was to "guarantee" return of 4½ per cent for annuity accumulations but not on a contractual basis. The new Association was not at present to deal with the risk of disability; "this will be provided for by the Carnegie Foundation." Although the Association was to be chartered to sell insurance and annuities of all types, it was to write only term insurance and deferred annuities. The report represents a victory for Pritchett. How much of this was due to Furst, who acted as the commission's secretary, is conjectural.

The preceding two years had been hard going for Pritchett and his colleagues in the Foundation, particularly Furst. The amount of correspondence, conferring, and negotiation they carried on is staggering. The trustees had to be convinced of the need of the new agency, the necessity of amending the Foundation's Rules, and the wisdom of the steps involved. Among those who had to be won over were Charles F. Thwing, secretary of the board, Henry C. King, Marion LeRoy Burton, Charles R. Van Hise, David Starr Jordan, Samuel B. McCormick, and Arthur T. Hadley, not to mention

Jacob Gould Schurman, who was very difficult to bring into line. Outside the board there were individuals, brilliant and vocal, like A. O. Lovejoy, who began by pecking away at the word "Confidential" as applied to the 1915 edition of Bulletin Number 9, Jastrow, Cattell, Cook, and many others equally sharp of pen. Certain faculties objected to parts of the report, and indeed it is doubtful if the proportion of clear approbation was even ultimately so high as Furst seems to have been led to indicate. The opposition of A.A.U.P. Committee P continued until after the new annuity association had been incorporated. The fact was that comparatively few college teachers really understood either the Foundation's problems or its proposal. A committee of the Actuarial Society of America, Arthur Hunter, chairman, gave guarded approval in February 1918, and about the same can be said of the committee of the American Institute of Actuaries, which incidentally attributed to the McClintock 4½ per cent tables "ample security." The attitude of the actuarial profession was on the whole sporting, considering how hard Pritchett had borne down on the great insurance companies during the Association's germination. It was nearer home that some of the greatest difficulties arose.

Carnegie Corporation, the Foundation, and the Association

Now, on December 3, 1915, the Corporation board requested of each of the Carnegie philanthropies, including the Foundation, a report on its respective affairs and financial needs. Pritchett, well assisted by Furst, prepared and submitted the Foundation's report to the Foundation's executive committee, January 21, 1916, with the notation that it had not yet fully considered the changes and plans for the new association that Pritchett was suggesting. The report and these caveats Pritchett forwarded to the Corporation on February 4, 1916. It was a comprehensive and unvarnished statement, and it made not too palatable reading.

By 1917 Mr. Carnegie's health and inclination were leading him to take progressively less part in Carnegie Corporation of New York. Among its trustees the group which had been most intimately connected with the details of its life since the early 1900's were powerful in matters of policy. Over their united tendencies, Senator Root's breadth of view and of nature appear not wholly to have prevailed. When, therefore, Pritchett transmitted to the Corporation board the results of the Foundation trustees' meetings of November 1916 and May 1917, in which the need of more money for the Foundation and of endowment for the proposed annuity association were writ pretty large, he encountered a tendency to make conditions upon which aspects of the negotiations should hinge. The result was that while agreement was reached, it was surrounded by various stipulations, some of which were thorns in the path forward. Despite all this, the attitude of the Corporation board as a whole was friendly, considerate, and generous—even open-handed—in providing funds, and such it has continued to be to this day.

On June 7, 1917, the trustees of Carnegie Corporation voted one million dollars for capital and surplus of the new Association. It thus became "the only agency that has put any money into the enterprise"; and hence the owner of all its stock except the very nominal amounts ultimately paid for by Pritchett and Franks. On November 7, 1917, in an all-day session, the Corporation board listened to Pritchett's statement of the Foundation's case, later much elaborated and detailed in correspondence. One result was its agreement to provide Reserve Fund Number One; the conditions were that the Foundation should contribute its one-million-dollar "surplus" while Carnegie Corporation would contribute five million at 4 per cent interest as of January 1, 1918, and subsequently annual payments of $600,000 during ten years, the resulting fund to become available principal and interest to the Foundation for pension purposes January 1, 1928. Current officers and staff members of other Carnegie philanthropies were to become eligible to participate in T.I.A.A. The Corporation board further furnished $1,000,000 to establish the Foundation's Reserve Fund Number Two to provide benefits for older teachers in institutions needing help in adopting T.I.A.A. retirement annuity contracts and assist otherwise to inaugurate the new contributory plan. These two grants the Foundation Executive Committee "gratefully accepted" on December 21, 1917, and also by transfer of $100,000 in unused resources set up the Emergency Reserve Fund of the Foundation. The Corporation had not closed the door to further requests for funds from the Foundation should they be needed. One price the Foundation had to pay was the revision of its Rules so that the benefits in prospect as of November 15, 1917, "shall not exceed the financial resources of the Carnegie Foundation."

The Teachers Insurance and Annuity Association of America was incorporated by the New York State Legislature March 4, 1918. In spite of much agitation, it was to be not a mutual, but a stock company, writing only nonparticipating policies. Pritchett

Part Two ⟿ 1918-1930

～ 6 ～

Relationships

OFFICES · A LEGAL QUESTION · OFFICERS AND STAFF MEMBERS, 1918-
30—THE SAYRE EPISODE, 1929 · ALL IN THE FAMILY—"THAT LUSTY
INFANT, THE ASSOCIATION"; RELATIONS WITH CARNEGIE CORPORA-
TION; CO-OPERATIVE INVESTING · THE ROCKEFELLER PHILANTHRO-
PIES · NATIONAL ASSOCIATIONS AND OTHER BODIES—ASSOCIATION OF
AMERICAN UNIVERSITIES; ASSOCIATION OF AMERICAN COLLEGES;
AMERICAN COUNCIL ON EDUCATION; COLLEGE ENTRANCE EXAMINA-
TION BOARD; COUNCIL ON MEDICAL EDUCATION OF THE AMERICAN
MEDICAL ASSOCIATION; NATIONAL EDUCATION ASSOCIATION; AMER-
ICAN ASSOCIATION OF UNIVERSITY PROFESSORS · REGIONAL AND SPE-
CIAL BODIES—CHURCH EDUCATIONAL BOARDS

IT WAS on August 11, 1919, that Andrew Carnegie died at
Shadowbrook, Lenox, Massachusetts. During his last years,
although the presidents of his philanthropies through personal
visits and annual reports kept him informed, he had taken small if
any part in the affairs of even Carnegie Corporation of which he
was president. Pritchett often said that Mr. Carnegie towards the
close of his life asked questions about only one of his philanthropies, "the insurance company"—that is, the Teachers Insurance
and Annuity Association. Time was, however, when at each annual
meeting he had entertained the trustees of the Foundation at dinner or at luncheon and, until war forced his absence in 1914, had
favored them with "quickening talks." To Pritchett in 1920 it
seemed "very desirable that among [those elected to fill vacancies
in the board] there should be some who were younger than the
group of men Mr. Carnegie had originally named. . . . The meetings that we used to have with Mr. Carnegie have passed into the
twilight of history. . . . These younger men will never have the

123

experience we had when we used to foregather with the Founder, himself."

At the annual luncheons given since 1907, at which the president of the Foundation is host, Mr. Carnegie sometimes said a few words on his theories of giving and related matters. For many years these luncheons were held at Delmonico's, and after 1923 at various clubs near the Foundation's offices. Since 1931 they have taken place at the Century Association. Until Pritchett retired in 1930, it was he who usually recalled Mr. Carnegie's purposes and characteristics to his fellow-trustees. Afterward, for more than a decade, Butler usually spoke; many of his pleasant talks were in their way masterpieces. Subsequently, the retiring or newly elected chairman of the board proposed a toast to the memory of Andrew Carnegie, and many of these talks also have been memorable.

By 1920 the old order was indeed changing. At the fifteenth annual meeting the places left by the resignations of Crawford, Peterson, Schurman, and Smith were filled by electing Ferry, Hibben, Neilson, and Vinson. As of November 1, 1924, T. Morrison Carnegie, a Founder-appointed trustee and the Foundation's first treasurer, resigned his trusteeship. Robert A. Franks, Mr. Carnegie's long-time financial associate, had some years before become treasurer of the Foundation.

Pritchett once wrote to a member of the board that "in Mr. Carnegie's life, it was his habit" to invite the trustees to dine on the Tuesday evening before their annual meeting. The habit does not appear to have been invariable. After his death, the custom almost lapsed, although Butler dined his fellow-trustees in 1921 and 1924 and again in 1930. In 1925 Thomas W. Lamont, who had joined the board in 1917, inaugurated the series of annual trustees' dinners that ended only with his death early in 1948. At each the guests of honor were always of eminence, frequently of ambassadorial status, and Lamont's inimitable hospitality, combined at table and afterward with some of the best talk to be enjoyed on this side of the Atlantic, made every such occasion a treasured memory. Since 1948 these dinners of trustees and guests have been held at the University Club.

At the beginning of the sixteenth winter, Pritchett saw the Foundation's business as lying in three fields: "1. The liquidation of the old retiring allowances. . . . This will require the expenditure of some fifty millions of dollars in the next thirty years for which . . . large reserves are being accumulated. 2. The development of the contractual plan of old-age annuities through the Teachers Insurance and Annuity Association, . . . a separate corporation. . . . 3. The work of the Division of Educational Enquiry." All of this business was soon to be transferred to new quarters. Since 1908 it had been conducted at 576 Fifth Avenue, where there had been more elbow room than formerly, but scarcely more pleasing accommodations.

OFFICES

In 1920 came the move with Carnegie Corporation of New York and T.I.A.A. to the tenth floor of 522 Fifth Avenue. Pritchett was intimately involved in the Corporation, and doubtless it was through his influence that the selection came about, although most of the planning and execution of the move fell to Furst. The office layout was to suggest the Foundation's scholar-like activities. One inestimable improvement was a private office for each officer and staff member. Thanks possibly to a hope expressed by Reed, the rooms were planned to suggest private libraries with glass-doored bookcases. In the taste of the day the furniture was dignified, with a tendency toward the massive, but the atmosphere was not luxurious except to those who, during the past decade and a half, had suffered the inadequacy of the former quarters, and men of affairs who called were accustomed to more elegant surroundings. Although weathered oak furnishings did not help the north lighting, and prolonged tinkering failed to abolish the need for electric light even on pleasant afternoons, still, except where educational studies expanded the service staff, the offices seemed spacious, even impressive.[1]

---

[1] The general atmosphere was cordial but not effusive. The visitor was pleasantly received by a personable and intelligent receptionist, who either answered questions out of her own knowledge or by means of reference books or else conducted him to the person he had come to see. Even those who had come on unwelcome or inopportune errands were never permitted to sense anything adverse in the air.

In spite of intimate personal relations between visitors on the one hand and officers and staff members on the other, there was no first-naming. There was none between the men and women who worked for the Foundation. In a decade of close association, the Foundation's third president addressed the secretary of the Foundation only once by his first name—on a North River pier near midnight when the younger man had met the older, returning from Europe, to deliver the news of the death of an intimate friend. The custom

Furst never tired of indicating to visitors that these were not business premises in the usual sense, but offices of an essentially academic institution. The president's room was long used as a meeting place for the trustees, who filled it to overflowing discomfort. Indeed, not one of the rooms, as designed by an interior decorator, was capable of functional adjustment.

A LEGAL QUESTION

From time to time in the Foundation's existence, question has been raised whether meetings of the Board of Trustees ought to be held in Washington where its "principal office" is located. At least three attorneys have seen no real necessity. One rule cited ran somewhat to the effect that where a statute of incorporation or the bylaws do not provide for meetings outside the state, none may be held; but both the charter and the bylaws of the Foundation "provide that meetings of the trustees may be held outside the District" of Columbia. Hence for the sake of convenience, as well as of tradition growing out of the days of Mr. Carnegie, the trustees have met only in New York City.

OFFICERS AND STAFF MEMBERS, 1918-30

On May 5, 1922, the executive committee, prompted by Butler, invited Pritchett to choose an artist to execute his portrait in oils. Pritchett selected Albert Herter. The canvas was completed at Santa Barbara in early April 1923, and until 1947 it hung in the Foundation's reception room. An excellent likeness (the hands are those of Pritchett the former baseball and cricket player), slightly under life size, it represents Pritchett seated in characteristic attitude, albeit Learned once remarked upon the "old fox" expression in the face—that is, an expression of quizzical skepticism.

During much of the period, Pritchett's health was not of the best. A persistent throat trouble was less disturbing in the milder airs of the West than in New York City. With the permission of

of addressing the president under the title "Dr." is said to have originated with Mr. Carnegie, but no president ever followed it in reference to himself. Pritchett was the most formal of the four in his self-reference to "Mr. Pritchett." Among themselves, staff members and others with a single exception spoke always of "Dr. Pritchett." The respect which this practice reflected was genuine.

the executive committee, Pritchett usually spent the summer and early autumn in California, November, December, January, and sometimes February in New York, with the return to California in the late winter or the spring. The business of the Foundation suffered little from this arrangement. With an energetic and devoted secretary in Furst, and three staff members of first-rate quality, the Foundation rather gained than lost through the uninterrupted days of meditation that Pritchett was enabled to give to its affairs. Delays sometimes occurred, and a few matters turned out to have been mishandled, but there is no doubt that Pritchett, chairman of the Santa Barbara Relief Committee after the earthquake of 1925, was sincere when he wrote to Furst September 2: "The experience I am now having makes me appreciate as I never did before what it means to have the co-operation of such an able and loyal group as you fellows are." He referred to Furst, Learned, busy with aspects of international education, Reed, and Savage, who was at the time in England asking questions about university sports. More than two years before, Kandel had returned to Teachers College, where wider opportunity summoned him—a severe loss to the Foundation—and Savage had become the third staff member.

For Pritchett those twelve years made trying times. Knowing that the Foundation's financial roots were loosening and weakening, he realized that its pecuniary salvation lay with Carnegie Corporation of New York and the development of the T.I.A.A., the former as a temporary resource, the latter as a permanent institution to assume the pensioning burden. Yet he never lapsed into compromise with quality or permitted it to his staff. He yielded not one inch to the principles he believed to be sound. This phase of his integrity was often mistaken for stubbornness and unreasoning conservatism. It was really a clear-sighted scientist's disinterested devotion to truth as he saw it. His dedicatory address, "An Act of Remembrance," at the unveiling of a tablet in the David Grey Community Building, Santa Barbara, February 6, 1929, reveals one spiritual side of Pritchett's nature that some of his intimates might not recognize for his.

The Sayre Episode, 1929

It is perhaps time to throw light upon one matter relating to the Foundation that has long been a puzzle. Monell Sayre had joined the Foundation in 1905, and for the ensuing eight years his versatility and industry touched practically every aspect of its work. As of December 1, 1913, he resigned almost overnight to become secretary of the Church Pension Fund of the Protestant Episcopal Church, a post which Pritchett had been influential in securing for him.

Until April 1919 relations continued cordial. Then to Sayre a caller quoted Furst as having said that the Church Pension Fund would "have to be two or three times" its present size to meet its accrued liabilities. Although Sayre called Furst to account for this, relations appeared friendly until 1928, when Sayre sent a Philadelphia correspondent a letter in part rather disparaging of the Foundation, and on the correspondent showing Furst a copy, Furst undertook to establish his own righteousness, although rather testily. In replying, Sayre referred to "the little darts scattered through the Foundation's correspondence and reports." Although the interchange flagged, Sayre apparently continued discontented. On April 12, 1929, in connection with an address he was giving in Columbus, Ohio, he released a prepared statement which began: "Extraordinary ineptitude on the part of its management has brought the $30,000,000 Carnegie Foundation for the Advancement of Teaching to a state of virtual bankruptcy, Monell Sayre, international pension authority, stated today." This slap at Pritchett looked very much like headline-hunting because the Foundation's athletic and other inquiries were currently attracting considerable newspaper attention. Pritchett and Furst tried with fair success to explain matters to newspaper reporters.

Again the correspondence flared. On July 25, 1929, Sayre wrote to Furst to the effect that the Foundation "regards the Episcopal Church rather lightly," and that, if desired, he would furnish certain data if they were used verbatim. Furst could not take this quietly; in his reply of August 9, he referred to "statements concerning this Foundation recently attributed to you," as "misleading," and added: "when therefore you appear indifferent to the effect that such statements may have on those from whom you received only consideration and opportunity when you needed such encouragement, I cannot understand your attitude. . . ." Sayre replied August 12 in defiant vein. There was no answer, but on May 8, 1929, Pritchett had gently laid the matter before his old friend Bishop William Lawrence of Boston. Thereafter the warmth of their friendship receded. Furst gave out a newspaper interview or two which did not help the Foundation's public relations in the long run. The only net result of the episode was the damage done by tempers lost in public.

"That Lusty Infant, the Association"

For a decade and more, Pritchett was president and Furst secretary of both the Foundation and the Teachers Insurance and Annuity Association, "first, because it brought down the overhead of the T.I.A.A. and secondly, of more importance, because through this arrangement," Pritchett stated some years later, "the T.I.&A.A. was put in touch with the great body of teachers. The Insurance Company got its policy-holders mainly through the Foundation." This was all true. The only question—and it cannot now be answered conclusively—is whether the Association might not have gained more policyholders if it had been completely separate from the Foundation in management as well as in name and corporate structure.

Probably the repeated "plugging" of the T.I.A.A. in Foundation Annual Reports was an important force in selling both its insurance and its annuities. At the same time, it prompted some raising of eyebrows, because certain statements adverse to both bodies led to a supposition that by using the Foundation Annual Reports for promoting the Association, the officers of the Foundation were trying to save their own skins, badly lacerated by repeated reductions of Foundation benefits. From about 1916 up to at least 1924, various printed documents such as Foundation Annual Reports and reports to the executive committee and the trustees somewhat implied that the Association was an adjunct of the Foundation. As a natural step, the Foundation's critics became critical also of the Association. Development of the Association in its earlier days was sometimes difficult because of a notion that it might be well to "wait and see" how the new company made out. In spite of this feeling, which certainly existed in some quarters, November 1925 saw Carnegie Corporation of New York proposing formally that the Foundation should take over its 498 shares of T.I.A.A. capital stock. The Foundation trustees declined the commitment because, as they stated, they recognized that "the ownership of the stock by the Carnegie Corporation with its large endowment has been a considerable factor in creating in the minds of teachers confidence in the future of the Association." It was a fortunate refusal, as future events demonstrated.

Although as the Association began to move ahead most of the great life insurance companies extended it a friendly hand, one, not in the New York area, distributed widely a hostile statement which Pritchett termed "thoroughly misleading." He replied in the Fourteenth Annual Report (1919) and in a pamphlet called *Some Misapprehensions Touching Life Insurance*, issued in midsummer 1919. This was a provocative and rather vituperative brochure which probably brought more bad feeling than benefit to anyone, although it did put the old-line companies on notice as to what Pritchett considered their shortcomings. Years were to pass before the scars fully healed.

Pritchett and Furst worked ahead at their dual jobs. By September 1921, the Association had written "five millions of contracts" and was "upon a sound and prosperous basis." Doubtless among the most persuasive reasons were action by the Foundation executive committee December 6, 1918, after long deliberation, looking to use of the new Reserve Fund Number Two and abandonment of the principle of compulsory annuity contributions in institutions to become associated; adjustment of this difficult problem was left to the universities and colleges themselves.

Without legal obligation the Foundation, in its Rules adopted by the trustees April 22, 1918, had undertaken important commitments in behalf of the Association: (1) to maintain until 1928 interest on the teacher's accumulations in the Association joint contributory deferred contracts at 4½ per cent; (2) to pay the Association's overhead if and as it ran above the income expected from securities set aside as capital and surplus, that is, it was anticipated, if overhead costs exceeded $50,000 a year, a provision which Pritchett thought would never involve any very considerable expense, but which up to 1933 cost the Foundation more than half a million dollars; and (3) to provide disability protection under Section C of its Rules. In addition, (4) by separate action November 21, 1917, the trustees had agreed to accept from Carnegie Corporation and to hold and disburse, principal and income, the new Reserve Fund Number Two in assisting institutions associated, or to be associated, with the Foundation in effectuating the Association's Teachers Retirement Plan of annuities. Although the first of these commitments never became operative, the second and third developed serious financial problems for the Foundation.

When in 1921 Angell, after one year in office, resigned from the presidency of the Corporation to go to Yale, Pritchett became the Corporation's acting president. Gradually, under the triple burden, he left details concerning direction of the Association to its board and officers, but its management still centered in Furst and the Foundation. Before Angell went, he, as president of the Corporation, named twenty T.I.A.A. policyholders who selected a committee of five of their members to nominate five policyholders of whom three were to be elected T.I.A.A. trustees. That policyholders were to have a voice in the management of the Association through their board members was thus assured. Although the T.I.A.A. had its growing pains its progress was steady in spite of the efforts of opponents and detractors.

Relations with Carnegie Corporation

While there is no clear evidence that the Carnegie Foundation suffered directly from Pritchett's holding three presidencies, 1921-23, some of its trustees had their doubts of the arrangement. One wrote to him: "I have always felt that the burden was altogether more than you should have assumed, but I suppose there was no help for it." From correspondence in 1912 and 1913 it is certain that Pritchett placed great emphasis and trust in the Corporation as a financial reservoir for Mr. Carnegie's philanthropies and that in Mr. Carnegie's mind it was one of the Corporation's "chief purposes . . . to stand back of the institutions he has founded." Moreover, Pritchett never entertained doubts of the Founder's intention in this matter. Senator Root seems to have held, as regards the Foundation, an even more explicit view, for on November 16, 1917, Pritchett wrote to Charles L. Taylor of Pittsburgh, identified with the Carnegie Hero Fund Commission: "as Mr. Root truly says, our Corporation should not assume to have any knowledge of what is fitting for the pension problem, but should only act on recommendations from the trustees of the Foundation." Inasmuch as most of the difficulties in handling the Foundation's pension load after about 1917 involved Carnegie Corporation of New York, these views and Pritchett's Corporation duties probably had much importance. Between 1921 and 1923 Pritchett, as acting president, of course conducted correspondence and interviews in the name of the Corporation. Certain Corporation trustees appear to have had misgivings about this, for Pritchett was at pains to note to Furst that he had undertaken these chores "not through any desire to interfere with the affairs of the Corporation, but in the endeavor to carry along until a competent head was chosen." That competent head was Frederick P. Keppel, who assumed the Corporation presidency October 1, 1923. This eased Pritchett's load by one office.

In 1926, with the Foundation Executive Committee's approval, Pritchett represented the Corporation at the dedication of the building which the Corporation presented to the American School of Classical Studies at Athens to house the library given by Dr. Johannes Gennadius, and also visited Egypt and Palestine for the Carnegie Endowment for International Peace.

Co-operative Investing

Pritchett's term as president *ad interim* of Carnegie Corporation showed him anew the difficulties all endowments face in investing their funds. Apparently at his prompting, Samuel S. Hall, Jr., a young member of the T.I.A.A. financial staff, prepared, April 28, 1923, a memorandum on the advantages of a central investment office for the several organizations founded by Mr. Carnegie. Fifteen months later the suggestion had received practical application if not formal adoption, for Hall, with Pritchett so to speak at his side, was handling the investments of the Foundation and Carnegie Institution of Washington, as well as those of the Association. Now Pritchett in 1925-26 held membership in the Corporation Finance Committee, which seemed to him too large for prompt action. In a memorandum to President Keppel of the Corporation dated December 22, 1925, later revised by Hall, Pritchett, or Furst for his signature, laid out a one-man central investing agency for the Corporation, the Foundation, the Institution of Washington, the Carnegie Endowment for International Peace, and the T.I.A.A. The investment committee operating for the Association was apparently to advise concerning types of security for investment, and from these issues Hall was to choose, at the behest of the representative finance committee, investments for the other philanthropies co-operating. Expenses were to be divided equitably among the patron bodies.

During the winter and spring, Mr. R. C. Leffingwell, a trustee of the Corporation having wide financial experience, gave much practical attention to the plan, and by June 29, 1926, Pritchett wrote formally to President Keppel of the Corporation "that it is desirable to set up the single investment agent to act for the Carnegie Corporation, the Foundation, the Institution of Washington, the Peace Endowment, and the T.I.A.A., such agent to work under the committee . . . now . . . serving for that purpose and to report work in each case to the financial committee of the several institutions."

To Senator Root, Pritchett pointed out that "while each of these institutions . . . must through its own financial committee be responsible for the investment of the . . . funds and have a constant scrutiny of its holdings, the actual work of getting the necessary information must be done by somebody who gives his time to it, who has been trained to the work, and who has access to the best advice of the banking people. We therefore conclude that next autumn it will be wise to appoint Mr. Hall an officer for the [five institutions] each of these institutions contributing to his salary. . . ."

The Foundation executive committee approved the recommendation November 5, 1926, the other bodies concerned also acted favorably, and the co-operative investment office began operations early in 1927, to continue, with changes in membership or personnel, for more than two decades.

THE ROCKEFELLER PHILANTHROPIES

For a number of years, Mr. Carnegie served as a trustee of the General Education Board. Early in the Carnegie Foundation's existence Butler gave a dinner for officers and certain trustees of the Rockefeller bodies and the Carnegie Foundation, which was of great assistance to those organizing the work of the new philanthropy. During those formative days Pritchett sought and received much opinion and advice from Mr. Frederick T. Gates and Dr. Wallace Buttrick, and these cordial relations were not affected by Flexner's leaving the Foundation to join the Rockefeller philanthropies in 1913. The record suggests the number of occasions upon which views were interchanged and counsel sought and given but the decisions which flowed therefrom were, even in every least instance, the decisions of the officers or the individual boards they represented.

An illustration of this fact is the approach to a study of agricultural education. On November 19, 1924, on Pritchett's prompting, the Foundation Board of Trustees received from the executive committee a recommendation for a study of agricultural education on which it took no action. Thereby it lost its chance, for on November 6, 1925, the executive committee learned, not without relief but with a touch of chagrin, that the inquiry was to be undertaken by the General Education Board.

NATIONAL ASSOCIATIONS AND OTHER BODIES

Relations between various representative associations and the Foundation began as soon as the Foundation commenced to acquire national reputation. The first of these groups to recognize the possibilities of the new agency was the Association of American Universities.

Association of American Universities

The initial communication from the Association of American Universities to the Foundation was sent by the association's then secretary, Frederick P. Keppel, and addressed to Pritchett. It invited Pritchett to attend all future meetings of the association. This he did for several years. Some of the matters he discussed with chairmen of association committees were important: American study in Europe, on which Pritchett wrote in the Second Annual Report (1907); policy regarding enlargement of the association's membership roll; the standing of various universities in other countries. Pritchett also served upon A.A.U. committees and subcommittees, and the Foundation in its New York offices provided them with a meeting place. In 1916 the Foundation's Associated List influenced the enlargement of the association's list of accepted colleges and universities. Conversely, it is possible that the association's use of the term "accepted" had something to do with the Foundation trustees changing in 1915 the designation of its own "accepted list" to "associated list." At the Foundation's annual meeting of 1916 the association took official part in discussions of plans for an annuity and insurance association and had representation on the commission of eleven which passed upon them. Foundation representation at association annual meetings continued under the Foundation's third president, Walter A. Jessup. The association discontinued accreditation in 1949.

Association of American Colleges

On November 16, 1914, the presidents of three mid-western higher institutions dispatched a circular letter proposing the organization of an Association of American Colleges on a denominational (Presbyterian) basis at a meeting to be held at Chicago, January 14, 1915. In view of the Foundation's nondenominational restrictions it is interesting to note that Pritchett was invited to attend the association's second meeting, 1916, although he had finally to decline. On request, the Association of American Colleges named its representative to serve on the commission of eleven to study the plan for the annuity association. In subsequent years there was much consultation and correspondence between officers of the Foundation and of the Association of American Colleges over diverse matters, such as the standing of certain colleges in the United States, especially with universities overseas, speakers for association meetings, various educational inquiries, including a study of curricula for which the Foundation supplied funds in 1920, the scope of college entrance requirements, honorary degrees, the geographical distribution of colleges, and theological institutions. At a number of the association's annual meetings Furst delivered statistical papers, and at that of 1930 Savage spoke on college athletics.

American Council on Education

The American Council on Education was, for education, among the best results of World War I. In 1923 the National Conference Committee on Standards of Colleges and Secondary Schools, organized some years before, which since 1908 had met at the Foundation's offices, voted to become the Committee on Standards of the American Council. Thereupon the Foundation was requested, without becoming a member of the council, to continue its co-operation with it and to nominate a representative on the new council committee. Accepting this invitation the Foundation executive committee named Furst, who served until his death in 1931.

College Entrance Examination Board

In April 1908 the College Entrance Examination Board invited Pritchett, as president of the Foundation, to sit with the board. This he did for a number of annual meetings. Thereafter the Foundation was long formally represented by Furst, who contributed several statistical and bibliographical discussions to the board's proceedings, and later by Learned. In 1922, on request of the board, Furst, Learned, and Reed studied its procedure and internal organization with Trevor Arnett, secretary of the General Education Board, whose special responsibility was the C.E.E.B.'s financial arrangements. Furst reported November 4 on the portion of the study carried on in the Foundation's offices. At the board's twenty-fifth anniversary dinner in 1925 Pritchett spoke on the question, "Has the College Entrance Examination Board Justified Its Quarter-century of Life?" About 1940 there seemed little reason to continue the formal representation at meetings, and upon Learned's suggestion it was terminated.

The parts of the board, the American Council on Education, and the Foundation in forming Educational Testing Service, Inc., will be sketched in Chapter 13.

Council on Medical Education of the American Medical Association

The point upon which turned the relationship between the Foundation and the American Medical Association's Council on Medical Education was the Flexner studies (1908-12). After their publication, co-operation continued. Pritchett spoke at association and council meetings, wrote on phases of medical education in his Annual Reports and elsewhere, had data collected on various topics, and counseled concerning numerous matters. One of his most successful Annual Report discussions pertained to medical cults. There were several requests for studies in the field—individual schools, medical licensing boards, procedure, etc.—none of which could be granted. When Dr. N. P. Colwell, secretary of the council, was at work upon the classification of medical schools in 1919, he corresponded much with Furst and Pritchett. The rapprochement continued active until about 1928, and then revived somewhat during the administration of Jessup, whose connections with medical education while president of the State University of Iowa had been close and who for some years was a "permanent" delegate from the National Association of State Universities to the Council on Medical Education.

National Education Association

During Pritchett's administration relations of the Foundation and the National Education Association touched principally upon two matters: teacher training, and pensions and retirement in public education.

Although Learned's Bulletin Number 14, *The Professional Preparation of Teachers for American Public Schools*, did not appear until 1920, sections on State Regulation of Higher Education and on Politics and Education in Iowa, by-products of Learned's advisory work, appeared in the Eighth Annual Report (1913). Among members of a committee reporting in July 1914 at the N.E.A. Normal School Department sessions at St. Paul, these discussions and the fact that normal school teachers were not eligible for Foundation benefits roused resentment. Pritchett was opposed to the normal schools' awarding the A.B. The committee accused "the Carnegie and Rockefeller foundations, agencies not in any way responsible to the people," of efforts "to control the policies of our state educational institution," to dictate courses of study, indirectly to endanger academic freedom, and thus to "defeat the primary purpose of democracy. . . ." Temperate denials from Pritchett and Learned, of course, resulted in correspondence with committee members; Pritchett suggested that it was "a little unfair" of one of them to take "political action" in the N.E.A. committee. Controversy continued. The Foundation was not without support in the N.E.A. membership although the *Journal of Education*, October 8, 1914, carried a bitterly zealous attack insinuating that "the Carnegie millions" were being used to punish "every state, every institution, every man who dares to have a mind of his own." Pritchett resigned in October from an N.E.A. committee to which he had been named in July. He renewed and extended his position in the Eighteenth (1923) and Nineteenth (1924) Annual Reports, questioning the increased cost of public education, its over-enrichment of the curriculum, its departure from simplicity and sincerity, its superficiality, and the direction of its progress. Many laymen and not a few educators agreed with him. Without receding from this stand, Furst tried to make it clear to J. W. Crabtree, secretary of the N.E.A., who had been a leader in the attack, and Crabtree disavowed any desire to injure Pritchett personally, although he continued guerilla sorties on Pritchett and the Foundation until Pritchett's retirement neared. When Suzzallo succeeded to the presidency cordial relations were resumed.

From 1916 onward, in the field of pensions and retirement, there was considerable co-operation between the Foundation and the N.E.A. Furst and Kandel prepared numerous reports on teachers' pensions and other topics and presented them at N.E.A. meetings. The connection gave impetus to the Foundation's own pension studies. Bulletin Number 12, *Pensions for Public School Teachers* (1918) by Furst and Kandel, an inclusive document with supporting data from the Vermont inquiry, was a report to the N.E.A. Committee on Salaries, Pensions, and Tenure. The United States Bureau of Education, through its editor W. Carson Ryan, Jr., in 1918 requested and received permission to use Furst's N.E.A. paper of 1916 as an appendix to its "brief bulletin on pensions." Joseph Swain, president of Swarthmore and chairman of the N.E.A. Committee on Pensions, etc., furthered the Foundation's pension studies and asked Furst for an inquiry into tenure, which Kandel two years later undertook. For the 1921 meeting at Des Moines, Furst and Kandel prepared jointly a report for the Committee on Pensions, but owing to the protests of a "lady member" the chairman deemed it advisable to omit their statement. After the research division of the N.E.A. was started in 1922 under the direction of Dr. John K. Norton, co-operation was close. Two years later, however, under new presidential policies, the N.E.A. began to work away from the higher level of education, although Swain in 1925 wrote warmly and appreciatively of the Foundation's work in the field which he had tilled "during ten years of pioneering faithful service."

American Association of University Professors

In December 1914, Otto Heller of Washington University had written to Pritchett that "an Association of American Professors" was forming. The tone of the letter suggests that the Foundation and Pritchett might look forward to an even rougher time than before. Indeed, it took less than two years for the Foundation's bitterest critics to become prominent in association affairs. The first public statements about the new body issued by Pritchett in the name of the Foundation were cordial. When the new plan for insurance and annuities, Bulletin Number 9, went out in the autumn of 1915 in a confidential edition for officers and professors in Associated institutions, Pritchett requested that a committee of the A.A.-U.P. study it. Accordingly, in February 1916, the president of the association appointed Committee P of twenty-four members, including Professor Harlan F. Stone of Columbia, chairman, and W. W. Cook, Heller, Jastrow, and Lovejoy. Its first report was issued September 30, 1916, its second in 1918, and a supplementary statement by two its members in 1919.

In general, despite the reasonable attitude of J. H. Wigmore, A.A.U.P. president, this committee was acutely, even painfully critical of the Foundation and all its works, particularly of the proposals to amend its Rules, to curtail benefits, and to form the Teachers Insurance and Annuity Association. The committee's first report had dealt comprehensively with the Foundation's shortcomings and demanded teacher membership in the Foundation board. The second report repeated several phases of the opposition expressed in newspapers, periodicals, and elsewhere. First and last, the committee emphasized the following matters: After citing resolutions of the A.A.U.P. December 28, 1917, adverse to the proposed T.I.A.A.,

Pritchett and the Foundation were censured for the 1918 changes in the Rules, made without consulting A.A.U.P. Committee P or representative teachers. Moreover, the control of the T.I.A.A. as set up was bad; it did not accord with Committee P's suggestions. Proposed premium rates were objectionable. Policies should be participating. The suggested use of Foundation surplus was offensive. Selection of risks would be faulty. Cash value should attach to annuity policies. There should be provisions assuring disability benefits and convertibility. The second report received a unanimous but numerically small vote of approval at the association's Baltimore meeting, December 28, 1918.

Thus Committee P made the central assault upon the Foundation, Pritchett, and the proposed association. Flank actions were conducted by Jastrow, Lovejoy, and others. Jastrow chanted his old war cries: a return to Mr. Carnegie's original aims, representation of the teaching profession on the Foundation board, steadfastness of purpose and stable policy for the Foundation. Lovejoy and Stone prepared an attack, published by Cattell (1919) in his journal *School and Society*, insisting that colleges allow their teachers to select the companies from which they would purchase annuities. The article was a direct attempt to cause the new T.I.A.A. to fail of its purpose. Cattell's volume, *Carnegie Pensions*, a bitter harvest of diatribe and malediction, appeared also in 1919. His advertisement announcing its publication anathematized the Foundation, Pritchett, and some of Pritchett's colleagues.

The results this uproar brought could have been achieved by quieter means. Although several of Jastrow's strictures were echoed in the first Committee P report, a circular letter from Cattell to each Foundation trustee February 22, 1919, which came down to a personal attack on Pritchett and a virtual threat against the board, contributed nothing but bad feeling. Cattell had already shot one of his last bolts when in *School and Society*, January 4, 1918, he had attacked "viciously"—the adverb is S. B. McCormick's—the new plan of insurance and annuities. It is possible that certain measures owed something to the long agitation: For example, policyholders and teachers were ultimately included in the T.I.A.A. board of trustees. But they were not placed as such in the Foundation's. The Association was not mutualized, and the Foundation's old service retirement rule was not restored.

In fine, the Foundation accepted the wishes of the A.A.U.P. and Committee P in raising the age at which its retiring allowances might begin, abandoning its proposal that its "free" pensions should go only to the older pensionables, giving over a requirement that younger men should take deferred annuity contracts, publishing certain actuarial estimates, permitting A.A.U.P. representatives to speak at Foundation trustees meetings, abandoning compulsory annuities, and providing through the Association more forms of life insurance, including decreasing term policies, than originally proposed, as well as accepting other measures affecting representation on the T.I.A.A. board and submitting the Plan to the two actuarial groups. At various universities such as Wisconsin, Washington University, and the Johns Hopkins, with which recalcitrants were connected, faculty votes of dissent and censure of the plan cropped up, to be answered patiently by Furst and Pritchett. "The assaults . . . on the T.I.A.A. by the Committee on Pensions and Insurance and by Professor Cattell . . . of course confused the minds of a good many teachers," admitted Pritchett to Provost Edgar Fahs Smith of the University of Pennsylvania, in March 1919, "but in the long run, it will take care of itself." By January 13, 1920, Pritchett could tell a correspondent in the Midwest that in his opinion the Association of University Professors had "about come to the conclusion that after all, it was a little premature."

Yet Cook as chairman of Committee P was still arguing for mutualization in 1921. Jastrow in 1925 appealed to Keppel as president of Carnegie Corporation about inadequacy of retiring allowances without result. The principal victory for these critics lay in the abandonment of Pritchett's suggestion that the Foundation's resources be used for teachers over forty or forty-five years of age and that young teachers be protected by T.I.A.A. contracts only.

Ultimately the break between the Association and the Foundation and the A.A.U.P. was healed. Today the offices of the A.A.U.P. use the joint contributory retirement annuity contracts of the Association. In recent years an A.A.U.P. committee visited the T.I.A.A. offices and apparently thought well of what they saw and learned. The controversy provided, as far as is known, the only protest Pritchett ever made, though not for publication, about editorial treatment of the Foundation or himself.

REGIONAL AND SPECIAL BODIES

Besides the national groups, the relations of the Foundation with certain special and regional bodies deserves brief note. Furst studied college entrance requirements and reported to the New England Association of Colleges and Secondary Schools and the Association of Colleges and Secondary Schools of the Southern States, 1920-25. After special inquiries he addressed also the Association of Colleges and Preparatory Schools of the Middle States and Maryland, the National Association of State Universities, and the American Council on Education, 1917-22. At the request of a special commission, Furst, in 1923, also produced a study of technical and higher education in Massachusetts, which he condensed to two tables and nine charts, and furnished a statistical chapter of the report, 1924, mainly on college entrance and promotion. Kandel spoke before numerous bodies and so also did Learned. Reed confined his oral reports to the field of legal education.

The winds of simplified spelling made a first mild flutter in Foundation Annual Reports in 1914. They blew also through the pages of Kandel's *Federal Aid for Vocational Education*, Bulletin Number 10, 1917. The more disconcerting simplifications recommended by the Simplified Spelling Board, of which Mr. Carnegie was an earnest supporter, did not appear in Foundation publications and the breeze soon blew itself out as far as it affected them.

From 1921 to 1923 Kandel handled in the Foundation offices the American Field Service Fellowships under which young Frenchmen were afforded study at the universities of the United States. In this matter his work was, as elsewhere, outstanding, although the fellowships are not referred to in meetings or Annual Reports. When Kandel joined the new International Institute of Education he took with him his responsibilities for the fellowships.

The Public Education Association had been founded in 1895 to organize the efforts of private citizens in furthering the welfare of New York City's public schools. This association had enlisted the interest of Pritchett and then of Flexner, and later Furst was their natural heir. He also devoted much time to the work of the New York City Pension Commission of 1927.

Church Educational Boards

Although the Foundation was prevented by both charter and Letter of Gift from paying pensions in denominational institutions, the influence it wielded in this direction was not inconsiderable. Pritchett and Furst maintained close touch with various denominational boards through their officers, encouraged them in their attempts to raise the quality of their education and of their retirement

~ 7 ~

Apogee

PENSION STUDIES, EXTERNAL · EDUCATIONAL STUDIES: BULLETINS—
ENGINEERING EDUCATION; LEGAL EDUCATION, THREE BULLETINS;
PREPARATION OF PUBLIC SCHOOL TEACHERS, THE "MISSOURI STUDY";
EDUCATION IN "THE MARITIMES"; COLLEGE ATHLETICS; DENTAL
EDUCATION; EUROPEAN AND AMERICAN EDUCATION: LEARNED'S COM-
PARISON · ANNUAL REPORTS · REQUESTS FOR STUDIES AND FOR THEIR
SUPPORT · A FRESH CONCEPTION · NEW VISTA

T HE last dozen years of Pritchett's active service brought
forth from the Foundation a stream of published material,
most of it of high quality, that in the public mind of the day placed
the Foundation's broader activities in educational and technical inquiry far above its work as a pensioning agency. This was a direct
outcome of Pritchett's views on pension plans acquired with the
growth of the Foundation, his earlier exploration of the general educational scene, particularly professional education, and his growing concern with quality in the educational process. The publications of the Foundation, 1918-30, dealt with a variety of topics and
their impact registered, sometimes not immediately, but always in
the long run.

In an unprinted address before the American Otological Society,
1927, Pritchett drew distinctions nowadays too often neglected. He
contrasted *arbeiten*, or exercises, with scientific research which implies "a different order of equipment for the individual and a higher
order of intellectual and personal performance." Research, which
"has for its object the advancement of human knowledge," presupposed (1) a problem of real significance worthy of the highest
effort, (2) prosecuted by men who are familiar with the territory
already occupied by science—"the adventure of the trained and

143

skilful experimenter and thinker"—(3) that demands "devotion, clear thinking, hard work, and absolute sincerity to face the facts." To approximate these ideals in the work of the Foundation, Pritchett had a small group of men on appointment without term: as Foundation secretary and second in command, Furst, with Learned, Reed, Kandel for five years, and later Savage as staff members; and on temporary association, engaged for particular tasks, Charles R. Mann, W. C. Bagley, William J. Gies, and W. Carson Ryan. Reginald Heber Smith and Henry Suzzallo were on a different footing from the others named. For separate studies, the roster was enlarged and strengthened by further recruiting of men no less well equipped, energetic, and devoted. Generally speaking, the work of eleven of these men appeared in sixteen Bulletins and parts of twelve Annual Reports and it presented, on the one hand, the technical results of certain pension inquiries and, on the other, the conclusions of several broader educational studies. The exception was Suzzallo's work in the field of graduate education which he did not live to complete.

PENSION STUDIES, EXTERNAL

Beginning about 1911 or 1912, the Foundation's studies of pensions and retirement shifted their main emphasis gradually from its own problems to a broader basis pertaining to teachers at all levels and even to employees in industry. In the hands successively of Sayre, Kandel, and Savage, with Pritchett and Furst in the triple roles of authors, editors, and chief critics, they dealt with every discoverable pension system in the countries of the world, and they contributed not only to the Foundation's knowledge of its own problems but to retirement theory and practice in an almost unlimited field. A section of the Annual Report was first set aside for general discussions of pensions in 1915. It continued until these pension studies terminated in 1930.

Bulletin Number 12, *Pensions for Public School Teachers* (1918), as prepared by Kandel and Furst, leant somewhat heavily upon Foundation Annual Reports (1914-17) and Bulletin Number 9 (1915-16). The preface is ascribed to Pritchett, who probably revised a draft put together by his colleagues. One of its sentences ran: "The only way in which absolute security can be obtained is for the contribution of the public as well as that of the teacher to be paid annually, credited to the individual teacher, and set aside

until the time of his retirement," a plan followed by the most enlightened teachers' retirement systems of today. The Bulletin has
already had attention in Chapter 5.

A request from the Virginia State Board of Education that the
Foundation study and report upon the pension problem in the public schools of the Commonwealth, presented in the autumn of 1922,
led to two and one-half years of work before results appeared in
Bulletin Number 17, *Retiring Allowances for Officers and Teachers
in Virginia Public Schools* (1926) by Furst, Raymond L. Mattocks,
and Savage, with a preface by Pritchett. Mattocks, an actuary of
the T.I.A.A., well versed in the science, made the calculations, Savage wrote the text, and Furst revised it and also devised the tabular
statement and form in which the plan was presented. The work owed
much to the criticism of "the best known students of pensions in the
country," as Pritchett called them in his preface. The study was well
received by the State Teachers Association, which had also sought
it, but many of its provisions failed of enactment. Cost was the
impediment.

Bulletin Number 22, *A Retirement Plan for Colorado Public
Schools*, 1928, was prepared by Savage and Edmund S. Cogswell,
Boston consulting actuary. A brief study grounded in principles
applied from preceding work, it made large concessions to practical
financing, particularly in suggesting a separate provision for disability allowances and withdrawal refunds. State legislation of 1909
and 1919 involving separate taxes to provide allowances ranging
from $30 to $50 a month imposed an obligation that was not always
met. The task was to frame a statewide retirement system which was
essentially sound but should not cut the benefits already promised.
Final estimates showed that with all teachers included, the proposals would cost the counties about $675,000 during the succeeding
thirty years, or about $22,500 a year, equivalent to 5 per cent of
the teachers' salaries. Although two attempts were made by the
Colorado Education Association to procure legislation, the plan
failed of adoption. The obstacle was the old barrier, cost.

Pritchett's discussion of *The Social Philosophy of Pensions* and
related matters in Bulletin Number 25 (1930) was his valedictory.
As the undersized volume was being published, his successor was
being chosen and he relinquished the Foundation presidency about
four months after publication. The format with its small page and
extra-leaded large type, leaves the impression that the treatment
is—in the language of food adulteration—"extended." Pensions,

Pritchett maintained, are justified by their improvement to service, not as charity to the individual; society owes no man a pension. The system that restricts freedom of employment or holds the worker to a particular job is indefensible. No pension system will work without individual foresight and self-denial, and because of cost no free pension scheme can be long sustained unless out of the "unlimited purse" of a government. The second part of the Bulletin reviews then-existing pension systems for professional groups: college teachers through the T.I.A.A., a few isolated independent college retirement plans, twenty-seven statewide and twenty-one city teacher retirement systems, the protection available to ministers of twenty-one denominations. This was scarcely a definitive covering of the professional field. At the elbow of Pritchett, writing without his accustomed kindling spark, out of his experience in Foundation affairs, both pleasant and difficult, stands T.I.A.A., insisting with the clamor of a twelve-year-old, that it be not forgotten. Although the Bulletin does not represent Pritchett at his best, in its day it was comprehensive and authoritative. Released for publication April 21, 1930, it drew no great public attention, but many students of pensions regarded it highly.

EDUCATIONAL STUDIES: BULLETINS

The principal educational studies associated with the name of the Carnegie Foundation have been published in its Bulletins and its Annual Reports. Usually Annual Reports issued during the progress of a study designed to be summarized later as a Bulletin contained articles relating to the study. The Twenty-fourth Annual Report (1929), issued July 14, 1930, contained the text of Bulletin Number 25 in full, on the theory that each type of publication reached a different group of readers. The theory was probably erroneous because both groups were covered by the same mailing lists.

Throughout the years under discussion it was usual for the Division of Educational Enquiry, the side of the Foundation designed to handle studies in the field, to have in its accounts considerable unexpended balances which, cumulated, reached $131,000 in 1926. These funds, together with Pritchett's imaginative selection of topics and the vigor of his general direction, account for the vast output in the Division of Educational Enquiry during the dozen years preceding his retirement.

No brief discussion or résumé can do justice to any Bulletin or

Report of the Foundation. The Bulletins were presented with utmost care, usually first in confidential proofs to be read and criticized by qualified persons, and then in a published version. The material in its day was fresh, even when publication was delayed, scrupulously worked over from many points of view, and not often dull. Texts were carefully planned, well written, and practically free from pedaguese, solecisms, or ambiguities; growing out of the garnered material, they were seldom tailored to a preconceived notion. On the whole, the tabular matter made sense. The Bulletins can scarcely be called simple—they were not written by or for simpletons—but without too perceptible an effort they let light and air into some of the obscure corners of American education. Taken together, they present for our higher education a conspectus, vigorous, frank, clear, that is unique in the field.

Of the twelve Bulletins issued during the period, only a few, and the studies out of which they developed, can be treated in detail.

Engineering Education, Bulletin Number 11, 1918

Pritchett had come to the Foundation from a school of engineering. Although by 1908 he had severed most of his former academic and professional ties, he still held membership in the Joint Committee on Engineering Education, which by questionnaire had collected much material bearing on its field. This, other committee members had few facilities for studying and Pritchett, approached in the spring of 1910, saw no way to handle it then in the Foundation's offices; but through Bowman, he found means to get the work done by Professor Thomas H. Harrington of Columbia. Now, in 1910, some 102 institutions were granting engineering degrees and the profession was over-full. A year later Pritchett looked forward to a "clear and incisive study" of the subject. By February 5, 1912, the executive committee of the Joint Committee on Engineering Education, under instructions of the full committee, was ready to help, but Pritchett found that he could not proceed until the autumn if a man for field work could be found. He had in mind Dr. Charles R. Mann, professor of physics at Chicago, who in 1908 had first come to his attention as secretary of the American Federation of Teachers of the Mathematical and the Natural Sciences and of Section L of the American Association for the Advancement of Science, both of which were concerned rather with instruction than with administration. Difficulty in finding the right person apparently stalled the whole enterprise in spite of requests from the Council on Engineering Education and "the various engineering societies," including the American Society of Civil Engineers and other influential bodies.

In February 1913, Mr. Carnegie's gift for the Division of Educational Enquiry made ample provision for this type of work, but the question who should make the study remained. Thanks to the Vermont inquiry, the engineering proposal dragged on until June 1913, when the Society for the Promotion of Engineering Education began gently to prod Pritchett. By autumn, when the Vermont study was being rounded into shape, the societies were showing justifiable impatience. At last, after long cogitation, Pritchett offered the task to Mann upon discussion of preliminaries and arranging all but finally for leave of absence. Mann was approved by the joint committee and finally accepted appointment February 7, 1914, to begin the inquiry March 17, and to enter upon full-time duties September 14. Furst sent him materials already collected, and Humphreys of Stevens Institute, a much-interested Foundation trustee, made available a German manuscript of a study of the field in Germany. On Mann's inquiry, Furst and Pritchett sketched the Foundation policy of making no statements about a study unless results of some sort could be set forth, a policy which Mann followed strictly in addressing the Society for the Promotion of Engineering Education at Ames, Iowa, in July. His appointment to the S.P.E.E. committee on committees followed shortly.

The ensuing months Mann spent in travel and inquiry. He selected twenty engineering schools for close scrutiny to obtain a cross section of the situation, but he gathered data from others. Work on these data progressed. By August 1915, Mann had constructed statistical tables which Kandel carefully reviewed, but with the generalizations from them Pritchett was not completely satisfied and so told Mann. Fortunately before the middle of February 1915 Mann had put together a working outline of his report.

Pritchett, "somewhat stunned" by Mann's first two chapters, was not unduly tough with them; they needed restatement at least. But the war was soon commanding much of Mann's attention. Working hard in New York City, he hoped to complete his typescript by the end of August 1917. At his request, Abraham Flexner of the General Education Board read parts of it and Mann thought well of his criticism except that he did not see how he could make the bulletin "easy vacation reading." Flexner's comments and Pritchett's disappointment set Mann a difficult task, but he acknowledged to

Pritchett that the "report in its present form is wholly inadequate. . . . All those who have read it have failed to grasp the main conception. . . ." In spite of war duties in Washington Mann pressed the rewriting on a part-pay basis. The study went into confidential proofs, which after being circulated were thoroughly discussed by the Joint Committee on Engineering Education at the Foundation offices. Pritchett, Furst, and Kandel worked the resulting suggestions into the text. Prefatory material was beaten into shape and set in type. A release date fixed as June 27, 1918, could not be met. Bulletin Number 11, *A Study of Engineering Education,* finally reached the public October 24, 1918. After Mann's Foundation connections ceased, he continued as consulting expert to the War Department until in 1925 he became president of the American Council on Education.

The effect of the Bulletin upon engineering education was wide though not revolutionary, and the support and appreciative resolutions of the S.P.E.E. spread what influence it had. For the engineering profession Mann's work opened the way to the founding of the Engineers' Council for Professional Development in 1932. For the Foundation there were two comparatively important results: First, the request of the engineering societies may have been a factor in Mr. Carnegie's decision to endow a Division of Educational Enquiry; secondly, Bulletin Number 11 was the first of the Foundation's studies to broach the use and construction of new-type tests through a special series of experiments conducted by Professor Edward L. Thorndike of Columbia, although Pritchett was skeptical of the results obtained.

Legal Education, Three Bulletins: 1919, 1921, 1928

Up to the close of World War I the only study in the field of legal education to contribute to the Foundation's series of Bulletins was Redlich's *Common Law and the Case Method,* 1914. It is singular that the most popular study that the Foundation ever published as part of its series relating to legal education contained only seven rather casual references to the topic: Reginald Heber Smith's *Justice and the Poor,* Bulletin Number 13, which first appeared in 1919 with subsequent editions in 1921 and 1928. Still another edition issued commercially. The origin of the studies was traced in Pritchett's introduction: "The presentation of the present report as a special bulletin . . . was suggested by the application of certain legal aid societies to the Carnegie Corporation for grants of funds.

The trustees of the Corporation . . . felt that a thoroughgoing report on the whole question of legal aid should precede any such action on their part. They agreed therefore to defray the expenses of such a report if prepared with the co-operation of the Carnegie Foundation in conjunction with its already partially completed enquiry" into legal education.

The Foundation's study of legal education had gone slowly. Reed, who had joined the Division of Educational Enquiry in 1913, realized that with extended travel, visits to all American and Canadian law schools, and hard office work, he was far behind his own schedule. He seems to have felt that Smith, in a draft of *Justice and the Poor* which Reed saw in July 1918, had annexed some of the ingredients of his own cake, which had scarcely passed the mixing stage. Among the schools, he had met general but not complete co-operation; some with memories of Flexner's exposé of medical education as yet unfaded, refused Reed information altogether. Reed was averse to acting longer as a "pacemaker" for others. Pritchett, becoming irked by the delay, fell back upon the opportunity the Corporation offered in order to get something published however questionable its relation might be to the field. With many others, Pritchett recognized that the connection between Smith's penetrating and much needed inquiry and the Foundation's studies of legal education was tenuous. Smith pointed out two chief defects in the legal aid program: lack of co-operation and centralization of the societies on a national scale, and paucity of funds for their support. There were to be found only two instances out of six in which co-operation between university legal aid bodies and outside agencies in the field brought praiseworthy results. Moreover, Smith apparently had small hope for the future in this regard, for he based his recommendations entirely upon extra-university legal aid organizations. Even with a foreword by Senator Root, the wisdom of hitching the noteworthy and useful Bulletin Number 13 to the Foundation's studies of legal education remains "not proven."

Meanwhile, Reed hammered away at his own typescript. By September 1919 it was in shape for the critical eye of Pritchett, who, reading it, was "pleased and satisfied. . . . It is an entirely different report from that which I had in mind when we started. . . . It is more scholarly and exhaustive." Reed continued to perfect his statistical data; a year after the draft of the text was typed, he was still at them. "The time has now come," Pritchett wrote, "when you should sacrifice, if necessary, the examination of details to the need for a prompt presentation of the results available." By the summer of 1921, Reed's task was accomplished, eight and a half years after the American Bar Association's Committee on Legal Education and Admission to the Bar had requested the inquiry.

As Pritchett stated in his preface, *Training for the Public Profession of the Law* (Bulletin Number 15, 1921) was not an educational survey in the common acceptance of the term. Reed dealt with the rise of law schools from proprietary independence to university affiliation, but it was to the bar associations that he looked for leadership in raising standards in the schools and among the examiners. He saw a "unitary" bar as impossible in any measurable time.

The whole subject of legal education was incredibly complex; what was called for was simplification. This Reed's treatment did not achieve. Among important points he argued that night law schools should be brought up to grade, not abolished one and all; that admission to legal practice should depend less on financial means of study and more on competence; that bar admission machinery should be tightened and improved. Upon the task implied, various legal groups set to work, notably the American Bar Association through its Conference of Bar Association Delegates 1922, and during the next decade much progress ensued. Reed's second Bulletin assisted materially.

While most of the Foundation's studies were addressed to the general reader—"the intelligent layman" was Pritchett's phrase for him—Reed's *Present Day Law Schools in the United States and Canada* (Bulletin Number 19, 1928) was addressed to lawyers and teachers of the law. A scholar in history, he leaned heavily upon the historical method with fine-spun reasoning and continual and sometimes disconcerting references to his preceding volume. The book of 573 pages is not invariably easy reading nor does it make its points sharply and unmistakably. The appendix material includes the bar admission requirements for each state, facts about the fees, history, requirements for admission and graduation, and attendance at each of 186 law schools, and much information about standards, recommendations, and rulings of various bodies connected with the profession. To lawyers, teachers of law, and law-school officers its thorough treatment probably seemed well worth waiting seven years for. The value of Reed's work in the eyes of the profession was attested by his election, 1923, as the only lay member of the American Law Institute.

Preparation of Public School Teachers, the "Missouri Study"

The work which culminated in Bulletin Number 14, *The Professional Preparation of Teachers for American Public Schools,* 1920, is clearly documented because it was carried on at a distance from the Foundation's offices. On July 18, 1914, Governor Elliott W. Major of Missouri formally invited the Foundation, through Pritchett, to undertake a statewide inquiry into the preparation of teachers at the state university, five normal schools, and elsewhere. Pritchett accepted tentatively on July 30 and the executive committee approved in the autumn. The earlier overtures had led to Learned's preparing a memorandum on the aims and methods of such a study. By November he was on the ground at work. After attending with Pritchett a state conference on teacher preparation November 24, Learned traveled up and down the state and by December 17 his "head was fairly bursting with plans for the study."

As nuclei of a staff, he chose Professor William C. Bagley of the University of Illinois to study the normal-school curriculum, and Professor Homer Josselyn of the University of Kansas to collect statistics on Missouri teachers. To Learned the study seemed to mushroom almost overnight. Under his direction, Josselyn had devised and dispatched a questionnaire on the teacher's training, and responses began to come in, though slowly. It was the first attempt of its kind to gather complete individual information on so large a scale. Learned also pressed the five normal schools for admissions data.

Then in the first week of March 1915 befell a major catastrophe: Quarters in the normal school at Warrensburg were "burned out completely," all the records of the study there were destroyed, and this portion of the work had to be transferred to Kirksville. In spite of all this, as April arrived the troubles in the normal schools and the causes were becoming clear. Learned discerned that the Kirksville Normal School illustrated difficulties prevalent throughout the state. The methods and possible results of the inquiry, becoming known, engendered statewide gossip. At the university admissions proved to be in no better order than at the normal schools, but Learned thought the Springfield school "a relief after Kirksville."

Part of the summer he spent at work in Missouri, part in the

East. The Kansas City schools were laggard with their data. During the autumn Learned journeyed up and down the state, sometimes on horseback, and into Kansas where he gained a high opinion of that state's public-school personnel. This led him to think well of Missouri teachers also, and perhaps was partly the reason he soon began to be "cordially received everywhere" with everyone anxious to talk.

Personnel and equipment for the study were expanding at an extraordinary rate. Most of Josselyn's Lawrence house was occupied by statistical workers from the University of Kansas and the Kirksville complement was growing steadily, while the New York offices of the Foundation became crowded to the point, seemingly, of bursting. Professors Charles A. McMurry of Peabody and George D. Strayer of Teachers College, Columbia, had become associated with the work. On May 13 and 14, 1916, Learned, Bagley, McMurry, Strayer, and Josselyn met to confer, and Learned quoted Strayer as remarking: "I see this is going to be a really great report." Walter F. Dearborn of Harvard undertook a new-type testing program in the St. Louis schools. At this point, Charles H. Judd of the University of Chicago began an independent four-week survey of this school system. Because of Judd's previous relations with Josselyn there was concern about possible effects upon the larger study, but on Learned's intervention matters were patched up and co-operation effected between the two enterprises.

Learned began to be pestered by both anonymous and personal protests about the collection of Kansas City data and other phases of the work. A minority group in the schools even engaged a lawyer to "protect their reputations." Learned, however, was getting his information and the protests made him only the more jubilant. A proposal to use psychological tests as a basis for eliminating unfit teachers, not actually vetoed but seriously questioned by Pritchett, was abandoned.

Having returned to New York in July 1917, Learned spent the ensuing thirteen months there and at Franklin, New Hampshire, shaping the report, in part helped by Bagley. In a letter of August 17, 1917, he summarized the work for Pritchett at Santa Barbara, laying special stress upon Josselyn's statistics from more than 18,500 teachers out of the nineteen or twenty thousand then at work in the Missouri schools. The individual items, tabulated by as many as eighteen clerks working in Josselyn's house, numbered between six and seven millions. Leonard Ayres, then of the Russell Sage

Foundation, an accomplished statistician, termed the volume of data "enormous." The weakest spot in the system Learned was coming to see as the 114 county superintendents.

Bagley in 1916 had issued a preliminary report on the curriculum. The close of 1917 found him engaged upon a more extensive analysis and construction which promised to be of immediate and lasting import and resulted in his widely acclaimed final curriculum proposals. Josselyn's census and Learned's school visits in twenty-five cities were yielding substantial information. Nevertheless, in Learned's view, the inquiry as a whole lacked background. In the spring of 1918 Pritchett thought the costs of the study were running high, and Learned proposed ways and means of reducing them, particularly through new-type testing.

It was at about this time that the study began to lag. Already it had far outrun Learned's preliminary memorandum. In New York, Kandel and Furst were preparing material on the national aspects of teacher training, but the matter of licensure was retarding their progress. Learned was suffering from fatigue; never a rapid or a ready writer, he found his burden much increased by the co-ordination and supervision he had to devote to the components of the report. Although Pritchett was looking forward to early termination of the work, that proved to be impossible.

Bulletin Number 14, *The Professional Preparation of Teachers for American Public Schools*, was released June 28, 1920, three years after Bagley's curriculum study had been published as a separate brochure. For the main volume, W. Carson Ryan, Jr., education editor of the New York *Evening Post*, prepared a press summary. Already one critic had christened the Bulletin "the normal-school Bible." Perhaps because it was used extensively as a text in teacher-training institutions, the first edition was soon exhausted. Printings ran to 12,000 copies. Learned thought the newspapers, nationally, treated the study well, but he was somewhat disappointed over their headlining "married teachers." In Missouri, he thought, personal comment was "mild but friendly," indicating a degree of guarded if tolerant adverse opinion. Many, though not all, of the proposals in the Bulletin were adopted by the state, in spite of one cardinal defect of the volume: The authors completely ignored school budgets and matters of finance. Total expenses of the inquiry were $184,350.

Education in "The Maritimes"

It was in the spring of 1921, after Carnegie Corporation had received from several higher institutions in the Canadian Maritime Provinces requests for grants, that the Corporation trustees felt the need of some sort of inquiry that should show how best to aid this group. On June 8, renewing a verbal request, Angell asked Pritchett for Learned's services and suggested that "a New England college man" be selected as his colleague in studying the situation. That New Englander turned out to be President K. C. M. Sills of Bowdoin, a native of Nova Scotia. He and Learned visited the Maritime Provinces and prepared a brief report. At a meeting in New York, April 13, 1922, officers of the Corporation, of which by that time Pritchett was acting president, together with institutional presidents concerned, heard these results. It was determined that the Learned-Sills report should become a Bulletin of the Foundation.

In that very brief monograph, Bulletin Number 16, *Education in the Maritime Provinces of Canada,* the authors contrive to set forth in nontechnical language their views of educational conditions in the Provinces, together with a cogent plea for reorganization at the higher level through confederation, which resembled a proposal by Lord Dalhousie made in 1818 but never operative. The initial cost they estimated at four and a half millions. As a succinct, persuasive presentation of a problem and a solution, with financial and other statistics in precisely the appropriate quantity, the Bulletin has few if any equals among Foundation publications. Aside from the cost of the proposal, it seems likely that denominationalism prevented adoption of its recommendations, but it was of service to the Corporation in handling Canadian requests and grants and it came to renewed life in 1930 in the area.

College Athletics: Bulletins Number 18, 23, 24, 26

Although repeated suggestions had been made that the Foundation study and report upon college athletics, it was November 16, 1921, before the matter reached the Board of Trustees through the executive committee and was referred back to the committee to be "kept under advisement . . . with the possibility of action in the future." At the next annual meeting the trustees nibbled again at the edges of the problem by discussing college athletics in general, but it was too hot a topic for concerted handling *ex tempore.*

Upon Chancellor Kirkland of Vanderbilt reporting that the Association of Colleges and Secondary Schools of the Southern States had appointed a five-man committee to study intercollegiate athletics in the area, the executive committee, January 6, 1922, referred the matter to Pritchett, who was to expend such amount as he should decide upon, "not to exceed $1,000," in meeting the expenses of the committee. He reported, May 2, 1923, that $438 of the authorized sum had been spent. The executive committee had declined to involve the Foundation in such a study at the moment.

There was talk but no action until late February 1925, when Dean Frank W. Nicolson of Wesleyan discussed with Keppel the possibility of a one-man inquiry into intercollegiate athletics with Foundation sponsorship and Corporation support. Accordingly, Furst procured from F. D. Fackenthal, then secretary of Columbia, a list of twenty higher institutions where, for one reason or another, athletics appeared worth studying. Savage presented the results of what was known in the office as the "Twenty-College Study" in three pages of the Twentieth Annual Report (1925), in which he laid responsibility for conditions, good and bad, at the door of the college president. It was less denunciatory talk than Pritchett had contributed to the Eighteenth Annual Report (1923) on the abuse of intercollegiate athletics, but it contained more facts.

Obviously, in view of the requests for an investigation from various representative bodies, it was only a question of time and tactics before a full inquiry would have to be undertaken. Pritchett, on learning that Savage intended to spend two weeks of September 1925 in England, handed him the assignment of finding out something about sports and games at British universities and schools. Savage was engulfed in these results, which Pritchett wished to issue as a Bulletin, when, on January 8, 1926, the executive committee accepted the invitation of the National Collegiate Athletic Association, which assured countrywide institutional co-operation, "to make an investigation of the whole question of intercollegiate athletics and its [*sic*] relation to modern education." After the meeting had dispersed, Pritchett put the study in Savage's hands.

The next two months were devoted mostly to the British material, outlining the American study, and procuring associates for the new work. The first chosen was J. S. Noffsinger, now head of the National Home Study Council, Washington, whose experience as college president equipped him to collect facts from various Pennsylvania colleges. He was the most economical traveler the Foundation ever had. The second selection was Harold W. Bentley, then a Columbia instructor. John T. McGovern, New York attorney, was associated (without compensation because he wished to retain a completely amateur status in England) to visit Roman Catholic colleges and to cover certain legal questions. Dean F. Smiley, M.D., of Cornell worked upon the hygiene of training and related matters. W. Carson Ryan, Jr., of Swarthmore was to read and report on the literature of college athletics. This procedure was Furst's suggestion.

After Noffsinger left the study for other duties, the field work devolved upon Bentley, McGovern, and Savage. They went to what now seems absurd trouble to establish a uniform point of view. Yet when they had attained it, they complained one to the other that each was agreeing with his colleagues and not one of the three was disputing conclusions of the other two. During the first year, more than fifty institutions were visited.

The results of the British athletic venture appeared in Bulletin Number 18, *Games and Sports in British Schools and Universities*, 1926. It was not one of the Foundation's revolutionary contributions to the field of American higher education. Through it the Foundation became somewhat better known in the British Isles, and a few American university classes in physical education used it as a supplementary text. Whatever may be said for its interest, it had little utility or effect beyond demonstrating a method of inquiry by visit and interview.

The typescript of Bulletin Number 23, *American College Athletics*, went to press June 1929 and was released on October 24, after the first and only full-length press conference ever held for a publication of the Carnegie Foundation. All told, 130 schools, colleges, and universities in the United States and Canada had been visited, some of them two or three times. No confidential proof was distributed, even to trustees; each presiding officer had received a data sheet setting forth what was found at his institution. The resulting protests were printed in footnotes to the Bulletin text which, in spite of its length, presented only a fraction of the material gathered. It was encyclopedic in scope, thorough in method, and unprejudiced in presentation. Its chief faults were its length and its detail; and yet without sufficient preponderance of evidence it would have failed of its purpose altogether.

The book of twelve chapters and 347 pages had a rousing reception in thousands of newspaper columns, speeches in support and in denial, and special articles. The only Foundation publication that rivaled it in controversial attention was Flexner's study of American medical education. There was praise and blame enough for all, yet not one of the myriad details of the volume was ever successfully refuted.

For the sake of the record, be it recalled that Bulletin Number 23 at no point proposed or favored the abolition of college athletics. What it called for was "not more law, but a more genuine regard for existing law," not uniform eligibility requirements, but better sportsmanship and plain common honesty in college sport. It scored, first, commercialism in athletics and, second, neglect by college officers of educational contributions that sports might be brought to make.

Those responsible for the study regretted that Pritchett in his preface chose to emphasize a view of his own that the paid coach was the root of all athletic abuses. Their view was that the paid coach was only one manifestation of commercialism and that he was a result rather than the inclusive source of this defect. Disappointed though they were with Pritchett's view, they nevertheless recognized the breadth of mind that allowed them to state fully and freely the conclusions to which their evidence had led them, without attempting even the slightest modification.

Results of the study were obscured by the countrywide economic clouds which greeted its publication. As with Flexner's first medical Bulletin, the two years of inquiry had produced changes at individual institutions before the report was issued. Some of these were noted in Bulletin Number 26. The onset of the depression began to make times hard for both the colleges and their sports. For a short time a view was current that "Carnegie money" would be used to improve college athletics. None was forthcoming, however, for the purpose; the study had uncovered defects and merits in the system which was left—as it belonged—to the institutions themselves: presidents, trustees, faculties, undergraduates, and alumni. Members of the study dispensed advice and counsel on request, and this continued *diminuendo* until 1950. Perhaps on an average of once or twice a year a voice has cried in the athletic wilderness for "another Carnegie investigation." Although Bulletin Number 23 has survived its usefulness, it will not stay decently dead. Roughly four college generations after it appeared, the National Collegiate Athletic Association undertook to compel observance of some of its principles.

The more immediate aftereffects of Bulletin Number 23 were set down in Bulletin Number 26, *Current Developments in American College Sport*, 1931, by three of the authors of the preceding study. The changes that were noted include the following items: In 1930, gate receipts were falling off, especially for football. A few college programs were being curtailed. Athletic accounting had been improved at six institutions. At fourteen, practice time was being reduced. Five universities and colleges were using or planning new physical education facilities, while twenty-two intramural programs were being expanded. At thirty institutions scattered over the country, student interest in intercollegiate contests was clearly declining. Observers attributed this development in part to undergraduate revulsion over the subsidizing of athletes, in part to a more serious student attitude toward academic work, in part to high prices for admission to contests. As a preliminary result of the inquiry, by October 1929, recruiting and subsidizing had been attacked in sixteen institutions; a year and a half later, thirty-eight more had started to clean up. Athletic conferences and representative associations were discussing rules and attempting to enforce them more stringently.

Off the campus, newspapers and sports writers, the taboo broken by the plain talk of "Bulletin 23," had begun to write oftener of the procuring and support of athletes. Some writers continued cynical, but the best of them gave the new changes, actual and proposed, their support. In 1930 the radio was not helping matters much, although broadcasts of sports events were improving. Commercialism in athletics, fanned by the depression, continued a pest. The years of athletic turmoil that were to precede and follow Pearl Harbor were not far distant. Perhaps if the course of international events had been peaceful, Bulletin Number 23 would have borne even better fruit. As it was, the Foundation's American Athletic Inquiry was the only study for which results, favorable and unfavorable, were formally summarized in the Bulletin series.

The least controversial document of the study was Ryan's volume *The Literature of American School and College Athletics*, Bulletin Number 24, 1929. Its 1,030 entries perhaps comprise the most complete analytical bibliography and digest ever made of a single phase of American education. Ryan's reading of this material revealed that the merits and the defects of American school and college sport had long been known. Many readers have recognized the irony its summaries suggest as well as the first-rate bibliographical skill and the industry that went into making it. Its total cost was $15,260.25, while that of the entire athletic inquiry was more than $110,000, met from funds of the Foundation.

Dental Education, Bulletin Number 19, 1926

The fact that between 1922 and 1926 the Foundation issued no Bulletins is due less to Pritchett's and Learned's work with Carnegie Corporation of New York than to the desire of those engaged upon studies to perfect them before publication. The precise date of the inception of the study of dental education is not clear. A formal request for the inquiry from the Dental Faculties Association of American Universities went before the executive committee November 5, 1920; a year less one day later, a study of dental education had been begun by Dr. William J. Gies, a biological chemist of wide repute and many scientific affiliations, who was professor of physiological chemistry at the New York College of Pharmacy and at Teachers College, Columbia University. The effort was, as Pritchett stated, to render for dental education "the same service that the Foundation undertook to perform for medical education—to survey the field, to state the essential facts, and to seek to draw such conclusions as may be helpful." Although Bulletin Number 19 bore on its title page 1926 as its year of publication, it was released June 27, 1927.

Gies visited each of the forty-four American and five Canadian dental schools, some twice and oftener. He consulted advisers in dentistry and medicine assiduously and wrote and spoke repeatedly at gatherings of dental teachers, administrators, and practitioners. His 240 pages of careful text and 417 pages of data and supplementary notes attest his industry and ability to accumulate facts. Submitting confidential proofs to each school delayed publication materially.

Gies's technique in treating his subject resembled that of the miniaturist. Opinions still differ as to the value and results of his work. Yet from the conflict emerge certain unavoidable conclusions: First, Gies practically singlehanded forced the elimination of the independent dental school from the American scene, a remarkable accomplishment even if many of the commercial aspects of dental education continued after certain proprietary schools had achieved university association. Secondly, he raised the stature of the profession by insisting that dentistry is an important component of health service. Thirdly, his influence at least rearranged curricular preparation for the practice of dentistry, even if it added few fresh devices. Fourthly, although he stilled few controversies and fanned others, nevertheless without his work the biological conception of dentistry which the next quarter-century was to introduce and propagate would certainly have been far longer delayed, and perhaps would not have come at all, had he not spaded and replotted the ground that received the seed of new concepts.

European and American Education: Learned's Comparison, 1927

A good part of the year 1924-25 Learned spent in Europe on what was supposed to be leave of absence and travel with his family. The trip turned into an attempt to account for the quality of European education. After returning to the United States in the autumn, Learned went back to Germany, France, and England for further inquiry, this time at the higher level. His letters to his office colleagues fairly burned with new ideas. In the meantime, E. Graham Savage, former Eton housemaster, subsequently H. M. Chief Inspector of Schools for the Board of Education and Chief Education Officer of the London County Council, made the Foundation's office his headquarters while on a secondary-school mission to the United States. So also did M. Saison of the French Ministry of Education. Learned visited Oxford, Cambridge, London, and some of the newer British universities and was back in the United States early in August with much of his report in typescript, although the French topics were giving trouble. The discussion was printed in the Twentieth (1925) and Twenty-first (1926) Annual Reports. It was issued as Bulletin Number 20, *The Quality of the Educational Process in the United States and in Europe*, in 1927.

Persuasively reasoned, employing a minimum of statistics, the Bulletin is no disgruntled attack upon American education; Learned credits the American high school and college with many merits which their most ardent proponents might hesitate to proclaim. The volume points out that the European student confronts an intellectual responsibility that he cannot and may not evade. His intellectual goals are clearly defined, and he must pursue them through demonstrated achievement. On the other hand, "the college or school that dully or carelessly strikes a mediocre average and invites all . . . to accept its mechanical imprint as though it were the mark of supreme excellence is scarcely satisfactory." This, of course, is a spark from Pritchett's hammering on intellectual sincerity.

The freshness and vigor of the Bulletin, distributed broadcast, excited much discussion in school and college faculties. Its precision and good temper won it wide influence which today could be appraised only in general terms, but it prepared the ground for a much more exacting tillage which Learned almost at once began— a study of the relations of school and college in Pennsylvania. The link between Learned's European analysis and the Pennsylvania Study is supplied by a statement in the Twenty-second Annual Report (1927) to the effect that at the annual meeting of November 17, 1926, the Board of Trustees received a report on "the present character and relations of schools and colleges in the United States as compared with those in several European countries; and authorized the continuance of the last inquiry in a specific study of the relations of the schools and colleges in the state of Pennsylvania."

The invitation to conduct this inquiry had come at an appropriate moment. Even as early as February 1, 1924, Pritchett, stirred perhaps by some of Learned's European interim reports, had informed Keppel that he was "constructing a scheme for the study of the High School and of the College from the point of view of their general tendencies rather than from that of . . . particular parts of the machinery. . . . As soon as I can lick it into fair shape," he added, "I mean to submit it to the joint criticism of Furst, Learned, Reed, and Savage. These sinners will probably tear it to pieces, as is their general habit with my writing. . . ." Up to 1927, under this policy, besides Pritchett's discussion of educational costs, integrity, and progress in the Annual Reports for 1922, 1923, and 1924 respectively, the Foundation had undertaken inquiries into three aspects of European schools and colleges: Flexner's study of medical education in Europe, Savage's account of games and sports in British universities, and Learned's discussion of the quality of the educational process. The Pennsylvania Study could not have been broached at a better time. It will be discussed in Chapter 10.

ANNUAL REPORTS

The twelve Annual Reports of the period now under consideration followed closely the pattern previously developed. Each contained a "plug" for the Teachers Insurance and Annuity Association, usually drafted by Furst, which in the earlier part of the period inclined to deal pretty summarily with objections and accusations affecting the Association and rather tenderly with statements that favored it. For each Report, Pritchett provided what he termed a "preachment," a discussion of some phase of education.

The most spectacular of these contributions began in the Seventeenth Annual Report (1922) with a section on the "Rising Cost of Education," continued in the Eighteenth (1923) with the "Teachers' Responsibility for Our Educational Integrity," and concluded in the Nineteenth (1924) on the "Direction of our Educational Progress." Of these three, perhaps the first, released in March 1923, attracted the widest attention, which lasted well into September; the *New York Times* even conducted a sort of symposium on the subject. Newspaper editorials and interviews over the country were legion, and letters to the editor abundant, East and West. It was in this series that Pritchett stressed his notion that the purpose of education was "training the habits and powers of the mind," a phrase that left him wide open to many an attack. In Annual Reports of the day, also, Pritchett vigorously opposed federal control of education, a secretary of education for the Cabinet, and large subsidies out of government funds to "equalize" educational opportunities over the land. His outspoken handling of these tender topics roused much attention, some of it highly unfavorable.

Learned and Reed treated for each Annual Report a phase of the study upon which each was engaged. So, also, after 1925, did Savage, who succeeded Kandel in providing the section on pension studies. Reed began his Annual Review of Legal Education in the Reports and later developed it as a separate enterprise. Furst usually put together the section related to administration. Everyone took a hand in reviewing the first three volumes of the Educational Finance Inquiry Commission in 1925. The practice of intensive, meticulous criticism of each writer's contribution by all of his office colleagues, begun by Bowman at least as early as 1909, was costly in effort and delay, but probably saved much vituperation after issue.

The lateness of some of these Annual Reports can be explained merely by this round-robin process. It was due also to extensive rewriting of proof, slow revision, tardy copy, sometimes procrastination, and sometimes plain bad luck. Even these obstacles hardly justified it for the Nineteenth (1924), in which Reed's contribution was dated November 1924 and Pritchett's signature October 15, or for the Twentieth (1925) which was released May 24, 1926, or for the Twenty-first (1926) distributed a full year after the close of the fiscal period it purported to cover.

The first by-line to appear in an Annual Report was Reed's at the end of a section on Legal Education in the Sixteenth (1921), not without hesitation on the part of Furst and especially of Pritchett, who had begun to feel that absence of by-lines was tending to credit him with information and statements for which he could not feel really responsible. Even so, it was some time before by-lines became general in Annual Report usage. The practice of printing as sections of Annual Reports material from Bulletins furnished ammunition for detractors even if it were economical of office time and effort. Publication of a fifty-six-page condensed version of the Nineteenth Annual Report (1924), by-product of a current passion for digests and conspectuses, amounted practically to nothing but increased expense.

Some account of other Annual Report sections of the day, dealing with the Foundation's own pension problem, is taken in Chapter 8.

REQUESTS FOR STUDIES AND FOR THEIR SUPPORT

The standing which the Carnegie Foundation was gaining during Pritchett's last dozen years as president generated proposals for a far greater number of educational studies than could be undertaken or even considered seriously with the personnel or the funds available. To enumerate all of these requests would be tedious; a selected list will suffice to show their general tenor and scope, and in some instances their ultimate disposal, but not the frequency with which some of them recurred. Requests (1919) for a study of "the condition of art instruction in American colleges and universities" from the College Art Association and for an examination of colleges of pharmacy from the American Conference of Pharmaceutical Faculties were declined by the executive committee. A hope that theological seminaries might be studied statistically (1920) got nowhere. In 1922-23 the executive committee regretted that it could not recommend early action upon studies of medical sects, the teaching of journalism and (again) pharmacy; in 1927 it declined requests relating to a study of educational experiments, Michigan primary and secondary schools, Negro colleges, colleges of pharmacy once more, and scholarships. In 1928-29 a testing project involving new-type tests in English schools, with Carnegie Corporation support and Carnegie Foundation supervision, was considered but not developed. In the same year a proposal to study material on postgraduate medical education, in part collected by the Foundation, which inclined towards emphasizing "team medicine" as the most important unit in medical practice did not eventuate. At a single meeting in 1930 Pritchett reported to the executive committee that the Foundation was not at present in a position to accept invitations to undertake studies of teaching in Negro schools, intercollegiate athletics in Arkansas, Indiana, and Texas, examination systems in various countries, student activities, the public schools of Fort Worth, state aid to Maryland schools and colleges, schools and courses in journalism, and the Haddonfield, New Jersey, school system as suggested by Alfred E. Driscoll, member of the Haddonfield Board of Education, later twice governor of the state.

Three proposals of 1927 bore fruit. President E. C. Elliott of Purdue, long interested in the organization of university boards of trustees, suggested that they be studied. Later a study of this subject, financed through the Foundation by Carnegie Corporation, resulted in the commercial publication of a volume of which he was one of the authors, *The Government of Higher Education.* Secondly, President David Spence Hill of the University of New Mexico, and Henry Suzzallo, former president of the University of Washington, suggested an inquiry under some such title as "Higher Education and the State," which subsequently was carried out.

Thirdly, President Keppel of Carnegie Corporation, in February 1927, asked Pritchett to consider getting Suzzallo to work on graduate education which had been under discussion for some months, and upon Savage preparing a memorandum on the subject, the Corporation's executive committee granted $10,000 to the Foundation for the purpose "if the opportunity should arise." Meanwhile, Keppel had invited Suzzallo, who accepted and started work in April. The venture continued in various forms under several hands for a decade. Pritchett was careful in noting that, at its inception, it was a Corporation enterprise.

A FRESH CONCEPTION

The year 1924 brought the beginning of a new phase in the relationship between Carnegie Corporation of New York and the Foundation and its Division of Educational Enquiry, in three Corporation grants for "joint projects," that is, educational studies or ventures which, in these instances, Carnegie Corporation desired to see undertaken and would finance, but which it entrusted to the Foundation to supervise and manage. The operating agencies which received the initial grants of $5,000 each, 1924-25, were the Co-operative Bureau for Women Teachers, a committee of the National Education Association on uniform standards and curricula in the public schools, and the University of the State of New York for experiments in applying a new type of examination. All three projects were initiated by the Corporation. The view is at least possible that the grants were so made as to involve the Foundation in their oversight because of convenience to the Corporation. In this aspect, the joint projects of this and later periods somewhat resemble the legal aid society study and the inquiry into education in "The Maritimes."

NEW VISTA

When Keppel in 1927 suggested Suzzallo as capable of undertaking a study of graduate education Pritchett had known Suzzallo for some years. From 1916 onward correspondence and personal talks between Suzzallo and Pritchett had developed firm friendship and mutual respect. In 1919 Pritchett thought so highly of Suzzallo that he brought his name into discussions of who should succeed Mr. Carnegie as president of Carnegie Corporation. Pritchett may or may not have named his own successor as president of the Foundation, but the trustees' choice of Suzzallo in November 1929, gave the older man great pleasure and satisfaction. Suzzallo's modesty in reply to Pritchett's news of his election was sincere and touching: "If I can only be effectively true to the spirit of your workmanship, I shall be most happy." What that spirit was as it operated within a part of Pritchett's grand schema of studies may be gathered from a sentence Reed wrote to Pritchett, January 27, 1921: "You are the finest example of the principle of academic freedom in higher education." The characteristic which Reed recognized was one of the important factors in Pritchett's development, and especially in the Foundation's climb to eminence.

~ 8 ~

Gathering Clouds

FACTORS AND PRODUCT—EXTERNAL FACTORS; INTERNAL FACTORS ·
THE TIDE ADVANCES—RULES, 1918; RULES, 1920, 1922; THE COL-
LEGES TAKE A HAND · STORM WARNINGS · CARNEGIE CORPORATION
INTERVENES—THE MACKENZIE COMMITTEE; THE MACKENZIE RE-
PORT; WAS IT INTERFERENCE?; THE FOUNDATION'S SPECIAL COMMIT-
TEE · SUGGESTIONS AND PROPOSALS—BORROWING FROM CARNEGIE
CORPORATION; THE FOUNDATION TO DISTRIBUTE ITS CAPITAL; FOUN-
DATION TRUSTEES, APRIL 3, 1928; WAS PRITCHETT JUSTIFIED?; THE
PURCHASE OF ANNUITIES · THE "FINAL" SOLUTION · RESIDUES ·
AFTER RETIREMENT, WHAT? · TWILIGHT OF AN ERA

WHILE the Carnegie Foundation through its educational
and pension studies, 1918-30, was winning golden opinions, as well as some not so golden, the situation regarding its own
retiring allowances and pensions was giving increasing concern. In
1918, when the fifth edition of Rules for the Granting of Retiring
Allowances had issued, the future had seemed fair. By 1926 skies
were graying.

FACTORS AND PRODUCT

Two sets of factors combined to cause deterioration in the Foundation's situation as a pensioning agency. One set was external to
the Foundation and quite beyond its control; the other set, internal
to the Foundation, could have been controlled if its Board of Trustees and its executive committee had recognized them as clearly as
its presiding officer read them.

167

External Factors

Consideration of available information leaves the doubt if in the Foundation's first years anyone concerned with it had a seer's conception of the future growth of the American college as to numbers of institutions or members of their staffs. Mr. Carnegie, having in mind primarily a gift to the old and honored teacher, now seems to have taken for granted that the college teaching personnel of 1905-15 would remain more or less stationary for a long time. Pritchett foresaw growth but not to the extent that eventuated. S. S. Hall, Sr., in 1909 assumed a five-year increase in the number of pensionables from 3,357 to only 3,400 by 1914. The growth that actually occurred was one manifestation of the inflationary tendencies that, beginning in the 1920's, penetrated every phase, financial and economic, of the nation's life. Riding the wave, not a few associated institutions, finding that under the Foundation's Rules certain persons could not benefit, changed academic titles to make them eligible. After World War I and especially about 1922, membership in college faculties tended to become stabilized; fewer professors left teaching for other callings and more settled down to continue college teaching until they could claim the retiring allowances Mr. Carnegie's generosity had provided. Indeed, when in 1918, 1920, 1922, and especially in 1929, the Foundation announced changes in its Rules, effective as of future dates, a rush ensued to retire before the reductions in benefits became operative. Then, too, Furst showed in the Twenty-third Annual Report (1928) college teachers, as represented by the completed lives of 358 Foundation beneficiaries, 1906-27, were living longer than the generality of men included in the mortality tables of the day; indeed, in 1922, mortality among men beneficiaries was only 80 per cent of that to be expected under the American Experience Table. R. L. Mattocks, actuary for the Foundation, discerned the same tendency in a larger group of beneficiaries. In 1927, fifteen persons ninety years or older were receiving benefits.

For much of the period the Foundation's return from its investments held high and steady. Its U. S. Steel Corporation bonds yielded 5 per cent at par and the average rate of return on its other securities was comparable. Not until 1926 was the possibility of a lower return recognized; in the Twenty-first Annual Report occurs the statement: "The rate of return for the future is problematical."

By all odds the most impressive factor in the external situation was the rise in college salaries that occurred in the inflationary 'twenties. Between 1907 and 1920, the tendency had established itself through increases of from 20 per cent to 60 per cent, and by 1922 even 80 per cent in smaller colleges, and the institutions were seeking more endowment to raise salaries. In the associated institutions median salaries jumped from $1,945 in 1917-18 to $3,869 in 1921-22, or about 98 per cent in four years. As Mattocks showed, it meant little that 15 per cent of the increase had come as a result of the advance in the age of the teachers; the salaries of thirty-eight persons retired in 1921-22 had increased from $3,450 in 1917-18 to $4,712 in their last year of active teaching. And the tendency continued and even intensified throughout the period, with a corresponding increase in the amount of each retiring allowance and widow's pension. So long as benefits were geared to salaries over which the Foundation had, of course, no control, no end could be foreseen for the spiral. About such factors in the Foundation's pension situation as have just been enumerated, the Foundation of itself could do little or nothing, short of revolutionary change.

Internal Factors

As to certain factors within the control of the Foundation's trustees and executive committee the question was different.

In the Rules for the Granting of Retiring Allowances lay part of the difficulty. Neither simple nor clear in phrasing, they were interpreted and given special meaning at so many points that over the years they became almost impossible to understand. Vagueness of phrase offered loopholes for differing interpretations. In ruling as to meaning and intent the executive committee now appears to have been liberal to the point of extravagance, probably owing to its desire to avoid or to refute accusations of unfairness. In numerous instances the committee probably ran counter to Pritchett's views and recommendations. Questions involving status of pensionables were generally decided in favor of the institution or the individual, seldom with the view to protecting the Foundation's resources for the whole body of teachers. Although at first instructors were considered ineligible, subsequently not only they but administrative officers as well were included among those whose service would duly qualify them for allowances. As late as June 1926 the executive committee considered ten status cases and decided half of them in favor of the pensionables, on the ground—scarcely justifiable in all cases—that they had been in public service during the war years.

After the war, in numerous instances expectations had been restored because of service with various organizations which in retrospect seem somewhat remote from the war effort. In each year up to 1925 from twenty-five to fifty names were "restored" for one reason or another to the list of pensionables.

In other technical matters a similar pattern is discernible. Although professors of agriculture had long been considered ineligible, those at Cornell were retired like other regularly eligible teachers. "Some twelve or thirteen" names were added to the number of Canadian pensionables for dubious reasons. Institutions were not held responsible for correctly reporting their own eligibles; if a name was omitted through institutional error it was promptly restored by the committee, which felt that the man himself should not be penalized for the mistake of his college. Gradually a practice known as "back-dating" allowances grew to the proportions of an abuse. Applications for allowances, filed by institutions from a day or two up to months after the allowance was to start, the committee would approve readily enough, and the allowance began as of the time requested, with consequently increased cost to the Foundation.

For a time the number of allowances granted outside the Associated List receded, only to rise again as policy vacillated or softened. Furthermore, between 1906 and 1917 grants of allowances and pensions in nonassociated institutions had averaged, according to Furst, $914 each and cost a total of $1,000,000. Pritchett once stated that "the granting of these small pensions . . . has gone far to satisfy the complaint that the pensions of the Foundation were not for the poor and faithful who most needed them." Moreover, from 1906 to 1924 there were granted in institutions outside the Associated List some 152 retiring allowances and 16 widows' pensions. In addition, over the years 1915-28 a total of 156 names were added to the list of pensionables, from which for one cause or another 31 were ultimately removed, leaving on this account a net gain of 125 names, possible widows not included.

Other special decisions, or the lack of decision, contributed to further inroads upon the Foundation's ability to meet its future load. The question whether teachers of engineering who received consultants' fees aggregating more than their salaries as teachers should be able to claim benefits was raised but not pursued far by the executive committee. Admission of institutions to the Associated List grew steadily to twenty-two in the decade after 1919 as criteria for institutional eligibility increasingly stressed adoption of T.I.-

A.A.'s contributory deferred retirement annuity contracts as a qualification *sine qua non*. Before 1918 all such admissions to the Associated List had implied a direct increase in the cost of allowances and pensions both immediate and future; thereafter most of the immediate or proximate cost was shifted to Reserve Fund Number Two, but the widening of opportunity for migration without loss of expectation lowered the withdrawals from the total group of pensionables. Incidentally, the use of Reserve Fund Number Two, 1918-21, was liberal perhaps to the point of extravagance. During those years, usually as a result of Furst's recommendation, nine colleges, beginning with Vanderbilt University's $30,000 in 1919, received from it grants ranging between $25,000 and $50,000 as contributions towards endowment funds of from $25,000 to $200,000 each in order to further adoption of the Association's retirement annuity contracts. In addition, grants of allowances from Reserve Fund Number Two for individuals too old for full contractual protection usually supplemented the outright gifts.

For several reasons it was impossible to compile or maintain a complete or accurate list of pensionables. This was partly the fault of the public institutions, which as late as 1921, the Educational Finance Inquiry Commission found, kept their accounts rather badly. It was perhaps more especially due to the Foundation's use of institutional budgets to determine eligibility and salaries. The consequence was that no one at any given moment could discover the precise number of pensionables in the group, or even with certainty at any component college.

As if these defects and deficiencies were not enough, the very basis of the Rules themselves was faulty and insecure. Retiring allowances for both age and disability, as well as widows' pensions, depended upon a percentage relationship to the average salary received during the final five (later ten) years of active teaching. During the period the trend of college salaries was upward. As the average salary rose—quite beyond the control of the Foundation—the allowance increased proportionately. The average retiring allowance in force jumped in a single year from $2,126 (1924) to $2,188 (1925). This defect could be remedied only by lowering the maximum of the allowance or, more simply, by "pegging" the allowances at one flat figure for all. In September 1927, Pritchett wrote to Furst: ". . . we must eliminate the uncertainty of future pay as a factor" in the retiring allowance. This uncertainty was the reason why "actuaries can have no sure basis for calculation on account of the Rules," which at their core were predicated upon an unknowable cost which was plainly rising to the point of grave danger.

The question may well be asked why the executive committee, reminded repeatedly of these factors, did not adjust all or at least some of them. The answer is that they made the attempt, but not drastically or inclusively enough. They saw themselves as condemned by the Rules to a course of action that might be modified but could not be changed except in comparatively minor details: The Rules of 1918, 1920, 1922 all displayed the same general structure. For years critics and dissidents had been accusing the Foundation, its governing bodies by implication, and Pritchett personally, of unfairness, evasion of responsibilities, infringement upon rights, and even outright dishonesty. Pritchett was no stranger to the situation; he knew only too well its causes and its inescapable consequences. He labored to convince both board and executive committee of the need for drastic action. But by far the largest concentration of persons eligible to benefit was to be found at six universities, and the presidents of all six were trustees of the Foundation.

After all, the Carnegie Foundation was a charitable and educational institution. Its trustees were trying to carry out the generous purposes of Mr. Carnegie. Already the Foundation had received large grants from Carnegie Corporation and it might again need Corporation help. The day of reckoning lay in the future. It had been known since 1909 that no rights accrued to individuals under the Rules, and with prospects of more than $30,000,000 in resources represented by Mr. Carnegie's gifts of endowments, totaling $16,250,000, the Corporation's contributions of nearly twelve millions, and all the surplus income and the profits from sales and exchanges of securities—well, it was simply inconceivable that any difficulty could not be surmounted. Finally, the Foundation was not a business concern but a philanthropic enterprise and the generous impulse of the Founder lighted a kindred flame in the breasts of many of his trustees.

THE TIDE ADVANCES

It must not be supposed that attempts to modify the effects of these factors, external and internal, were not made.

Rules, 1918

In an endeavor to articulate the Foundation's retiring allowances with the contractual retirement annuities of the newly formed

Teachers Insurance and Annuity Association, the Foundation's Rules, as amended by the trustees April 22, 1918, divided teachers of associated institutions into three groups: *Group A* consisted of those eligible teachers who on November 17, 1915, the date the Foundation trustees took action looking to a contributory plan, should reach age sixty-five on or before June 30, 1923. *Group B* comprised those who would not reach the age of sixty-five on June 30, 1923. *Group C* was composed of teachers entering the service of associated institutions after November 17, 1915, who participated in the contributory annuity plan of T.I.A.A. For those in Group A the allowance was to be half of the active pay during the final half decade of service plus $400 up to the maximum allowance of $4,000. For Group B, the allowance was scaled down by postponing the date at which retirement on the maximum allowance became possible. For both groups disability benefits and widows' pensions remained intact. For Group C, containing naturally the youngest persons of all three groups, who entered associated institutions after November 17, 1915, as well as teachers in institutions later admitted to the Associated List, to all of whom T.I.A.A. contracts were available, the Foundation in effect closed its eligibility to "free" pensions unless one became disabled and assigned one's T.I.A.A. annuity contract to the Foundation.

The Rules of 1918 thus embodied the first attempt to stem the tide of mounting costs. They were also the first to carry a heading in which it was clearly stated that they were not contractual and that benefits depended upon the resources then available to the Foundation. Under their provisions, endowment requirements for entering the Associated List were raised for the future from $200,000 to $500,000, paralleling those current for classification as colleges in New York State and Pennsylvania. In addition, benefits were scaled down very considerably. Pritchett called these Rules "simple and definite." Technically, that may have been so; in practice and administration they were neither.

Rules, 1920, 1922

The tide continued to rise and to call for other precautions. Further reductions in benefits were written into revisions of the Rules in 1920 and 1922, the second of the two versions being based upon more conservative actuarial tables and assumptions. The 1922 Rules reduced the maximum for future allowances from $4,000 to $3,600 at age seventy, and based the allowances on the last ten service years' salary instead of the last five. These changes, hung on the framework of the 1918 Rules, represented attempts to meet the drain upon the Foundation's resources caused by the continuing rise in college salaries, but they did not go far in that direction and reflected no very general desire in the board or the executive committee to deal stringently or definitively with the mounting pension load.

The Colleges Take a Hand

Meanwhile, associated institutions, exhorted in Annual Reports and in correspondence, were attempting measures to supplement the prospective allowances of their professors. By 1925 eleven large and smaller were adding increments at their own cost, while seven nonassociated institutions, whose teachers had no expectations from the Foundation, were increasing their formal retirement provisions. Thus the responsibility for making available a means of retirement gradually began to rest where it belonged—upon employer and employee jointly and not upon a charitable agency.

STORM WARNINGS

Up to 1919-20, actuarial work upon the Foundation's resources and liabilities had been jointly done by men engaged for the occasion, who had worked with the best information available. As of April 1, 1920, R. L. Mattocks of T.I.A.A. made new calculations for the most thoroughgoing valuation thus far attempted. The data for the 4,552 pensionables were, of course, defective. Future rates of return on the Foundation's investments, probably seen through other eyes than Mattocks's, proved later to have been established at too high a figure. He employed McClintock's 4½ per cent tables which were still in good repute. To offset some or all of these factors he introduced safeguards as to withdrawals and future salary assumptions. His conclusions were partly to the effect that as of April 1, 1920, the Foundation's resources, amounting to some $26,000,-000, would meet its existing responsibilities, providing salaries did not rise sharply and other factors worked out according to calculations.

Perhaps it was only natural that many who on May 21, 1920, heard Mattocks's report as presented to the executive committee, and later examined it, should be less impressed by its cautionary clauses than by the fact that resources in sight might suffice to meet the load. Mattocks had particularly emphasized the danger in the general rise in college salaries and the comparatively low mortality rate as contrasted with what might be expected from both the McClintock and the American Experience tables.

During the ensuing eight years, Mattocks made actuarial valuations or calculations in seven. In 1922 he first broached "pegging" the allowances. In 1924 he emphasized his view that expenditures had exceeded the figures expected first and principally because salaries, and therefore individual allowances and pensions, had risen higher than anticipated, and secondly, because many names, omitted from the list of eligibles through institutional oversight or misunderstanding, had been restored on petition to the executive committee. Even if investment returns held up well, he expected from 1944, when Reserve Fund Number One should be exhausted, to 1962 a deficiency of $13,000,000.

Reviewing his calculations in 1926, he again called attention to the unpredictability of the variables embodied. If current benefits were continued for five years they would then have to be cut by 40 per cent; if for ten years by 65 per cent. As the ultimate maximum allowance, following a downward scaling, he suggested $1,800 at age seventy. The worst of it was that his figures had been "very close to the actual experience so far." By 1927 he was stressing the need of borrowing to meet the load. Mattocks's work was thoroughly conservative and in findings boldly pessimistic. It influenced discussions prepared by Pritchett and Furst for most of the Annual Reports of the day. Its results showed plainly in the Rules of 1922. Still, the general structure of the Rules remained as it had been, perhaps because they, as Pritchett wrote in the Seventeenth Annual Report (1922), "could not now be changed without adopting an arbitrarily fixed scale of salaries," which would amount practically to making available the same allowance to all pensionables. This step no one seems to have been prepared to take.

Evidence is clear that from 1922 to 1926, Pritchett, independently of others than Furst and Mattocks, tried patiently to get the Foundation trustees to face the facts. He was not wholly successful. For them a letter and memorandum on the Foundation's pension load and resources, November 5, 1926, pointed out the necessity of reducing benefits to accord with the funds then in sight and called upon them to face their "clear and necessary duty" towards future beneficiaries. It convinced some trustees but not all; more than a few "hoped" for another solution. To Butler, who inclined to rely upon Corporation money to bridge the gap between load and resources, Pritchett wrote November 10, 1926, in part: "This thistle will be a bigger one and harder to pull four years from now. I feel under obligation to get it settled in my time and to share myself whatever odium may come from the operation." Pritchett saw his own retirement as in the not distant future.

The settlement of 1918 between the Foundation and the Corporation had been understood as not closing the door against further requests from the Foundation for Corporation assistance in meeting the pension load, but as stipulating that such requests must originate with the Foundation. This understanding Pritchett and his trustees had respected and maintained; there is no evidence that from 1918 to 1925 any other course received Pritchett's serious consideration. He was probably taken aback when early in February 1925, at Santa Barbara, he received from President Keppel of the Corporation, through Furst, an inquiry as to what future aid the Foundation might require from the Corporation. This inquiry Keppel later explained as having been prompted by a desire within his board to determine future policy affecting other Carnegie agencies.

The Mackenzie Committee

Within a fortnight Keppel had constituted a committee to study the Foundation pension situation: Professor Michael A. Mackenzie of the University of Toronto, an experienced actuary; Dr. Frederick L. Hoffman, actuary of the Prudential Life Insurance Company and dean of the Advanced Department of the Babson Institute, Wellesley Hills, Massachusetts; and Professor E. B. Wilson of Harvard. In correspondence Pritchett was somewhat reserved in his comments, but in conferring with Keppel in New York on April 6, 1925, he expressed willingness that the committee should serve and discussed its work with Keppel and its members on June 4. It was strictly a Corporation affair and the Corporation executive committee approved it and made a grant for its work on June 12.

The committee's first six months were spent in discussing and trying to determine what they were to study. In June a request for many data was filed with the Foundation. Assembling, arranging, classifying, carding, and transcribing these data in the Foundation offices took almost three years—until May 1928. Between October and December 1925 a Babson student prepared for Hoffman a report on the Foundation from its first five annual reports, which, although it bore heavily upon wavering policy, was fair and penetrating as far as it went. Wilson, as Mackenzie wrote to Furst, was not versed in actuarial science, but he undertook certain machine tabulations of data. Mackenzie himself tended to become involved in minutiae and correspondence. For this there was a measure of justification; the data, as collected, were faulty, fragmentary, spotty, and discrepant, sometimes nonexistent altogether. Furst drove himself and the office staff strenuously at the task but he could not really satisfy the meticulous Mackenzie. The committee reported January 12, 1928.

The Mackenzie Report

Other members of the three-man committee had apparently not seen Mackenzie's figures when he filed the committee's report. Among his underlying assumptions were 5 per cent interest during the lifetime of living beneficiaries and up to the retirement of existing pensionables; 4 per cent interest during the lifetime of any person who became a beneficiary after November 17, 1931; a reduced separation or withdrawal factor; the Rules of 1922 to remain unchanged; no salary, 1925-26, to exceed $7,200 to impose a maximum of $3,600 upon all allowances; widows' pensions of one-fourth pay; administration to consume the income on $2,000,000. On these assumptions the Foundation's liabilities totaled $35,162,200, with the prospect of $28,476,000 to meet them. As of November 17, 1925, the prospective deficit was computed at about $8,686,000; as of November 17, 1927, interest being accrued, it had grown to $9,576,000. The committee recommended pegging the allowances— Mattocks had advocated this as long ago as May 5, 1922—and ceasing to add to the "already overloaded list" of pensionables. Differences between these figures and Mattocks's occasioned questions, but when the technical counts and expectations were canvassed, the two actuaries were seen to be in practical agreement.

Was It Interference?

In some minds the appointing of the Mackenzie Committee and not a little of its activities added up to an attempt on the part of Carnegie Corporation to call the tune for the Foundation. Although evidence to the contrary exists, the fact remains that a number of steps ran counter to Senator Root's view expressed some time previously that the Corporation should not presume to special knowledge of the affairs of Mr. Carnegie's other philanthropies, and in framing action for their support and assistance should depend upon their respective and presumably expert recommendations. At any rate, it can be said that the motives of certain Corporation trustees in seeking to ascertain the Foundation's needs were of the kindliest and of the highest. Be that as it may, Pritchett appears to have blamed some of the Corporation trustees *ex officio* for the move, and he clearly warned Keppel that Keppel might ultimately find them "somewhat embarrassing." The Corporation executive committee's suggestion to Keppel, transmitted to Pritchett May 21, 1925, that in its judgment "the retiring allowances granted by the Foundation should be limited to the names which appeared on the pension list . . . November 17, 1915," although courteously answered for the executive committee by Pritchett, citing Mr. Carnegie's "expressed wish" about allowances for teachers in institutions not accepted or associated, did nothing to stem a foreboding as to motives and methods.

The Foundation's Special Committee

On Pritchett's initiative, the trustees of the Foundation at the twenty-first annual meeting, November 17, 1926, discussed the question of future resources and called upon the chairman of the board to appoint a special committee to consider "the relation of the resources of the Foundation to the liquidation of its obligations, this Committee to lay the situation as they see it before the Carnegie Corporation and to report back to the Foundation one year hence." Robert E. Vinson, president of Western Reserve, chairman, appointed as members of this committee Presidents Josiah H. Penniman of the University of Pennsylvania, Frederick C. Ferry of Hamilton, Sir Robert A. Falconer of Toronto, Rush Rhees of Rochester, and Frank Aydelotte of Swarthmore.

This special committee seems not to have begun its work at any great speed, although its members corresponded among themselves and with Pritchett and Furst. It met on May 27, 1927, and on June 10 Pritchett supplied it with various memoranda requested of him at its May meeting, dealing *inter alia* with salary increases, numbers of men and women pensionables and eligibles, and a note concerning the deficiency of $8,400,000 which Mattocks had computed as of January 1, 1927, on the basis of the Rules of 1922, together with summaries and an explanation of differences between previous actuarial estimates and the actual experience. On October

19, 1927, the special committee saw Pritchett and Keppel separately and reached conclusions on several matters: It would be unwise to change the 1922 Rules. As a wise action, the whole matter should be laid before the Corporation board with a view to obtaining help on that basis. The Foundation in meeting its obligations should expend capital as well as interest, or it should get the Corporation to underwrite the deficiency until 1965 and then terminate the Foundation, or else the Foundation should mortgage its resources to the Corporation and repay the loan from whatever income and capital might remain after 1965. Pritchett did not like these conclusions. After pointing out certain weaknesses in them, he contended that before approaching the Corporation board, the special committee should report progress to the Foundation trustees, who directed its appointment, and look further into the matter.

Pritchett carried the day. On November 16, 1927, at the twenty-second annual meeting, the special committee reported progress, asked that it be continued in order to consider new actuarial and other material then in preparation, and requested authority to lay its findings before the president and the trustees of the Corporation. Pritchett read a fifteen-page memorandum stating his position. By that means he at least gained time to contest the issues which by now seemed pretty clear. He stood for so revising the Rules as to reduce the load of future pensions to a figure which the Foundation could meet from resources currently in sight.

Much correspondence and conferring ensued. On February 7, 1928, the special committee met with Keppel on his invitation. Keppel was convinced that the Foundation was under a moral obligation to expend its capital in meeting the load, and to this end he made several related proposals which the committee favored. These, on February 23, 1928, Keppel laid before the Corporation's executive committee, which invited the special committee of the Foundation to a discussion. The inviting resolution did not mention Pritchett or suggest his presence or a deputy's at the discussion. The Mackenzie Committee's report had been submitted January 12, 1928. Out of all these documents and actions there emerged various suggestions for a solution of the problem. Certain of these demand consideration, one or two extended attention.

In the course of various discussions and much correspondence after January 1927, a number of solutions were proposed, a few of which deserve more than passing notice although not necessarily in their order of appearance or always in the somewhat extended phrasing in which they were couched.

Borrowing from Carnegie Corporation

Mattocks, as has been noted, had previously mentioned the possibility of the Foundation's borrowing from Carnegie Corporation to meet the pension deficiency. On February 27, 1925, Pritchett in two letters, one to Keppel, the other to Furst, referred somewhat uncertainly to this course, but neither correspondent appears to have commented in reply. The special committee on October 19, 1927, also discussed "mortgaging the resources of the Foundation to the Corporation" and repayment of the loan.

The Foundation to Distribute Its Capital

On February 1, 1928, Keppel in a memorandum laid before the Corporation's executive committee for consideration several propositions, some of which were predicated upon the idea that the Foundation ought to rid itself of the burden of pensions and pensioning. This was to be accomplished mainly by ceding back to the Corporation one-half of Reserve Fund Number One ($6,214,000) and by accepting from the Corporation for nine years $600,000 annually as it had "been doing for the past ten years" thus the "present pensions could be provided for." This would leave $16,104,189 capital and accumulated interest plus the other half of Reserve Fund Number One, a total of $22,318,189 to be distributed among the colleges, which would also have to put up collectively, according to Mackenzie's figures, an additional $2,273,710. Keppel termed this a "co-operative solution" which "would definitely enhance Carnegie prestige." "The Foundation could go forward upon its work in connection with contributory insurance [surely Keppel meant annuities] and continue the educational research unhampered by this incubus."

This proposal had had the attention of the attorneys, on Keppel's request, and also of the Foundation's special committee on his initiative, both in October 1927. The special committee discussed it with Keppel also on February 7, 1928, as "a moral obligation." It was recognized by all that distributing the capital funds of the Foundation or, broadly speaking, using them for any purpose except the production of income, would require court action, which was recommended as being advisable to seek. It should be noted that the view behind this proposal was almost precisely the opposite of Mr. Carnegie's in setting up the Foundation, which for many years he saw as primarily a pensioning agency with educational inquiry as an ancillary function at most.

The expenditure of principal by the Foundation had been proposed in 1916. One of the members of the Foundation's special committee had recurred to it in December 1926. Pritchett had opposed it each time it had appeared; on February 28, 1928, he wrote to Keppel that "it could only be done by obtaining a judgment of the Court, and would constitute in my judgment so grave a breach of trust as to be definitely barred from consideration." To Furst he termed it "apparently illegal and highly immoral," and Furst drew six "strong" arguments against it. To Penniman, Pritchett stated the view, March 5, 1928, that inasmuch as many of the trustees were to be beneficiaries "they would as trustees distribute the principal of Mr. Carnegie's gift to themselves and their institutions. . . . The proposal is unthinkable." Upon Butler appearing to favor distribution of principal, Pritchett sought to disabuse him of the notion by citing Mr. Carnegie's known views and purposes. Through Penniman, Pritchett hammered hard the attitude of the special committee in choosing "the wrong path when they undertake to administer a trust of which they or their institutions are beneficiaries," and added, "I will consider it my own duty to oppose your recommendation."

Probably Keppel saw how the situation was shaping. At any rate, he adopted towards Pritchett a mollifying attitude while still keeping the issues joined. Mr. Root's opinion was to the approximate effect that while the Foundation could not then distribute principal, the way could be cleared by action of the New York State Supreme Court; Keppel had not intended to use this opinion "unless or until the Foundation had decided to take up the question. . . ." Pritchett, girding himself for a Foundation trustees meeting on April 3, 1928, wrote to Furst March 20:

I have no question that this matter will be settled honestly in the end. One can understand how well-meaning men, whose personal interests are affected, could bring themselves to the point of believing that a valuable privilege was a vested right, and that they had a sound reason for laying hands on Mr. Carnegie's endowment and distributing it to themselves. I cannot understand why Mr. Keppel should be taking up this matter with his Executive Committee before the trustees of the Foundation have had a chance to consider it.

He termed the proposal an "immoral and futile expedient," and added: "We will see a merry fight before the spoliation is accomplished." To Mackenzie he called it a "gross breach of trust." Before Keppel, Pritchett laid carefully and precisely the grounds of his stand. Keppel accepted the responsibility for reopening the question, and with good temper gave justificatory reasons for his views. To each of the two men, the differences in aims, purposes, and means to accomplish them seemed clear.

Foundation Trustees, April 3, 1928

The trustees of the Foundation met April 3, 1928, in an atmosphere of tension—and no wonder. Penniman reported for the special committee, which recommended (1) adherence to the 1922 Rules as well as (2) requesting continuance for nine years of the currently operative Corporation grant of $600,000 annually; (3) early announcement to institutions that allowances would be reduced after the period 1929-38; (4) scaling down of allowances after 1938; (5) consideration of the purchasing of annuities for retiring pensionables from T.I.A.A. or some other companies. Under (2) they requested that the board adopt a closed list of pensionables and peg allowances on a progressively downward scale as a means of removing uncertainty. The special committee, he added, had considered the distribution of the Foundation's capital which counsel had said would probably prove feasible if no objection were raised and if a strong case could be made out for expenditure through the colleges; this he doubted. The report was clear but guarded in tone, and all present identified the forces and views it reflected.

The meeting then heard and considered a special report of the president analyzing the situation at length, putting the question involved up to the trustees, laying much of the blame on "the uncertainty of future salaries" and advocating "pegging the salaries at a fixed level" as a basis for calculating allowances, but only by implication suggesting that the allowances themselves be pegged. The special report made no reference to the proposal to distribute capital or to that proposal's collapse. Probably to the special committee it gave the impression that in it Pritchett was showing them how their own report should have been written. At any rate, the board concurred in five sections of the special committee's report, but ignored the question of distributing capital. On the president's special report it took no action. To Mackenzie on April 23, Pritchett wrote that "the proposal to allocate capital . . . to a few institutions was a distinct shock to many of the trustees." To those trustees whose institutions would not share, it never occurred that the "favored beneficiaries" in a few institutions "would also claim the right to divide among themselves the permanent endowment." He added that a fixed scale was considered for pegging salaries at the 1922 level, but not carefully enough.

Was Pritchett Justified?

All available papers and correspondence that Pritchett prepared or was responsible for in this interchange show clearly his view that in opposing distribution of capital he was contending for the very life of the Carnegie Foundation. He appears to have realized by March 1928, that he held the whip hand in the matter, which Mackenzie termed "an awful thing" if it reached the courts. Twenty years after the event, it appears that Pritchett went the limit in his imputations of immoral self-seeking, when the final result could have been reached by pointing out to the individuals concerned the consequences, to themselves and to others, of a course which could be shown to have the appearance of evil. In the spring of 1928, the events merely suggested above followed one upon another with great rapidity and they all focused upon Pritchett. It is difficult to censure him for the stand he took; lesser men would have yielded before he began to fight.

The Purchase of Annuities

The Foundation special committee's report suggested that the purchase of life annuities be studied as a means of alleviating the difficulties. This matter had been in the air since December 1926. It was kept there by several variables involved in the expectations of the pensionables, including the unpredictable cost linked to future salaries, pensions for widows, the disability provision, a complicated withdrawal factor, and the necessity of using cash in annuity purchases. In February 1928, however, Keppel proposed this possible solution anew to the special committee, perhaps encouraged by a suggestion of Mackenzie. Life insurance company officials, approached in the matter, balked at "too many unknown quantities." By June 1, Keppel was considering and getting figures on the purchase from T.I.A.A. of group annuities of a special type to be reinsured at Corporation expense. Pritchett opposed this proposal on various grounds: among others, the separation it would bring between the Foundation and its beneficiaries. Partly because of the costs involved in purchasing individual annuities, Keppel came increasingly to favor a group treatment. It was Butler who, October 22, 1928, suggested "a second and complementary allowance . . . on a contractual basis" purchased by Carnegie Corporation from T.I.A.A. for each pensionable. Pritchett seems to have thought there was something in this, but not much; he looked forward to a scaling down of Foundation allowances and felt that any added Corporation funds which might increase them should be given outright to the Foundation if at all.

The Corporation executive committee even went so far as to express willingness to grant, 1928-37, a total of $5,400,000 to purchase a paid-up group annuity policy for present pensionables through the Association, though realizing "that this recommendation runs counter to the judgment of the officers of the Carnegie Foundation. . . ." On November 19 Pritchett and Keppel discussed individual annuity contracts carrying options for surviving widows similarly provided, instead of a group policy, and Keppel expressed willingness to recommend this arrangement to his board and try to get his executive committee to agree. It did, and so also did the Corporation board on November 22. These supplementary annuities, purchased at retirement, were to be available at age seventy to those present pensionables who should reach age sixty-five on and after January 1, 1931.

Keppel's intentions were still fixed upon group annuities. Professor Henry R. Seager of Columbia supported Pritchett in his objection to use of the group principle in this situation. Finally, individual contracts prevailed. They were to yield $500 a year on the whole-life basis if purchased at retirement, and to carry actuarial equivalents between the ages of seventy and sixty-five and also widow-survivor pensions on option. At last upon this form of contract agreement came, although Pritchett pointed out that "an unforeseen breakdown of economic conditions would . . . prevent the Corporation from carrying out the promise." The fact that on January 26, 1929, Furst and Mattocks wanted to reserve the freedom of T.I.A.A. to change rates of supplementary contracts to accord with the Association's future interest earnings and mortality experience called forth from Keppel to Pritchett the comment: "I think I am justified in feeling that you and I have gotten beyond the state of mind that this paragraph reveals. . . . According to Mackenzie it is a theoretical rather than a practical matter, as there is an unusually wide margin of safety." Nevertheless, under the clauses of the New York State Insurance Law, the reservation stood.

THE "FINAL" SOLUTION

The present discussion pretends to be only a distillate of the mass of correspondence, notes, rejoinders, plans, counterproposals, resolutions, data, and other details that led to the ultimate adjustments and decisions which turned out to be probably the best that could be achieved in a discordant situation. The Corporation executive committee gave "full and sympathetic study" to a letter of Pritchett's to Keppel written after things had quieted a bit. Mattocks wanted to see the allowance pegged at $1,000 at age seventy, with the Corporation supplementing this sum by a $500 straight-life annuity contract. Officers of the Foundation hoped for a continuing investment return of 5 per cent in spite of the default in interest on Chicago, Milwaukee, and St. Paul Railway Company bonds held in the General Endowment Fund that had occurred in the spring of 1928. Reinvestment of proceeds resulting from the sale of the Foundation's remaining holdings in United States Steel Corporation 5 per cent bonds had increased both principal and income of the fund. On November 2, 1928, the Foundation's executive committee reported to the board on two plans for reducing benefits; at the twenty-third annual meeting the board adopted the more conservative which, on a sliding scale of ages, would in five years reduce the maximum allowance available at age seventy to $1,000 in 1937, and authorized communication to the presidents of the associated institutions of this action and its effect, including revised Rules, upon each future individual allowance. The matter was laid before a gathering of college presidents on November 16, 1928.

Two months later a draft of a formal legal agreement between the Corporation and the Teachers Insurance and Annuity Association pertaining to supplementary annuities for most of the Foundation beneficiaries had been worked out, and on January 24 a new version of the Foundation Rules was in draft form. Counsel cleared the legal aspects on or about February 6. On the next day, Keppel for the Corporation sent to presidents of seventy-six associated institutions, a printed statement of what the Corporation had agreed to do for 2,968 Foundation beneficiaries through T.I.A.A. by way of purchasing supplementary annuities, and Pritchett dispatched to them a letter enclosing copies of the new Rules, a list of each institution's pensionables, 3,422 in all, showing each individual's expectations from the Foundation. Supplementary letters contained the expectations of seven other pensionables. At last, four years after Keppel's entry into the matter, a solution had been achieved.

That solution, stated in briefest terms, was essentially as follows:

For all of the 3,422 pensionables, the Foundation out of its resources would pay retiring allowances based upon Rules still resembling in awkwardness and obscurity those of 1922 but scaled down to yield a maximum allowance of $1,000 at age seventy in 1932 and thereafter. Carnegie Corporation would purchase for each of 2,968 beneficiaries retiring for age a straight-life annuity from T.I.A.A. on an individual contract supplementing the $1,000 Foundation allowance by $500, with actuarial equivalent values for those retiring between age seventy and age sixty-five when the supplementary annuity would amount to $300 on the straight-life basis. Thus the total retiring stipend for 2,968 pensionables claiming it on the basis of age in 1932 and onward would be $1,500 a year at age seventy and $970 at age sixty-five, with provision for a widow continued by the Foundation as before, but available under the supplementary contract on an optional settlement. The prohibition upon teaching by retired professors was continued, and the Foundation's liability for certain T.I.A.A. annuity-contract holders in case of disability and for maintaining the 4½ per cent interest on Association annuity contracts still stood.

RESIDUES

Although no public announcement of the new scale of allowances was to be made until May 1, 1929, Pritchett's and Keppel's letters of February 7 produced an immediate effect. A few weeks after their dispatch Furst wrote to Pritchett at Santa Barbara: "There have been several appreciations of what the Foundation has done and will still do, and only three criticisms" from college presidents.

"A number of them somehow received the impression from the Rules that widows were no longer provided for. . . . There are numerous requests to have names put on the list, even now, and a very general desire to have a considerable number of the three hundred men who could have retired under the 1922 Rules still do so with a larger allowance. . . ." And later: "Correspondence with the colleges has been very large particularly with regard to retirements before May 1 and also with regard to contributory deferred annuities to supplement provisions by the Foundation and the Corporation. . . ." By mid-May new arrangements to supplement both Foundation allowances and Corporation annuities had been made by five institutions, while twenty-one were working on the matter.

Retrospectively Pritchett wrote: "It is interesting to note that the two boards at the end of three years of discussion have done the thing that I tried originally to get them to do;" and "I have some curiosity to know approximately at what the maximum allowance could have been placed had the trustees of the Foundation acted three years ago when I originally made the recommendation." The answer was "about 20 per cent higher than that which was finally adopted," that is, $1,200 at age seventy instead of $1,000. Indeed, Mattocks's figures turned out to have been more conservative than Mackenzie's, particularly because they were based upon data subsequent by three years to Mackenzie's and they seem to have more nearly forecast actual experience after January 1, 1928, in spite of Mackenzie's insistence upon minutiae and both actuaries' too liberal assumptions as to interest rates. Both men agreed upon certain other possible ways of cutting the load.

To Butler, Pritchett wrote somewhat bitterly: "Keppel with the best intentions has delayed us for nearly two years by his desire to regulate the details of the administration of the Foundation. He knows almost nothing of the questions involved. . . . The committee [of Foundation trustees] . . . accept any dictum from the president of the Corporation because they hope that in such agreement there lies a satisfactory appropriation."

And Furst reported that "a recent graduate of Harvard has just called to say that two professors there suggested he might find employment with us, in connection with 'Mr. Keppel's reorganization of the Foundation.' "

AFTER RETIREMENT, WHAT?

The Foundation's Rules, including those of 1929, had never permitted term-time college teaching during receipt of an allowance. The theory had been that the allowances were large enough to make this unnecessary. The prospect of the 1929 reduction brought a loud protest.

Organized at the University of Wisconsin, where Jastrow was teaching, the protest soon spread to twenty-six associated institutions, from which teachers assembled in New York City on April 13, 1929, and passed a resolution requesting the withdrawal of the prohibition on teaching in retirement contained in Rule 10. Jastrow had a valid case. After much correspondence and consultation, the executive committee recommended to the trustees that the ban be relaxed, and on November 20 the board amended Rule 10 to permit "teachers on the retired list to do part-time teaching for part-time remuneration." It was up to the executive committee to interpret the amendment.

For Furst, who bore most of the load of administrative detail, the vague phrasing of the Rule brought difficulties and vexation. At last, on September 20, there came a concrete request that a beneficiary be permitted to teach half-time for half-salary. The executive committee's decision was negative. There the matter hung; what the amended Rule 10 seemed to grant, the ruling appeared to refuse. Furst went on as best he could. The tangle was unsnarled only after Suzzallo took office as President.

TWILIGHT OF AN ERA

With the adoption of the Rules of 1929 and of the Corporation agreement to supplement allowances, Pritchett acted upon his growing determination to retire. At the twenty-fourth annual meeting, November 20, 1929, the trustees accepted his resignation, effective June 30, 1930, or later as he chose; elected Suzzallo as his successor; and, reluctant to relinquish Pritchett's administrative wisdom, voted him emeritus status with consultative functions and a generous retainer. They never showed greater wisdom. At first, Pritchett, although he felt the retiring allowance he was to receive was justifiable, was reluctant to accept the retainer. Furst, for his colleagues on the staff, reassured him, and so also did Suzzallo on several occasions. These views overcame Pritchett's apprehensiveness lest the stipend be regarded as too generous and make for prejudice against the Foundation. He relinquished the presidency to Suzzallo August 1, 1930.

For once the grounds of a resignation were clearly stated. Pritchett's letter cited the condition of his health which then made it advisable for him to remain outside New York City during most of the year, and his sincere conviction that, with the final adjustment of the Foundation's pensions, direction of the Foundation might well be entrusted to a younger man.

Although at one time or another Pritchett's views on various subjects had differed from those of almost every one of the trustees, all united in their appreciation of his services. As President-emeritus William Lowe Bryan of Indiana once wrote to Jessup: "No more severe criticisms [of Pritchett] were made than by members of the Board of Trustees in the meetings. . . . Dr. Pritchett found himself (as every executive does) in situations where he could not make explanation but must take criticism in silence." Moving to accept the resignation, Butler spoke with feeling of the man and his work mainly from the academic point of view. In seconding Butler's motion, Lamont, as a layman, praised Pritchett's educational discussions in the Annual Reports for their "store of information, opinion, and inspiration." Penniman opened a statement prepared for himself and his colleagues with these words: "The Carnegie Foundation was the joint creation of Dr. Pritchett and Mr. Carnegie, as were also the Carnegie Corporation of New York . . . and the Teachers Insurance and Annuity Association. . . ."

Certainly among Pritchett's greatest services must be reckoned the guidance he gave, sometimes very forcible, to Mr. Carnegie. Although both were men of strong will and independent thought, it has been indicated by one who should know, that in only one situation did their relations approach rupture. Pritchett's "role of diplomat in Carnegie interests," as Walter M. Gilbert put it, stood out "in interrelations of the various Carnegie organizations in which he had responsibility" and not infrequently "he served as interpreter of the Founder's wishes and interests." It is clear that one of Pritchett's best contributions was the form and force with which at innumerable points he sought to carry out Mr. Carnegie's benevolent intentions. Lamont emphasized a wider influence: ". . . While we naturally think of Dr. Pritchett first as a philosopher in education . . . in the world of affairs we look to him for clarity of thought and wise counsel. While Dr. Pritchett's repute has been enhanced by his direction of the Carnegie Foundation, we should remember also that he has brought added distinction to the Foundation through his outstanding service in other fields."

One who reads Pritchett's contributions to a quarter-century of Annual Reports recognizes them as the product of wisdom acquired through action and observation, long thought, ability in marshaling and bringing home facts, and the sincerity which arises from belief that a good cause is worth fighting for. It is true that they contain dogmatic passages, but those passages took the side of the angels. For Pritchett there was no compromise between what seemed right and just and what was or might prove to be popular.

Pritchett, for his part, valued the attitude of his board. "The trustees of the Foundation," he wrote just before he retired, "have given their executive the widest measure of freedom in the discussion of educational causes. At the end of twenty-five years of service, a retiring president can give no higher praise than this testimony."

With the coming of August 1930 an era closed in the life of the Carnegie Foundation.

Part Three ~ 1930-1945

~ 9 ~

Another Day

FUNCTIONAL APPRAISAL—AN ADMINISTRATIVE BUDGET; MEETINGS OF
THE TRUSTEES; WORK OF THE EXECUTIVE COMMITTEE · THE WORK-
ING OF THE NEW RULES—THE LIST OF PENSIONABLES · COMMIT-
MENTS FOR T.I.A.A.—ASSURANCES ABOUT T.I.A.A. OVERHEAD; DISA-
BILITY AND ASSOCIATION ANNUITY CONTRACTS · PENSION STUDIES OF
THE FOUNDATION · PROBLEMS OF RESERVE FUND NUMBER TWO ·
THE NEW BROOM AND EDUCATIONAL ENQUIRY—FINANCE; FOUNDA-
TION AND CORPORATION; STUDIES UNDER WAY · EXTRAMURAL ·
DEATH · INTERIM

HENRY SUZZALLO took office as second president of the Carnegie Foundation August 1, 1930, nearly ten months
after his election. His coming had been delayed by his commitments to the National Advisory Committee on Education, of which
he was director, and by certain editorial tasks. When he entered
upon his Foundation duties he had at hand Pritchett, president
emeritus, for counsel and advice, Furst, as the experienced secretary of the Foundation, three seasoned staff members—Learned,
Reed, and Savage—and a skilled group of assistants. All welcomed
him warmly.

Pritchett had followed Suzzallo's career with deep interest from
his early service at Teachers College, Columbia University, through
his brilliant presidency and its painful termination at the University of Washington, his return to Teachers College, a connection
he preferred above a number of eastern college presidencies, his
election as trustee of the Foundation in 1919, and his chairmanship of the board 1926-27. The Corporation-inspired inquiry into
graduate education was also in Suzzallo's hands. Although his own
and Pritchett's careers, points of view, and philosophies of educa-

193

tion contrasted sharply at many points, the esteem of the two men was mutual. Always modest, Suzzallo possessed immense intellectual curiosity and capacity for accomplishment, but his ambitions were never self-centered; his loyalties were to his predecessors, his colleagues, and the institutions he served. This devotion played like a forced draft upon the energy that he brought to his new tasks, an energy which, freely expended for both Foundation and Corporation, all too soon burned him out, but not until his accomplishments as scholar and philosopher in education, as teacher, and as administrator, not to mention his endearing personal qualities, had won him reputation throughout the land. Probably in no other quarter of the globe could a man of such humble origins have climbed so high in the affectionate respect of his fellows.

With the coming of so galvanizing a force to the Foundation operational changes were inevitable. During Suzzallo's first six months as president the faithful Furst, with nearly twenty years of experience, served as the Foundation's secretary. This fact, coupled with Pritchett's availability and Suzzallo's tact, effectually bridged the gap between administrations. But the operational load of the preceding five years had exacted from Furst a fearful toll, and Suzzallo began to feel that administrative improvement—if, indeed, any could be brought about—must come very gradually. Then, late in January 1931, Furst was stricken with a fatal illness. After consulting Learned and Reed, Suzzallo nominated and the executive committee, February 6, 1931, confirmed Savage as acting secretary. Furst died on leave of absence March 6, 1931, and on May 1 Savage succeeded him. So well did Suzzallo handle changes in the inner workings of the Foundation that the office group was scarcely conscious of them as they came to pass, in spite of being fully informed of them in advance.

FUNCTIONAL APPRAISAL

It was Suzzallo's conviction, grounded in many years of successful experience, that administration should be planned and conducted on a functional basis. Of this view the Carnegie Foundation of 1930 was scarcely an outstanding example. The situation teased Suzzallo, but he knew enough of recent Foundation history to realize that since 1925 for Pritchett and Furst the struggle had been not to operate on any theoretical basis but to get things done at all. On learning that Savage, Furst's fledgling successor, had started a detailed inventory of Foundation personnel, Suzzallo not only encouraged him but extended it into other phases of operations. As results began to emerge Suzzallo at once put them to work, using a large notebook of jottings and diagrams that he constructed in his characteristic green ink. Among first results was a table of office organization, which he discussed somewhat apologetically with Savage as "a sledge hammer used to kill a mosquito," but which immensely clarified duties, procedures, and relationships.

An Administrative Budget

Not since the early days had the Foundation operated upon an administrative budget. Furst had regarded budgeting as impossible because, he pointed out, no one could estimate from year to year the annual load of retiring allowances and pensions. Suzzallo approached the matter from the other end of the maze, by insisting that administration was the first charge upon income, for without administrative personnel and machinery no benefits could be paid.

One morning in mid-April 1931, Suzzallo asked Savage if he intended to have a budget for the fiscal year 1931-32 ready to present to the executive committee at its meeting of May 1. The reply was negative, as Suzzallo, of course, knew it would be from previous talks with Furst. "All right," said Suzzallo and his eyes held an anticipatory twinkle, "we'll make one." And president and secretary set about the task. While Savage reviewed the expenditures for the preceding five years, Suzzallo drew up a budget form, complete and entirely logical if somewhat cumbersome, which with simplifications and adaptations has been in use ever since. Savage developed a system of detailed controls and checks, and on May 1 the president secured executive committee approval of a serviceable summary and of a suitable accounting procedure.

This budget totaled some $131,200. Its operation gave the first demonstration of clarification through definition of function that the Foundation had had for at least twenty years. At once it pointed the way to a more economical conduct of the work, but equally important was its smoothing of operations even regarding the Board of Trustees and the executive committee.

Meetings of the Trustees

Suzzallo's views on the value of functional organization and administration amounted almost to a prepossession. The time between his coming to the Foundation and the twenty-fifth annual meeting was too short to alter trustee procedure, long established, and Pritchett's presence at the last such gathering he expected to attend made Suzzallo reluctant to introduce changes. Nevertheless, the annual meeting of 1930 was the first for a quarter-century in which the minutes were kept by a professional secretary; Furst, in the words of the record, was "appointed to act as recording secretary for the meeting."

For the meeting of 1931 Suzzallo prepared himself thoroughly. Somewhat as Pritchett had done in 1920, he set forth in detail his conception of the functions and work of the Foundation. The minutes, kept by Savage as Furst's successor, digest his remarks:

> Upon the death of Mr. Furst, who served as secretary of both the Foundation and the Association, and the consequent promotion of Mr. Savage to the secretaryship of the Foundation, the resulting vacancy in the staff was not filled. There has followed a redistribution of functions in the activities of the Foundation, which now may be classified under two general heads: first, those relating to the retiring allowances and pensions of the Foundation; second, those pertaining to educational enquiry and consultation. Under the second heading there are now three divisions of work: (1) studies and efforts looking to the improvement of instruction, with which Mr. Learned is principally concerned; (2) studies bearing upon professional education, with which Mr. Reed is principally concerned; (3) studies concerning organization and administration in higher education, with which the president and Mr. Savage are concerned. The resulting emphasis upon the functions of the staff is proving itself to be useful not only to the Foundation but also to Carnegie Corporation of New York and especially to those who as administrators in numerous educational institutions have occasion to consult members of the Foundation's staff.

One or two points here suggested require emphasis: First, Suzzallo looked forward through a transitional stage to the complete administrative separation of the Teachers Insurance and Annuity Association from the Foundation and to closer co-operation with Carnegie Corporation of New York, processes already well under way, as will be shown later. Secondly, the functional approach had broken the ruts into which the Foundation's work had begun to fall. Thirdly, whereas Pritchett had had to devote his concluding years in office to pension problems and much of the annual meetings to detailed and rather technical discussion of them, Suzzallo, mindful of the settlement of 1929, seized the opportunity to open the windows upon a wider vista which refreshed the somewhat jaded board and imparted new emphasis and meaning to its sessions. Lastly, whereas Pritchett's later practice had been to hold his own remarks and those from the floor strictly to the business in hand, Suzzallo with his magic persuasiveness gave the trustees their heads in discussion and let them talk, even up to the point of irrelevance. To a group accustomed to think aloud this proved welcome indeed. The impetus carried over through the twenty-eighth annual meeting, when Pritchett presided after Suzzallo's death, and even into the presidency of Jessup.

In the Twenty-sixth Annual Report (1931) Suzzallo wrote, and meant:

> It is the Foundation's function, now and in the future, to aid the educational profession and the public to define and solve [important current problems in education] by careful survey, scholarly inquiry, scientific research, skillful demonstration, and, above all, by careful analysis and constructive suggestion based on all the accurate facts at hand.

This was probably the most carefully reasoned statement of the Foundation's function in educational inquiry that had been made up to that time.

Work of the Executive Committee

Upon the proceedings of the executive committee, where Foundation policy and operation centered, Suzzallo exercised an influence at least as vivifying as he exerted upon the board. Results of the 1929 adjustments in the Rules, coupled with the general economic situation and its bearing upon the financing of the Foundation, coming under Suzzallo's close scrutiny in the course of his operational inventory, invited his attention. Once he had acquired a working knowledge of the Foundation's problems he sought to meet them with speed and precision through executive committee action.

Up to March 1931 he accomplished little. Thereafter he hewed fast and hard. He was fortunate in dealing with a seasoned committee, of whom three were Founder-appointed trustees (Butler, Franks, and Vanderlip), two (Ferry of Hamilton, and Penniman) were, like Butler, thoroughly experienced academic administrators, and none was inhospitable to change. By carefully planning each meeting and leaving nothing to chance, by introducing both provisional and final agenda containing as many drafts of votes as possible, especially for routine action, and by resorting to no surprise proposals Suzzallo was able to reduce the frequency and length of meetings. A new form for minutes and references to them proved useful. For the first time the dates of regular meetings were set a year and more in advance—for the Fridays nearest the seventh of January, May, and October, a schedule adhered to strictly for nearly two decades with benefit to all.

Suzzallo's growing concern with the possible effects of the deepening financial depression upon both principal and income of Foundation funds led to designation, January 8, 1932, of a subcommittee of the executive committee to oversee the investments of the Foundation, operating through S. S. Hall, Jr., assistant treasurer and investment officer, and reporting to the executive committee. Consisting of Vanderlip, chairman, Franks, the Foundation treasurer, and, ex officio, Suzzallo, the Finance Subcommittee was to hold office at the executive committee's pleasure. The group held its organization meeting January 14, and for some time thereafter met once a fortnight or oftener. It intensified for the Foundation alone the work of the finance committee of the T.I.A.A., which since 1924 had passed upon lists of securities from which approved investments suitable to the purposes of the Foundation had been culled for purchase.

With Suzzallo as president the executive committee's work, while increasingly conservative, began to gain in definition and effectiveness through the vigorous precision with which he attacked operational problems. This sort of thing is reflected in the handling of budgets under the working of the Rules of 1929, in coming to grips with four commitments of the Foundation to the Association, and in extension and modification of the work of the Division of Educational Enquiry.

THE WORKING OF THE NEW RULES

Round about the Rules for the Granting of Retiring Allowances 1929 there existed, as it were, a delimiting relationship with Carnegie Corporation of New York. The Corporation's agreement of March 1929 to supplement with immediate Association annuities most of the Foundation's retiring allowances, as well as its gift, since 1918, of two Reserve Funds, imposed upon the Foundation a certain restraint, tacit for the most part but perhaps the more potent for that reason, which bred a more conservative policy in granting allowances and recognizing eligibility. As early as April 3, 1928, the board had voted "not to add any further names to the list of those eligible for retiring allowances," and this action appears to have acquired some of the force of a consideration in the Corporation's decision to supplement Foundation benefits. Certainly Suzzallo regarded it as such and guided his executive committee to observe it.

Furst had wrestled long and hard with individual cases involving term-time teaching after retirement, which had resulted from the relaxing of Rule 10. Suzzallo had planned to lay the matter before the executive committee on February 6, 1931. Furst's illness deprived the committee of his help and advice, but on Suzzallo's pressing for some sort of solution it voted that beneficiaries might teach part-time in an academic year "provided the work given at no time exceeds something less than half a full-time load, and that remuneration is also something less than half of the full salary."

This was a step, albeit hasty, in the right direction, but it left unanswered two questions: What is a full-time load, and, What is *the* full salary? In the two cases decided as precedents discussion showed that the committee clearly had in mind the last active academic salaries. As the months went by, cases arising demonstrated that in view of the wide differences in salary scales of associated institutions the key to the puzzle was the individual record. Over the problem Suzzallo and Savage toiled, and then consulted individuals of the executive committee. At last the officers decided that there was only one way to approximate fairness for all: The last active year of teaching provided the measuring sticks for both compensation and program under "the part-time interpretation" of Rule 10 which obtained until about 1940.

The List of Pensionables

No rent in the administrative fabric seems at this writing to have been too small for Suzzallo's attention. He sought and procured executive committee action upon a number of questions, all previously discussed with Pritchett, which now appear mere odds and ends but which, clarified, contributed much to smoothness of operation: the size of editions for publications; publications in storage; the vacating of Learned's absurd title of "assistant secretary," which had honored neither Learned nor the Foundation; the title of "actuarial consultant" for Mattocks, tardy enough recognition of his work; the question whether the board should next meet in Washington, under Cadwalader's not very positive opinion of twenty-five years before; reaffirmation of the vote of 1926 to pay benefits through institutions; payment of Canadian allowances; bargaining for places on the list of pensionables through substitution of names; a positive prohibition of back-dating, which Mattocks had long favored. None of these matters now seems to have approached in importance Suzzallo's handling of the eligible list.

In this he had at the back of his mind the new and intensified relation between the Foundation and Carnegie Corporation of New York. After the distribution, February 7, 1929, of the lists of institutional eligibles, the trustee policy of 1928 not to add names to these lists had been adhered to, except for restoration to eligibility of persons omitted through other errors than their own. A considerable number of these cases, always vexatious, had arisen up to the spring of 1931.

Now, Mattocks had long favored a closed list of pensionables and had won Savage to his view. The barrier had been the fear of possible injustice in omission of names by institutional error. With the restorations occasioned by the distribution, verification, and return of the lists of February 7, 1929, subsiding, Mattocks and Savage laid the whole matter before Suzzallo. Although they stressed the fact that no new names had been added since June 7, 1930, probably the argument that convinced him was that the Corporation had based its March 1929 agreement with the Association on a closed and final list for supplementary annuities. At last Suzzallo asked Savage if he could compile a definitive list of Foundation pensionables. The task, although laborious and exacting, took a comparatively short time, but in the face of custom a deal of nerve to authorize. Then came the proposal to print the list and distribute it confidentially to institutions. Over this Suzzallo did not hesitate. Pritchett thought well of the notion. On May 1, 1931, a printed roster of 3,190 names was laid before the executive committee, which on Suzzallo's recommendation adopted it as in fact a Closed List of Pensionables, to which no restorations or additions have since been made. The principle that institutions themselves were to sustain the consequences of their omission of names followed almost as a corollary. The extent to which this single vote and its results simplified the administration of the Foundation's benefits almost passes belief.

COMMITMENTS FOR T.I.A.A.

Even with the clarification of many matters internal to the Foundation there remained for solution a number of problems related to the Foundation's offspring, the Teachers Insurance and Annuity Association. Pritchett's resignation as the Association's president raised anew the old question of dual presidencies. It was debated warmly. President Keppel, of the Corporation, wanted the Association completely separated from the Foundation, with no administrative officers doubling in duties; he argued that this was fundamental to winning anew the confidence of the teachers. Pritchett did not agree; he believed that inasmuch as the close relation between the Foundation and the Association had brought the Association many policyholders the two posts ought to be as intimately related in the future as they had been in the past. How far he pressed this view does not appear. The issue was decided otherwise by the Association's choice of Professor James W. Glover, head of the Department of Mathematics at the University of Michigan, with the financial blessing of Carnegie Corporation. Thus, the Association appeared to be freed of that Foundation influence which in some quarters may have retarded its advancement. In these matters it is doubtful if Suzzallo was much consulted.

He was not slow to see that the economic depression then besetting the nation might seriously affect the discharge of certain commitments of the Foundation in behalf of the Association. These had long been of record. The potential seriousness of some of them Pritchett seems never to have fully appreciated, although for one or two he had laid a groundwork which might ultimately have proved palliative. The fact now seems to be that both he and Furst habitually referred to certain "guarantees" by the Foundation in behalf of the Association which were not guarantees at all, but declarations of intent, with safeguarding conditions expressed or implied. On the abrogation in 1928 of one such provision, Suzzallo's concern was as to how far other declarations might or should be made effective.

Assurances about T.I.A.A. Overhead

On April 22, 1918, the Foundation trustees had voted measures designed to assure the new Association, first, an annual return of 4½ per cent on deferred annuity contracts purchased by certain teachers in associated institutions, and second, ultimate self-government through election of its governing board by its policyholders. The first of these measures had been terminated as of January 4, 1928, on the ground that no occasion to apply it had arisen. The second, which affected both Corporation and Foundation, was by 1930 well on the way to caring for itself. But on the same day also the trustees of the Foundation had resolved to take up the slack when the reasonable expenses of T.I.A.A. should exceed the return from the invested capital and surplus provided by the Corporation; in other words, when they passed $50,000 a year. The first payment by the Foundation under this resolution was made June 7, 1918, for legal services. By 1925 such expenditures had come to be regarded as an annual burden, and by 1931 they were amounting to a considerable sum each year, paid from the Emergency Reserve Fund.

Now, by June 30, 1931, this fund had receded from about $525,000 in 1925 to $319,094, owing to drafts for studies in the Division of Educational Enquiry but especially to appropriations for Association overhead. In 1929 there had been talk of the Corporation's taking over this load, but Keppel preferred, in view of certain Corporation commitments to the Foundation, that the Foundation should carry the Association's excess overhead until October 1933. By January 1931, total payments by the Foundation on this account had reached $283,733.

Keppel had the impression that the Emergency Reserve Fund, like Reserves One and Two, had come from Carnegie Corporation of New York. The fact was that over the years it had been built up out of unused income from the Foundation's General Endowment Fund. Although it was badly titled it was the only Foundation reserve which could be spent for general needs as they arose.

Grants for Association overhead were depleting it too rapidly to suit Suzzallo. At his urging the executive committee discussed the matter in January and May 1932. The Corporation did not see its way to pay the excess overhead of the Association beginning in October 1932. Meanwhile the question of a reserve against liabilities under Section C of the Rules had been solved, but only by earmarking for the purpose a considerable portion of the sum remaining in the Emergency Reserve. Indeed, the situation had become so serious that in April 1932 Suzzallo and Keppel concluded negotiations under which book values of Emergency Reserve Fund securities, as sold under the necessity of meeting Foundation payments to support the Association, were to be underwritten by the Corporation. According to this agreement, the Corporation made up differences totaling $17,383 for certain sales. The Foundation's final payment on account of Association overhead was made in December 1932. As of the end of that month these payments had totaled $508,795.97. Thereafter the Corporation assumed the burden which under Corporation trustee action had impended since 1924.

Disability and Association Annuity Contracts

The initial decision that the Teachers Insurance and Annuity Association should not offer disability protection (as the term is usually understood) had been taken largely in deference to Pritchett's views. As a means of meeting the teacher's need of some such protection the Foundation's Rules of 1918 and thereafter have contained a provision to the general effect that besides the regular disability-retirement privileges afforded pensionables, the Foundation in the case of certain nonpensionable Association annuity-contract holders would pay an allowance for life, to the disabled policyholder only, provided he assigned his annuity contract to the Foundation. This arrangement was to be open to those entering associated institutions after November 17, 1915, up to January 1, 1938. As of April 1931 the single case in which it had been invoked had cost the Foundation $335. But the protection it afforded was apparently much appreciated by those eligible, and the publications of both the Association and the Foundation, under Pritchett and Furst, had frequently stressed it.

Now, disability insurance had long troubled insurance companies and with at least one it had wrought havoc. Since 1928 Mattocks had been apprehensive regarding costs under Section C because of the potential unknowable risks involved for the Foundation. In the spring of 1931 he discussed it more than once with Suzzallo and Savage; his view was that "while the absolutely safe thing to do would be to terminate this provision as early as consistent with dignity," in any event the terminal date should be shifted forward five years. Pritchett saw "no real reason for this action," but Suzzallo, mindful of the drain, past and prospective, upon the Emergency Reserve Fund for underwriting the Association's excess overhead and for certain sums that had been drawn from the Emergency Reserve for studies and publications in the Division of Educational Enquiry, wished fervently to reduce the risks. After deliberation he followed Mattocks's counsel in proposing that the terminal date for those eligible to the privileges of Section C should be advanced from 1938 to 1933, and that the capital of the Emergency Reserve Fund should be brought up to $200,000, which should be earmarked to sustain the section. Both executive committee and board acquiesced in appropriate measures. The board went even further: It authorized the recodification of Section C, for purposes of clarity only, and by early 1933 the whole matter had been adjusted. Thus, by January 1933, mainly through Suzzallo's farseeing efforts, the Foundation had been freed of two perilous burdens which many believed it should never have assumed: the responsibility for the Association's overhead, and half a decade of a latent but incalculable financial commitment.

Five years later the success of the codification of Section C led to further clarification of all the Rules.

PENSION STUDIES OF THE FOUNDATION

Since 1905, even before the New York State incorporation, the Carnegie Foundation had studied pensions and retirement. Results had been published in each Annual Report and in five Bulletins. These studies and discussions had been prepared by Pritchett, Bowman, Sayre, Furst, Kandel, Mattocks, and Savage, in succession and also in co-operation. They dealt in more or less detail with 688 pension plans: for college and university teachers 45; for other teachers 246; for clergymen 45; for industrial, business, military and naval personnel, and for other professions than teaching 300; in other countries than the United States 32; governmental old age pensions 20. The world had been combed for material. It included all known available discussions in the field, all discoverable plans or proposals and comments thereon, all obtainable material on insurance company offerings, all legislative enactments and bills, municipal, county, state, and governmental, all reports, printed or otherwise, all systems in operation, including company reports in which pensions were referred to. The Foundation's pension collection was widely known, and its discussions of retirement reached an influential though never a large body of readers. As Pritchett approached his own retirement he had written that the Foundation's publications in the field of pensions "constitute the most complete review of the pension problem to be found in any one source. They have been prepared with great care and have proved invaluable for the use of colleges, schools, state systems of education, and even for

pension systems in industrial and commercial organizations. They
have perhaps done more to inculcate sound principles in retirement
legislation than any other single cause." No one has ever questioned
this statement and it is doubtful if it could be refuted. The most
valid objection to its purport has been that the forty-odd discussions, which run to at least 1,000 printed pages, vary in estimating
the values of individual provisions in some of the plans they treat,
a variation explicable by the number of hands that prepared them
and the advance in knowledge during the quarter-century they
cover. These discussions and the advisory services which comple-
mented them, pertaining to at least 2,000 pension plans and proposals, were unique in extent, utility, and influence.

Useful though these studies proved to the Foundation in its own
functions and in the devising of T.I.A.A., as well as to others who
benefited from them, by 1931 the development of pension theory
had pretty well caught up with them, their nature and preparation
had begun to partake of the routine, not to say the perfunctory,
and their utility had certainly waned. All this Suzzallo regretfully
discovered through talks with Pritchett, Savage, and others, and
through his own scrutiny. What to do?

The answer came partly from his functional approach to all such
problems, partly from necessity. Savage's work as secretary of the
Foundation and director of the fading athletic inquiry left him
scant time to study pensions, reflect and write upon them, and consult about retirement provisions, old and especially new. Indeed,
advisory activities were already taking precedence over all phases
of this work. On the other hand, the Association was well suited
in both purpose and personnel to carry it forward. Talks with
Pritchett, Glover, Savage, and others quickly brought Suzzallo to
the decision upon which he acted. As of June 30, 1931, he transferred the Foundation's external pension studies to the T.I.A.A.,
where Dr. R. B. Robbins, secretary, pursued them for a number
of years, and the office of the Foundation knew them no more.

These pension studies of the Foundation had proved their value
in four directions: First, in shaping Foundation policy, framing
rules, and administering both; secondly, as blazing the trail towards
T.I.A.A. and emphasizing the merits of contractual annuities, fund-
ing pensions in advance, the legally enforceable contract, and strict
actuarial supervision; thirdly, the financial relations with Carnegie
Corporation, as first demonstrated in 1925-26, and their utility to
the Corporation traceable in a Corporation grant, 1916-17, of more

than $324,000 to a denominational pension fund. Fourthly, outside the Foundation and the Corporation these studies affected provisions for teachers retirement in most states of the Union. To their influence are traceable many of the soundest provisions in industrial and company pension plans, especially those reinsured through life insurance companies. They probably indirectly influenced some of the better provisions of Federal Social Security Acts. It is not clear that they had much restraining effect upon veterans' pensions or upon the United States Civil Service or other federal plans. In the spring of 1943 the Foundation's collection of pension materials, containing well over a thousand items, was deposited in the New York Public Library.

After 1931 the Foundation took even more of its own medicine in intensifying scrutiny, actuarial and expert, of its own problems; it was in Suzzallo's administration that Mattocks completed the first real study that had been made of Reserve Fund Number Two.

PROBLEMS OF RESERVE FUND NUMBER TWO

During the autumn of 1931 Mattocks argued for an actuarial valuation of Reserve Fund Number Two. Bent upon exploring every cranny, Suzzallo readily acquiesced. Data were as of December 31, 1931.

The work was not wholly actuarial. Examination of the terms surrounding some of the Reserve Two grants revealed loose ends in three for which terminal action of some sort appeared overdue. With executive committee approval, Suzzallo at once pressed for adjustments and got them. They, of course, increased very materially the estimated value of the resources remaining in the Fund.

Mattocks estimated that the present value of the Fund's obligations, as against par value of bonds amounting to $699,000, left a possible leeway of about $97,000, which he held to be an "absolute minimum" as a factor of safety under existing conditions. A larger study pertaining to the whole pension load underlay measures taken during Jessup's administration, although Suzzallo laid it before the executive committee May 5, 1933, and Pritchett presented it to the Board of Trustees after Suzzallo's death.

THE NEW BROOM AND EDUCATIONAL ENQUIRY

Suzzallo's explorations soon led him to the Division of Educational Enquiry. His functional rearrangement of responsibilities and fields for himself and members of the staff was only one of the results. Other contributions to the division's operations manifested themselves in its financing, in a new relationship to Carnegie Corporation of New York, and in its studies.

Finance

Between 1927 and 1929 costs of studies and publications had almost obliterated the Division's accumulated surplus. In 1929 some $40,000 had to be loaned, as it were, by the Emergency Reserve Fund to the Division for tests used in the Pennsylvania Study. During the next twelvemonth an additional $35,000 was advanced from the same source to help defray printing costs for the American athletic bulletins and to assist the Pennsylvania inquiry. After going thoroughly into this situation Suzzallo raised it with the Finance Subcommittee, with and through which he often worked in other matters than investment, and it agreed with him that these sums should be restored to the Emergency Reserve, particularly in view of possible drafts on account of Section C of the Rules. This the executive committee directed, and it was accomplished forthwith.

If Suzzallo had lived longer a recommendation he originated with the Subcommittee might have had important results. It was to the effect that "the policy be adopted of defraying in advance the cost of issuing bulletins and other publications of the Division . . . , earmarking funds over an appropriate number of years in advance of issue." The recommendation lapsed at his death.

Foundation and Corporation

It became increasingly clear, first, that the income of the Division's endowment, about $50,000 a year, might be endangered by defaults in certain interest payments, and that, secondly, even if it were not, it would be insufficient for Learned's costly Pennsylvania Study, to which the Foundation was heavily committed. Suzzallo devised with Keppel an interrelationship between the Corporation and the Foundation in which the Corporation not only furnished most of the funds needed for that study, but developed a program of joint projects which is more fully described in Chapter

10. Financial stringency forbade repetition of such a grant as that which the Foundation in 1926 had made, in the amount of $5,000, to the Institute of International Education for publication of a *Handbook for American Students in France* and "other purposes . . . germane to the purposes of the Division of Educational Enquiry," one of the very few direct grants for projects ever made by the Foundation.

Studies Under Way

During Suzzallo's years as president he accomplished several difficult tasks which, probably by agreement, Pritchett had left for him. In the spring of 1931 he wisely terminated the American athletic inquiry before it went to seed. Yet its counseling functions continued; between January 8 and May 6, 1932, it advised with fourteen universities, two associations, one four-year college, and one junior college about minor changes in the structure and conduct of athletics or physical education. The whole six-year enterprise had taken close to $115,000, all costs included. Suzzallo also, as of April 21, 1931, terminated the study of dental education, which had cost only $64,520 during its nine years, and which was producing more discords than harmony. Freed of these two encumbrances Suzzallo pressed on to other work.

For Reed he nominally had opened the field of professional education, although Reed clung to legal education and continued to prepare his Annual Review, which the National Conference of Bar Examiners wanted expanded to meet certain statistical needs, largely its own, a request upon which the executive committee took no action —this in spite of one resolution commending Reed's work from the Pennsylvania State Board of Law Examiners and another from the National Conference itself. On formal request of the provincial university Learned, in the midst of expanding his Pennsylvania Study, found time under the auspices of Carnegie Corporation to undertake with Chancellor E. W. Wallace, of Victoria University, Toronto, a short informal inquiry into higher education in Saskatchewan, which resulted in the thirty-page Bulletin Number 27. Its bearing on the humanities was close to Suzzallo's heart.

Local Provision for Higher Education in Saskatchewan, 1932, by Learned and Wallace, foreword by Suzzallo, is a gem of clarity, discernment, brevity, and tactful decision. Familiar with the problems it treated, Wallace collected most of the material, while Learned wrote the text. On the questions involved Learned brought to bear all of his American and European experience in a document of sound educational advice. The Bulletin had no superior among publications of the Foundation. Its best testimonial was the fact that most of its advice was accepted. To the cost of publication Carnegie Corporation contributed $400.

There was occupation aplenty for all. A review of memorandum files from 1931 onwards reveals an astonishing amount of advisory and historical work by Foundation staff members that was directly or indirectly related to the work of Carnegie Corporation. In that year, for example, Pritchett prepared a paper, unpublished, which although principally devoted to the inter-relationships of the Corporation, the Foundation, and the Association, would rank high in any appraisal of foundation policy-making. As for the monumental Pennsylvania Study, under Learned, it was making excellent progress in spreading the gospel of new-type comprehensive examinations and the cumulative record covering the full period of secondary preparation for college. In addition to assisting two western state universities to adjust to statewide educational plans, Suzzallo himself provided the motive power for a study of state higher education in California, 1931-32, supported jointly by that state and by Carnegie Corporation of New York, the excellence of which, discernible in the state-published Report of the Commission of Seven, deserved a better fate than befell it. With work of such magnitude and difficulty consuming Suzzallo's time and energy, he and the executive committee naturally saw no way to make other surveys of particular institutions or of higher education in other states, however challenging requests might appear.

EXTRAMURAL

It was perhaps to be expected that Suzzallo's geniality and administrative wisdom should draw to his office large numbers of visitors seeking advice upon the organization and operation of universities. His suggestions as to the filling of college and other presidencies met with what now seems to have been notable success. In more than one instance he sought to deter college officers from resigning, a somewhat unusual course. Relations with academic associations and societies took color from his cordiality. With the National Association of State Universities, the American Council on Education, especially its Problems and Plans Committee and its Central Committee on Personnel, the National Education Association, and even with the American Association of University Professors, whose Committee on Pensions in March 1930 had issued a report somewhat less intransigeant than usual, Suzzallo worked influentially and wholeheartedly. Pritchett's services to Carnegie Corporation Suzzallo both supplemented and himself extended; here as elsewhere he filled time and again the role of pacificator. The burden of these relationships rather increased than diminished during his thirty-eight months incumbency. At no time did he fail to carry it with acumen and good humor.

DEATH

The pace that Suzzallo maintained must have told upon an even stronger constitution than his. The summer of 1933 he spent at Palo Alto in hopes of rest and quiet, hopes that could not be fulfilled. In the second week of September he and Mrs. Suzzallo started for New York City via Winnipeg, taking a steamer from San Francisco to Seattle. While at Palo Alto, he had shown evidences of strain, and during the voyage he suffered from a certain restlessness. On September 18 he was so weak that he was taken from the ship and placed in a hospital for rest and diagnosis. At first he appeared to improve, but his already impaired heart failed him, and on September 25 he died.

The shock to his colleagues and friends was extreme. His death left the Foundation without a directing head, no successor being provided for in the bylaws, but, thanks to help and counsel from Livingston Farrand, chairman of the board, and Butler, the work went forward. Pritchett hastened back from Santa Barbara to New York. On November 15 the executive committee "agreed informally that Dr. Pritchett [should] continue his present special services until the new president takes office"; he might well have been designated acting president, as he assumed he had been.

In Milbank Memorial Chapel, December 18, 1933, about three hundred persons attended a service in Suzzallo's memory arranged by Carnegie Corporation, of which, of course, he had been, ex officio, a trustee. Keppel presided, and the speakers were Dean William F. Russell, of Teachers College; Arnold Bennett Hall, of the Brookings Institution, Washington; and President Butler of Columbia. A brochure containing the proceedings in full was printed by the Merrymount Press, at the expense of Carnegie Corporation, and issued by the Foundation in 1934.

INTERIM

Pritchett's main task was now to find a successor to Suzzallo, a difficult matter at best but especially exacting in view of the relations, financial and otherwise, with Carnegie Corporation. If refutation were to be sought for the charge that Pritchett was autocratic it could be readily found in his long talks with Learned, Reed, and Savage, and the closeness with which he listened to their opinions and suggestions. He sought also the views of each individual trustee. The response was generous in quantity and, prevailingly, in quality, as regards Foundation policy and qualifications to be sought. By November 25 one candidate was clearly leading. Six days later a name was presented to the executive committee, which had already authorized preliminary negotiations and had directed that the ballot be taken by mail. Voting proceeded until December 8, when, the choice thus far being unanimous, Pritchett formally tendered the presidency of the Foundation to Walter Albert Jessup, president of the State University of Iowa, a trustee of the Foundation since 1932 and Suzzallo's intimate friend. A vote or two that straggled in up to December 15 only reinforced the unanimity of the board, and public announcement was made at once. The only adverse comment within the board, as far as known, was the suggestion by a single trustee that the process of choice was a device to narrow the list of candidates to the executive committee's own man. The record clearly shows that this was not the fact. Jessup took office May 1, 1934.

～ 10 ～

Harvest

CROP FOR THE REAPING · INTERNAL PROJECTS OR "TO" GRANTS—
STATE HIGHER EDUCATION IN CALIFORNIA; THE PENNSYLVANIA
STUDY: "THE STUDENT AND HIS KNOWLEDGE"; "AN EXPERIMENT IN
RESPONSIBLE LEARNING"; GRADUATE EDUCATION: "STUDIES IN EARLY
GRADUATE EDUCATION"; MERITS OF THE JOINT PROJECT ARRANGE-
MENT · EXTERNAL PROJECTS ON "THROUGH" GRANTS—THE EURO-
PEAN EXAMINATIONS INQUIRY; SECONDARY SCHOOL AND COLLEGE—
THE "EIGHT-YEAR STUDY"; THE OWATONNA PROJECT; FOR THE
SOUTH; OTHER "THROUGH" PROJECTS; PROJECTS WITH "SUPPLE-
MENTARY PUBLICATIONS"

MUCH of the buoyancy and pleasurable activity that characterized Suzzallo's regime, especially as regards educational inquiries and projects of Carnegie Corporation and the
Foundation, was due to the impact of his personality upon conditions that already existed in August 1930 when he came to the presidency. Thanks partly to Pritchett, by that time a pattern was
already in being. It is not to be supposed that Suzzallo lacked discernment or invention, or that he was ever content to let matters
wander their own way without trying to guide, develop, and improve them. The facts need emphasis that in reference to educational undertakings on grants Pritchett had countenanced and fostered a series of relationships which, while far from perfect, had,
by and large, high merit and promise, and that thus Suzzallo was
freed to develop and adapt those which most commended themselves
to his energizing imagination.

In other words, Suzzallo apparently sensed that for three or
four years his work would resemble the cultivating, weeding, and
partial reaping of a crop that had begun to sprout before Pritchett

relinquished active duty. This is not to imply that Suzzallo accepted the situation, or any other for that matter, without thorough initial examination. Such would have been alien to his every quality. Instead he analyzed, often graphically, and pondered, terminated some activities, such as the studies of college athletics, pensions, and dental education, and chose for development those inquiries and relationships which he deemed most promising for his own day and for the future of the Foundation, the Corporation, and the American public and its educational welfare.

CROP FOR THE REAPING

The situation was not simple. Following Mr. Carnegie's intention, many times expressed, Carnegie Corporation of New York had twice protected the Foundation from financial disaster to its pension load. At the same time, the Corporation was not averse to utilizing the Foundation's prestige in educational inquiry and its experience, already considerable, in handling external projects. The income of the Division of Educational Enquiry was at most insufficient to support certain very costly work that was both pressing and highly promising. On the other hand, the Corporation, especially Keppel as its president, saw possibilities in boldly undertaking certain ventures which the Foundation was well fitted to supervise and sponsor. The Corporation scarcely needed outside financial help. For its fiscal year 1930-31, income from the total capital assets in its main fund of more than $145,859,000 exceeded $6,-609,000. It could be spent only in the United States. For the corresponding period the Foundation's Division of Educational Enquiry had total assets whose market value had dropped to $1,144,-225, although its annual income was holding up well at $53,675 in spite of two comparatively heavy investments somewhat questionable as to future return. Whether or not the matter had been discussed previously by Keppel and Pritchett, at any rate Suzzallo and Keppel devised a sort of compact under which, with formal approval, the Corporation was to furnish the Foundation $100,000 annually for joint and special projects. To Suzzallo this must have seemed a godsend and it probably was, even if not dissimilar arrangements were made at the same time between the Corporation and other philanthropies associated with Mr. Carnegie's name. For the Corporation and the Foundation the advantages were many and mutual.

Roughly the projects affected by this co-operative arrangement fell into two categories: (1) those internal to the Foundation, carried on partly or wholly by Foundation officers or staff members, in which the Foundation exercised full control of expenditure of funds once received, and results of which were generally published by the Foundation, usually as Bulletins; (2) those external to the Foundation, whether initiated by it or by the Corporation, for which the Foundation received Corporation funds and transmitted them to other operating bodies, and over which the Foundation might and often did exercise a modicum of advice or persuasion. For the second type, results were issued sometimes by the Foundation in supplementary publications, more often by other bodies or publishers. This statement, however, involves numerous exceptions and represents rather a theory than invariable practice.

To the first type of project belong the Foundation's California inquiry—although full results were published by the State—the Pennsylvania Study, which brought forth two Foundation Bulletins, Numbers 29 and 31, and the study of graduate education, as Suzzallo relinquished it, and as reported in Bulletins Number 28 and 30 and one volume issued as a supplementary publication, and in several other documents thus classified. These three ventures yielded extended discussions in several Annual Reports. Among external or "through" joint projects may be numbered some which might have been more closely connected with the Division of Educational Enquiry had its staff been larger, and for which results were instead published in the supplementary series. Other external projects operated entirely outside the Foundation.

This attempt to classify the ninety-odd joint or special projects of the Foundation and Corporation deals in generalities only, which exceptions test at almost every point. The policies and modes of procedure which the classification, however faulty, reflects endured much longer than the men who devised them.

INTERNAL PROJECTS OR "TO" GRANTS

Beginnings of three studies carried on within the Foundation offices have already been suggested in Chapter 9: the California Study, completed in less than ten months; the Pennsylvania Study, which ran for as many years; and the study of graduate education begun by Suzzallo in 1927, which contributed even to the enterprise terminated in 1948 by the merging of the Graduate Record Examination project with Educational Testing Service, Inc.

State Higher Education in California

Suzzallo felt that the heyday of the educational survey was over and that the Foundation ought not to conduct more of such enterprises. In this view Pritchett concurred. Yet almost as soon as Suzzallo had begun to formulate this policy word came to him indirectly that California would ask some such study, and that the state would pay at least part of the cost. On talking the matter over with Keppel, who favored the undertaking, he received assurances that the task would not have to be financed by the Foundation. Suzzalo, a native of California who had received much of his education in the state and had lived there for some years, knew most of its educational problems at first hand, and the opportunity of helping to solve some of them challenged him. He again consulted Pritchett, whose verdict was: "I suppose you'll have to do it." Pritchett, a legal resident of the state, knew the seriousness of its position and his change of attitude removed for Suzzallo the last preliminary impediment. Suzzallo at once began to lay out the study and to consider names of persons who might form a commission to deal with it. When, therefore, on September 22, 1931, Governor James Rolph, Jr., acting under legislative resolution passed in May, formally requested the Carnegie Foundation to survey the state's "present system, plan of organization, and conduct of public education of higher than high-school grade," and proffered $25,000 already appropriated for the purpose, Suzzallo was ready to proceed.

On October 9 he laid the request before the executive committee which "without precedent as to the Foundation's making surveys of state educational problems," instructed him to accept the invitation for the Foundation on the terms Governor Rolph had indicated, and, the Corporation having made available for the work the same sum as the state, authorized the expenditure upon it of as much as might be needed of the $50,000 thus available. On the following day the Governor was notified and work began.

By October 19 Suzzallo and Savage were on the ground for a preliminary gauging of issues, problems, and possible procedures. The ultimate purpose was the framing of specific recommendations "to give the tax-supported higher schools of the state both social and educational effectiveness." Hearings and conferences in Sacramento, Los Angeles, and Berkeley drew representatives of various bodies and institutions, not to mention citizens at large. It was soon clear that the success of any report would depend upon the quality and extent of local co-operation, official and lay. Apparently, this was accorded in an unusual degree, save for occasional temptations to resume partisan or regional contention. It was a fevered period of planning and negotiation, and it furnished the kind of stimulus that was the breath of life to Henry Suzzallo.

To supplement office resources in personnel he appointed two able staff associates: Paul E. Webb in California and Dr. David Spence Hill in Washington, with Thomas Fansler as assistant in the Foundation office. He also organized a Commission of Seven to pass upon issues and facts as collected and distilled by officers, staff members, and staff associates, and to make the necessary recommendations as to a course the state might follow: Chancellor Capen of the University of Buffalo, chairman; President Coffman of the University of Minnesota; Dean Judd of the School of Education, University of Chicago; President O. R. Latham of Iowa State Teachers College; Professor A. B. Meredith of the School of Education, New York University; Dr. James E. Russell, dean-emeritus of Teachers College, Columbia University; and President George F. Zook of the University of Akron. This group turned out to be one of the best working bodies ever enlisted in such an enterprise. In March 1932 they visited California higher institutions, public and private, and then under Capen's chairmanship held a series of meetings and executive sessions. Although Suzzallo with his own hand drafted the essentials of their report they worked them over, backwards and forwards, in general and in detail, until the result reflected unanimity. The process was remarkable for the vigor and interest with which each commissioner participated; there was not one "yes-man" or "passenger" among them.

The inquiry was scarcely a survey in the usual sense of the term. Suzzallo thought of it rather as a study and appraisal, with heavy emphasis upon future measures, and certainly the techniques employed and the principles set forth in the report depended more upon wisdom than upon undigested statistics, although many numerical data were gathered, distilled, and used in reaching conclusions. The report was sent to the Governor June 24, 1932, and published by the state in August.

Most of its forty-eight recommendations, which had been drafted by Suzzallo, were choked by the tares of institutional and regional self-interest. Only a little more than a third reached fruition, although the legislature ultimately created a state Council for Educational Planning and Co-ordination. The conflict in influence and authority between the University regents and the State Board of Education was not resolved, and the teachers colleges continued to press forward into four-year colleges of liberal arts. Duplication of functions among institutions abated little, if at all, and many of the economies that might have flowed from the recommendations were neglected. Had Suzzallo lived, more recommendations might have prevailed. It has often been said that the report, through its clarity and its inclusive statement of principles, had greater influence upon American education outside California than within the state, and this is probably true. The commission had unanimously enjoyed the work and the conditions under which it was done.

The Pennsylvania Study

To Learned's study of the relations between secondary and higher education, begun in 1921 and by 1930 supported principally by Carnegie Corporation, Suzzallo gave stimulus through his kindling interest. A new venture had originated in 1925-26 in discussions bearing upon the relations of secondary and higher education in the Commonwealth carried on by the Association of College Presidents of Pennsylvania. These discussions led to the appointment of a commission composed of representatives of this association and the State Department of Public Instruction, which invited the Foundation to study and report upon the matter. Learned's European work, summarized in the Twenty-first Annual Report (1926) and in his Bulletin Number 20 (1927), *The Quality of the Educational Process in the United States and Europe*, as mentioned in Chapter 7, made him the natural choice to direct the new inquiry, and on consultation it was agreed that he should have complete co-operation within the state and seven years in which to complete the task. One eligible instrument for educational measurement Learned knew to be new-type objective testing, which had been considered for the Missouri study of teacher education and also for Mann's work in the engineering field. Learned associated with his operations an expert technical authority on testing, Dr. Ben D. Wood of Columbia University, probably the best possible choice. They planned to test the same group of students with the same examinations, comprising perhaps 1,800 questions, at three points in their school careers: at entrance to secondary school, at the end of the secondary-school course, and near the end of college work.

The Pennsylvania tests, as Kandel points out in Bulletin Number 28 (1936), numbered four: (1) an intelligence test; (2) a "general culture" test in 1,222 questions graded as to difficulty and covering general science, foreign literature, fine arts, general history, and social studies; (3) a test in English; (4) a mathematics test. Subject matter was not confined to materials customarily presented in college courses; it was intended to measure fairly the permanent acquisition of knowledge attributable to the working of the student's desire to assimilate ideas, from whatever source acquired. This formed the basis of the study's assault upon the course credit system.

By means of a cumulative record card with graphic analysis, the invention of Dr. Wood, the progress of groups of students and of each individual among them could be traced and appraised. The union of the two devices and the long-time range of the operation were unique in that day as applied to more than 55,000 individual students in forty-odd colleges and eighteen school systems. About 3,000 took the tests more than once. As procedures finally developed, college seniors underwent the tests in 1928, college sophomores in 1930, repeating them as seniors in 1932.

The closeness required in the work was extraordinarily demanding, especially as pertaining to individual students. To achieve it necessitated the employment of a greatly expanded staff, many of whom had to be trained to their duties. Space generously provided by Carnegie Corporation, soon packed to overflowing, continued to overflow for the duration of the inquiry. Results of the main study appeared in four Progress Reports and two reprints issued as supplementary publications, in the current Annual Reports, and in Bulletin Number 29. A second Bulletin, Number 31, embodied further results.

THE STUDENT AND HIS KNOWLEDGE, BULLETIN NUMBER 29, 1938

The title of the first Bulletin recalled Keppel's book, *The Student and His College*, published some years earlier. After a decade of work Learned and Wood between them prepared a volume of 392 pages, with index, interpreting the outcomes of their venture. The introduction of the Bulletin, "Summary of Results and Conclusions Drawn from the High-School and College Examination," is sufficiently described by its title. Part I is termed "An Academic Inventory of the Baccalaureate Mind." Based upon the results of the 1928 senior tests it shows by graphs and explanatory text just

what that mind contained. Part II, "Academic Growth of the Baccalaureate Mind," rests upon the two subsequent testings; through
the same and similar means it demonstrates how seniors "got that
way" in school and college.

The Pennsylvania Study was one of the few educational inquiries,
whether made by the Foundation or by any other agency, that can
appropriately be called revolutionary, for it proposed a complete
bouleversement of American higher education. Starting with the
premise that knowledge is the dominating feature in any educational outcome, it demonstrates that knowledge is important only
as it is representative, permanent, and available. The tests of the
study were proved to be highly reliable instruments of educational
measurement. They revealed great variability among those who
took them and also among and within the co-operating institutions.
Graduation was taking place on a basis of time-serving rather than
demonstrable achievement. The growth of the college student's
knowledge as among individuals was shown to be variable to the
verge of absurdity. Some gained, some lost; many non-college high-
school graduates showed higher ability than college sophomores, or
even seniors. In all this the controlling principle was self-education.
Until the study's introduction of the cumulative record card into
the co-operating colleges existing records were highly inadequate.
Colleges did not understand their students and, to judge from one
experiment, some did not choose to and even avoided the effort. This
situation the cumulative record card corrected. Through its use,
Learned and Wood insisted, the student can be advised and guided,
through fully accessible and flexible curricular offerings, with better
contact between student and teacher and student and college,
towards augmented resources of knowledge which is the raw material of thought and action. They argued vigorously for the abolition
of units and credits as criteria of college selection and graduation,
and for far-reaching changes in almost every phase of college education, which, they insisted, would help to improve both college and
high-school teaching and infuse self-reliance, reality, and directness into education, which after all is a continuing process.

The foregoing excerpt of conclusions is, of course, an inadequate
patchwork. The force and weight of Bulletin Number 29 affected
American higher education profoundly. The volume was widely distributed and intently read. It wrought many changes in its own
right, but it led, more or less circuitously, to many more. It established objective testing as both respectable and highly useful. It

induced the perfecting of the first effective test-scoring machine. It led directly to Learned's Co-operative Graduate Testing enterprise and related projects, and to the forming and endowing of Educational Testing Service, Inc. It provided source material for at least two books and many magazine articles. Beyond question it made practicable and validated many of the tools which gave the war work of the American college distinguished success in providing military and naval personnel. Among educational studies it maintains very high place.

An Experiment in Responsible Learning, Bulletin Number 31, 1940

One of Learned's staff assistants for the Pennsylvania inquiry was Mrs. Anna Rose Hawkes, who, with Learned, prepared a further account of one project (1929-38) of the study in appraising secondary-school progress. Eighteen Pennsylvania school systems had introduced annual objective testing and cumulative records. Of these systems, three formed special classes and dispensed with "the old credit structure": Altoona High School, Cheltenham Township High School at Elkins Park, and Radnor Township High School at Wayne. A fourth, Reading High, co-operated but not completely. All told, the experiment affected 140 pupils. It began, 1928-29, in their junior high-school days, tested them annually through the twelfth grade, and thereafter in at least one college year, the senior, 1937-38, although many took also sophomore tests in 1935-36. At first the Stanford achievement tests and later the objective tests of the Co-operative Test Service were employed. Subsequently the work was brought to depend upon selected comprehensive objective examinations of the Pennsylvania study. Cumulative records were used throughout, and with special adjustment of schedules regular teachers were assigned to the entire program. The experiment thus reflected for the first time the findings of the Pennsylvania Study in practical use.

Results pleased all of the administrators and the teachers involved. As for the students, they ought to have been pleased with their own cumulative records, and, to judge from their achievement, most of them probably were. Sixteen cumulative records supplement the running text of the Bulletin, with explanatory notes on each case. Unless these youngsters' attainments went to their heads the sixteen subsequently made the bright spots in many a college classroom.

Whether the principles developed through the Pennsylvania Study have been introduced in such a degree and on so comprehensive a scale in other school systems is not recorded. This particular experiment in responsible learning was probably far in advance of its time, but the odds are that in due course it will have many followers and adapters.

In the Thirty-sixth Annual Report (1941) a section, "The Wages of Scholarship," written by Learned, put a finishing touch upon the Pennsylvania Study. Some 1,227 male alumni, graduated in 1928 from Pennsylvania colleges, had been persuaded to give the facts of their subsequent experience. At graduation all had taken an identical twelve-hour examination covering nearly the entire range of liberal-arts studies. Learned compared the individual success in this examination with position and income achieved in a decade of professional or business life. The two sets of data turned out to be disparate. While the average grade in college or "an examination of mastered knowledge" usually has importance in predicting post-college success, both measures fail to explain a student's power or weakness. "It is too much to expect that the financial rewards of life will ever arrange themselves outwardly in accordance with any reasonable scale of 'just desserts.' " Predictions would gain validity "were we to take the whole student into account; were we not only to find out what and how much knowledge he possesses, but also to observe what his knowledge means to him and how skillful he is in putting it to work."

The Foundation's Pennsylvania inquiry in all its phases cost more than a third of a million dollars, most of which came from Carnegie Corporation. Although from one point of view it represents a single phase in the development of Learned's genius, it stands among the great studies in American higher education.

In the midst of the Pennsylvania inquiry Learned, as a member of the Educational Advisory Committee of the New York State Economic Council, found time and energy to help study the Niagara Falls, New York, public school system. The committee's report, dated January 17, 1935, recommended numerous economies and changes in methods of instruction, some of which stemmed from Learned's Bulletin Number 20 and his long experience in the field. The report produced wide discussion, much of it unfavorable, and few reforms.

Graduate Education

While the Pennsylvania Study might be termed an operational project, the Foundation's studies in graduate education were descriptive in nature except as they merged with Learned's Cooperative Graduate Testing Program to be discussed in Chapter 13.

Since the Foundation's early days study of graduate education had been under consideration. Aside from Pritchett's including it in his grand *schema* of studies, Cooke in Bulletin Number 5, *Academic and Industrial Efficiency* (1910), had glanced at the field in relation to physics, and in the Sixth Annual Report (1911) Pritchett had expressed the hope of studying the whole area; indeed, in the same year Flexner made preliminary preparation for such an inquiry. With his move to the Rockefeller Foundation the matter lapsed but was not forgotten. In 1916 the executive committee considered inviting Professor Wilhelm Rappard from Germany to do for American graduate schools something resembling Redlich's work on the case method in our law schools.

The matter again came alive in 1927, when Savage prepared for Pritchett, on request, a detailed memorandum and budget for a two-year inquiry. This related to Suzzallo's connection in the same year with a project which was stimulated by Keppel and undertaken for the Corporation, but in which the Foundation nominally sponsored Suzzallo's efforts. Before he came to the presidency in 1930 he had gathered much material; thereafter he greatly increased his store. All of this work, progressively impeded by his duties as president, lapsed at his death. Repeated attempts to revive his study were not, as Jessup later put the matter, "of outstanding success." Jessup nevertheless persisted in his interest and effort. His university service had shown him the importance of the graduate school, and he knew well its shortcomings and its merits. The year 1936 found him pressing forward, with Corporation money, three ventures in the field: W. Carson Ryan's inquiry into the beginnings of graduate education in the United States, started in the Foundation offices in 1936; Learned's graduate testing project, the relation of which to the Pennsylvania Study has already been suggested; and certain statistical inquiries by Dr. Marcia Edwards, then assistant professor in the College of Education, University of Minnesota, which had broadened from one study into three. Dr. Edwards's results, distributed by the Foundation as a supplementary publication, are to be discussed briefly below, as such. The Graduate Record Examination project is treated in Chapter 13. Dr. Ryan, again temporarily associated with the Foundation after his work with the American Athletic Inquiry, prepared the first de-

tailed, full-scale account of the beginnings of graduate education in
the United States.

STUDIES IN EARLY GRADUATE EDUCATION, BULLETIN NUMBER 30, 1939

In the course of Ryan's inquiry he went to great lengths in his
use of original sources, but he also interviewed in person or through
correspondence a number of people who possessed documents related to his subject or were themselves concerned directly in the
developments of which he writes. Consequently, Bulletin Number
30 exhibits a rare combination of qualities: the vividness and zest
of the skilled newspaperman and the meticulousness of the accomplished scholar. The treatment was historical. It began with Princeton's early attempts at graduate education, as early as 1760, traced
the development through offerings at Yale, Michigan, Harvard,
Columbia, and Brown since 1825, and emphasized particularly the
flowering of scholarly training at the newly organized Johns Hopkins (1870-76) under Gilman, Clark University (1888) under G.
Stanley Hall, and the University of Chicago (1890) under Harper,
reorganized under postnatal benefactions from John D. Rockefeller, Sr. It is the stories of these three college presidents and
their graduate institutions that Ryan relates: the early vicissitudes,
the uncertainties, never of purpose, the struggles, discouragements,
and ultimate success.

Ryan used the biographical method of developing his theme. All
three men, he showed, "began with the very definite conviction that
American universities and colleges were not meeting the needs of
society. . . ." In efforts to change this situation the three pioneers
put men before buildings, material equipment, and administrative
machinery. They emphasized informality in teaching and in learning, with the result that freedom of instruction and research came
to characterize the three graduate schools they created under a determination to achieve "the highest possible quality in the educational process." Ryan's studies in graduate education, 1936-39, cost
a total of $22,100. On their conclusion Ryan's immediate concerns
shifted from work on the beginnings of American graduate education, fostered successively by both Suzzallo and Jessup until 1938,
over to explorations in the field of mental hygiene and education,
undertaken at the behest of Keppel in the Corporation and concluded two years later. While all of Ryan's unitary assignments as
staff associate centered in the Foundation office, their results benefited both Foundation and Corporation.

Merits of the Joint Project Arrangement

Viewed in perspective the Corporation-Foundation joint project program had, and still has, as its paramount advantage the utmost flexibility. That quality made it possible in the year 1931-32, the second of the new financial arrangement, for the Foundation to sponsor for the Corporation no fewer than sixteen projects of wide range in higher education. A project could be initiated by the approval of either body. Its prospective duration might be long or short, its probable cost low or high; the total of single grants ranged from $1,500 or $2,000 upwards to more than half a million. Sometimes the work involved has been the direct responsibility of the Foundation in its own offices. More often it has been carried on at a college or a university, or by a committee of a state or national body, or by a governmental agency. The round figure of $100,000 a year, to be devoted to such enterprises, now seems to have been about right in its day. Although it ruled out some ventures of promise, it was large enough to enable the responsible officers to take a chance if encouraged by the quality of the personnel concerned, and small enough to require careful examination of every proposal whatever its size. After executive committee action, May 1933, joint projects became for the Foundation administrative matters to be reported only once each year as action taken. The joint-project compact seems to have been an almost ideal working arrangement to meet a multitude of contingencies.

EXTERNAL PROJECTS ON "THROUGH" GRANTS

By far the greater number of joint projects have been conducted on grants made by Carnegie Corporation to the Carnegie Foundation and then transmitted by the Foundation to the responsible institutions or bodies for the uses of scholars, administrators, or others working in their own environments. All external as well as internal grants have been listed and discussed and costs and results set down in the Foundation's Annual Reports. They have made possible a wide variety of undertakings that for a quarter of a century have penetrated almost every cranny of American higher or secondary education. Some account of four of these enterprises may illustrate their variety as to type.

The European Examinations Inquiry

Kandel has well limned the background of the European Examinations Inquiry in the appendix to Bulletin Number 28, *Examinations and Their Substitutes in the United States.* The initial impulse probably originated with Keppel, 1930-31, whose natural interest in European education, whetted by his own experience, was further sharpened by Learned's work and Suzzallo's imagination. Discussion soon revealed the impracticability of attempting to organize a project of this nature under European sponsorship. If, however, it were to be administered in the United States it might operate under American auspices and receive financial support from the Corporation through the Foundation. Neither body under its charter could make direct payments of the type contemplated, but both could pay the costs of American sponsorship to an American institution. The happy solution was found in placing the project under the administration of Dr. Paul Monroe, and making and transmitting grants to the International Institute, Teachers College, Columbia University, of which he had long been director. He accepted the responsibility and organized the work. The first conference of the project was held at Eastbourne, England, in May 1931. Twenty-eight interested delegates attended from England, France, Germany, Scotland, Switzerland, and the United States. Except for general descriptions of the educational systems of the countries represented there were no prepared papers, an absence which made for informal and spontaneous discussion.

Differences in language proved no barrier to a statement and appreciation of examination problems faced by each delegation in its own land. The direct result of the Eastbourne Conference was the appointment of national committees in England, France, Germany, and Scotland, and the undertaking of various studies of examining in England, France, and Switzerland.

For some of the national groups the going was rough, but a directors' interim conference held in London, June 1933, showed that progress and enlightenment towards a wider examination concept had begun. Further reports were presented at a third conference at Folkestone in June 1936. The English committee had dealt with subjective examining at various educational levels and in numerous subjects, with a variety of techniques for marking, checking marks, and other procedures. Somewhat similarly the French committee focused its attention upon the crucial *baccalauréat* and one hundred papers in six subjects of that examination. Beyond these tests the French group ranged widely, with the result that they declared themselves, as Kandel shows, "more modest and less dogmatic" about the infallibility of their examinations.

The Scottish committee displayed in their work a lively enterprise. The results of their examination in new-type testing of more than 87,000 children born in 1921 and enrolled in Scottish schools were published in 1933. This report constitutes one of the most sympathetically humane documents in the field of new-type testing. The 1932 intelligence tests for Scottish children were repeated in 1947 with encouraging results; there was a significant rise in the test scores and hence in the average I.Q. The Scots studied also examination problems of university entrance and prognostic values.

The work of the German committee, promising at its inception, faded beneath the Hitler regime, and only one delegate from Germany attended the Folkestone conference. The final assembly of the delegates, this time from England, Finland, France, Norway, Scotland, and Sweden, as well as the United States, met September 16-18, 1938, at Dinard, France, almost under the very clouds of war. Each national group had issued one or more volumes, and even the newcomers had made notable advances in defining, attacking, and some in resolving their difficulties. The published reports of the committees united in pointing the breadth of the examination problem. While only the Scottish documents rest upon new-type testing processes, nevertheless the American student of examinations can acquire from the national reports a unique knowledge of the examination problem in other lands. How many of the benefits that were flowing from the European Examinations Inquiry survived events of the period 1939-45 cannot be determined, or even guessed. Grants in behalf of the project by the Corporation, 1931-39, totaled $185,400.

Secondary School and College—The "Eight-Year Study"

About the success of the Progressive Education Association's "Eight-Year Study" of the relation between secondary school and college opinions have differed widely. The study had its inception in or about 1930 with appointment by the association of a commission of twenty-eight persons, which, however, appears to have had small if any financial support until Suzzallo became interested in its aim "to bring about a more effective co-operation between secondary schools and liberal arts colleges," and recommended, September 21, 1931, a Corporation-Foundation "through" grant of

$20,000, payable half in 1931-32, half in the following year. This grant was made. Ten days later a special committee on testing was announced for the study, and Learned sent to the chairman of the main group a batch of material pertaining to Pennsylvania Study tests. No acknowledgment is of record. Learned's colleague, Dr. Ben D. Wood, laid before the smaller group his own testing plan, which was not adopted.

By the end of 1932 the whole enterprise was being greatly expanded. Although space could not be found for it at "522," Learned helped with many suggestions as to personnel and schools which might be included in the work, and approved most of the preliminary efforts of the commission, of which both he and Wood were members. Suzzallo considered the venture promising, and the Corporation ultimately brought its contribution up to $70,000, the major appropriation for which was made after Suzzallo's death. Over 200 colleges and 30 representative secondary schools, more than half of them private, were enlisted in the experiment. Learned began to feel uneasy about the loose organization of the enterprise, the absence of control groups, and other matters. His points seem to have been well taken, for he was encountering and solving a multitude of similar problems in the Pennsylvania Study and knew the advantages to be gained from meeting them boldly and decisively. For years his prime interest had been the individual student and he had found no valid way to appraise the results of school or college work except as it affected available knowledge. The study, on the other hand, was concerning itself with other criteria in judging its component colleges and schools, and depending less conclusively upon new-type objective testing. By the end of 1934, indeed, the testing element had been dropped from the program. The General Education Board, however, had begun to make very substantial contributions, far larger than those of the Corporation, to the work.

Upon a delegation's seeking further "Carnegie money" in the autumn of 1936, Jessup called upon outside advisers to assist in framing a decision. The reports were negative. These reinforced, albeit on different grounds, Learned's growing convictions concerning the enterprise, although some of those directing it recognized the need to develop a secondary and higher program that should emphasize and study the student himself. The chief implement of inquiry was not objective testing but the subjective rating of pupil personnel, behavior, and characteristics, and of institutional programs, plant,

and equipment. In 1941 results began to be published commercially
in several volumes.

It was stated in 1936-37 that "hundreds of secondary schools are
now seriously rethinking the problem of their responsibility to their
students. . . . A new spirit of co-operation between schools and colleges has definitely been established." The basis of this somewhat
inclusive statement must have been very broad indeed; perhaps it
rested upon new educational efforts in California, Georgia, Michigan, Ohio, Oregon, Utah, and the State of Washington, which were
referable to the study, let alone Pennsylvania. At this distance of
time it is impossible to differentiate among the local effects of the
eight-year study, and of certain aspects of the Foundation's Pennsylvania Study, and of the two projects taken in concert. Both were
conceived and dedicated to serve much the same ends, but through
radically different approaches and means. Total grants to the eight-
year study exceeded $691,000, of which Carnegie Corporation,
through the Foundation, contributed $70,000.

The Owatonna Project

On October 11, 1932, the Corporation board of trustees made
available to the University of Minnesota, through the Foundation,
an initial grant for researches, under the direction of Dean M. E.
Haggerty, into the "validity of psychological and educational assumptions prevalent in the field of art education."

The grant was predicated upon an unusually promising set of
conditions: At the time Lotus D. Coffman, trustee of the Foundation, was president of the University of Minnesota. Suzzallo, who
knew him well, was interested in art education, a subject that was
one of the enthusiasms of President Keppel of the Corporation.
Haggerty was a farseeing and capable administrator. The project
throughout its existence exemplified what can be done in a recep-
tive environment by workers possessing *élan*, tact, and skill.

The community chosen for the experiment was Owatonna, Minnesota, situated in an agricultural section, with printing and jew-
elry-making industries and a population numbering some 7,000 persons of varied national background.

For purposes of the project Owatonna was practically virgin
soil. After eighteen months of work such progress had been made
that not alone the schools of the community but groups of adults
were showing a very material increase in the realization that art
had its place not alone in education and industry but in daily life

and the homes in which it was lived. Application for additional funds led to a continuation grant for further demonstration, devising a school curriculum in art and its use in the public schools, and preparing for the Minnesota State Board of Education a course of study in art for the schools of the state as a whole. Besides working in the schools and the life of the city the project issued two publications: "Art a Way of Life," by Dean Haggerty, and "A City That Art Built," by Professor August C. Krey. By 1936 the staff consisted of two lecturers, two specialists, and five other appointees.

After Haggerty's death acting Dean W. E. Peik, of the Minnesota University College of Education, supervised the venture. Publications increased; one particularly useful document contained material for public-school art courses not hitherto available to teachers. Corporation grants through the Foundation for the project continued. By various partially objective means, statistical and otherwise, it was proved that the project had transformed the life of the community and its schools with respect to art and its implications in daily living. Haggerty before his death had completed a monograph entitled "Enrichment of the Common Life." Another monograph outlined the project as a whole and its results—"Owatonna, the Social Development of a Minnesota Community," by Dr. Edgar Bruce Wesley, 1938. When the project terminated, out of grants totaling $43,000 there remained more than $5,000 to be devoted to further purposes of the venture.

Distinguishing features of the Owatonna project were the competence with which it was planned and carried out, in spite of obvious pitfalls for such a task, the completeness and unpretentiousness with which results were analyzed and reported for the lay reader, and the clarity with which its influence is traceable within the state.

For the South

In the Foundation's early days the accusation was not uncommon that it had neglected higher education in the southern area of the United States. Adding to the Accepted or the Associated List the Tulane University of Louisiana (1907), the University of Virginia (1911), Vanderbilt (1919), Fisk University and Washington and Lee (1921), the University of Alabama (1922), and George Peabody College for Teachers (1923), as each successively met the requirements of the Rules, did much to mitigate the charge but did not wholly refute it. During the spring and autumn of 1931 the Social Science Research Council's Regional Committee, which had been constituted two years earlier, matured plans for developing a keener interest in social science research and a finer productivity among higher institutions of the area. The committee had early realized that this matter rested upon such fundamentals as the supply and retention of college teachers, their salaries, living conditions, and teaching load, and various problems of administration as well as of instruction. On these and related questions the committee focused its attention. It was hampered by lacking even the moderate funds it foresaw as necessary for its work.

Approach was made to Carnegie Corporation and the Carnegie Foundation. Keppel and Suzzallo became keenly interested. On October 13, 1931, the Corporation board granted, for payment through the Foundation, $5,000 for the Southern Regional Committee's "study of the elements affecting efficiency and economy in the organization of colleges and universities in the southern region." This phrasing was Suzzallo's; it reflected his concern about the whole question of economy and efficiency in higher education. Upon the committee's consulting him, he helped to plan its procedures and methods.

Professor B. B. Kendrick, of the Woman's College, University of North Carolina, headed the committee. W. F. Ogburn of the University of Chicago, L. L. Bernard of Washington University, and H. W. Odum also of North Carolina, co-operated. Ogburn had outlined the general problem and suggested ways to approach it. Active work began in early December. Data were secured from ninety-nine southern institutions, large and small, through questionnaires which were notably clear and direct. Almost complete response was obtained. In March 1932 at a meeting in Tuscaloosa, Alabama, a preliminary statistical report of conditions in the area, presented to the Southern Regional Committee and a dozen officers of southern colleges and universities, startled the hearers by its revelations.

At once the question arose how to spread the information it contained and cure the situation. The first step was seen to be interpretation of data and publication of results. This took the form of a volume written by Professor Wilson Gee of the University of Virginia, with one chapter prepared by Professor Bernard, entitled *Research Barriers in the South* and published commercially in the autumn of 1932. It not only delineated the situation clearly in its treatment of the "drag" out of the South, college salaries, living costs, teaching loads, and other matters, but suggested ameliorative measures. In this connection Professor Gee wrote: ". . . there must be an increased emphasis upon research and the support, financial and otherwise, necessary to its achievement," a prophetic demand that foreshadowed Corporation-Foundation efforts in this direction more than a decade later.

But publication was not enough to satisfy the Southern Regional Committee. In the winter of 1933-34 it constituted Professors Odum, Ogburn, Gee, and Kendrick a subcommittee to sponsor discussion of local problems on a number of campuses during visits paid by Professor Kendrick. A continuation grant of $5,000, May 18, 1933, furthered the work. Thus the impact of the project was brought home, with the result that a provisional plan for co-ordinating and strengthening graduate study in the South took form. This not only exerted an immediately good effect upon the region but laid the groundwork for the larger subsequent venture.

Although the results of the project have been appraised only subjectively they have benefited both university and college administration and also graduate work and research in the area. Total grants amounted to $10,000.

Other "Through" Projects

It must not be assumed that all of the scores of projects for which Carnegie Corporation made grants transmitted through the Carnegie Foundation have proved successful. Some had little or no effect. Others, badly publicized or unskillfully conducted, died aborning. One or two could not even be started because death took those who had devised them and were to see them through. The majority of them—probably the great majority—succeeded. The criterion of success was never completely formulated but it probably would have run something like this: Did the project do what it set out to accomplish? Did it, within the field to which it pertained, provoke discussion or action, or give help to persons working therein? The ultimate success of the grant in no way depended upon its size or its production of printed matter. The relation of purpose to accomplishment appears to have provided the sole test, in most cases subjective, of the success a project achieved.

Other grants for projects of this type, concerning which full data may be found in the Annual Reports of the Foundation, include:

American Association of University Professors, for work of a special committee, William B. Munro, Harvard University, chairman, to bring about improvement of instruction in American colleges and universities, $20,000 in 1931; "Report of the Committee on College and University Teaching," published by the Association, 1933; discussion in more than fifty Association chapters.

American Association of University Professors, to enable its Committee Y to study the effect of the depression on higher education, F. K. Richtmyer, Cornell University, chairman, $13,500, 1935-37; *Depression, Recovery and Higher Education*, Report of Committee Y, prepared by M. M. Willey, University of Minnesota, 1937.

American Council on Education, for its Modern Language Committee, Robert H. Fife, Columbia University, chairman, total grants, including those for a study of English as a foreign language, $76,650, 1930-42; results published in Coleman, *An Analytical Bibliography of Modern Language Teaching*, 1933; Keniston, *Spanish Syntax List*, 1937; and other volumes.

American Council on Education, for the Committee on Measurement and Guidance under the direction of Dean Herbert E. Hawkes, Columbia University, in its national teacher-testing program, which affiliated in 1948 with other testing enterprises in Educational Testing Service, Inc., $100,000, 1939-41.

Harvard University, for a study of factors causing reading disability in children and adults, under the direction of Walter F. Dearborn, $10,000, 1933-35; "Aniseikonia as Related to Disability in Reading," 1938, and other publications.

New York University, for an inquiry into factors in the failure or success of college teachers, using the appraisals of college administrators, by Anna Y. Reed, $2,500 in 1933; *The Effective and Ineffective College Teacher*, 1935.

Psychological Corporation, towards support of the work of the Psychological Institute in outlining and demonstrating a curriculum in English usage and composition for grades from primary through the junior high school, under the direction of L. J. O'Rourke, $39,200, 1931-35; *Rebuilding the English-Usage Curriculum to Insure Greater Mastery of Essentials*, 1934; *English and Everyday Life*, four volumes, 1934-37; and other publications.

The list might be expanded to include grants in all sections of the United States and of all sizes, small and large.

Projects with "Supplementary Publications"

Besides Annual Reports and Bulletins the Foundation since 1906 has published a variety of other documents, which in office talk were termed "supplementary publications." The category developed into a sort of catchall for monographs, volumes, or matter which was reprinted from Bulletins and Annual Reports, or which explained the Foundation and its work, or was prepared by persons not holding Foundation appointment, or was judged to be timely but not likely to have enduring utility. None of these criteria was inviolable and each had one or more exceptions. The list of fifty-eight "other" or "supplementary" titles can only be termed miscellaneous. Before Suzzallo's presidency the documents thus published were roughly of a stature that was deemed to preclude publication as Bulletins or as sections in Annual Reports, unless as reprints. Such were the *Plan for the Exchange of Teachers with Prussia* (1908), the ten editions of the Foundation's charter and bylaws, beginning in 1906, the list of publications itself in some twenty printings all told, beginning in 1917, and Reed's *Annual Review of Legal Education* in nine numbers 1927-35; a reprint of Pritchett's Preface to Bulletin Number 23, adaptations of certain sections of Annual Reports. On analyzing and reflecting upon these "supplementary publications," Suzzallo, seeing an opportunity to serve a public that might not be reached by the Foundation's regular publications, and confronted with a tradition that with few exceptions documents classified as Bulletins should be prepared by regular Foundation appointees, readily determined to utilize the "supplementary" classification in attacking broad current educational problems. His resolve had its roots in the countrywide depression of the early thirties.

It chanced that the United States Office of Education had at hand many data which it could not publish because the depression had cramped its appropriations. Grants from Carnegie Corporation under the special-projects compact soon provided funds for the purpose and for bringing material more nearly up to date. Subsequently these arrangements seemed to have opened the way for a grant in 1940, paid through the Foundation and the National Education Association, which bore directly upon the work of the Office during those days of national emergency.

From the earlier grants two volumes resulted: *The State and Higher Education, Phases of Their Relationship*, by Fred J. Kelly and John H. McNeely, of the Office of Education, 1933, and *Economy in Higher Education*, by David Spence Hill, Foundation staff associate, and Dr. Kelly, 1933. Meanwhile, Hill was engaged upon a subject over which Suzzallo was much concerned and which Hill treated in *Control of Tax-supported Higher Education in the United States*, 1934, published in the series. The foreign distribution of this volume was exceptionally large, thanks to the State Department and the Institute of International Education.

The success and utility of these ventures led Suzzallo to pursue the underlying policy further. His friend, Edward C. Elliott, president of Purdue University, had long had a lively interest in the legal grounding of higher education as related to its administration and cognate matters, and had collected much pertinent material. The two friends consulted, and Dr. Elliott formally associated Dr. M. M. Chambers, legally trained, then a fellow at Ohio State University, with the work, conducted under a series of Corporation grants "through" the Foundation, initially to Purdue. This union of minds and talents proved to be among the most fruitful in the Foundation's history. Its first product was *Charters and Basic Laws of Selected American Universities and Colleges*, 1933. There ensued a useful series on *The Colleges and the Courts*, the initial volume of which, issued in 1936, achieved a second edition six years afterwards and was followed by two shorter studies by Dr. Chambers, bringing the discussion up to 1945. A fourth volume carries it through 1950. Not a few college and university administrators and even lawyers have testified to the usefulness and accuracy of these studies and the reception has been very favorable.

The Elliott-Chambers team produced also, in 1939, a volume (litho-printed) on the documents basal to certain American philanthropic endowments which, owing to conditions attached to some of the material supplied, had to be held to private distribution only. A second study with the same title, *Charters of Philanthropies*, containing observations on the types and legal status of American endowments, without restricted material, was published by the Foundation in 1948. This treatment of selected trust instruments, by-laws, and court decisions, for which Dr. Elliott wrote the foreword, maintained the usefulness, clarity, and authority that characterized other volumes by the same writers.

Another "supplementary publication," begun in Suzzallo's day under a Corporation "through" grant and issued by the Foundation, suffered restriction in distribution because of a suit for libel —Dr. Walter C. Eells's *Surveys of American Higher Education,* 1937—but not until it had established its place for serviceableness, comprehensiveness, and precision as a reference volume.

A limited excursion into graduate education was intended to carry forward the Foundation's interest in the subject. With the start in 1936 of Learned's Co-operative Graduate Testing Program, which later became the Graduate Record Examination project, and with Ryan's inquiries into early graduate schools well on its way, Dr. Marcia Edwards of the University of Minnesota accepted the Foundation's invitation to study parts of the field under a Corporation-Foundation grant to the University. Her work commenced with statistical treatment of data from 712 colleges, accredited and nonaccredited, bearing on their graduates' success over a five-year period in thirteen American graduate schools. Urged on by Jessup to a second phase, Dr. Edwards then dealt with records of 12,647 students who entered six graduate schools in three years. In a third phase she visited, 1937-39, a dozen such schools and talked with officers and students who discussed conditions and problems freely with her. The materials thus assembled led Dr. Edwards to certain rather cautious generalizations and suggestions. These Jessup, in his introduction to her *Studies in American Graduate Education* published by the Foundation in 1944, about three months before Jessup's sudden death, extended and sharpened. That introduction, grounded in Jessup's long experience and deep interest in the field, stands among the best critical commentaries associated with his name. While its direct effects are problematical, it bore a clear if not a demonstrably causative relation to changes in policies and procedures adopted by the Association of American Universities during the six years following its publication. Certainly by this emphasis upon new-type testing at the graduate level Jessup advanced the progress of the Graduate Record Examination project. Dr. Edwards's studies cost $8,556, of which publication and distribution required $1,301.

Most of the Foundation's "supplementary publications" appeared in heavy paper bindings. Editions ranged from perhaps a thousand to three thousand copies. A few of the volumes presenting the results of studies—say one hundred in an edition—were bound in cloth, usually blue buckram. Like the Annual Reports and Bulletins, "supplementary publications" were distributed without charge.

~~ 11 ~~

Workaday Decade

THE "TENTH-FLOOR" GROUP · CHANGES IN THE BOARD · INTERNALI-
TIES—THE BOARD OF TRUSTEES; RESIGNATIONS FROM THE BOARD;
THE EXECUTIVE COMMITTEE; CODIFICATION OF THE BYLAWS, 1940;
STAFF RETIREMENT PROVISIONS · PENSIONS AND RETIRING ALLOW-
ANCES—PENSION STUDIES, NEW STYLE; RULES, 1938 · THE COURT
ORDER, 1939 · INVESTMENT AND FINANCE—THE HANDLING OF IN-
VESTMENTS; RESERVE FUND NUMBER TWO VALUED; RESERVE FUND
NUMBER ONE TERMINATED; ENDOWMENT, DIVISION OF EDUCATIONAL
ENQUIRY · STUDIES, PROJECTS, AND RESULTS—A STUDY OF EXAMINA-
TIONS; OTHER STUDIES: REQUESTS; JOINT PROJECTS · FAMILY TIES
AND OTHERS—T.I.A.A. COMES OF AGE; THE CARNEGIE CENTENARY;
OTHER RELATIONS · THE FOUNDATION AND WORLD WAR II—THE
RULES AND THE WAR; WARTIME PROJECTS · JULY 5, 1944

ALTHOUGH in some ways antithetical as to nature and methods, Suzzallo and Jessup, devoted friends, had in common
at least three qualities: knowledge of educational administration,
loyalty, and kindliness. Where the one was quick but not hasty of
decision, with a tendency to grapple with difficulties almost before
they materialized, the other inclined to a more unhurried pace, seldom acted without long—perhaps protracted—consideration, and
frequently waited for the future to solve its own problems. Their
experiences as university presidents were very different: Suzzallo's
brilliant incumbency at the University of Washington ended in un-
happiness; Jessup's success at the State University of Iowa brought
him a degree of content.

As presidents of the Carnegie Foundation both repeatedly demonstrated that they respected their predecessors, their efforts and
qualities, their accomplishments, and the traditions they had built.

236

The two men's respective contributions to the work of the Foundation were very different. Suzzallo's fiery sympathy for his fellows consumed immense energy. Jessup, no less sympathetic, operated with far greater deliberateness. The administrative loads that both men carried were heavy but Jessup bore his with less evident wear and tear. His personal appearance seemed of itself to invite confidence and he was one of those rare individuals who know the uses of silence. Both men had an untimely death, but each left his legacy of skill in negotiation, of mastery of very different techniques of operation, and of abiding loyalties and friendships.

In a comparatively brief time Walter Jessup grew into the presidency of the Foundation as few men could have done—witness the increasing wisdom of his contributions to successive Annual Reports. In most educational matters his was a qualified optimism. He thought in words and his initial views on almost any subject usually differed widely from the conclusions he reached through his oral reflections. This characteristic he repeatedly demonstrated during his first seven years as president of the Foundation; thereafter, when he assumed the added burdens of the Corporation presidency he carried it with him.

THE "TENTH-FLOOR" GROUP

Even before Jessup took up his duties as president of the Carnegie Foundation, May 1, 1934, he appreciated his good fortune in being elected to lead a group of experienced and loyal men and women. Pritchett, happy in the Jessup selection, set an example to all the rest in cordiality and adaptability. "When a man has served his time as an active officer of one or more of these creations of Mr. Carnegie, and retires to the sidelines as a spectator," Pritchett told Jessup not long after the new president had taken office, "I think he ought to remember that he has had his play and ought not therefore to interfere with the game. This much I have tried hard to observe. . . ." Pritchett was even bent upon relinquishing his honorarium as president emeritus. This matter Jessup, much as he valued Pritchett's wisdom, did not try to argue with him; instead, he referred it to the executive committee, which refused to change either the relationship or the payment. In no single year did Pritchett on emeritus status fail to earn his stipend. His counsel, freely given but never proffered out of hand, served as the bridge between Suzzallo's and Jessup's administrations.

During the first seven years Jessup was with the Foundation he nominally gave full time to its work. Actually the relation of the Foundation to Carnegie Corporation, of which Jessup was both trustee and adviser, consumed much energy and time. With the Corporation and its president, Jessup worked conscientiously and steadily; the talent of each man seemed in many ways to complement the other's. That Jessup's services to the Corporation were well regarded is plain from his being chosen its president in 1941. For the next thirty-one months the Foundation had less than a moiety of his time and attention, an arrangement which now clearly seems to have been less fortunate for the Foundation than Pritchett's term, 1921-23, with the Corporation, even including Learned's work as his assistant.

Under Jessup the work of the Foundation's staff members, Learned and Reed, and of Ryan as staff associate 1936-40, was at least as fruitful as it had been under Suzzallo. Throughout Jessup's term of office, Savage was Foundation secretary, and after 1937 treasurer as well, and Jessup came to depend upon him increasingly with the years. Indeed, after November 1941 it could not have been otherwise. Hall, skilled assistant treasurer and investment officer, was succeeded in the spring of 1939 by Devereux C. Josephs, whose enterprise, grasp, and capacity won him rapid advancement within the Carnegie philanthropies and elsewhere. Jessup's administration was characterized by a general stability except for his own shift and for enforced changes in the Foundation's treasurership and its Board of Trustees.

CHANGES IN THE BOARD

During Jessup's decade death took seven members of the Board of Trustees: in 1935, Albert Bledsoe Dinwiddie after twelve years of trusteeship, and Robert A. Franks, Foundation treasurer since 1910, who had been appointed by Mr. Carnegie; in 1937, Frank A. Vanderlip, another original trustee, who, intimately associated with the beginnings of the Foundation, had served as treasurer for two years; in 1938, Lotus Delta Coffman after eight years on the board; in 1939, Livingston Farrand, whose ten-year service had bridged three administrations; in 1940, Ernest H. Lindley after only six years membership; and in 1941, Josiah Harmar Penniman, elected in 1924. Pritchett died August 28, 1939, and Jessup himself July 5, 1944, while holding the two presidencies.

Franks's work as treasurer of the Foundation, Carnegie Corporation, and the Teachers Insurance and Annuity Association, together with his life trusteeship of the Corporation, had, in Jessup's words, "contributed to make his services invaluable." Vanderlip had been associated only with the Foundation and with T.I.A.A., as its chairman, but his work and counsel for both had been outstanding. The loss of Pritchett was even more grievous; the memorial minute concerning him stressed his bringing to the Foundation's organization and development "great qualities of mind and character: the power of penetrating thought, adventurous enterprise, courage, steadfast integrity," and testified to "his powers of discernment, his devotion to right and truth as he saw them, his humor, his tolerance, and his frankness. . . . The impact of his mind and character upon our ideals of education will long endure." At the thirty-fifth annual meeting (1940) Butler, who knew whereof he spoke, emphasized Pritchett's part in the genesis of the Foundation 1904-05: Pritchett, he stated, more than anyone else "was responsible for casting into definite form the more or less indefinite ideals which were the outcome of those early discussions" between Mr. Carnegie and his friends. Both tributes to Pritchett's memory were just and valid.

INTERNALITIES

As might be supposed Jessup, a respecter of tradition, moved rather deliberately in matters involving changes in internal procedure and policy.

The Board of Trustees

As part of each annual meeting Suzzallo had encouraged individual trustees to participate in discussions of timely problems touching higher education. Jessup recognized the value of this but as time passed he saw that the trustees might welcome information about the work of the Foundation, for he recalled that before he himself became president he had attended only one meeting after his election to the board in 1932. The twenty-ninth annual meeting (1934) considered the effects, mainly financial, of the depression upon the colleges; only two trustees stressed the immense changes then being wrought in the total educational structure. At the thirtieth (1935) Jessup enlightened the gathering about the administration of the Foundation and the need of clarifying Section C of the Rules, relating to disability annuity provisions for T.I.A.A.

annuity contract-holders. In 1936 the question of reviving the American athletic inquiry was canvassed. Thereafter topics included the chances of the United States being drawn into another World War (a not very prophetic discussion), the war itself and the colleges, the preservation of liberal education (a somewhat heated session), university research and its support. The last subject proved to be the most enlivening of all. Usually Jessup touched briefly also upon the history of the Foundation and its services to the nation under Pritchett and Suzzallo; he believed that the more the trustees knew about such matters the better.

Resignations from the Board

In the days of Charles W. Eliot tradition had indicated that upon relinquishing active academic connections trustees should resign from the board. In the later 1930's Jessup faced the fact that if this course were followed he should lose some of his most useful board members, including President Ferry, Neilson, and Penniman, almost simultaneously. These three men, somewhat to their own embarrassment, he persuaded to stay on, but he released them as soon as it was practicable. The episode profited the Foundation temporarily but it almost killed a useful tradition which a decade later was revived with difficulty.

The Executive Committee

Three days after Jessup took office he brought again before the executive committee the old question whether the Board of Trustees should hold at least one annual meeting in Washington. Discussion produced no very cogent reason for assembling there. It was Butler who settled the matter when he "referred to Mr. Carnegie's care to keep his endowments away from the business of government in the public mind," apparently forgetting for the moment that both the Carnegie Endowment for International Peace and Carnegie Institution of Washington had their principal offices in the capitol city. Jessup did his best to prevent meetings of the executive committee from becoming routine affairs. While he took pains to inform its members fully about all aspects of the Foundation's work, nevertheless the closing of the list of pensionables in 1931 and the simplification of the process of granting disability annuity allowances (January 1934), and later all benefits (May 1934), had almost removed one formerly important item of business, namely, discussion of the status of eligibles. With the rise in the number of "normal" cases the committee tended increasingly to leave decisions on them to the officers, who reported them only for ratification. This meant, in effect, centralizing practical responsibility for retiring allowances and pensions in the secretary of the Foundation. Customarily the president called upon the secretary to present unusual or complicated cases to the executive committee for final action; only one truly irregular case arose in eighteen years. Gradually the executive committee assumed towards the secretary's decisions an attitude of acceptance reflected, for one instance, in a remark of a member: "Well, I have trusted your judgment in so many things that I suppose I'd better trust it in this." In partial justification it might have been pleaded that although agenda for each meeting, mailed a week beforehand, contained full information about every case that was to come before the committee, that member was exceptional who could find time to study the list in detail. While this mode of operation expedited committee business and saved time for other matters, it nevertheless tended to concentrate in the officers, and especially in the Foundation's secretary, a responsibility which was rightly the committee's alone, no matter what the recommendation in the case.

The successful codification (1933) of Section C of the Rules for the Granting of Retiring Allowances led to three other codifications, only two of which pertained primarily to administrative procedure and policy. These two dealt with the Foundation's bylaws and with retirement provisions for officers and staff. The third involved the Rules for the Granting of Retiring Allowances, and while it antedated by two years the other two, it is more appropriate for discussion in another connection.

Codification of the Bylaws, 1940

In 1940 the Foundation's bylaws had endured for almost thirty-four years. Since 1906 only two amendments had been adopted: In 1908 the requirement of an administrative budget was rescinded, and in 1916 the beginning of the fiscal year was changed from October 1 to July 1. By 1939 the Foundation was operating as much in spite of its bylaws as under them, and the number if not the seriousness of discrepancies between theory and practice increased. To these shortcomings Jessup became increasingly sensitive and although reluctant to tinker with them, at last, mindful of the two successful operations on the Rules, told Savage to see what he could do to bring the bylaws into consonance with current administrative usage without drastic alteration of their form or substance.

The most important changes that Savage's drafts suggested involved recognition of the existence of the secretary of the Foundation, custodianship of its property and seal, sharper definitions of officer functions and responsibilities, the need of a finance committee, restoration of the budget, and means of meeting certain requirements for ownership, transfer, and registration of securities. A number of lawyers, investment people, bankers, and other qualified persons gave much careful attention to details of the draft. Jessup, too, worked over it and liked it. The legal proceedings of 1937-39, discussed below, lent impetus to the matter. On May 10, 1940, Jessup laid it before the executive committee, which designated Penniman and Dr. Wriston, then secretary of the board, to report upon it at the committee's October meeting. At that time the executive committee recommended the draft to the board and, notice being duly given, the trustees, thanks to Dr. Wriston's presentation, adopted the codification at their thirty-fifth annual meeting, and also voted certain formal assurances to stock transfer agents and registrars. The bylaws of 1940 stood intact for nine years.

Staff Retirement Provisions

About two years after the Teachers Insurance and Annuity Association had received its charter the Foundation executive committee passed a somewhat vague vote adopting the Association's contracts for purposes of staff retirement, on a 5-and-5 per cent joint contributory basis. Employee participation was made voluntary. At the time, Learned and Kandel among the officers and staff members elected to participate; probably Pritchett, Furst, and the executive committee felt that in view of the $4,000 maximum retiring allowance then set by the Rules of 1918 and 1920 provision for themselves was ample and compulsion hardly justifiable. The structure developed flaws. Both Savage (1923) and Jessup (1934) held T.I.A.A. joint contributory retirement annuity contracts when they joined the Foundation. Neither had expectations of a "free" Foundation retiring allowance. The service staff was covered on the voluntary basis, thanks to the prospective use of Reserve Fund Number Two in some instances. Learned had both expectations of a retiring allowance and a T.I.A.A. contract, and so also did Kandel; Reed had expectations but no contractual coverage. Amid such complications as these, accrued during twenty years, the situation was in need of clarification, for while it seemed to be understood by the interested parties, it lacked definiteness and it rather resembled the predicament of the proverbial shoemaker's barefoot children.

Decisive impulse towards action came in the spring of 1940 when T.I.A.A. suggested that the Foundation join with that Association and with Carnegie Corporation of New York to form out of the employees of the three bodies a group that could be covered by T.I.A.A. collective insurance. The proposal led Jessup and Savage to examine carefully the whole matter of old-age and insurance protection for Foundation employees, not to mention the Foundation itself. The most readily available remedy appeared as codification of requirements and practice, and accordingly after the strands of the fabric had been untangled and rewoven Jessup brought to the executive committee, May 10, 1940, a satisfactory codification of retirement and insurance provisions for Foundation employees on a compulsory basis. It passed the committee without dissent and is still in effect, with necessary and permitted adjustments as to amounts of contributions and supplements in individual cases.

PENSIONS AND RETIRING ALLOWANCES

Jessup's leaning towards stability soon encouraged Mattocks to state his dissatisfaction over the looseness of the 1929 Rule III on widows' pensions. He and Savage persuaded Jessup to bring the matter before the executive committee in May 1935, with suggestions as to clarification of the committee's intent, with board action in November and executive committee interpretation in January 1936. The provision was restated, and ultimately some thirteen male beneficiaries who had married since their retirement were exempted by name from the restrictions that had long been intended but never precisely phrased.

Doubt concerning the utility and maintenance of a list of institutions formally "associated" with the Foundation had been growing in Jessup's mind. When, therefore, in 1936 a board member raised with him the question of what advantage was to be gained for an institution through being "associated," Jessup was not unprepared for action. Indeed, the new autonomy of the Teachers Insurance and Annuity Association had focused the matter for both him and the executive committee in January and it had received sufficient attention to invite scrutiny at the thirty-first annual meeting (1936) when the whole matter of accrediting lists was briefly discussed. The subject of the Associated List was referred to the executive committee, which requested thorough study.

In the meantime, codification and simplification of all the Rules was being canvassed and this topic involved directly the Associated List itself. After prolonged consideration the executive committee voted to recommend that the board act to discontinue the printing of the Associated List as such and instead to specify the institutions formerly termed "associated" as a group of universities and colleges within which migration and transfer would have no effect upon expectations of retiring allowances. The fact was that the Associated List was constantly being confused as to purpose and purport with the accrediting lists of various associations and bodies, and was being abused in a number of ways, including use for college advertising and the acquisition of prestige. The board in November 1937 adopted the recommendations of the executive committee. Thereafter the list, known as the "Specified List," was published only in the pamphlet containing the Rules, without suggestion or connotation as to the basis of former "association," the rating of any institutions, or accreditation. The Associated List, however useful in its day, had outworn that usefulness. Abuse of it continued even after Savage and Miss Edythe Maslen thoroughly exposed it in the Thirty-eighth Annual Report (1943).

Pension Studies, New Style

After 1931, except for actuarial calculations, the Foundation's studies of its own pension and retirement problems lapsed. True, each year's operations were closely checked from the general administrative point of view, but generalizations remained unpublished, and although Mattocks, Savage, and Miss Maslen worked, both together and separately, upon a number of problems, it was 1938 before results of one inquiry could be summarized in the Thirty-third Annual Report, in a section on "Completed Lives of 1,280 Foundation Beneficiaries." To this same Report Mattocks contributed a paper on "Life Insurance for College Teachers" in which he approached the well worn subject from a new point of view. For the Thirty-seventh Annual Report (1942) Savage wrote on "Supplementing the Foundation's Retiring Allowances and Widows' Pensions," and for the Thirty-ninth (1944) "Work After Retirement," combining here three studies in one presentation.

From either the actuarial or the statistical point of view Mattocks and Miss Maslen investigated (1942-44) recipients of disability allowances, beneficiaries paid individually (that is, not through their institutions), recipients of age allowances and service allowances, widows, and work after retirement, but results although administratively important appeared somewhat technical for use in Annual Reports. Mattocks made actuarial studies of the Foundation's pension load as groundwork for the court proceedings of both 1939 and 1945.

Much of his work was done *ad hoc*, while Savage and Miss Maslen were usually able to proceed more leisurely with topics of their own selection. These studies, however, had important bearings. For instance, in 1935 they influenced clarification of requirements as to widows' pensions.

Parenthetically, although many recipients of Foundation benefits lived into their nineties, only one, Professor Robert Hallowell Richards, of the Massachusetts Institute of Technology, born August 26, 1844, has ever attained, at this writing, a full one hundred years; retired July 1, 1914, he died October 6, 1944.

As early as 1913 the trustees had recorded their view that the endowment of the Foundation "should not be used to pay the salary of a college teacher or officer under the form of a pension," and the executive committee on several occasions had reinforced this view by decisions in doubtful cases. In the spring of 1943 Miss Maslen, combing college catalogues for data on post-retirement teaching, discovered patent irregularities in which at one institution Foundation retiring allowances had been used as part of compensation for active teaching by emeritus professors. An overpayment of $40,000 had resulted. The bulk of this sum was recovered by the Foundation. The discovery and ultimate adjustment of the matter was the most exciting bit of detective work since the American athletic inquiry.

Jessup fully comprehended the bearings of all these studies. At the thirty-eighth annual meeting (1943) he spoke in part to the following effect: The Foundation at this stage must be administered with an undeviating regard for the mathematics of its existence. The need for detailed information about its allowances and pensions is constant and must remain constant for the record of the future. In very truth detailed mathematical, financial, and statistical data underlay the revision of the Rules for the Granting of Retiring Allowances 1938 and the court proceedings of 1939.

Rules, 1938

The 1929 edition of the Rules, although faulty and cumbersome, endured for a decade, the longest period any version had stood. The amendments and interpretations it had undergone had made for obscurity of meaning rather than for clearness, and few persons outside the Foundation's offices could divine the purport of the regulations with any clarity. Jessup by 1935 had become acutely aware of the situation, and in October, at his initiative, he was authorized by the executive committee to "direct the completion of the codifying and arrangement of the Rules" in addition to those portions that bore on widows' pensions and disability annuity allowances, "the general sense and effect to remain as at present." The actual process of reconstruction was almost completed within six months; delay arose from the formalities attending the birth of the new Specified List and the necessity of testing each phrase in relation to applications as filed. On November 17, 1937, the board, following recommendation of the executive committee, formally authorized and directed that the Rules be recodified and distributed. Final action by the executive committee, to which the board had referred the whole matter, came in the following January and the new edition, the ninth, caused scarcely a ripple when issued.

THE COURT ORDER, 1939

The adjustments, 1929, in the Foundation's Rules, and the related agreement between the Corporation and the Teachers Insurance and Annuity Association concerning supplementary annuities, had resulted in stabilizing and closing the list of pensionables by 1931, the elimination of final average salary as a basis for future benefits, and reduction of the maximum allowance to $1,000 a year at age seventy. There remained only one extremely important problem: the decrease of yield from investments which had dogged the Foundation since 1927. As early as February 27, 1924, Mattocks, foreseeing likelihood of loss of income with the call of the Foundation's 5 per cent United States Steel Corporation bonds, had pointed out the possibility of the Foundation's borrowing, without interest, during the period of reduced income and repaying later as the pension load dropped within income. He set no source for the loan. A year afterward Pritchett mentioned to Keppel the possibility of the Corporation's lending the money. The Mackenzie Committee also, in

1927, touched upon this possibility, among others, and Furst even devised a rough tentative schedule for borrowing and repayment. But in that day, with nearly $13,000,000 in Reserve Fund Number One and income at 5.01 per cent from all funds, the day of reckoning seemed far removed.

The depression brought reductions of both principal and yield of the Foundation's invested resources. In the spring of 1933 Mattocks had completed one of his actuarial studies, which, although he had assumed interest at 5 per cent with otherwise "very conservative factors," showed that if Reserve Fund Number One were exhausted in 1946 borrowing would be inevitable. Still he made no reference to the Corporation as the possible source of funds. This report Suzzallo presented to the executive committee May 5, 1933. Impressed, that committee directed him to transmit it to Keppel. For the moment the net result was that, taboo being removed, the matter of borrowing, heretofore referred to as it were in whispers, came out into the open.

Meanwhile the Foundation's assets were shrinking more rapidly than had been expected. Jessup, seeing this fact as of first importance and roused by Hall's investment reports, bade Mattocks pursue his inquiries further. Mattocks proceeded on even more conservative assumptions, especially as to investment returns, with the result that he moved forward the date of exhaustion of Reserve Fund Number One to 1945, and possibly earlier. Obviously to Keppel, the sources for possible borrowings could be only two: one, the Corporation; the other, an unrelated organization such as a bank, a trust company, or perhaps an insurance company. For nonactuarial study of the entire matter Keppel engaged an expert consultant with special knowledge of interest rates.

The resulting report, filed October 7, 1935, after five months of work, while thorough and exhaustive suggested no fresh, miraculous solution. It was fully discussed by both Corporation and Foundation, boards and officers, and at last there was constituted a Joint Committee on the Pension Load, to which Keppel for the Corporation selected Thomas S. Arbuthnot of Pittsburgh, and Henry James; and Jessup for the Foundation Livingston Farrand of Cornell, and William Allan Neilson of Smith. Among this group of six persons James alone, chairman of T.I.A.A., had had first hand and technical experience with retirement and pensions, although most of the others had lived with the pension problem.

To the Corporation board in March 1937, the Foundation executive committee in May, and the Foundation trustees in November, Jessup read for the record a review and analysis of the situation as it had developed since 1905. Then the joint committee went to work in earnest. Although it held only two or three formal meetings it progressed steadily, and by April had framed a tentative plan to meet the coming emergency. That plan rested upon two questions: First, could the Foundation borrow from its own General Endowment Fund to meet part of its needs, and subsequently restore the borrowings so that the principal of the fund would ultimately become again intact? Secondly, could the Foundation for the same purpose borrow, at first equally and then in larger amounts, from the Corporation, these borrowings also to be repaid over a period of years as the receding load released income for the purpose? No interest charges were contemplated. The crux of the plan was borrowing and repayment of the Foundation's own funds, on the one hand, and similar simultaneous procedure with the Corporation, on the other. The inventor of this device is not now identifiable.

The fundamental issue called for decision by a court of law. In April 1938 Jessup requested opinion about the tentative plan from Elihu Root, Jr., Esq., of Root, Clark, Howland and Ballantine. Then began eighteen months of consultation, deliberation, drafting, revision, and re-revision. The case was developed round the doctrine of *cy pres:* If it applied, could Mr. Carnegie's original ten millions be regarded as a gift in perpetuity, and could the five millions he subsequently gave to the Foundation be borrowed and restored? As the necessary technical assumptions were determined, Mattocks made several actuarial estimates. His ultimate calculations indicated that Reserve Fund Number One would be exhausted in 1943, that between 1943 and 1951 borrowings from the General Endowment Fund, if permissible, would total $5,000,000, and that the amount to be borrowed from the Corporation would reach $14,430,000.

After detailed study Mr. Root, December 1938, for his firm sent Jessup a letter of opinion which answered both of the questions underlying the tentative plan with a provisional and guarded affirmative, and charted a course of action to be followed.

In special session called by the executive committee, the first special board meeting held in eleven years, the Foundation trustees, January 27, 1939, approved the plan and authorized "such proceedings as might be necessary or suitable to establish in the Foundation authority to carry it out." They also authorized the officers of the Foundation, upon counsel's advising that the way was clear, to take the necessary steps to this end. It was March before the Corporation trustees took similar action; they then at Keppel's suggestion set the limit of the aggregate future advances to be made by the Corporation at $15,000,000. With the Foundation furnishing much actuarial, financial, and educational data, counsel's draft of a Petition to the Supreme Court of the State of New York was by May 1939 approaching a final version.

But inasmuch as New York State legislation had been so revised long after the Foundation's District of Columbia Charter had been granted by Congress as to bring charitable corporations within the requirements of the State's General Corporation Law, counsel decided that the Foundation ought to obtain a Certificate of Authority to carry on its activities in New York State. A Statement and Designation of Authority was duly executed and filed. Then counsel procured from the New York State Tax Commission a ruling to the effect that the Foundation is subject to neither the license tax on "foreign" corporations nor the franchise tax on business corporations. With these technical but highly important matters disposed of, counsel on October 19, 1939, filed the necessary petition.

Thereafter legal details received more rapid adjustment. On being required to show cause why the petition should not be granted, the Attorney General of the State answered that for the purposes of the proceeding all the allegations of fact in the petition were admitted and that he interposed no objection to Supreme Court action. Furthermore, on November 15, 1939, the Foundation Board of Trustees had duly voted without dissenting voice, under requirements of the Foundation's charter, that the purposes of the Foundation should "include the purpose and power of expending that portion of the principal funds . . ." called for by the plan.

Next day counsel filed his brief. On the seventeenth Mr. Root and the Solicitor General of the State called informally upon Justice William T. Collins, then of the New York State Supreme Court, in his chambers, and on the eighteenth Justice Collins issued the necessary Court Order, which was entered two days later. Jessup on November 21 expressed to Mr. Root appreciation "for the services which you and your firm have rendered not only to the Foundation and its Trustees, but also to those in receipt of benefits from the Foundation and to those who have expectations of future benefits. . . ." By March 1940 the Corporation had begun to implement the plan by setting up reserves against the funds required.

The newspaper treatment of this episode was of first quality, thanks probably to the knowledge and background possessed by the reporters assigned to cover the story, and the frankness with which the attorneys met the writers. The proceedings almost invited sensationalism but none appeared, and by grace of one wire service the news coverage was nationwide. The editorials, though comparatively few in number, were well done.

INVESTMENT AND FINANCE

In the effect of the depression upon the Foundation's security holdings, almost exclusively in bonds, and its income therefrom, Jessup as president inherited a financial problem of the first magnitude. The finance subcommittee and the executive committee followed the resulting recessions with growing concern through Hall's periodic summaries of values for each fund. Railroad bonds, of which the Foundation owned many, had declined materially, and bonds of foreign governments even more; almost every security held by the Foundation had felt the downward pressure. Income, of course, suffered correspondingly. The situation, especially in the General Endowment Fund, Reserve Fund Number One, and the endowment of the Division of Educational Enquiry, was serious and growing graver month by month.

The finance subcommittee examined and discussed it at numerous meetings of 1934 and 1935. Rather soon the fact became clear that radical countermeasures were necessary, and the subcommittee decided after much deliberation that it should depart from long-established policy and invest in common stocks. But in Vanderlip's view investment in common stocks was, for a foundation, debatable policy. The subcommittee believed that so wide a break with tradition should be discussed by both the executive committee and the Board of Trustees, and that certain restrictions as to proportions of common-stock investment should be set up and followed. Already Carnegie Corporation of New York had entered the equity field and its example had influence with both of the Foundation's committees and with the board. A full exposition of the matter, by Vanderlip as acting-treasurer, and by Jessup, November 27, 1935, at meetings of the executive committee and of the Board of Trustees, elicited no objection or dissent from the proposal, and the finance subcommittee went to work on a policy which reached provisional form by January 1936. Funds to carry it out had to come from sales and redemptions of securities. By October 1, 1936, results began to appear in a rise of market above book values in the funds affected amounting to about 1.88 per cent, but a probable decline in General Endowment income by as much as $50,000 for the year 1936-37.

The Handling of Investments

Various developments, 1936-40, led to adjustments in the technical processes related to the Foundation's investments which now seem to be of comparatively minor importance. In 1936 the coming of a new treasurer to Carnegie Corporation conduced to the fidelity bonding of Foundation officers, a revival after many years that would have horrified Franks but rendered those who followed him in the Foundation's financial affairs more comfortable in their posts. At the same time the arrangements for the Co-operative Investment Office and the shared services of the investment officers among the Corporation, the Foundation, the Carnegie Endowment for International Peace, Carnegie Institution of Washington, and Teachers Insurance and Annuity Association were reaffirmed and formalized. In 1937, Savage, on being made acting treasurer and then treasurer after Vanderlip's death, began to emphasize the fact that the Foundation treasurership was a custodial office, not directly related to the investment of funds. Upon codification of the bylaws, 1940, the finance subcommittee became the finance committee, thereafter to deal rather with investment policy and selection than with broader financial procedure and concepts, although its functions changed again with the coming of Josephs as investment officer.

Reserve Fund Number Two Valued

Mattocks valued Reserve Fund Number Two as of December 31, 1941. Against assets of about $386,000 he showed liabilities of about $359,000, with a possible ultimate balance of $27,000 after the Fund had met all of its obligations in assisting institutions to adopt T.I.A.A. retirement contracts and paying certain allowances charged against it with this purpose in view. He used a "most conservative" table of mortality and assumed future interest at 2½ per cent. No grants had been made from this Fund for a number of years and his results showed one bright spot in a dark general situation.

Reserve Fund Number One Terminated

On April 19, 1944, Reserve Fund Number One ceased after more than a quarter-century of existence. Authorized and established by the Board of Trustees in November 1917, in response to a communication from the Corporation, and in use for pension purposes since 1928, it had received from the Foundation, by transfer of unused income, more than a million and a quarter dollars in cash, and from Carnegie Corporation securities, cash grants, and income ascribable to those sources totaling more than $10,737,800. In the sixteen years of the fund's use, these resources had provided more than $18,000,000 all told.

With the exhaustion of Reserve One borrowing under the Plan for Completing Payment of the Foundation's Retiring Allowances and Pensions and the Court Order of 1939, began as of May 1, 1944.

Endowment, Division of Educational Enquiry

In the meantime, the receding tidal wave of the depression had swept over the Division of Educational Enquiry. Its endowment, received in 1913 from Carnegie Corporation, shrank from a market value of $1,150,000 to $498,135 in May 1942. Default of interest, beginning in 1936, on $1,000,000 of 4 per cent railroad bonds, and the sale of these securities over a period of more than five years, not to mention conservative reinvestment of the meager proceeds, reduced endowment income of the Division from about $50,000 a year to some $11,800 in 1942. This misfortune led to the Foundation's depending more and more upon the generosity of the Corporation for the support of educational studies. Although, after 1942, when the fund was reconstituted, its allocated income rose to some $23,300 in 1950-51, it is still insufficient to enable the Foundation to undertake certain types of educational projects or the more costly sort of inquiry without Corporation help.

STUDIES, PROJECTS, AND RESULTS

During Jessup's administration, thanks in part to appropriations from Carnegie Corporation of New York, the internal activities of the Foundation's Division of Educational Enquiry continued high if not fevered. Each Annual Report of the ten years contained a discussion signed by the president and sections on various studies on which staff members were engaged. Among other topics Jessup treated the spiritual resources of our colleges, college registration and the student, our itinerant students, and phases of the war effort as related to the American college. Reed about 1932 had begun to shift his emphasis from legal education to the broader field of professional education. Although some of his views on standards and accreditation did not coincide with Jessup's no restriction fell upon expressing them. In the Thirty-second Annual Report (1937) Reed examined the current revolt against standards and standardizers operating by and through accrediting lists. In this he anticipated some of the reasoning that underlay action of the trustees in 1938 abolishing "association" with the Foundation and setting up a Specified List for migration and transfer. Learned's contributions during the decade dealt with selected material as it accrued from his Pennsylvania Study and his Graduate Record Examination project begun in 1937, in a sort of continuing progress report. Ryan's inquiry into our early graduate schools netted only one Annual Report section.

A Study of Examinations

I. L. Kandel, who in 1923 had transferred from the Foundation to a professorship at Teachers College, Columbia University, prepared the first Bulletin to be published in Jessup's presidency: *Examinations and Their Substitutes in the United States*, 1936. The work was undertaken at the request and with the support of the Corporation in the hope that it might result in a unified account of American experience in the field as related to the European Examinations Inquiry discussed in Chapter 10. This hope was amply fulfilled.

Kandel found that the examination problem essentially resolves itself into devising methods of discovering the right education for the right pupil. Neither examinations nor teachers' judgments furnish trustworthy bases for educational distribution. In the United States approach to this matter has come through, first, intelligence tests, and then tests of achievement and aptitude. Subsequently, cumulative records formed sources for the profitable educational guidance of individuals. Results, Kandel noted, are not yet final and educational values still await adequate definition. But clearly society has a stake in the kind of education an individual receives, and that individual ought to be measured as to his needs, capacities, and possible future bent.

Having established this point of view Kandel traced the history of the traditional examinations in the United States from 1869 and the development of new-type tests, with particular attention to the work of the New York State Regents, the College Entrance Examination Board, and the Foundation's Pennsylvania Study. He insisted that "the problem of examinations strikes at the very roots of the whole meaning and significance of education for society," and poses the question whether it is not the function of an educational system "to promote the best happiness of the individual by putting him in the way of the highest development of which he is capable and which will contribute to the best progress of society itself"; the justification of an educational system rests upon using examinations as a means of adapting work to the ascertained abilities of its pupils. Kandel's treatment joins with Learned's in opening new vistas for the mastery and use of enduring and usable knowledge. His Bulletin Number 28 presents in nontechnical language the best comprehensive account of examinations and tests, academic and scholastic, ever produced for the United States.

Corporation grants for the study and its publication totaled $9,500.

Other Studies: Requests

The effects of the Foundation's American Athletic Inquiries were very much alive when Jessup came to the presidency. In May 1934 some forty-two higher institutions appeared to be making honest and somewhat successful efforts to keep college athletics decent, while six others were moving in the same direction. Eighteen months later the National Association of State Universities "urgently and unanimously" requested a supplementary study in the same field, but the executive committee followed Jessup's counsel in not authorizing the task. Indeed, January 1937 saw the Foundation with ten live proposals for projects and inquiries related to athletics, none of which appeared practicable in the current stringent financial situation or for other reasons.

At the time the most that could be done was twice to assemble informally presidents of some thirteen higher institutions, or their deputies, for discussion of a possible inquiry into eligibility for intercollegiate contests. It soon appeared that one or two institutions were not enthusiastic and even pressure brought by more than one trustee did not cause Jessup to pursue the matter beyond the exploratory stage. At last he buried it, as he hoped, once and for all.

Suggestions for studies of other matters than athletics involved library schools in the United States and teacher training. Neither these nor several equally important proposals could be accepted for the reason just indicated.

Joint Projects

During 1934-35 policy underlying Corporation-Foundation joint projects and their support took a new turn, whether on Jessup's or on Keppel's initiative but certainly to their mutual satisfaction. Attempt was made to bring to conclusion studies already under way which promised significant results, rather than to embark upon new inquiries. Among the ventures affected two may be mentioned here: Professor Arthur Pope's inquiry into art education, begun in 1934, which resulted in the publication, 1937, by a university press of his volume, *Art, Artist and Layman;* and Frank Aydelotte's description of honors work in the American college, which cost $4,710 to make. It was published commercially without subsidy. Other results and publications are noted in Chapter 10 and in the Appendix. It is significant that in 1938-39 the Corporation increased its allotment for joint projects to $150,000 annually. By 1942 practically all of the joint ventures being pursued outside the Foundation offices were contributing to the war effort, whether or not they were initiated in connection with it.

FAMILY TIES AND OTHERS

The executive committee minutes of 1936 note that in the preceding year much of Jessup's time and attention was given to the co-operative activities and grants of the Corporation and the Foundation. During subsequent years this relationship intensified through Jessup's Corporation trusteeship and his advisory work in numerous connections. It culminated, 1941, in his election to be president of the Corporation and his service both in that capacity and in the Foundation presidency for almost three years. This matter Jessup first broached to the executive committee by letter in July 1941, as Keppel's retirement began to seem inevitable. On October 10 the executive committee discussed it favorably: "It was pointed out, without dissent, that no union of the Foundation and the Corporation is contemplated and that the two endowments, each with Dr. Jessup as president, will remain separate and distinct entities." Jessup added the Corporation presidency to his burden

November 18, 1941. Thereafter he necessarily gave increasingly less attention to Foundation affairs and more to Corporation matters, perhaps a not unnatural change which brought more benefit to the Corporation than to the Foundation.

T.I.A.A. Comes of Age

In Chapter 5 reference was made to a demand by a committee of the American Association of University Professors that the stock of the Teachers Insurance and Annuity Association should be owned by its policyholders. As matters turned out it became for more than twenty years the nominal property of the Carnegie Corporation, Pritchett, and Franks. In the presidency of T.I.A.A. Pritchett was succeeded by James W. Glover, and Glover by Henry James, whose title was, first, chairman of the board. When James retired from office Devereux C. Josephs succeeded him, to relinquish these duties in 1945 when he became president of Carnegie Corporation, and R. McAllister Lloyd president of T.I.A.A. One of James's best services proved to be the creation, 1937, of a corporation, Trustees of T.I.A.A. Stock, to hold that stock, the outstanding two shares of which the corporation acquired from Keppel and James. Thus, the Association achieved complete autonomy both legal and actual. The Thirty-eighth Annual Report of the Foundation (1943) contained a section on the first quarter-century of the Association's work congratulatory in tone but more subdued than earlier discussions of related matters in Foundation publications.

The Carnegie Centenary

On November 25-27, 1935, Mr. Carnegie's philanthropies in the United States, England, and Scotland celebrated the one-hundredth anniversary of his birth. In New York City the festivities were arranged by Carnegie Corporation. With the Corporation there joined the Carnegie Institute, of Pittsburgh (1896), Carnegie Institution of Washington (1902), Carnegie Hero Fund Commission (1904), the Carnegie Foundation for the Advancement of Teaching (1905), the Carnegie Endowment for International Peace (1910), and Teachers Insurance and Annuity Association (1918), together with representatives of other philanthropies associated with the name. The centenary program consisted of a concert in Carnegie Hall, November 25th, by the New York Symphony Orchestra and the Oratorio Society of New York, Dr. Walter Damrosch master of ceremonies; a memorial gathering at the New York

Academy of Medicine, Butler presiding; and a centenary dinner at the Waldorf-Astoria on the twenty-seventh, for the trustees and friends of Mr. Carnegie's philanthropies, Jessup presiding, with Keppel, Conant of Harvard, and James as speakers.

Every Carnegie library in the United States and the British dominions and colonies, as well as many other educational agencies, received from the Corporation a framed reproduction in color of a portrait of Mr. Carnegie by Mr. Louis Mora, and the New York Public Library displayed books, pamphlets, and periodicals associated with the Founder's career. The Dunfermline weaver's son had come a long way in a short hundred years.

Other Relations

Jessup continued Suzzallo's care of the relationships existing between the Foundation and other educational bodies. Like his predecessor he was a member of the Educational Policies Commission of the National Education Association, the Problems and Plans Committee of the American Council on Education, and the Cleveland Conference. Jessup worked also with the National Association of State Universities, urging moderation and tolerance in that association's attitude towards colleges, their aims and standards, and he reported as a permanent delegate to the Council on Education of the American Medical Association. With the American Council on Education relations remained especially close; in 1940 and afterwards, discussion bearing upon tests and testing, in which Jessup and Learned took part, bore for American education perhaps more useful fruit than any other similar efforts. Jessup rendered long, active, and sympathetic service on the Board of Education of the Methodist Episcopal Church. In 1943 a committee of the American Association of University Professors presented a report on the relations between the Foundation, Carnegie Corporation, and T.I.A.A., the tone of which differed vastly from that of earlier pronouncements on the same or similar subjects.

THE FOUNDATION AND WORLD WAR II

Pearl Harbor and the advent of hostilities exerted upon the Foundation effects far stronger and more complicated than World War I had brought in 1917. Internal measures which events induced included organization, drills, and supplies for possible air raids, and the duplication and vault-storage of essential records until May

1944. The payment of retiring allowances and widows' pensions of noncitizens, under government regulations, gave trouble, partly through blocking of accounts, but infinitely less than would have accrued had benefits been transmitted directly instead of through disbursing offices of institutions. A plan of supplementary emergency compensation was adopted for members of the service staff. The emergency greatly intensified the care and efforts in investment of the finance subcommittee, the finance committee, and the co-operative investment office. Increased purchases of United States Government securities—measures stimulated by the Foundation's potential creditor relationship to the Corporation—cut income but assured principal. The Foundation lost no personnel to the war effort, except that Mr. Lovett's active duties ceased while he held appointment as Assistant Secretary of War for Air, an inevitable but serious blow. Fortunately, he retained nominal membership in the Board of Trustees during his years in Washington. The board by resolution adopted temporarily a two-year term for its chairman. Of the annual meetings 1940-45 national events became the standard topic for discussion, probably to the benefit but no great comfort of members of the board.

The Rules and the War

The restrictions in the Rules on work after retirement were soon seen as having an adverse effect upon the supply of personnel for college teaching and administration. To alleviate the difficulties the executive committee, January 7, 1942, voted that the officers for the duration of the war and the national emergency were so to administer the Foundation's Rules as "to facilitate temporary service connected with the National Defense without loss of benefits or of expectations. . . ." Moreover, the committee "unanimously agreed that this vote is to be interpreted with catholicity," and that beneficiaries should be free to undertake temporary service in the national defense, including term-time college teaching or administrative duties, without modification of benefits, and that services thus performed by pensionables associated temporarily with certain specified war-connected organizations should count as professorial service towards retirement under the Rules. The first two of these three actions constituted an almost complete reversal of the policy of strictness under which the Rules had previously been administered. Many beneficiaries rendered wartime service under these measures, principally through term-time teaching.

One wartime episode resulted in failure. The Foundation became involved in a proposed exchange of scientists between Great Britain and the United States which appears to have been originated by Lord Hankey. Carnegie Corporation looked with favor on the project, which was developed for the Foundation by Stephen Duggan, then president of the Institute of International Education, but because of American reluctance to release the scientists concerned the scheme fell through.

A decline in office consultation and interviewing enabled Jessup to serve on a reviewing committee of the National Defense Research Committee, Office of Scientific Research and Development, which considered policies and arrangements with universities about N.D.R.C. contracts for 1941-42. This duty might have proved burdensome if it had come to Jessup after he became immersed in the duties of the two presidencies; as it was, he took it in stride.

Wartime Projects

Of the joint projects which served the ends of war two deserve special mention at this point: In 1940 the Corporation granted through the Foundation and the National Education Association $15,000 for work of the United States Office of Education in special educational services. The grant was used chiefly for the Office's Information Exchange on Education in Wartime, which issued loan packets of material for elementary, secondary, higher, vocational, and adult uses. As for the Graduate Record Office, Learned was quick in seizing opportunities to further the national cause through co-operative testing in the field of engineering education and later in facilitating postwar attendance under the so-called G.I. Bill of Rights.

JULY 5, 1944

The strain of the war years and of dual responsibility told heavily upon Jessup's rugged health. During the winter of 1943-44 he was ailing but he concealed his troubles from his colleagues and worked at full speed. He and those of his family whom war service permitted were planning to pass the summer of 1944 in Vermont. On July 5 in New York City, where he was to have attended to certain Corporation duties, he died in his sleep of a heart attack. His sudden and tragic death left both Foundation and Corporation without presidents.

The memorial minute stressed three services he had rendered to the Foundation: fostering and concluding the Pennsylvania Study, opening up the Graduate Record Examination project, and for both "the Foundation and the profession of the teacher [what was] perhaps his greatest achievement . . . the addition to the Foundation's resources to meet its continuing pension load made possible through the generous action of Carnegie Corporation of New York." As Edward C. Elliott, chairman of the board, wrote in the Fortieth Annual Report (1945): "His influence upon American higher education was probably more far-reaching than the quiet geniality of his character and methods may now suggest."

Part Four — 1945-1950

~~~ 12 ~~~

Giving Place to New

FOUNDATION AND CORPORATION, 1944 · INTERREGNUM—COMMIT-
TEE ON THE PRESIDENCY; MEETINGS: TRUSTEES, EXECUTIVE COM-
MITTEE; PUBLICATIONS; THE COURT ORDER AMENDED, 1945 · CHOOS-
ING THE PRESIDENT · A NEW HAND—ANNUAL MEETINGS · TIME OF
CHANGE—STAFF MEMBERS, OFFICERS; SERVICE STAFF; OFFICE AC-
COMMODATIONS, ADMINISTRATION; FINANCIAL ARRANGEMENTS · THE
CHANGING SCENE · STUDIES, ACTIVITIES, PROJECTS—JOINT PROJECTS
REVIVED; THE SOUTHERN PROGRAM OF GRANTS-IN-AID · THE BOARD
OF TRUSTEES, 1945-50

FROM November 1941 to February 1946 the Carnegie Foundation for the Advancement of Teaching lacked a full-
time chief administrative officer. The burdens of the Corporation
presidency, much increased after Pearl Harbor, progressively curtailed the attention Jessup could spare for Foundation matters.
Although in the closing weeks of 1941 he was able to divide his
efforts with apparent equality between the two endowments, the
spring of 1942 found him devoting increasingly more time to the
affairs of Carnegie Corporation, and consequently less to those of
the Foundation. For several months before his death in July 1944
he seemed perforce content that the Foundation should proceed
under its own momentum.

At the roots of this growing situation lay a number of matters.
The work of the Corporation and problems related to Keppel's retirement combined to produce an undoubtedly irresistible challenge, and Jessup had been selected against the field to deal with it.
As for the time he could devote to visitors, few who called distinguished between the Corporation and the Foundation, and indeed
the business of both bodies coincided at many points. Usually

263

Jessup was accessible for brief office chats on Foundation affairs even if he could no longer find opportunity to initiate these talks himself. Learned and Savage—Reed having retired in 1940—were seasoned to their work and had able assistants. But those extempore, unhurried, face-to-face discussions, the best fruits of which are fresh ideas and which form a vitalizing core of the service that an endowment like the Foundation can render, grew fewer and fewer as the months went by.

Jessup's death deprived the Foundation of both an activating spark and the means whereby new procedures and policies could be wrought. Savage's duty, 1944-46, was to keep things moving; the executive committee expected him to "carry on," not to initiate, in order that Jessup's successor might take over as nearly as possible where Jessup had left off. The loss of Jessup, however, meant more than this. The memorial minute stressed "his personal participation in every phase of the Foundation's affairs . . . , his firm and farsighted handling of its problems, and his ready guidance in the fulfillment of its opportunities . . . he made his office, through his wisdom and friendly understanding, the resort of men in all branches of education . . ." and one trustee termed him "the wisest counsellor I ever had."

FOUNDATION AND CORPORATION, 1944

In some ways the loss of Jessup affected Carnegie Corporation no less than the Foundation. Through the years the relationship between the two endowments had grown closer. While on the one hand the Corporation had enabled the Foundation to meet its pension load, on the other the Foundation, in a sort of *quid pro quo*, had been conducted with conscientious regard to its obligations, financial and ethical, not alone to its own constituency, but especially to the Corporation. For at least fifteen years the Foundation's every policy, every action had been pretested before adoption by the light of this dual relationship. In one way Jessup's presidency of both Foundation and Corporation simplified the relationship between the two bodies, although for his successors it implied complexities, especially as affecting the dependent Foundation. Some of these began to appear during the year following his death, while his successors were being chosen.

Just as after Suzzallo's death Farrand helped in the conduct of the Foundation with friendly advice and consultation, so also, after Jessup's, his friend Edward C. Elliott, at the time chairman of the Foundation's Board of Trustees, went to even greater lengths of sacrifice and help for those in the Foundation upon whom the burden rested for more than a year and a half. Neither of these men hesitated to give aid and comfort in an emergency, and both were selfless in the service they rendered. Pritchett himself had bridged as president emeritus the gap between his own administration and Suzzallo's, and at the behest of the executive committee between Suzzallo's and Jessup's. Between Jessup's presidency and his successor's there was no bridge over which administrative continuity might proceed; there was a ford, and thanks to Dr. Elliott that gap was passed.

Committee on the Presidency

The executive committtee came to grips with the situation in October 1944. Its discussion early emphasized the fact that Jessup's work for and with the Corporation during the preceding thirty-two months had been grounded not in principle but in expediency and convenience, and the committee's feeling that in future the respective presidencies probably ought to be held by two different individuals. On these premises the executive committee authorized Dr. Elliott, who began meeting regularly with it, to appoint a five-man committee, of which he should be chairman and which should consist of four other trustees, two from the board at large and two from the executive committee membership itself, to consider "all matters and problems" connected with Jessup's death and the selection of a new president, and to confer with the corresponding committee already constituted by and for Carnegie Corporation. From the trustees at large Dr. Elliott chose Dr. Capen and Dr. Snyder, from among the executive committee Mr. Lamont and Dr. Sills. The question whether the Foundation ought to elect its president before or after the Corporation acted was left for discussion by the new committee.

Meetings: Trustees, Executive Committee

Almost every page of the minutes of the Foundation's thirty-ninth annual meeting (1944) reflects the loss of Jessup: official cognizance in the memorial minute; re-election of the officers of the board as a step towards preserving administrative continuity, a report of the progress made by the Foundation's committee on the presidency, constituted six weeks earlier, and trustee discussion of the qualities of mind and character that the new president should possess, particularly for the sake of continued co-operation with Carnegie Corporation of New York and with the president it was to choose. The committee planned to proceed very deliberately and encouraged no hopes of an early report. From the comments of individual trustees its members received confirmation of their own views, as outlined above, but little new light on the problems they faced. Two matters became clear: The committee was proceeding with due care and consideration, and its thoughts and attitude were constantly reverting to the relation of the Foundation to the Corporation.

Aside from natural stress upon reports of the committee on the presidency, the executive committee at its four meetings of 1944-45 faced prospective difficulties connected with the operation of the Court Order of 1939. These came as something of a shock to some of its members, but in January 1945 the executive committee, acting upon recommendation of the finance committee and the investment officer, Mr. Josephs, authorized the officers to seek in the name of the Foundation amendment to the Court Order which should smooth its practical operation. This matter receives attention on subsequent pages of this chapter.

On July 12, 1944, Dr. Elliott, after conferring long with Savage, had passed to him a letter of instruction which, being confirmed by the executive committee at its October meeting, was judged, taken together with the bylaws of the Foundation, to furnish a frame in which the Foundation's work might continue effectively. Certain committee members expressed concern over the fact that the chain of administrative responsibility at the time extended downward no further than the secretary, who was concurrently carrying his own jobs as secretary and as treasurer and many of the duties which the bylaws allotted to the president. Discussion suggested safeguarding further the succession of responsibility by appointing an assistant secretary, but no action ensued.

During the interregnum Dr. Elliott, by request, presided over meetings of the executive committee. January 1946 saw Mr. Robert A. Lovett, newly released from duty as Assistant Secretary of War for Air, elected to the finance committee. Administrative and certain financial functions proceeded much as before. So, too, did the remaining business of the Foundation. The Co-operative Graduate Testing Program, to which Chapter 13 will be mainly devoted, was attaining a success which surpassed even Learned's hopes and certainly the expectations of Jessup. The Rules of 1938-40 and the executive committee's instruction of January 1942 as to "catholicity" had facilitated the employment of both pensionables and beneficiaries as instructors for A.S.T.P. and V-12 programs, and the committee learned that at least 171 beneficiaries had performed war-related work after retirement.

Publications, 1944-46

Although in the period under discussion the Foundation issued a number of supplementary publications bearing upon the Co-operative Graduate Testing Program, its work and activities continued to be reflected most clearly in the two Annual Reports that came out after Jessup's death. To the Fortieth (1945) Dr. Elliott contributed what was really a public report of progress for the committee on the presidency. One sentence will illustrate the comprehension with which that committee was working: "The role of the Foundation in the years to come, whether in relation to the Carnegie endowments or to our higher education, depends to a large extent upon two factors: the quality of its presiding officer and the degree of success achieved in maintaining a Board of Trustees whose membership principally represents American higher education in action." That sentence was in full accord with the traditions of the Foundation and its Donor.

Admitting, as Dr. Elliott wrote, that "the Foundation's functions had long since passed their pioneering stage and become settled in pattern," its studies of its own pension provisions continued, especially from the actuarial point of view. Mattocks went forward with his annual scrutiny, and at each annual meeting Savage as treasurer discussed briefly the pension load and the working of the Court Order of 1939.

The Court Order Amended, 1945

For almost five years after the court order of 1939 issued the prime concern of the Foundation's finance committee and investment officers, as well as of the executive committee, continued to be improvement of quality and maturities of holdings. Income appeared to be of only slightly secondary importance. Among those most concerned there perhaps lay a feeling that the Foundation's relations, financial and otherwise, with Carnegie Corporation presupposed this emphasis. Between June 30, 1939, and June 30, 1943, the average rate of income from all securities held by the Foundation fell by somewhat irregular stages from 3.56 per cent to 3.19 per cent. By October 1943 the co-operative investment office, envisaging the day when under the Court Order the Foundation would be no longer able to expend principal, was becoming increasingly concerned with market values. Termination of Reserve Fund Number One in April 1944 seemed to advance that day and increase the concern, and the commencement of borrowing from the Corporation and the General Endowment Fund sharpened the prospect. For weeks before Jessup died actuarial and financial calculations concerning this matter were under way, and within the ensuing two months Mattocks began still another actuarial study of the pension load. His task was complicated by the changes in the interest rate he was bidden to assume, but at length the underlying assumptions were settled. Other data were as of June 30, 1945.

In the preceding January Josephs, as assistant treasurer and investment officer, had emphasized before the finance committee and the executive committee the following points: At that time the General Endowment Fund contained something over $15,000,000. Of this total the Court Order of 1939 permitted the use of $5,000,000 and more, principal and interest, for benefits, equal amounts to be advanced concurrently by the Corporation. The Order required that the prospective $10,000,000 remaining in the General Endowment Fund should stand intact, only its income to be used.

This invested capital was, of course, subject to market fluctuations. In some seven or eight years all of the $5,000,000 would probably be spent. During that period, if and when market value of the larger portion should fall to $10,000,000, then under the Order use of Foundation capital would have to cease. As the total of these resources approached the $10,000,000 downward limit the utmost care and attention would be required in investing only in nonfluctuating securities readily convertible into cash. This would certainly reduce the rate of return. The heart of the difficulty lay in the fact that no one could tell whether this would actually happen and if it did when it would occur. The finance committee and the investment officers were bedeviled by the bond redemptions they foresaw. These implied reinvestment. But in what securities? At what prices? At what rate of income?

The only possible safeguards, Josephs and the finance committee suggested, lay in (1) stabilizing the amount to be borrowed from the General Endowment (an amount which in January 1945 exceeded $5,000,000) in a legally separate portfolio, and (2) investing the remaining $10,000,000 in such securities as should produce the utmost income, assure eventual safety, and decrease concern with market fluctuations. Although this was, in 1945, a clear necessity, it could not have been foreseen in 1939 when the nation was at peace, however pressing it had since become.

The executive committee combed the problem to shreds, and reached the same conclusions as the finance committee. It went a step further; it authorized the Foundation's officers—in fact only two, Josephs and Savage—to seek, with the consent of the Corporation if obtainable, an amendment to the Court Order, the sooner the better.

About midway in this process the Foundation suffered its second impairment of administrative personnel within a year: Josephs took office, June 1, 1945, as president of Carnegie Corporation of New York. This might have proved serious had not Parker Monroe succeeded Josephs as Foundation investment officer, but with Josephs at hand for endless consultation the cloud turned out to have a golden lining.

It was Josephs who first consulted counsel in the matter. For the requisite actuarial calculations Mattocks was given a rate of return of 3¼ per cent. The long-drawn process of determining the actuarial and financial background turned largely into a matter of trial and error, in which, as one member of the executive committee pointed out, the chances of success came to rest rather upon investment skill than upon actuarial or other usual procedures. Clearly, to achieve the income rate of 3¼ per cent for the whole General Endowment Fund would demand close adjustment between quality of investments and rate of return—even some sacrifice of quality. Clearly also the whole matter was too highly technical to be submitted to the full Board of Trustees, especially without the competent steering of a skilled president. To secure clearcut, speedy action the officers could, under the bylaws, go to the six-man executive committee, of which two were members also of the finance committee and therefore fully informed on the matter. In May the executive committee took the necessary action; late in June counsel presented to the Supreme Court of the State of New York a Petition, with supporting documents, to modify the Court's Order of 1939.

Already a new element had entered the proceedings. The Attorney General of New York State was the statutory representative of the Foundation's beneficiaries; if any questions or impediments were to be introduced it would have been his duty to bring them in. On consultation the Attorney General suggested that if the respective amounts in the General Endowment to be retained intact, on the one hand, and to be used up, on the other, should be separated, then the two groups of securities should be segregated as of a date already past, if the influence of future eventualities was to be shaken off completely. For this step the investment officers were ready with a schedule showing securities classified as if they had already been segregated as of June 30, 1945. Careful timing and foresight speeded the final steps. Justice David W. Peck granted the petition to amend and it was entered August 2, 1945. In the proceedings the Court set June 30 for segregating the "permanent" portion of the General Endowment Fund and the expendable portion. On October 5 the executive committee approved and the Foundation could face a future freed from the tension of market values, unpredictable a decade or so in advance.

CHOOSING THE PRESIDENT

The Foundation's committee on the presidency met first on October 21, 1944, and thereafter on several occasions. Its members also consulted and corresponded among themselves and with their fellow trustees, energetically seeking ideas and suggestions. The composition of the group guaranteed that the choice of the Foundation's next president should be no star-chamber affair.

From the start there was apparently no notion that any one man should be president of both Foundation and Corporation, as Jessup had been, but at a joint meeting with the Corporation's committee, January 4, 1945, agreement was reached that the Foundation's choice should be made after the Corporation's, and after that date, in the Foundation's committee increased emphasis fell upon the necessity of continuing close relationship between the two philanthropies. Among the matters which the Foundation committee churned over were, first, the views that Jessup had really been loaned by the Foundation to the Corporation, that the charter purposes of the two endowments were separate and distinct, and that they ought to kept so; and, secondly, the suggestion that although the presidency of the Foundation as Jessup had left it was not a full-time job for a vigorous man, his successor could make it such if the Corporation continued its annual earmarking of $100,000 for projects. Dr. Elliott, in the Foundation's Fortieth Annual Report, summarized the central problems before the committee: "First, how can the Foundation, as its Charter requires, best continue its widely recognized service to the cause of higher education and the profession of the teacher in the United States, Canada, and Newfoundland with the limited resources at its command? Secondly, how best can the Foundation make available to Carnegie Corporation of New York in the future [a] co-operation at all commensurate with that extended over the past thirty-odd years?"

By April 15, 1945, certain members of the Foundation's committee were becoming somewhat disquieted "by the apparent inaction" of the Corporation group. They had planned to present their report in June at a special board meeting, but "unforeseen circumstances" canceled this hope. On May 14 Devereux C. Josephs, president of the Teachers Insurance and Annuity Association, was chosen president of Carnegie Corporation of New York, to take office June 1. Thereafter matters moved more rapidly. Even at long range there was developing a singular unanimity among Foundation trustees as to who should be their next president, a unanimity that in view of national and academic conditions made a special board meeting supererogatory. For the second time in the life of the Foundation resort was had to balloting by mail, as permitted by the bylaws. Each member of the board was particularly instructed that he might vote for a different candidate from the nominee of the committee on the presidency, and reminded that the new president was expected to devote the major portion of his time to special advisory services for the Corporation, and to be compensated proportionally.

Balloting, begun July 14, concluded September 1, 1945, with the unanimous election of Oliver Cromwell Carmichael, chancellor of Vanderbilt University, a Foundation trustee since 1938, to be the fourth president of the Carnegie Foundation. Official announcement was made twelve days later.

It is notable that this selection refined upon the Foundation's charter provision regarding representation from all parts of the country in its Board of Trustees. Pritchett had come to the Foundation from New England, Suzzallo from the West Coast, Jessup from the Middle West. Carmichael's previous service in the South completed a geographical pattern probably unrecognized by those whose ballots elected him.

A NEW HAND

O. C. Carmichael, graduate of the University of Alabama, and Rhodes Scholar at the University of Oxford, with a research degree in the School of *Litterae Humaniores* and a diploma in anthropology (1917) had been for nine years president of Alabama College before going to Vanderbilt as dean of the Graduate School and the Senior College. After a year's service as vice-chancellor he had succeeded in 1937 as chancellor James Hampton Kirkland, trustee of the Foundation 1917-37. Firmly identified with education in the southern states, especially at the higher level, Mr. Carmichael since 1939 had served as a trustee of the Teachers Insurance and Annuity Association. His participations had also included the Central Committee of the American Red Cross, the American Council's Problems and Plans Committee and also its Committee on the Relationships of Higher Education and the Federal Government, the board of the Nutrition Foundation, and the Advisory Council of the War Production Board.

Annual Meetings, 1945-50

By invitation the president-elect attended and participated in his first executive committee meeting November 14, 1945. On the same day he presided over discussion at the fortieth annual meeting and, as special adviser to Carnegie Corporation, sought views of his fellow Foundation trustees upon the Corporation's projected postwar program, and some of its bearings upon higher education.

Those views, as expressed, had value for the Corporation in shaping policy. On invitation of the Foundation board three Corporation officers attended the forty-first annual meeting (1946) to hear discussions of international studies and of testing at the higher level.

The first of these two topics bore upon the Corporation's plan for area studies that had been proposed in a memorandum drawn by the new Foundation president and the establishing of American centers of research in the field, the second upon development of the Graduate Testing Program and ultimately of Educational Testing Service, Inc., with a large grant from Carnegie Corporation. This was the first occasion in thirty years when others than officers and trustees of the Carnegie Foundation had attended an annual meeting, and the first time in an even longer period that an annual meeting had both morning and afternoon sessions.

These annual meetings began to resume the characteristics of a unique forum in the field of higher education. For the forty-second (1947) the topics were plans looking to the formation of a national testing agency, international studies, the impact of college upon the undergraduate, and balance in university education; for the forty-third (1948) recruitment, selection, and training of college faculties, including promotion policies and practices, as well as the working of the Selective Service Act 1948; for the forty-fourth (1949) the improvement of college teaching, and the program of the Association of American Universities. With few if any questions of Foundation policy or procedure to settle this use of part of the yearly gathering received unanimous approval among the Foundation's trustees. Close co-ordination of topics, on the one hand, with the daily experience of board members on their own campuses, and, on the other, with programs of the Corporation or of the Corporation and Foundation jointly; assigning of topics in advance and preliminary information as to their nature and probable handling; close timing of sessions; and the informed co-operation of the trustees themselves, vitalized the gatherings. Jessup had made a beginning in this direction which, however, by 1943 he had allowed to flag for fear of formalization. The newer handling has, on the contrary, brought increased spontaneity into the discussions.

TIME OF CHANGE

Those who, with the coming of a new chief executive, had expected considerable changes in the administration of the Foundation found their anticipations fulfilled during the ensuing five years. Some of these changes were ineluctable, others were matters of policy and choice.

Staff Members, Officers

After a third of a century as staff member, Learned, in June 1946, relinquished active responsibilities. The scope and variety of his work and of its influence upon American education had been the most extended and probably the most notable of all those who had served the Foundation, with the single exception of Pritchett himself. The fact that neither Reed nor Learned had a successor in the staff was a tribute to the unique value of their achievements. In February 1949, at the suggestion of President Carmichael, Savage resigned as secretary and as treasurer to devote full time, as staff member, to studying the history of the Foundation. Robert M. Lester, secretary of the Corporation since 1934 and the Foundation's associate secretary in charge of the joint grants-in-aid project, 1946-50, added the duties of secretary of the Foundation to his other work, while C. Herbert Lee, Corporation treasurer since 1942, became also treasurer of the Foundation.

Service Staff

For some years, as the business of the Foundation became more or less settled in pattern, it had been operating policy not to replace those members of the service staff who resigned or retired. During the period of recovery after World War II the number of assistants was still further reduced. Concurrently with these and other changes in officer and staff personnel, the need of office space was cut materially and certain overhead charges which formerly had been met by the Foundation were assumed by Carnegie Corporation of New York.

Office Accommodations, Administration

It had long been true that few persons without special knowledge could distinguish, or took the trouble to discriminate, between the Corporation and the Foundation. For a number of years affairs of both philanthropies had been conducted in part by the same persons —and benefactions by the two bodies had grown to be referred to as "Carnegie money," whatever its source. After 1946, as Carnegie Corporation extended its operations into the field of higher education, the business and educational relationships of the two endowments tended increasingly to coincide, and attempts to emphasize their individuality waned. In the summer of 1947 the office space shared by the two bodies was completely remodeled and consolidated. Subsequently office management and policy were unified under a single secretary working out a single set of principles, although each of the two philanthropies continued to operate under its own charter, bylaws, boards, and committees. All of these measures promised to reduce the cost of administering the Foundation; probably to some extent they reflected views which had received new emphasis in the two years succeeding Jessup's death.

Financial Arrangements

At the October 1945 meeting of the executive committee a proposal suggested by the co-operative investment office and recommended by the finance committee was adopted: to amortize on a "straight-line" basis premiums on the newly segregated "permanent" portion of the General Endowment Fund, probably because of the view that the process would assist in computing income available for payment of benefits and administrative expenses. After Mr. Lovett resumed his active connection with the Foundation, scrutiny of investments was conducted with increasing vigilance. The year 1948 broadened the changes in financial operations.

First, in January, the finance committee recommended and the executive committee approved in principle the "pooling" of four of the Foundation's funds. This resulted, on a date subsequently determined to be April 1, 1948, in combining the "permanent" portion of the General Endowment Fund, the endowment of the Division of Educational Enquiry, Reserve Fund Number Two, thenceforth designated "Contingency Fund," and the Emergency Reserve Fund, thereafter known as "Reserve Fund," in a single unit for purposes of investment, although the Foundation's accounts were expressly "to maintain and reflect the integrity of the respective funds." The step had been suggested some years before by the Foundation's auditors. Its final adoption brought a reduction in the number of banking accounts necessary and an ultimate simplification in accounting procedure.

As of June 30, 1948, the Foundation ceased to participate in the co-operative investment office and began to utilize in its investment work the advisory services of J. P. Morgan and Co., Incorporated. All these and other financial matters receive attention in Chapter 14.

THE CHANGING SCENE

With the coming of two new presiding officers to Carnegie Corporation and the Carnegie Foundation respectively, in spite of the fact that the president of the Foundation was much concerned with advisory services to the Corporation it seemed important at least to attempt to diminish the confusion in the public mind about the character and functions of the two endowments. This may have appeared especially desirable because the Corporation in its fresh emphasis upon one of its charter purposes, the diffusion of knowledge and understanding, began to deal increasingly and directly with the instrumentalities of higher education, the field to which the Foundation's charter specifically restricted it. Accordingly, in 1945, the Corporation arranged with a firm of public relations counselors a more or less formal undertaking with this end in view. Previously the Foundation, except in its very early days, had left press relations in the hands of its staff members and its officers, the former for the studies, inquiries, and publications which respectively had been their own prime concern, the latter for more general matters reflected principally in Annual Reports. The directness and informality characterizing this practice had savored of a certain amateurishness, which nevertheless had brought acceptable results. With the Corporation embarked upon its new policy there seemed no good reason, barring the tradition of independence, why the Foundation should not accept a generous offer to include it in the more professional arrangement. Accordingly this came to pass. Although the more modern practices thus implied fairly soon reached working order their value in results, as compared with that of the previous methods, has not as yet been completely established.

For forty years after 1908 repeated evidence led to the conviction that the typographical excellence of the Foundation's publications had contributed to good will on the part of readers and desirable standing and reputation for the Foundation. During that period its Bulletins, Annual Reports, and many of its other issues had been printed by D. B. Updike, the Merrymount Press. To this master of printing types and to Mr. John Bianchi was due the typographical distinction of more than one hundred Foundation publications. The printer's chief problem in this work Mr. Updike outlined in his *Notes on the Merrymount Press* (1934): "This printing required ingenuity in its arrangement and in the co-ordination of the material, and accuracy as absolute as can be attained. The Foundation has shown the Press much consideration; the Press in its turn has given the best it has." This fortunate relationship ended December 31, 1948, when the Merrymount Press ceased operations, and the Foundation's printing had to be taken elsewhere. Its latest list of publications had issued in 1947.

The form and display of the Foundation's minutes had been a special care of the Merrymount Press. Since 1922, with the exception of a single meeting, they had been drafted by the Foundation's secretary. In 1949, with the coming of a new hand to this task and with the shift in printers, it was natural that the minutes should exhibit changes in form and emphasis.

Much the same was true in respect of the Annual Reports beginning with the Forty-fourth (1949). In them the president and the secretary had presented yearly summaries of matters pertaining to their respective duties and work. The Reports continued to present full and detailed information about financial matters and investments, and a regrouping in the treasurer's section made the material clearer and more easily available. Statements concerning projects in operation and complete data on the retiring allowances and pensions of the Foundation continued. A list replaced the biographical sketches of deceased recipients of retiring allowances, which as "De Mortuis" had formed part of each Annual Report since the Second (1907), but the names included in the lists appeared no less distinguished and the services which their bearers had by inference rendered to American higher education no less faithful or important than those of their colleagues of other days.

The index was omitted from the Forty-fourth Annual Report, which contained sixty-one pages, and the Forty-fifth with sixty-seven, as contrasted with the much more extended format of preceding years.

By 1949 the bylaws of the Foundation had remained unaltered for nearly ten years. At the forty-fourth annual meeting, after study by counsel, they were revised and amended to provide for certain contingencies which if not treated specifically might conceivably involve questions of legality. The secretary of the board disappears from the new version, the finance committee becomes the investment committee after the pattern of the Corporation, while Roberts's Rules of Order make their debut among the more technical provisions.

During the past five years the payment of retiring allowances and widows' pensions has followed in the main the established pattern, which the closing of the List of Pensionables 1931 and codification of the Rules made possible, except that the administration of provisions for work after retirement appears to have been tightened.

Since 1931, when Suzzallo devised a formula for fixing dates of executive committee meetings, the committee had assembled regularly on the Friday nearest the seventh of January, May, and October, with a brief special session on the morning of each annual meeting. This schedule held until 1950, when other commitments by executive committee members began to impair quorums. The January meeting was then omitted, and other sessions, while approximating the former schedule, were called at the convenience of members.

STUDIES, ACTIVITIES, PROJECTS, 1945-50

The pensioning experience of the Foundation continued to invite intensive study. Mattocks went forward with his actuarial analyses, paying particular attention to the relations between load, mortality, and resources. By 1944 various factors, including longevity at the older ages, promised to increase somewhat the Foundation's liabilities, and Mattocks's studies contributed much groundwork for the amendment to the Court Order in 1945. A year later the executive committee considered a renewed proposal from him on abolishing the practice of continuing allowances and pensions in force for thirty days after the death of beneficiaries but no action was taken. As early as 1941 Savage, treasurer, prompted by Mattocks, had noted before the board that benefits might cost more annually than anticipated. For the next several years this came to pass, even though administrative expenses were held to a figure much below that which Mattocks had allowed for.

Nonactuarial pension studies were reported in two discussions by Miss Maslen and Savage, prepared for Annual Reports: in the Forty-first (1946) "A Record of Experience with the Closed List," and in the Forty-second (1947) "Senior Beneficiaries of the Foundation." While the first stressed the astonishing stability of the group of pensionables, the second was the more sensational; it showed that out of 4,383 beneficiaries (1906-46) a total of 63 had been recipients for twenty-five years or more, and that of all types of beneficiaries widows tended to receive benefits for the longest time.

The extended duration of allowances paid on the basis of disability was startling.

Meanwhile Carmichael, in addition to his exacting duties as special adviser to Carnegie Corporation, was working with the President's Commission on Higher Education, as vice-chairman of the Young commission on a state university for New York, and as chairman of the board of the State University of New York from its inception in 1949, public services which demanded almost infinite time and patience. His efforts in behalf of work conferences in higher education sponsored by the Southern Association of Colleges and Secondary Schools were recognized by resolution of that association.

In the Foundation's Annual Reports the president's discussions of educational topics attracted renewed attention by their timeliness and their directness. The thesis of the section in the Forty-first Annual Report (1946) was: "The final educational result depends upon the teacher. In our educational planning he should be exalted, the importance of his role emphasized and magnified." The next stressed the importance of "international studies" and possible means of supporting them. The piece for 1948, "Towards Better College Teaching," emphasized promising current efforts to further that end and the need of recognizing good teachers as more important than material equipment. The section in the Forty-fourth Annual Report (1949) dealt with "Education in Values" in a truly free and democratic society, while that in the Forty-fifth (1950), presenting "A Century of Higher Education—A Review," pointed the need of a "consistent, clearcut philosophy of American higher education," and wise formulation of objectives in the light of modern conditions.

Joint Projects Revived

The new administration re-emphasized the scheme of joint projects financed by Carnegie Corporation and sponsored by the Foundation in its Division of Educational Enquiry. The most recent assures the preparation by Dr. M. M. Chambers of a volume in the series on *The Colleges and the Courts*, dealing with the years 1946-50, under the auspices of the Foundation. Two other joint projects, operational in nature, on "through" grants, pertain also to higher education: one in the amount of $50,000 to the University of Missouri, March 17, 1949, "to improve undergraduate instruction in Missouri colleges," the other, November 1949 and 1950, totaling $45,000, for a study of general education in California community colleges sponsored by the American Council on Education. Results were published in 1952 in B. Lamar Johnson's *General Education in Action*. A fourth grant, May 9, 1947, "to" the Foundation, enabled Dr. R. B. Robbins, formerly vice-president of T.I.-A.A., an experienced and recognized authority in the field, to prepare a study of the contribution of the Foundation to pension and retirement theory since 1905.

The Southern Program of Grants-in-Aid

The last joint project to be considered here, but the first in order of time for the initial grant and in historic relationship to the Foundation is the Program of Grants-in-Aid for teachers in colleges of the southern area, first discussed concretely by President Carmichael at the forty-first annual meeting (1946) in relation to the initial Corporation grant. It seems almost like the harvest of a seed sown by Flexner, 1925-26, in an unpublished working memorandum in which he advocated "a system of fellowships for younger scholars of promise and a system of grants to older men who deserve and need a renewal of inspiration. . . ." Moreover, Wilson Gee, in *Research Barriers in the South*, 1932, had called attention to the need of increased emphasis on research and its support, as demonstrated in the work of the Southern Regional Committee, Social Science Research Council, under a Corporation-Foundation grant. The first attempt to meet on an extensive scale the problem Flexner and Gee had defined, came on March 21, 1946, when the trustees of Carnegie Corporation granted $700,000, payable $140,000 in each of five years, for a "co-operative, experimental program of grants-in-aid to institutional staffs in the Southeast" under the direction and management of the Foundation. Robert M. Lester, secretary of Carnegie Corporation, long familiar with higher education in the southern states, was named associate secretary of the Foundation to co-ordinate and oversee the program in the thirty-three participating higher institutions, divided into regional groups. After a promising start the Corporation, November 19, 1946, by an additional grant of $235,000, payable $47,000 annually for five years, made possible the extension of the project to thirteen Negro colleges and universities. Further funds, May 17, 1949, and one more participating institution brought total Corporation grants on this account up to $955,000. The number of co-operating institutions in 1950 stood at forty-seven, and their own contributions had already amounted to $260,000.

During the fourth year of operation the local faculty committees which select recipients and determine the amounts of their stipends had made allocations to approximately one thousand teachers, to help them supplement their teaching by carrying on research and creative activity of their own choosing, in fields of their own individual interest and competence. The ultimate purpose is to advance higher education in the area by vitalizing it and improving its quality. Opinion at regional meetings held during each year of the program has indicated that the project is producing valuable results and achieving its purposes.

The co-operative experimental Program of Grants-in-Aid in the South was received with approval and appreciation by the Committee on Higher Education of the Southern Association of Colleges and Secondary Schools. One of the participating institutions is already engaged in establishing an endowment to maintain local provisions after termination of the grant. On October 29, 1950, Yale University announced an anonymous gift of $1,000,000 to be used to assist younger faculty members in establishing themselves as productive scholars at a period in their careers when teaching programs are usually heaviest. Although this gift is not directly connected with the Southern Program of Grants-in-Aid, possibilities for such projects over the country at large appear very great, by whatever means results may be appraised.

It is notable that in the period 1924-50 grants by Carnegie Corporation "to" or "through" the Foundation for ninety-odd projects totaled more than $3,360,000, with an average approximating $129,390 for each year.

THE BOARD OF TRUSTEES, 1945-50

Initially Carmichael inherited a somewhat unusual situation in his Board of Trustees. During the war years resignations had been submitted by five of its members on relinquishing active academic service. For various reasons, mainly connected with the war, none of these resignations had been accepted, and at Jessup's personal request in each case the trustees involved had retained their seats, not without embarrassment over this contravening of tradition. With subsidence of the national emergency most of the resignations were pressed. Clearly the Foundation stood to profit in the long run through the replacements they implied. Instead of acting hastily, the board referred the five resignations to the executive committee, which, meeting more frequently than the board, might deal with them the more deliberately. Of the five, four were accepted and one withdrawn, although its author attended no more board meetings.

In the course of the years 1945-50 a majority of the Board of Trustees was replaced through election of no fewer than fourteen new members. Death took Butler, Lamont, and Fox. Resignations upon relinquishment of academic duties accounted for eleven other vacancies. The resulting elections were as follows: 1945—Harris of Tulane, Valentine of Rochester; 1946—Compton of Washington University, Davidson of Union, Fred of Wisconsin; 1947—Josephs of Carnegie Corporation, who resigned after taking the presidency of the New York Life Insurance Company two years later; 1948— Allen of the University of Washington, Lowry of Wooster; 1949— Millis of Western Reserve, Gustavson of Nebraska, Thomas S. Lamont of New York City; 1950—Arthur S. Dean of New York City, Eisenhower of Columbia, Griswold of Yale. In the board as a whole on November 15, 1950, the presiding officers of institutions of higher education in the United States numbered twenty-one, in Canada one; the laymen three.

As of June 30, 1950, the average age of the Foundation's Board of Trustees was 62.9 years. The oldest in both years and service was Denny, whom Mr. Carnegie had selected, the youngest Davidson. Five members were less than fifty years of age, but only one was under the average age of the original group when chosen by the Founder. The ages of the eleven trustees chosen 1945-49, inclusive, averaged 49.6 years at the time of election; of the three chosen in 1950, 52.0 years. For all of the fourteen new trustees elected 1945-50, inclusive, the average age at election was 50.1 years. For the whole board as it stood after the elections of November 15, 1950, the average age was 57.5 years, as contrasted with the figure for November 15, 1905, namely 45 years.

Experiment in Graduate Testing

ROOTS—PRITCHETT'S CONCEPTS; THE FOUNDATION AND EARLY NEW-TYPE TESTING; THE FOUNDATION AND WRITTEN EXAMINATIONS, 1923 · RISE OF THE GRADUATE RECORD EXAMINATION PROJECT · EARLY DAYS—PURPOSE OF THE PROJECT; NATURE OF THE EXAMINATION · PROGRESS—THE CENTRAL PROGRAM; BRANCHING OUT; ENGINEER-ING MEASUREMENT AND GUIDANCE; MEDICAL APTITUDE TESTS; INDE-PENDENT STUDENT-TESTING PROGRAM; PUBLICATIONS · DOLLARS AND CENTS—MACHINE SCORING; QUARTERS; ACCOUNTING · A NATION-WIDE TESTING AGENCY · PICKING UP THE PIECES · FIVE YEARS OF E.T.S.

O NE who seeks in this chapter a complete or a technical discussion of new-type objective tests or a history of the science and art of examining will be disappointed. He will find only a summary of an experimental testing project conducted by the Carnegie Foundation and financed mainly by Carnegie Corporation of New York. That experiment had complex origins, unusually wide range, and important results for American education.

ROOTS

The history, philosophy, and procedure of examinations in America have had able treatment in Kandel's *Examinations and Their Substitutes in the United States* (1936), Bulletin Number 28 of the Carnegie Foundation. Others also have shown that testing as we know it today goes back to Sir Francis Galton's *Inquiries into Human Faculty* (1883), and was developed for North America through the work of James McKeen Cattell, J. M. Rice, Edward L. Thorndike, H. H. Goddard, who in the 1890's and early 1900's applied the scales and principles of Alfred Binet, Lewis M. Terman, Daniel Starch, Edward C. Elliott, F. J. Kelly, and many others. During the year 1917-18 War Department use of the Army Alpha Tests, involving two or three million persons, added impetus to the movement. The reliability of marks for old-type discursive examinations came increasingly under question and scrutiny, and by the 1930's new-type objective testing had made its way into every educational level—indeed, into almost every school and college—in America.

Pritchett's Concepts

Thorndike's *Mental and Social Measurements* appeared in the year preceding Mr. Carnegie's Letter of Gift. While the volume attracted much attention its principles did not gain full acceptance overnight. Pritchett knew of it, but in the Foundation's first three years his attention was fixed upon what then were considered broader aspects of higher education. In November 1908 he proposed to the executive committee that the Foundation undertake studies of professional education, including graduate schools, and the executive committee's approval of his "pet idea," as Vanderlip termed it, in effect set up a grand *schema* of inquiries that was to endure for some four decades.

To Pritchett Jessup ascribed a second fertilizing concept. In the Preface to Bulletin Number 28 he connected the origins of the Pennsylvania Study with Pritchett's plea in the Nineteenth Annual Report (1924) for "an ideal of education which rests upon simplicity, sincerity, and thoroughness," and related this ideal to the quality of education, a matter fundamental to the Pennsylvania Study. Jessup thus brought the chain of ideas down to 1926 and to Learned's preoccupation with the quality of education in the United States and in Europe, the theme of his Bulletin Number 20 (1927).

The Foundation and Early New-type Testing

Ten years before the Pennsylvania Study began the Foundation took its first step into the field of objective examination. In May, June, and October 1916, as part of its teacher-training inquiry, Walter F. Dearborn, professor of education at Harvard, sponsored in the experimental school of the University of Missouri appraisals in arithmetic, spelling, penmanship, reading, and English composition, using recognized tests, procedures, and scales, and a statistical treatment that though comparatively crude was indicative.

Five graduate students did the work, and results appeared in Learned's Bulletin Number 14 (1920).

The second step into the area came at about the same time. For Mann's study of engineering education, E. L. Thorndike of Columbia gave to forty-one Massachusetts Institute of Technology freshmen, forty-one engineering school freshmen at the University of Cincinnati, and thirty-four Columbia students all or parts of several objective tests in mathematics, English, and physics. The Columbia group served as a rudimentary control. While Professor Truman L. Kelley, who made the correlations, averred that seven of the tests used together had prognostic value, Pritchett in his Preface to Bulletin Number 11 (1918) was skeptical: "It is quite clear that the trial of these tests is not sufficient to demonstrate their trustworthiness" in prognosis of fitness for engineering study and practice. But, he added significantly, "There are few devices connected with teaching more unsatisfactory than our present day examinations, whether used as tests for admission or as criteria of performance on the part of the student."

The Foundation and Written Examinations, 1923

Two other steps retraced old paths. The first was taken under Furst's initiative. After the operations of the College Entrance Examination Board had been studied in the Foundation's offices, the executive committee in May 1923 authorized the New York Public Library to prepare a bibliography and synopsis of the literature concerning written examinations at a cost not to exceed $2,000. The task was related to an exploratory study of the teaching of English financed by the General Education Board, leading lights in which were Chancellor Samuel P. Capen, newly come to the University of Buffalo, Principal Wilson Farrand of Newark Academy, and President Frank Aydelotte of Swarthmore, American Secretary of the Rhodes Trust.

The next step was the selection of a group of Oxford dons chosen by former Rhodes Scholars suggested by Aydelotte, to comment upon certain College Board examinations—the questions not the answers. Few of the dons had knowledge of American examination problems or practices, and the views of the group, which Furst discussed in the Twentieth Annual Report (1925), had little pertinence. During this period the National Conference on Uniform Entrance Requirements in English, with which Furst was involved, was working on related matters side by side with the College Board.

These jottings bring the record of the Foundation's interest in examining and its techniques down to the inception of the Pennsylvania Study in 1926. That record may appear disparate for it touches Pritchett's interest in the quality of our education, his suggestion that graduate education be studied as associated with professional education, his discontent with current examining practice, the Pennsylvania Study as related to quality in the educational product, two tentative steps in the direction of new-type objective testing, and two rather niggling approaches to old-type discursive examinations. Learned's concern with the quality of education paved a direct route to the Foundation's inquiry into the relation of secondary to higher education in Pennsylvania. From this uneven soil, fertilized by long interest in graduate education and the rise of comprehensive objective tests, the Graduate Record Examination project was to grow.

RISE OF THE GRADUATE RECORD EXAMINATION PROJECT

As if the matters just enumerated did not yield sufficiently complicated sources for the Graduate Record Examination experiment, another must be traced.

By 1934, new-type testing, variously pursued, was booming through American primary and secondary schools and turning longtime conceptions of curriculums and methods topsy-turvy. Carl C. Brigham had brought the College Entrance Examination Board to using scholastic aptitude tests. This change, together with the rise of the Co-operative Test Service of the American Council on Education, pretty well accounted for the secondary level. After eight years of experience the Pennsylvania Study, under Learned and Ben D. Wood, was spreading new-type tests throughout the undergraduate level, not only within the commonwealth but at numbers of other colleges over the country, where it was bringing successful and revealing results. As early as 1931 Learned and Wood had envisaged a national college testing program, but it languished, partly for lack of funds, although in the following year the National Teacher Examination of the American Council on Education got off to a good start. Among colleges using the Pennsylvania tests some were eager to give them in the senior year. The dean of one graduate school in the South suggested that they might even be used for admission to graduate work. To Learned and Wood this notion was as tempting as fine marble to a sculptor and they worked it over in many a session. For Learned especially it opened an enticing vista of testing in the hands of a single unifying body from the first school grade to the last year of college and the very gates of the graduate school. Only the graduate school itself stood outside the charmed circle, but if the suggestion of the dean, as mentioned, were developed the graduate school itself might be brought to use objective tests, to its own great advantage, and ultimately a single body might offer a new-type testing program for every school, college, and university in English-speaking North America.

The more Learned and Wood played with this idea the more it fascinated them. During the winter of 1935-36 Learned discussed it with his office colleagues, Jessup, Keppel, Reed, Savage, and to them it almost sold itself. Really, as Wood and Learned came to see with increasing clarity, it had two components: The first was the development and establishment of objective testing at the graduate level, the second the uniting of all testing bodies in a single agency. Difficulties loomed as very great but not insurmountable. In the autumn Jessup asked Wood, with whom he and Keppel had discussed the matter, to prepare a written statement about it, and in December 1936 Wood completed a brief but comprehensive plan setting forth the advantages of a nationwide nonprofit educational testing agency.

In the meantime, however, Learned had reached the conviction that an objective graduate examination could not be inaugurated on, so to speak, a wholesale basis, that the best chance of success lay in interesting four of the greater American graduate schools through their deans, and that the co-operation of the College Entrance Examination Board was essential to both components of the project. Accordingly, he laid the whole matter before the graduate deans of four northeastern universities: Dr. George B. Pegram of Columbia, Dr. George H. Chase of Harvard, Dr. L. P. Eisenhart of Princeton, and Dr. Edgar S. Furniss of Yale, who conferred twice as a group and far oftener as individuals in the spring of 1936, Learned being present, and once in December when the presence of Jessup, Learned, and Wood brought renewed life to the undertaking. Conditional approval from the group opened the way to the development of the general plan. Keppel was strong for it, and that seemed to assure money for the experiment. Dr. George F. Zook, president of the American Council on Education, although taken by the notion thought the time for it was not yet ripe. An approach to the College Entrance Examination Board through

Brigham at first promised success, but afterwards stalled, with the gradually emerging result that the proposals for a single testing agency had to be laid aside in January 1938.

Earlier events had left the four deans approving the project in principle but stymied as to graduate testing. In the Foundation offices the outlook for both phases was dimming. A suggestion from one of the four co-operating deans saved the day. It was to this effect: "We are ready to go. Why wait? Let's get on with the examinations."

This suggestion appealed to all concerned and the matter moved off dead center. Wood and Learned went to work on the long task of getting the examination constructed. Discussions with members of the American Council's Committee on Measurement and Guidance accelerated the process. The first Graduate Record Examination was offered in the graduate schools of Columbia, Harvard, Princeton, and Yale in October 1937.

EARLY DAYS

From the Pennsylvania Study in its closing phases to the new Graduate Testing Program Learned took his colleagues Wood and Charles R. Langmuir, and many of his service staff. For a decade they had been associated in the earlier work, had developed and revised it, and knew it root and branch.

Purpose of the Project

Learned traced the purposes of the Co-operative Graduate Testing Program in his contribution to the Forty-first Annual Report (1946). In 1936-37, he noted, American graduate schools were threatened with a great influx of students formerly held back by the economic depression. The A.B., which had long since ceased to draw the line between the fit and the unfit, still had one discriminating feature: "It marked the upper limits of an area completely dominated up to that point by 'credits.'" A good graduate school stood to gain by using "the findings of a well-made external examination as turning the scale for the admission of a student, or at least for granting him a scholarship or a fellowship." In the initial stages of the experiment students were examined only after they had been admitted to graduate work; later, as use of the examination spread, it became accepted as furnishing revealing information about candidates for entrance, and some graduate schools required it before admission, while many depended considerably upon it for various purposes. Scores, reported in graphic profiles for each individual performance, facilitated comparisons of many sorts. Results of the examination and of the whole experiment, it was agreed, were to be published only with the consent of the co-operating deans.

Nature of the Examination

Both the Pennsylvania tests and the Graduate Record Examination were of the comprehensive objective type. They employed true-false, multiple-choice, and other recognized forms of question.

The original Graduate Record Examination had a more immediate purpose than the Pennsylvania tests described in Chapter 10, in that it sampled a student's organized knowledge with a view to determining his fitness to undertake graduate study. Comprising seven tests, to be taken complete in two half-day sessions totaling six hours, it dealt with mathematics, physical sciences, social studies, literature and fine arts, one foreign language, and the verbal factor. All examinees took all of these tests and the scores of each were recorded on a chart based on the average scores of a standard group of first-time graduate students.

The first revision of the examination divided the physical science section into two tests: physics and chemistry; literature and art into general literature and the fine arts; while by reduction the social science section was restricted to history, government, and economics, and the foreign language was omitted.

The second revision, 1938-39, added for students with special knowledge an advanced examination in fourteen fields of learning in which to demonstrate their capacity.

Each of the elementary and the advanced tests was framed and revised under the direction of a committee of four scholars for each subject, one appointed by the dean of each of the four co-operating graduate schools. The four scholars collected and screened material, pretested it, and passed upon its final use and arrangement. The question-and-answer books were carefully guarded by a system of hand-to-hand receipts. By 1940 the time for the whole examination, both elementary and advanced, including recesses and optional extensions, was lengthened to comprise two periods of four hours each. Further revisions and changes were made during 1945-46.

PROGRESS

During the period 1936-47 the Co-operative Graduate Testing Program was not the only activity under way for the Foundation's Division of Educational Enquiry. Several other projects were proceeding with grants from Carnegie Corporation. Roughly these projects pertained to the general fields of inquiry to which the Graduate Record Examination related: graduate education as represented by Dean Edwards's inquiries concerning graduate student records, and Ryan's studies of early graduate education in the United States; and testing and examining, as exemplified in the Pennsylvania Study, American participation in the European Examinations Inquiry, and Kandel's investigation of examinations and their substitutes which terminated with the publication of Bulletin Number 28 in January 1937. Beneath all of these efforts taken together the essential pattern is clearly discernible. The Co-operative Graduate Testing Program paralleled most of them, as two five-year glances at it will show.

The Central Program, 1937-42

The G.R.E. was first given in the graduate schools of Columbia, Harvard, Princeton, and Yale in October 1937. Brown University joined the group in March 1938. The revised tests were administered in these five graduate schools in 1938, '39, and '40. In 1938 Wisconsin and Rochester also tested graduate students, and in 1940 the graduate schools of four state universities used the tests: Iowa, Michigan, Minnesota, and Wisconsin. Meanwhile, three institutions had employed the tests at the undergraduate level—Brown 1938, Rochester 1939, and Hamilton 1939—and in 1939-40 no fewer than fifteen colleges and universities were following their example. By 1942 the examination had spread to fourteen graduate schools in which 12,704 students had taken it, and to twenty-six colleges with 14,948 undergraduates, a total thus far of 27,652 examinees. In addition, for the Association of American Universities Learned had directed the examining of 2,639 undergraduates at twenty colleges in connection with applications for admission to the Association's "Approved List." All of this work had been supported by Corporation grants totaling $357,100. In a conference held in October 1940, ample evidence had shown that colleges were finding the examination "serviceable not only as an aid to counselling seniors but also as a source of significant evidence about students and curricula," as Learned indicated in a memorandum to members of the test committee.

The first five years were a mixture of cloud and sunshine. One of the four deans found his hands full in keeping his faculty in line because of their fears of premature publicity. Of course, under the initial agreement announcement of results rested with the co-operating deans. By 1940 the notion was developing that the individual profiles showing performance in the tests could and—tentatively— might well be used as credentials for graduate school entrance, a view which Dean Pegram had expressed during the preceding year. The four deans had met upon several occasions; at their meeting of January 1940 they were gratified and probably relieved to hear from Jessup, Learned, and especially Langmuir, a most skillful tester, that "there should be constant study and revision of the tests," a task upon which the technical committee was soon engaged. Two years and more later Langmuir was able to state, in the Thirty-seventh Annual Report (1942), that results indicated "that the examination scores alone are approximately as useful as transcript records taken alone, and the two combined in a manner which uses the test results as a supplement to other evidence of students' qualifications yield a better basis for classifying students than either one used alone." In June 1942 work with the examination was reviewed by the deans of ten co-operating graduate schools, with unanimous agreement as to the worth of the program and the desirability of extending it at the undergraduate level.

Incidentally, in 1940 the enterprise had acquired its own local habitation and a new name for its quarters, the Graduate Record Office.

Branching Out, 1942-47

Thus even before 1940 the program, the basal purpose of which related to the improvement of graduate education, had been extended downward to the undergraduate level, and by 1942 undergraduates were in the majority among its examinees. The shift in examined personnel increased costs materially. The rapidity with which the use of the examination spread amazed all those involved. Much of the expansion was the product of the persuasive attitude of the men directing the work and their hospitality to suggestions for improving and increasing the service it was rendering.

By 1944 some fifty graduate or professional schools or divisions, in accordance with the statement of the ten co-operating deans two years earlier, were requiring or inviting applicants to submit results as an auxiliary credential for admission. A year later the sponsoring institutions, or schools within such institutions, numbered ninety-eight. Of these, thirty, including thirteen medical schools and four schools of law, required the Graduate Record Examination for all or some classes of matriculants. Centers at which the examination was available had increased to 208, of which 11 were in Canada. By 1947 the program included more than 175 higher institutions, for which it had furnished test results for upwards of 115,600 Graduate Record examinees. It had been suggested that the examination might be used for senior students in the institutions of the Southern Association of Colleges and Secondary Schools. The Foundation's challenge of 1906 concerning higher education in the South had surely been met.

As the colleges began the task of reconstruction after World War II and faced the problems of caring for increased attendance, it seemed likely that the use of suitable examinations might aid considerably in charting future instructional procedures. With a new general-education section of the G.R.E. (the "Profile" tests) to become available for use in the spring of 1946, it was essential to obtain fresh norms for purposes of comparison. Both to supply this need and at the same time to provide colleges with an inventory of each student's educational development, the opportunity seemed too useful to neglect. Accordingly, the Graduate Record Office planned an ambitious program to involve 20,000 students at fifty-odd accepted colleges and universities in giving the revised examination during the spring of 1946 and again in 1947. Results of the first testing were duly and promptly reported to the participating institutions. Although scores were not published, they probably made their contribution to the solution of a variety of institutional problems on many a campus, and the G.R.O. got its new norms.

The program in its second five years, responsive to needs and requests, overflowed into several other fields than graduate and general undergraduate education.

Engineering Measurement and Guidance

In the spring of 1943 the Society for the Promotion of Engineering Education and the Engineers' Council for Professional Development, long interested in problems of the professions they represented, applied to the Foundation for help in solving them. To this step they were prompted partly by difficulties aggravated by World War II and related to student selection, curricula organization, and the outcomes of instruction. These matters focused upon the subject of examination, and Jessup and Learned willingly hearkened to the call, with the result that there was inaugurated a project to deal with measurement and guidance in engineering education, sponsored co-operatively by the Society, the Council, and the Foundation. The general aim was to design certain objective examinations to assist in selecting and guiding engineering students, to determine the effectiveness of these tests, and, if possible, to provide instruments and methods that should aid in adjusting the engineering student to his initial study.

A somewhat elaborate organization of institutions and committees was set up. Work on the tests began in the spring of 1941, with contributions of material from fifteen engineering institutions, and by July 1, 1943, active work commenced, initial use of the examination being scheduled for the autumn of 1944. An earlier analysis of the educational practices of a hundred engineering schools aided materially. Learned reorganized the Graduate Record Office to accommodate the project and placed it in charge of his associate, Dr. K. W. Vaughn, who, however, continued to direct the National Teacher Examination of the American Council on Education's Co-operative Test Service until July 1, 1946.

Vaughn's vigorous pursuit of his new assignment led to the devising of a comprehensive new-type entrance examination termed the Pre-engineering Inventory, which in its revised Form A consisted of seven tests: general verbal ability, technical verbal ability, ability to comprehend scientific materials, general mathematical ability, ability to comprehend mechanical principles, spatial visualizing ability, and understanding of modern society. Aside from the diagnostic and other general purposes of the inventory at participating institutions, the tests were employed to a limited extent as aid in selection of scholarship holders, as the official selection test for the United States Merchant Marine Cadet Corps, and especially in statewide programs bearing upon the admission to engineering study at the state universities in California, South Dakota, Utah, Washington, and Wyoming. Ultimately the project was expanded to offer two aptitude examinations and two series of achievement tests and certain high-school guidance tests for the field. Up to December 1947 a total of 75,946 examinees had undergone the inventory. Funds had come from partial reimbursement of costs through fees, a money contribution from the E.C.P.D., and Carnegie Corporation-Foundation grants.

Medical Aptitude Tests

For some years certain schools of medicine made use of the Graduate Record Examination for or at admission of candidates to medical study. All told, more than a dozen schools had employed the tests. This led in 1945-46 to the Association of American Medical Colleges requesting the Graduate Record Office, in co-operation with the association's Committee on Student Personnel Practices, to prepare and administer for a reimbursing fee a comprehensive test designed to reveal aptitudes for undertaking the study of medicine. A nationwide program of testing for medical schools commenced January 1, 1947. By June of that year 14,307 applicants for entrance had been tested, and the number ultimately rose to 23,096 while the examination was administered in the Graduate Record Office. Vaughn directed the program up to March 1948.

Independent Student-Testing Program

As soon as the Co-operative Graduate Testing Program began to take hold, those interested realized that if the examination was to be made widely available to persons not in active university connection, the number of points at which it was administered would have to be very materially increased. Development of this policy encountered difficulties in establishing new examination centers; staffing each with an examiner and later with assistants, as well as furnishing instructions in order to assure uniform administration of the tests; supplying question books, reassembling them in New York City with the questions answered; paying the examiners; collecting the reimbursing fees; not to mention co-ordinating the whole process and its multitude of details. In all this there was always the example of the College Entrance Examination Board, which since 1900 had extended its examining centers over the world, and later the experience with the not dissimilar system of the Association of American Medical Colleges.

For the Graduate Record Examination project earlier organized effort to increase the number of centers beyond the campuses of institutions making direct use of the test began intensively about 1940. By 1943 it had received fresh impetus in connection with

Army personnel records and assignments, the possibilities of under-graduate and professional study accorded to service personnel re-turning to civil life under the so-called G.I. Bill of Rights, and the work of the Armed Forces Institute. Whereas in 1937 there were, of course, only 4 centers for the single examination given in that year, in 1943 the examination was administered at 40-odd centers, and in 1946 at 317. By July 1, 1947, the number had swelled to 743, of which 711 were in the United States, 17 in Canada, and 6 in territorial possessions or other countries. At each of these centers were available the Graduate Record Examination itself, the Pre-engineering Inventory, and the tests for medical aptitude. It was hoped that ultimately this expansion, together with reimbursement of costs through fees, might make the whole G.R.E. project self-supporting. Partly owing to the increase of centers the program by 1947 had grown to include more than 175 higher institutions, to which it had furnished results for upwards of 214,000 examinees.

Publications

The first circular related to the Co-operative Graduate Testing Program was distributed in March 1938. It contained general com-ment on the examination of 1937 and its results and selected anony-mous group and individual profiles growing out of the initial test-ing. Learned wrote much, if not all, of the interpretative matter. There followed a rather steady flow of material, duplicated or printed, that kept pace with the work of the whole project as it advanced. The less formal publications, principally mimeographed or planographed, included instructions to examiners and others, reports to and from advisory committees and groups, and much related information. More formal matter, mainly printed from types, comprised, 1941-46, some eighteen publications and reprints. Of these, five, including four Occasional Circulars, were reports of progress 1943-45; six dealt with the Graduate Record Examina-tion in general; four pertained to its use by returning service per-sonnel, and one, prepared for the fifty-sixth annual meeting of the Association of American Medical Colleges, illustrated the employ-ment of the examination in appraising applicants to medical schools. The service reflected in the documents bearing upon the appraisal of returning service personnel from World War II, while probably small in proportion to the number of servicemen and servicewomen who resumed their studies, had high importance.

DOLLARS AND CENTS

Even before the spring of 1937, when the first Graduate Record Examination had been inaugurated, the attempt was made to budget the financial needs of the experiment. Although the implied requirements were made flexible almost to the point of absurdity, the rapid development of the project, the high cost of devising and revising tests, the expansion and training of personnel to administer them, hand-score them, analyze the results, construct individual and group profiles, and perform the thousand and one other tasks required, made it impossible to forecast the amount of money to be needed during any ensuing year, or even six months. New suggestions for rendering service and spreading the good work, even after sifting them and discarding many, opened fresh but costly opportunities month by month, even week by week. Projections of policy were outgrown almost as soon as made. Although Learned's was not essentially a mind for detail, his vision, keenness, and persuasiveness, Wood's enthusiasm and perseverance, and the vigor of their younger associates, held the project together and rolled it forward.

By spring of 1940 Jessup was much disturbed by the mounting costs. So also probably was Keppel, but he held to his course and won his board's support for piecemeal grants. Between 1915 and 1937 upon thirty-three projects concerned directly or indirectly with testing and examining the Corporation had expended the round sum of $4,081,000. By 1940 the terminating Pennsylvania Study had been supported by the Corporation to the extent of more than $227,000, some of which had been granted before 1937, and between that year and June 30, 1940, Corporation grants for the Graduate Record Examination project had exceeded $172,000. It was becoming increasingly clear that in the matter of objective testing the Corporation had a bear by the tail. It required no revelation to show Jessup, who, of course, was a trustee of Carnegie Corporation, that in spite of attempts to restrain the project's costs they were soaring continuously.

For the first three years the accounts of the project were kept by the Foundation's bursar, H. C. Duryea. It made a load heavy with detail and vexation, and the Foundation's accounting system, excellent and serviceable for its own purposes, was not suitable to the type of bookkeeping the project required and was trying to get through its own set of books.

Jessup's deliberations led him to emphasize to Learned and Savage on March 22, 1940, the necessity of getting administrative and service operations of the Graduate Record Examination out of the Foundation's offices at an early date, tentatively by 1942. He protested the high costs and charged Learned to reduce them during the next two fiscal years. A suggestion that all test-scoring and reporting should be put into the hands of the American Council's Co-operative Test Service, with Learned in a consultative and advisory capacity, fell through. Jessup canvassed and negatived the incorporation of a new body, to be named the Educational Research and Statistical Service, which should take over the whole enterprise, on the ground that it would merely complicate the problem, not solve it.

The upshot was that the Graduate Record Examination project revised and intensified its own accounting procedures and introduced a system of reimbursement of costs through a three-dollar fee collected from each examinee. From the start these fees failed to meet the actual costs.

Machine Scoring

For both the Pennsylvania tests and the early version of the Graduate Record Examination much of the tabulation and statistical work was procured at cost from the Columbia University Statistical Bureau. In December 1939 this arrangement became impossible to continue. Langmuir, in charge of that phase of operations, suggested a contract with the International Business Machines Corporation under which the project should rent for its own use punch-card machines and related equipment. When that came to pass in 1940 expenses for this phase of the work materially subsided. Until much later, the Graduate Record Examinations, like the Pennsylvania Study tests, were scored by hand, a cumbersome process that required a comparatively large clerical force.

The development of the International test-scoring machine merits a history of its own. In the course of the Pennsylvania Study Wood and Learned had been troubled by the high cost of hand-scoring, which undoubtedly was retarding the progress of new-type testing. A year's study of the matter showed them that the solution of the problem through electro-mechanical means depended upon the inventive and financial resources of a large engineering laboratory. Accordingly, they laid the matter before Mr. Thomas J. Watson, then president and now chairman of the board of International

Business Machines Corporation and a trustee of Columbia University. Through a substantial gift Mr. Watson had made possible the establishment and maintenance of the Columbia University Statistical Bureau, with the main purpose of finding means to reduce the costs of statistical work in educational and other fields.

Once Mr. Watson was shown the importance of this problem for guidance and research in education he generously assigned it to the I.B.M. engineering staff and research laboratories for study and experimentation. Through the years of economic depression work on it was not permitted to flag, with the consequence that the first successful working model was put in operation in 1936. Numerous persons and organizations in the educational field contributed suggestions and encouragement, and the I.B.M. technical men at last perfected the first electrical device that successfully scored new-type tests and cumulated the scores. In 1937 the International test-scoring machine was ready for contract rental, but several years passed before, on Vaughn's initiative, it went into service for the revised Graduate Record Examination.

This is not all of the story. By devising two attachments, Mr. Watson's engineers converted the machine into a powerful instrument for test construction and for research in the constitution of human abilities, such as Professor L. L. Thurstone was pursuing in his University of Chicago laboratories under a Corporation-Foundation joint project grant. During World War II the machine proved invaluable to both the Army and the Navy. Considered expert opinion is to the effect that its use in the analyses it performs for a fraction of 1 per cent of the cost of earlier methods has saved vast sums and advanced very materially the cause of educational measurement and guidance. Its development is an outstanding illustration of what business vision, intelligence, and skill can accomplish in co-operation with educational knowledge and perception.

Quarters

Early work with the Graduate Record Examination centered in the Foundation's tenth-floor offices at 522 Fifth Avenue. There, as activities increased, it outgrew space loaned by the Corporation on the tenth floor and overflowed to the eleventh. Rental charges augmented the cost of the project. At last office space was generously provided by Columbia University in the old P. and S. Building at 437 West 59th Street, which already housed the Educational Records Bureau and other ventures in education and research, and the Graduate Record Office came into being.

Its new quarters had their defects, and not a few were serious, as none knew better than the University authorities themselves, but space was ample and served the purposes of the project and its fifty-odd employees after a fashion, with the important advantage that it was rent-free. With office equipment the Graduate Record Office was handsomely supplied.

Accounting

If budgeting for the Co-operative Graduate Testing Program proved illusory, so also did its accounting systems, at least two of which it outgrew almost as they came into operation. As the study branched, examinees increased in numbers and checks poured in from individuals and institutions by the scores of thousands. Personnel problems impinged upon financial. A cost-accounting system could scarcely keep accurate pace with the requirements it was designed to serve. For a considerable time the G.R.O. had its own banking and checking accounts, an innovation in the operation of a Foundation study.

A NATIONWIDE TESTING AGENCY

When the proposals of Learned and Wood for unifying testing in the United States were relinquished about 1938, they were not completely abandoned; on the contrary, their advocates merely laid them aside and awaited more propitious days. Both the Foundation and Carnegie Corporation in the spring and late summer of 1945 acquired new presidents, and changes in outlook and policy were to be expected.

In the autumn Learned reopened the matter with President-elect Carmichael of the Foundation, and upon his request transmitted in December a full analysis of the situation as it pertained not only to the functions of the Graduate Record Office but also to the work of "other enterprises of a related nature": the College Entrance Examination Board, the Co-operative Test Service of the American Council on Education, and the Educational Records Bureau. Learned had had preliminary discussions with certain graduate deans as to ways and means of establishing the G.R.O. on a basis independent of Corporation support, or else of amalgamating it with one or more of the other three bodies, and no insurmountable obstacles had appeared. Moreover, conditions and personalities involved in the "enterprises of a related nature" had changed with the years, and the persons now controlling them appeared guardedly hospitable to the whole notion of combining forces.

The Co-operative Graduate Testing Program from its inception had been seen clearly as a terminable demonstration, not a permanent operation. When, therefore, Learned discussed with President Josephs of the Corporation the possibility of combining the G.R.O. with one or more of the three other bodies he found an attentive listener. As matters were developing it seemed important to consult Nicholas Murray Butler, who had fathered the College Entrance Examination Board at its inception and who during its early years had been prominently associated with its development. Concerning the proposal to include the board in the new amalgamation, which he termed "another long step forward," Butler wrote: "I shall cooperate to the full in all possible ways. . . ."

Plans began to take form. Rather early, it had become increasingly clear that the Educational Records Bureau by reason of its purposes, clientele, and operations ought not to join in creating the projected central agency and negotiations looking to its participation accordingly ceased. In March of 1946 Carnegie Corporation voted a substantial sum to facilitate the combining of three of the examining bodies in "a single non-profit national testing agency," and to assure means of conducting research. Negotiations moved forward through discursive but not unduly protracted stages. On May 10, 1946, President Carmichael laid the matter before the Foundation executive committee, with special emphasis upon the Corporation's appropriation. The fact that he had already set about forming a committee on testing to lay the basis for the merger met strong approval. Before this committee really got down to work, Learned retired from his duties as staff member of the Foundation, a post he had filled with distinction for more than a third of a century, and the direction of the G.R.O. and all its ramifications passed to his colleague, Vaughn.

The committee on testing consisted of nine members, of whom six were college presidents and three were educators of national standing. It met twice in September under the chairmanship of President Conant of Harvard, who since Learned had consulted him in 1937 had thought favorably of a unified central testing body. A preliminary report, issued in October, endorsed the principle of consolidation and recommended the establishment of a new agency in which the College Entrance Examination Board, the American Council's Co-operative Test Service and National Teacher Examination, and the Graduate Record Office should join. It further recommended that in addition to assets to be contributed by these bodies not less than $750,000 should be provided through foundation grants. This finger pointed plainly at Carnegie Corporation.

There ensued nearly seven months of further discussion and correspondence. Gradually opposition yielded and the three interested agencies advanced through various stages, some doubting, some favorable. Officers of the Carnegie Corporation acted in a catalytic capacity—"honest brokers" was Josephs' phrase. At last all united in a common cause which promised more profit to American education as a whole than any of the agencies alone could bring.

Negotiations reached final stages in time to be reported to the Foundation's trustees at their forty-second annual meeting, November 19, 1947. The Corporation raised its grant to provide the entire $750,000 the committee on testing had judged necessary. Each component body voted to contribute according to an appraisal to be made of its property and effects. Articles of agreement, in which the Corporation joined, were signed, sealed, and delivered as of December 3, 1947. Sixteen days later the Board of Regents of the University of the State of New York granted a charter to Educational Testing Service, Inc., as a perpetual, nonstock, nonprofit body, and the new board of trustees met, organized, elected officers, and performed all other tasks necessary after incorporation. In the evening President Josephs produced after dinner the Corporation's check for $750,000, and Educational Testing Service was nearly ready to begin operations January 1, 1948.

The establishing of E.T.S. was a process truly mutual and co-operative. By agreement, the three components, the College Entrance Examination Board, which had begun operations in 1900, the American Council on Education for its Co-operative Test Service, inaugurated in 1930, and the Carnegie Foundation for the Graduate Record Office, youngest of the three, under various agreements made over to Educational Testing Service their contracts, leases, rights in certain technical and physical properties, and certain other assets. While for administration of tests the C.E.E.B. and C.T.S. preserved their separate entities, the G.R.O.'s activities and identity were completely merged in the new organization. Research was pooled. Thus the College Board and the Council came to contribute about $450,000, which with the Corporation's contribution on behalf of the G.R.O. assured E.T.S. of initial assets approximating $1,200,000.

It is noteworthy that during the two decades beginning in 1928 Carnegie Corporation of New York contributed through the Foundation to measurement and guidance in American education $227,-950 to the Pennsylvania Study and $774,800 to the Co-operative Graduate Testing Program. In addition, towards the establishing of E.T.S. the Corporation made a "through" grant of $750,000. The total contribution of the Corporation to the American measurement and guidance movement in the preceding twenty years is, therefore, to be reckoned at $1,752,750. And more was to come.

PICKING UP THE PIECES

With the Graduate Record Office safely amalgamated into the new Educational Testing Service, Inc., there remained the task of closing the gap in the Foundation's affairs. This was principally financial in nature. Under the agreement of December 3, 1947, the G.R.O.'s contribution to E.T.S. included all its assets except cash and accounts receivable. With questions as to ownership of the Pre-engineering Inventory readily solved, an appraisal had valued these assets at $71,549.

The Foundation's auditors undertook the task of valuing the outstanding accounts, both credit and debit. Fortunately, on Vaughn's leaving the project for technical duties in American-occupied Germany in March 1948, Langmuir after almost four years absence for war-connected work was able to help in resolving the remaining affairs of the G.R.O. Owing to personnel difficulties the new system of bookkeeping, which had operated for perhaps six months, helped little in untangling the financial strands, and it took nine months to straighten them out completely. The knottiest problem lay in the accounts receivable. Two grants totaling $100,000 from the Corporation to the Foundation, one of which was recoverable, adjusted all deficiencies.

Mr. Carmichael's co-operation in starting the new testing agency on its road to success, the patient negotiation, conferring, and discussion that he carried forward during its formative period, and especially after its inauguration, belong almost as much to the story of Carnegie Corporation as to that of the Foundation.

With the last refund on the recoverable grant, December 30,

1948, the ten-year Carnegie experiment and demonstration in graduate testing terminated. On the tenth floor at "522" the only matter for real regret was that Learned's active service with the Foundation had ceased before his and Wood's idea of a national examining body reached full development.

FIVE YEARS OF E.T.S.

After almost half a decade of operation it may be appropriate to glance at a few of the many phases of the development of Educational Testing Service, not, however, with any attempt to appraise them.

At the organization meeting of E.T.S. December 20, 1947, functions and policies of the new corporation were carefully considered by its board of trustees. Besides carrying on certain operations previously performed by its component bodies, and ruling out others, the board determined that E.T.S. was to attempt continuously to improve its own tests and testing programs, chart and conduct research in the major testing areas where research is desirable, and maintain high standards in all such activities. As for policies, it was agreed that close relationships must be maintained with educational institutions as well as various representative bodies and educational interests. New tests and new sources were to be developed, and current problems in the field faced and attacked. The trustees hoped to stimulate research in testing and provide counsel and advice to "those who feel a need for guidance in the selection, use, and interpretation of tests." Lastly, it seemed best to the board of trustees that the first five years of Educational Testing Service, 1947-52, should be regarded as a trial period.

The breadth of the enterprise was indicated by Mr. Carmichael:

> The formation of Educational Testing Service culminates years of effort among educators and testing experts to establish such a centralized agency. Equipped with facilities broad enough to set increasingly high standards of testing, the ETS will also concentrate on research in the theory and technique of testing, and in the development of new types of tests for the measurement not only of aptitudes but also of personality, social attitudes, and effectiveness of various teaching methods. Such techniques, designed to measure factors other than intelligence, are urgently needed for selection and guidance of students and to clarify the goals of education.

At the conclusion of the fifth year of operation, the trustees of E.T.S. placed the organization on a permanent footing. This action was amply justified by the success with which E.T.S. tests met. In its supervised testing programs for 1950-51 a total of 703,086 tests were scored; its institutional testing programs accounted for 427,-099 tests in that year. Supervised testing programs numbered twenty-six, including the Graduate Record Examination, the College Entrance Examination Board and College Ability Test, the Medical College Admission Test, an admission test for law schools, the National Teacher Examinations, Preliminary Actuarial Examinations, and other tests for governmental agencies and departments, not to mention three sets of qualification tests for Selective Service covering about 335,800 tests.

In addition there were meetings and conferences on testing and examining, much consultative work, and a very considerable amount of research and publication. E.T.S. operates through two offices: in Princeton, New Jersey, and in Chicago. These facilities serve both the United States and Canada as well.

On the administrative side, the relation of the Carnegie Foundation for the Advancement of Teaching to Educational Testing Service is now to be assured through continuing membership ex officio of the Foundation's president in the E.T.S. board. For the first five years Dr. Carmichael had served as chairman of the executive committee.

It is safe to say that there is scarcely a college or a university in the United States and Canada that has not felt in some way the impact of E.T.S. and its work. The service of E.T.S. has extended not alone to the national defense, but also to the Department of State and to scholarship and other programs carried on by business concerns as well. Although the annual budget is not published, from the number of tests involved it would appear to exceed $2,800,000. Thus have flowered the hopes and aspirations of those who participated in the development of the first nationwide nonprofit educational testing agency.

~ 14 ~

Notes on Investment and Finance

CONDITIONING FORCES · THREE PHASES—"GOOD OLD DAYS"; ALMOST
AS GOOD; COMMITTEE RULE; IMPROVING QUALITY OF HOLDINGS ·
CONCERNING THE FIVE FUNDS—GENERAL ENDOWMENT FUND; EN-
DOWMENT OF THE DIVISION OF EDUCATIONAL ENQUIRY; RESERVE
FUND NUMBER ONE; CONTINGENCY FUND (RESERVE FUND NUMBER
TWO); RESERVE FUND (EMERGENCY RESERVE FUND); CONSOLIDATION
· MISCELLANY—CANADIAN PROBLEMS; EXEMPTION FROM INCOME
TAXES ON BENEFITS; AMORTIZATION; NEW TURNING.

M ANY of the facts which make up the financial and investment history of the Carnegie Foundation have found
chronological place in earlier chapters of this study. The purpose
of the present notes is therefore less to add fresh details than to
summarize matters, already recorded, that may contribute to understanding of one aspect of the Foundation's experience.

CONDITIONING FORCES

During the forty-odd years of the Foundation's existence it at no
time operated, so to speak, in a vacuum. Indeed, of all the American
philanthropies founded by Mr. Carnegie himself his "gift to the
teachers" touched most directly the national fortunes and the concerns of the people it was to serve, and hence lay most widely open
to the influences of general economic conditions on the one hand, and
of the Founder's restrictions as to purposes on the other. While all
philanthropic bodies are subject to the effects of good times and
bad, few if any of the larger agencies are held by conditions of gift
to promises which, once initiated, must endure as long as the lives of
those for whom they were made. Destined by lack of precedent and

experience to pioneer almost without chart or compass, the Carnegie Foundation from its inception was compelled to undertake long-standing commitments which could not in honor be revoked.

By and large, four forces, not by any means equal in potency, have influenced the Foundation's financial course. Of these, probably the most powerful sprang from the changing background of events, nationwide, even worldwide—economic, political, social—against which it has existed since 1905. The influences of this background, its lights and shadows, have affected every American philanthropy or trust.

Before this national background has operated a second force: institutional tradition. Originating in Mr. Carnegie's own views and acts, this commanded the respect of those who shaped the policies and activities of his philanthropic creations. Not alone for the Foundation but for other groups, Pritchett, long influential as president and trustee, played here an important and sometimes strenuous part in interpreting the Founder's aims and interests. Coupled with these special circumstances a wider tradition affected, though less directly, the handling of the Foundation's finances: the investment theory and practice of American colleges and other philanthropic and educational interests.

Thirdly, the most cogent force in the Foundation's still developing financial situation, the conditions inherent in its major purpose of pensioning college teachers, emerged even before the Letter of Gift was dispatched. That document fixed the primary object of the Foundation for an unforeseeable period, limited its field of operation, and set for it a role that could be only exploratory, whatever its motives, resources, and results. This pioneering purpose affected the lives and personal finances of a special group whose number remained indeterminate for years, and involved a cost that depended partly on human volition but especially upon the probabilities of survival. These probabilities have changed greatly during the Foundation's lifetime and the instruments for measuring them have immensely sharpened. Conditions for participating in the benefits implied had to be set up; hence the Rules for the Granting of Retiring Allowances. Thus very early in the Foundation's history it had to develop a procedure from which even in the face of financial facts it could not deviate in principle, whatever modifications it might introduce.

Finally, from 1918 onward there has operated with increasing strength the debtor-creditor relationship between the Foundation and Carnegie Corporation of New York, "Andrew Carnegie, Incorporated." This relationship, intensifying with the passage of time, cannot be regarded as coercive; rather it has been ethical or moral; but as the "reservoir" functions of the Corporation as regards the Foundation have grown they have had increased influence in the shaping of the Foundation's investment procedures.

Such are the principal forces which, acting with others upon the personalities involved, have fashioned the financial history of the Carnegie Foundation.

That financial history may be the better understood if it be regarded as comprising essentially three phases, none of which is clearly marked in time, but each of which reflects one or more aspects of American economic experience. The first phase lasted from the time of Mr. Carnegie's promise of endowment in 1905 until about 1918, the second until the early 1930's, the third from that time until the present.

"Good Old Days"

The first phase partook of the economic stability that, broadly speaking, then characterized the nation. Mr. Carnegie's initial $10,-000,000 gift, and part of his $5,000,000 subsequent gift were made in fifty-year United States Steel Corporation registered 5 per cent gold bonds that he had taken in payment for his business. These were long-term securities, but they were callable before maturity at 115. Between June 9, 1906, and April 30, 1908, unused income made possible the acquisition of other bonds in the amount of $797,-882, with an average interest rate of 4.3 per cent. Much of this sum was invested in railroad bonds, then regarded as among the safest and best of securities because of the long-standing prosperity of American roads and their huge financial success. The national currency was on a gold basis. Looking back upon the time when the steel and other equally high-grade bonds characterized the Foundation's portfolios, Pritchett in 1933 might well write that "there was no investment problem." The first finance committee, somewhat informally constituted, consisted of Pritchett, who after 1910 had acquired experience of foundation investment through his membership in the finance committee of Carnegie Institution of Washington, Vanderlip, who was highly regarded in financial circles, and T.

Morrison Carnegie, the putative representative of the Founder, who was succeeded by Robert A. Franks, Mr. Carnegie's financial associate.

It is doubtful if other securities than bonds were ever seriously considered for investment. Although the Foundation was a District of Columbia corporation, New York State life insurance companies and savings banks were restricted to bonds, and indeed Mr. Carnegie himself had endowed the Foundation with that form of security. The yield on government obligations was low, but sound industrial and railroad bonds produced good returns, could be redeemed in gold, and were held to be generally satisfactory as investments for the Foundation. The finance committee set the practice that the Foundation should hold no more than 5 per cent of the bonds of any corporation, and this restriction seemed to fulfill current requirements for diversification by broadening the base of the Foundation's holdings. The pattern of bond investment was strengthened when the Foundation received from the Corporation in 1913 Mr. Carnegie's endowment of the Division of Educational Enquiry, consisting of a million in railroad bonds and a quarter-million in other gilt-edged securities.

Mr. Carnegie's first two gifts, totaling $15,000,000, had been made with the single immediate purpose of providing retiring pensions for college teachers. The endowment of the Division of Educational Enquiry, as accepted and received, could not by the terms of gift be used for pensions; its income was dedicated to studies and investigations. The two endowments, being separate in purpose, were kept separate as to investment and financial treatment. By this means was removed every slightest possibility that the purposes of the two funds were being, or ever could be, confused. To judge from the action of certain other American philanthropies this segregation of funds to accord with their separate purposes reflected not alone Mr. Carnegie's own views but good current practice within the philanthropic group as well.

During this first phase only a few notes were struck that had for a time anything resembling an ominous ring. In the autumn of 1909 S. S. Hall, Sr., Pritchett's actuary friend, having examined the Foundation's Fourth Annual Report, thought the fund ought to be built up to $20,000,000, because when it became necessary to reinvest, it probably "will have a lower interest rate than 5%." Perhaps this advice led to nothing because a return of, say, 3½ per cent, which Hall mentioned, lay outside the adult experience of those who received it. Be that as it may, as early as 1913 the U. S. Steel Corporation made proposals to purchase up to $1,000,000 of the Foundation's Steel bonds for its sinking funds "at such times and under such conditions as the . . . Steel Corporation may be willing to retire the bonds." In 1917 Professor E. B. Wilson of the Massachusetts Institute of Technology, in another connection, advocated to Pritchett the desirability of increasing the Foundation's capital, through Corporation grants, to an estimated $100,000,000, in view of "the rapid increase of wealth in this country and the rapid rise of prices, which will make any foundation whose capital stands still, retrograde in importance very rapidly."

Events of 1917-18 led to at least one important change in Foundation policy: They brought United States Government securities in the form of Liberty Bonds with their 4½ per cent interest rate into the range of investment possibility. Before World War I the Foundation had no "Governments" among its gilt-edged holdings. The relatively higher return on "Libertys" opened a new category for investing, on which, patriotism being in the air, it was not slow to seize. The new availability of government bonds had influence upon the investment policies of the 1930's and 1940's.

Professor Wilson's suggestion pertained directly to the events of 1916-18 which led to the founding of the Teachers Insurance and Annuity Association. More important for present purposes, those events brought new money from Carnegie Corporation into the Foundation's hands, to be used, after the manner of two previous gifts, for several distinct objects. By the time it came, the Foundation's pattern of finance and investment had been matured and the new money took its place in that pattern. Whereas at the close of the fiscal year 1916-17 the General Endowment Fund contained about $14,493,000 and the endowment of the Division of Educational Enquiry about $1,282,000, reckoned at book value, at the end of June 1918 the corresponding figures were $13,356,400 and $1,274,000. In addition, Corporation gifts had been received: for Reserve Fund Number One $2,148,175, and for Reserve Fund Number Two $1,000,000; while to the Emergency Reserve Fund the Foundation had transferred $100,000 and to Reserve One $1,248,-805 in unused income. All three Reserve Funds were to be expended principal and interest, the first two for purposes already fixed, the Emergency Reserve as the Foundation trustees or executive committee might direct. On the principle that under terms of establishment the five funds had their respective purposes, each was regarded as a financial entity, and no direct sales or transfer of securities were made from one to another thereafter.

Finally, it may be noted that during the years intervening between the Foundation's beginnings and the incorporation of the Teachers Insurance and Annuity Association the terms *inflation* and *deflation,* except in references connected with overissue of Federal Reserve currency, scarcely touched the financial consciousness. By and large, the times were "good." Whatever their vexations and difficulties, the Foundation's first decade and a half, more or less, was comparatively plain sailing on the investment sea, and its securities were of the highest grade.

Almost as Good

The phrase "Inflationary 'Twenties" came to be applied to that decade only after its passing. Gold bonds still offered golden opportunities. The wide development of electric power attracted numerous investors to the securities of utility companies, although it was some time later that the implications of the differences between holding and operating companies were really comprehended. Most of the country's railroads, after government operation during World War I, started the decade well. In 1925, as far as concerned the Foundation, came the first rumblings of financial difficulties in the default of interest by a western railroad on certain twenty-year 4 per cent debentures, of which the Foundation holdings totaled some $850,-000, and of which half a million had been acquired through gift of the Corporation, the remainder by purchase. A short receivership was anticipated, together with "recovery of most, perhaps all, of the investment, and possibly back interest." Although the last installment of $200,000 on Mr. Carnegie's gift of $5,000,000 for the state universities was not received until 1920, the Corporation had duly paid to the Foundation annual interest on outstanding amounts.

During the twenties there issued four versions or editions of the Foundation's Rules for the Granting of Retiring Allowances. Only the last, which appeared in 1929, drastically reduced future benefits; the others, as has been shown, brought minimal relief from the anticipated pension burden, and no version helped much to lighten current load.

In 1924-25 the United States Steel Corporation acted upon its previous proposal with a proposition to redeem a considerable number of the bonds with which Mr. Carnegie had endowed the Foundation. Negotiations between Judge Elbert H. Gary, chairman, and Pritchett were protracted; Pritchett was about to accept a somewhat lower redemption figure than he felt the terms of the bonds justified when his patience was rewarded by an offer that approximated the stipulated 115 and accrued interest. The Foundation delivered $5,500,000 of those securities, and received guaranteed coupon bonds of Steel Corporation subsidiaries to the value of $5,620,520, plus $616,290 in cash. More than once Pritchett remarked that the negotiations with Judge Gary, although always amicably conducted, formed one of his most harrowing experiences.

This redemption raised the Foundation's total holdings by a par value of about half a million dollars, its annual income by about $50,000. By 1929 all of the bonds had been redeemed, and thereby the principal of the General Endowment Fund had been increased by about $1,866,000 to a face value of $17,065,855, including cash, and its current annual income by some $95,000.

At the founding of the Teachers Insurance and Annuity Association three widely known financiers with excellent business connections consented to become trustees and to serve as its investment committee. Although they met only occasionally they performed invaluable service, and each held himself ready to consult with Foundation officers as desirable. In those days the Association's business was conducted in the offices of the Foundation under Pritchett and Furst.

Now, as of March 1919, Samuel S. Hall, Jr., was appointed assistant treasurer of the Association. Later, under a plan drafted by Pritchett, he became investment officer of Carnegie Corporation, Carnegie Institution of Washington, the Carnegie Endowment for International Peace, T.I.A.A., and the Foundation. This lightened for Pritchett a grave and growing responsibility.

In general, the scheme operated about as Pritchett had planned it and as sketched in Chapter 6. From lists of securities prepared primarily to suit the investment purposes of T.I.A.A. and revised about twice a year—oftener as occasion arose—Hall and Pritchett selected certain bonds that seemed to fill the requirements of the Foundation, and Hall then purchased them for cash, had them delivered, and reported to the executive committee. Each transaction usually involved several firms and as a rule was conducted "over the counter" in order not to disturb the market through large purchases. This method of procedure became firmly established. The work of the "Advisory Finance Committee" was thus available to all of the five organizations named above. The advisory list, in one sense regarded as a limitation upon operations, was not held as authorizing purchases without searching independent investigation of each seemingly eligible security by Hall, and for the Foundation he discussed each purchase or sale with Pritchett before making it. The first executive committee action upon a recommendation of the "Finance Advisory Committee" came in January 1927 when it approved investment of portions of the Foundation's reserve funds in dollar bonds of Belgium, France, and Italy.

On certain matters the committee and Pritchett took a negative stand. In the autumn of 1928 Pritchett in a memorandum noted that the "Finance Advisory Committee" had recently discussed "whether a proportion of trust funds might not wisely be invested in common stocks" and the conclusion, whether of Pritchett or of the committee, was that "it is questionable whether the trusts established by Mr. Carnegie would be justified in such investments." At this time Pritchett likewise held that "ground rents are a questionable investment for such institutions" unless some twenty or thirty millions were available to "obtain a fair spread of real estate investments." "Alert personnel is more important to quality of service in behalf of foundations than markedly increasing income through investments"—evidently a generalization prompted by Hall's success. What such alertness might accomplish, Pritchett implied, the Foundation had demonstrated through purchasing readily marketable bonds having prospects of improvement in value, and "as fast as these bonds ripen to a point where the yield on the market price falls below a certain figure, to sell and reinvest in similar promising bonds." This, he noted, had "netted [for the Foundation] over half a million dollars in realized profits, mainly for Reserve Fund Number One."

The foregoing notes stress many of the essentials which would underlie a financial history of the Foundation from about 1918 to about 1930, when Pritchett relinquished the presidency to Henry Suzzallo. Although during the period the Foundation had sustained losses of both principal and interest, they appeared neither considerable nor serious in view of its gains in resources. As of June 30, 1930, its assets at face value totaled $32,130,000 and more. The General Endowment Fund contained $16,866,000 in investments, including Mr. Carnegie's gifts totaling $15,000,000; the endowment of the Division of Educational Enquiry, originally $1,250,000 as received from the Corporation, was $1,254,700; Reserve Fund

Number One to which the Corporation had contributed $10,773,831 in 1918-28, stood at about $12,337,000; Reserve Fund Number Two, as originally received from the Corporation totaling $1,000,-000, had been drawn down to $768,700; and the Emergency Reserve Fund, which the Foundation had transferred from unused income, contained nearly $535,000. Remaining assets were in cash and accrued interest and dividends receivable. Profits on sales and exchanges of securities increased the original endowments and gifts. As of the corresponding date the year before total assets stood at $32,310,000, or about $80,000 higher. During 1929-30 sales of investments had netted the General Fund some $11,286 profit, Educational Enquiry $10,439, and Reserve One $97,169, while accumulated profits on sales of securities all told stood at about $2,552,300, including the profit on the redeemed Steel bonds. The only equities held were represented by 1,600 shares of prime 7 per cent cumulative preferred stocks in the General Fund, which amounted to less than 1 per cent of its portfolio as valued. The record spoke for itself.

Committee Rule

During much of Pritchett's incumbency it had been he and Hall who really shaped the Foundation's investment policies and the executive committee had discussed procedures, albeit as a rule somewhat sketchily when they involved individual securities. Suzzallo's innate modesty precluded his making any pretensions to investment knowledge, although he had more than he ever was ready to admit. He soon realized that the Emergency Reserve Fund was in danger of impairment as securities had to be sold to provide support for T.I.A.A. Accordingly, in the autumn of 1931 negotiations with Keppel, as president of the Corporation, led to the Corporation's buying back certain bonds from the Foundation and making up the difference between fair market values, with accrued interest, and book values.

Suzzallo was becoming increasingly convinced that in face of the financial perils which he saw closing in, the Foundation should have its own finance or investment committee. With this view the executive committee readily agreed, and on January 2, 1932, it named a subcommittee of its own members, consisting of Vanderlip, Franks, and Suzzallo "to pass upon purchase, sale, and exchange of securities of the Foundation." The subcommittee met and organized on January 14, and at once got down to its work.

Under the bylaws, fortified by long usage, the executive committee, operating through the investment officer, had the responsibility of managing and directing the Foundation's financial affairs and property. The work had actually been done by the president and Hall. The responsibility had been delegated to the new finance subcommittee, but not, as Vanderlip and Suzzallo saw, the necessary authority. Hence on December 1, 1933, upon recommendation of Vanderlip as chairman of the subcommittee, the executive committee voted to its subcommittee full authority to direct the investments of the Foundation, and the actual operations were accomplished first through Hall as investment officer, and later through the Co-operative Investment Office. This procedure has obtained in principle ever since. In 1940, under the codified bylaws the finance subcommittee became the finance committee, and in 1949 the investment committee. Its membership has always consisted of the president, ex officio, and, except for a brief period as will be shown, two other members from the executive committee. Those who have thus served have been Vanderlip, Pritchett for a time after Suzzallo's death, Franks, Thomas W. Lamont, Wriston, Lovett, and Thomas S. Lamont. During Suzzallo's administration he used the group not only for investments but for framing fiscal and administrative policy through budgeting and other measures and matters. Minutes were sent to all members of the executive committee.

The three-man group, under its various names, has almost always included one or more men of high financial standing and business experience. The collective knowledge possessed by their associates, the Corporation officers and finance committee, and the co-operative investment office has been made generously and readily available. Every measure adopted or considered by this committee, every purchase, sale, or exchange of securities, was a product of mature consideration, the collection and analysis of many data, and the sifting of expert opinion. A cynic once remarked that the minutes of these discussions could scarcely fail to improve the private investments of every member of the executive committee if he had his wits about him, and his institution's portfolio whether he had them or not.

In 1932 the finance subcommittee clarified certain operational matters. It decided as a policy that no security should be held in an amount of over half a million dollars in the Foundation's total holdings without special authorization, but that "the present holdings of the Foundation be not disturbed" under this ruling. By recommending a limit upon the amount of General Endowment income that should be used for paying benefits in any one fiscal year, ways and means of building up the Emergency Reserve Fund, and a maximum for operating costs, it brought to the executive committee a framework within which the Foundation could move economically and effectively towards a practicable budget. Through Hall as investment officer, it employed a procedure from which in 1936 developed the Co-operative Investment Office and kept the Foundation a participant in it for more than a dozen years. In 1938 it brought about study by counsel of the simplified District of Columbia Rule of Equity Number 48, which in its bearing upon the investment of trust funds for a time gave serious concern to the Foundation. Although it reviewed and discussed segregation of the Foundation's five funds as separate entities, it recognized and emphasized the differing status and purposes of each, even when opportunity and events indicated advantage in transferring securities from one fund to another. Throughout its first decade it strove against the effects of dwindling returns from investments and defaults in bond interest. And aided by the wide information available from the co-operative investment office and the business associates of committee members and their firms, the group has canvassed innumerable technical details relating to the securities it considered for purchase or sale.

Improving Quality of Holdings

Between 1929 and 1932 the quality of the bonds held in Reserve One had been raised considerably, partly through the fund's being frequently utilized somewhat as a trading account, a mode of operation that permitted profits to be treated as income for investment. The new finance subcommittee early appreciated that this rise in quality should be extended to all portfolios, particularly in view of the situation developing in railroad bonds. But signs of inflation were appearing, and by December 1933 most financial people seemed to think that second-grade bonds and other securities were more apt to appreciate from threatened or actual inflation and the devaluation of the dollar than securities of the highest grade. Loss of income, or the threat of it, appeared as the danger that ought to govern sales. Yet in spite of accumulated profits of more than $2,658,000 for all funds, the total market values were some $6,718 below book. The year 1934 increased the confusion in the bond market. With the gold clause invalidated by the Securities Act of 1933 chaos was come again, and by December the finance subcommittee began extensive purchase of government securities. Meanwhile, defaults of interest on railroad bonds mounted; by May 1936 they had affected twelve issues owned by the Foundation.

Late in 1935, Thomas W. Lamont, trustee since 1917, thanks to Jessup's persuasion accepted membership in the subcommittee, and his views quickened those of his colleagues about the improvement of quality in holdings, even at the cost of lower returns from investments. As related in an earlier chapter, the subcommittee's proposal to invest in common stocks, which Pritchett first regarded adversely but subsequently seconded, had met no opposition in the executive committee or the Board of Trustees, perhaps owing in part to the restrictions proposed: (1) that the Foundation's common-stock holdings should not total more than one per cent of any stock issue; (2) that a maximum investment in any one stock should not exceed $200,000; (3) that the aggregate amount to be placed in common stocks should not be more than $5,000,000 of the General Endowment, Reserve One, and perhaps the endowment of the Division of Educational Enquiry. Already Carnegie Corporation of New York had in operation a not dissimilar program, equally venturous.

Subcommittee meetings of December 1935 and January 1936 were given over to discussion of the new principle. Lamont, after noting that "today investors are fortunate to receive three and one-half per cent from common stocks," proposed a tripartite platform: (1) investment in high-grade bonds; (2) increased investment in preferred stocks for increasing income; (3) investment in good common stocks. He stressed the first of these planks, but he and Vanderlip agreed to all three, to an initial proportion of 10 per cent, or about $3,000,000, of the Foundation's investments to be placed in common stocks, and to an attempt to convert high-grade, long-term bond holdings into medium- or short-term issues. After protracted discussion, a list of stocks in various fields (e.g. metal mining, oils, chemicals, manufactures, etc.) was compiled by the investment office, desirable proportions for each field were set, and Hall was authorized to purchase after clearing with Vanderlip and Lamont.

Operations began at once, in spite of a general situation clouded by possible currency inflation, the soldiers' bonus proposals, and uncertainty in the attitude of Congress towards money and finance. By February 1, 1936, the General Endowment and Reserve One contained $2,609,000-worth of common stocks and convertible bonds, purchased from proceeds from selling bonds of "a grade somewhat lower than the best," and other bonds sold or redeemed. By May some $3,110,000 of the two funds was in stocks. By November 1936 purchase of "preferreds" had begun, and a second phase of the stock-purchasing program commenced from approved lists. Other steps followed.

The immediate effect of these operations was to raise market value of the Foundation's holdings, but to decrease income, and thus to throw a greater pension-load burden upon Reserve One. Early in 1937 several imponderables marked the general investment situation, including labor, politics, and the possibility of a European war. The stock-purchasing program was lagging, but it was completed by May. In the following year, by use of a revolving fund, it was gradually resumed with higher upward limits and extended more actively to the "preferreds." When, after Vanderlip's death, Lovett in 1938 succeeded him on the subcommittee, the policy of improving quality received a decided impetus. While at one time it slowed materially, to the satisfaction of everyone involved the quality of all portfolios affected rose demonstrably, and with extensions and modifications the general principles of conservative common-stock investment and improvement of holdings have been maintained ever since. Under repeated scrutiny that principle has proved immensely and readily adaptable to meet such varying needs as those connected with the Court Order (1939) and its Amendment (1945), and with World War II and its aftermath.

By May 1946 the somewhat depleted finance committee recommended steps whereby the framing of investment policy and its routine functions might under the bylaws be exercised by the executive committee. These the executive committee adopted, and after October 4, 1946, the finance committee did not meet formally until January 9, 1948, when it discussed President Carmichael's suggestion to pool investments. This on that date it approved in principle, and the executive committee directed. In thus temporarily assuming the finance committee's powers and functions the executive committee predicated action upon the understanding that "the Finance Committee may still act in its discretion if action be judged desirable or necessary." On and after January 9, 1948, the finance committee, or as it was subsequently redesignated, the investment committee, resumed its meetings as occasion dictated.

CONCERNING THE FIVE FUNDS

As indicated in Chapter 2, up to 1913 the Foundation had only one fund, variously called but usually referred to as "the endowment." It then became the General Endowment Fund. In that year the endowment of the Division of Educational Enquiry was set up, followed five years later by three additional funds, denominated Reserve Fund Number One, Reserve Fund Number Two, and the Emergency Reserve Fund. Each had its separate functions and entity. With purposes and origins already outlined on earlier pages, a glance at each fund is perhaps in order, beginning with the two endowments.

General Endowment Fund

From the main fund of the Foundation only income was expendable up to 1939, when the Court Order permitted the use of principal in the payment of benefits. Thereupon it was divided into two portfolios, "A" and "B," the former expendable, the latter to remain intact, with the value of the nonexpendable portfolio to be fixed as of an indeterminable future date. The Amendment of the Court Order (1945) fixed this date as June 30, 1945, and divided the fund into two parts: the "permanent" portion, containing about $10,000,000, representing Mr. Carnegie's original gift, and the expendable portion, consisting of the remainder and including his second gift of $5,000,000 and certain realized profits. The investment of both portions has been so conducted as to serve the ends for which each was respectively created. The General Endowment Fund was at its highest in 1929, with principal of $17,065,855, book value. On June 30, 1950, it contained an allocated $12,276,800 in both portions.

Endowment of the Division of Educational Enquiry

When on April 29, 1913, Carnegie Corporation turned over to the Foundation the new funds for studies which Mr. Carnegie had promised on the preceding January 13, the endowment of the Division of Educational Enquiry contained at par value $1,250,000, in two sets of bonds. By April 20, 1925, with investment of unexpended income its par value had risen to $1,346,000, and book value to $1,312,452. On December 27, 1938, book value stood at $1,153,500, but market value had dropped to $472,430. As of June 30, 1950, this endowment was allocated a value of $555,374, with annual income of $22,095.

The history of this fund reflects the fortunes of not a few other restricted endowments, particularly in relation to the ups and downs of the thirties. As of June 1931 its principal included a million in railroad bonds, having a market value of $870,000, which was already shrinking. To trace in detail the decline and fall of this particular security would serve no useful purpose. Whereas effects were felt in the General Endowment and Reserve One they were most serious in Educational Enquiry endowment, where at book value they involved about four-fifths of the fund. The much-dreaded default in interest came at last in the autumn of 1936. Owing principally to market conditions, several years passed before these bonds were disposed of; during a considerable period there was no demand at almost any price. Indeed, as late as September 1940 more than nine-tenths of them still remained unsold, although their price had turned upward. A year later, Josephs having become investment officer, the remainder had been sold and the proceeds placed in United States Government securities. From this calamitous reduction of annual income, from more than $50,000 to about $11,800, the Division and its work have not yet recovered, although under executive committee policy the Foundation to 1950 has gradually increased principal by about $73,000, and annual income by more than $10,000.

Reserve Fund Number One

Of the Foundation's three reserve funds, created in November 1917 to be spent, principal and interest, for specific purposes, the largest was Reserve Fund Number One. From Foundation "surplus" it received $1,248,805 in cash, and from Carnegie Corporation direct gifts of securities at book value amounting to $4,487,831. Unexpended balances of the Corporation's annual cash contributions of $600,000 to this reserve increased it by $1,534,848. With this principal sum augmented annually by other items, including interest and bond discounts of $6,423,375 and profits on sales of securities amounting to $649,377, it reached its maximum in 1928, a total of $12,905,000 in cash and securities.

In that year Reserve One became available for use. It lasted until April 19, 1944, about two years longer than revised actuarial computations had indicated. Its total yield was $18,064,255, or about 39 per cent of the Foundation's total expenditures, $46,250,000, for retiring allowances 1906-44. At several periods it was utilized somewhat after the fashion of a trading or revolving fund, inasmuch as not only principal and interest, but also profits from sales and exchanges of securities held in it, could be spent or retained as occasion warranted.

320   FRUIT OF AN IMPULSE

Contingency Fund (*Reserve Fund Number Two*)

In accordance with trustee action November 21, 1917, the executive committee one month later established a second reserve fund "not [to] be deemed a trust fund," to further the use of the joint contributory retirement annuity contracts of T.I.A.A. Its initial resources comprised $1,000,000 given by Carnegie Corporation of New York. Costs of appropriations from Reserve Two averaged about $100,000 annually during its first four years, but since 1931 the executive committee has made no new grants from it. In 1948 its title was changed to Contingency Fund. During the year 1949-50 drafts upon it for allowances and pensions, which totaled $14,-220, exceeded its income by $3,400 drawn from principal, but its total allocated resources were $272,000. It is subject to actuarial scrutiny.

Reserve Fund (*Emergency Reserve Fund*)

The initial source of the Emergency Reserve Fund, 1918, was the transfer of unused income of the General Endowment Fund, which 1918-26 built it up to $425,000. Peak resources, 1927, totaled about $623,800. Its heaviest disbursements in any one year were $135,400 in 1929-30, of which $100,000 went to T.I.A.A. for overhead above income from its paid-in capital and surplus. In 1932, on recommendation of the finance subcommittee, as suggested by Mattocks, $200,000 of the Emergency Reserve was earmarked to sustain disability annuity allowances under the Rules. As of June 30, 1950, this fund by allocation contained $308,833 under its later designation, Reserve Fund. During the preceding twelvemonth expenditures from it totaled $4,540, of which $2,540 went towards disability annuity allowances.

Consolidation

Aside from the reasons that led, 1948, to the amalgamation of the Foundation's funds and the actual process of pooling as discussed in Chapter 12, other considerations pointed to advantages that might be gained by consolidating the Foundation's holdings for investment and administration.

In the first place, with the expendable Reserve One out of the way, the funds remaining to be considered in this connection, after the Court Order 1939 and its Amendment 1945, were the two endowments, the "permanent" portion of the General Fund and the endowment of the Division of Educational Enquiry, and two reserves, namely, Reserve Fund Number Two and the Emergency Reserve Fund. Because ultimately, and probably by 1953, the expendable portion of the General Endowment would have gone the way of Reserve One it was not considered as suitable for pooling.

There were real disadvantages in continuing a policy of segregation. Clearly, it was not necessary to keep the funds separate on the grounds of purpose, if the books of account were so adjusted as to reflect the individual status of each fund. The aggregate amount involved was little more than a third of the Foundation's total holdings in 1929 or 1930. As each expendable fund further receded it became increasingly difficult to obtain for it the diversification that was judged necessary under the accepted views of today. Furthermore, of the five funds, the principal of the two endowments was to be preserved and even increased. Reserve Fund Number Two was approaching a point at which expenditures from it could be met from income rather than from income plus returns from sales of securities, and the same was true of the Emergency Reserve—indeed, as matters turned out, by 1950 the Emergency Reserve (Reserve Fund) was the first of the two to attain this status.

Finally, there were persuasive reasons for consolidation as exemplified in the practice of Carnegie Corporation of New York and of certain other philanthropies, as well as numerous universities and colleges, each with many times the resources of the Foundation. Contemporary financial policy for educational and similar undertakings thus favored pooling and profiting from it; Dr. Carmichael himself had seen at first hand its favorable operation for Vanderbilt University. Only the expendable portion of the General Endowment would lie outside the consolidation.

Matters were so planned that along with actual pooling, titles of two of the funds, which from inception had been only weakly descriptive and unsatisfactory designations, should be made more indicative, although the purposes of the funds were to remain intact. Reserve Fund Number Two was to become "Contingency Fund" and the Emergency Reserve Fund merely "Reserve Fund." The basis of consolidation would be book values as of June 30, 1947, and, after pooling, income, profits, and losses were to be allocated to the respective accounts on a basis proportional to book value of each portfolio as of that date.

Cash requirements, a matter of brief concern to some of the trustees, would be met by sales of securities and rights, sales and payments from the expendable portion of the General Endowment Fund, redemptions, income from investments, and sums borrowed in cash from Carnegie Corporation, suitably apportioned among the respective fund accounts.

The sums that pooling involved, including cash, totaled $11,-357,958. Calculations and consultations led to fixing the following proportions for allocations of income, amortization upward and downward, etc., for the fiscal year 1947-48: General Endowment "permanent" portion, 90.1 per cent; Division of Educational Enquiry, 4.9 per cent; Contingency Fund, 2.4 per cent; Reserve Fund, 2.6 per cent. These percentages were made subject to revision as desirable or necessary.

Such was the general plan of consolidation that went into effect June 30, 1947. After a brief period of readjustment its advantages became manifest and no material alterations have since been made. Even the original proportions for allocation among the funds have remained unaltered because no real reason to change them has appeared. The annual reports of the Foundation's treasurer continue to exhibit that completeness of information which has long characterized them.

MISCELLANY

An assortment of financial matters calls for brief emphasis, which in some cases may appear as mere enumeration, but which cannot be omitted if the present notes are to have anything resembling logical completeness.

Canadian Problems

At the fifteenth annual meeting, November 1920, the Board of Trustees, under urging of one of its more liberally minded members, decided rather on the spur of the moment to depart from long-standing practice and to pay Canadian benefits in New York funds. Upon investigation this procedure showed itself to be absurd, and Pritchett in December proposed, in a memorandum to all trustees, "to pay all retiring allowances already in force in New York exchange" and "retiring allowances going into effect after January 1, 1921, in Canadian checks." The differential appears to have been about 9 per cent in favor of United States currency, and the Foundation held some $800,000 in Canadian securities, of which about $100,000 was payable in Montreal. Correspondence showed only two trustees dissenting from the conclusions Pritchett threshed out in his memorandum, and in the spring of 1921 a Canadian checking account, which had been authorized in 1919, was opened to facilitate payments in Canadian funds, a process that has obtained ever since. Difficulties as to the Foundation's Canadian holdings arose in 1940 under restrictions of the Foreign Exchange Control Board, Ottawa, but were soon ironed out. In 1942 the Dominion Department of Internal Revenue, Income Tax Division, on application declared itself to be "prepared to recognize that [the Carnegie Foundation is] exempt from Canadian income tax" under the current tax convention between the United States and Canada.

Exemption from Income Taxes on Benefits

Although the status of the Foundation as to federal income tax was supposedly settled through correspondence conducted by Cadwalader in 1913, the matter of taxation of Foundation benefits came to life in the year 1919-20, when the Massachusetts collector in a ruling assessed federal income taxes of 8 per cent against beneficiaries not resident in the United States. The Foundation paid taxes for each such beneficiary, totaling $3,333 up to June 1, 1920. To both the Foundation and its recipients the matter was serious and counsel took it up vigorously. After months of correspondence and negotiation a new ruling, July 2, 1920, reversed earlier decisions and exempted all Foundation retiring allowances and widows' pensions from federal income tax, regardless of residence of individual beneficiaries, on the ground that they are in the nature of gifts and therefore are not taxable income to beneficiaries. New York State took a similar stand in October, Canada in December, while the Massachusetts Supreme Judicial Court rendered a decision, subsequently followed by a Commissioner ruling, to the same effect in 1927. Today it appears to be nationwide practice to levy no income tax upon the retiring allowances and widows' pensions paid by the Foundation.

In December 1920 the tax money paid by the Foundation while the matter was under adjustment was returned by the Treasury, and penalties assessed in the amount of some $833 were abated.

Amortization

Although various earlier treasurer's reports contained occasional items related to "bond discount" in the General Endowment Fund, these reflected auditors' work rather than official policy. In 1932 the finance subcommittee twice discussed amortization and decided against using it. Continuous policy as to amortization of premiums and discounts for investment holdings dates from 1942, when the endowment of the Division of Educational Enquiry was reconstituted.

For the succeeding three fiscal years that fund was debited with amortization ranging from about $28 to about $109 annually. After the amending of the Court Order in 1945, the finance committee, at the suggestion of the co-operative investment office, recommended and the executive committee voted to amortize the "permanent" portion of the General Endowment Fund. Details were left to the co-operative investment office until 1948, when the funds were consolidated. On May 7 of that year the executive committee voted to amortize both upward and downward for the resulting composite portfolio. For the ensuing two years an average of $2,593 was annually debited to the General Endowment. The downward process has been continued since 1948 with only small amounts involved.

New Turning

In the spring of 1948 President Carmichael suggested that J. P. Morgan and Co., Incorporated, might well act as financial advisers to the Carnegie Foundation, a capacity in which they had for some time served Carnegie Corporation of New York. Full discussion in the finance committee brought out views to the following effect: With recent changes in the membership of both that committee and the executive committee both groups lacked members with intimate practical knowledge of investment matters. Community of financial interest between the Foundation and the Corporation under the amended Plan for Completing Payment of Retiring Allowances and Pensions implies the closest sort of co-operation between the two bodies. Without competent external advice the finance committee could scarcely do more than merely approve steps taken by the investment officers, however sound those steps might appear. Consolidation of Foundation funds had brought new conditions, which, it was hoped, would simplify and more nearly regularize investment problems.

The suggestion found favor in the executive committee, which with regret and reluctance discontinued the Foundation's participation in the Co-operative Investment Office, which for many years had served it diligently and effectively, as of June 30, 1948, and began to rely for investment advisory service upon the Morgan group. The ensuing results now appear to have justified the change.

The Carnegie Foundation throughout its existence has made use of the best financial advice available to it. Its investments have been well and carefully handled. In more than one period those responsible for them have exercised unusual foresight, an outstanding example of which was investment in common stocks during the doubtful days of the mid-thirties. Even in 1950, when common stocks had become a routine, even a leading investment for educational funds, the proportion of the Foundation's common-stock holdings to its total composite portfolio was far from high. With one or two exceptions, the timing of its operations has been excellent. The downward course of its funds has been due mainly to conditions over which it had no control: the changing economic scene, the abolition of the gold clause in bonds, variations in the value of the American dollar, the purposes set by its charter and the Letter of Gift, and its inability to extricate itself with justice from the net of declining mortality and interest rates. It may be concluded that the Foundation's investment and financial policy has been shaped with a conservative boldness.

Of Men and Measures

TRUSTEES AND TRUSTEESHIP—OFFICERS OF THE BOARD; DUTIES,
FUNCTIONS · THE EXECUTIVE COMMITTEE IN ACTION · MEETINGS
AND PROCEEDINGS—THE BOARD; THE EXECUTIVE COMMITTEE; THE
INVESTMENT COMMITTEE · MINUTES · ADMINISTRATIVE PERSONNEL
—OFFICERS; STAFF MEMBERS; STAFF ASSOCIATES; THE SERVICE
STAFF; THE REWARDS OF SERVICE · PRESS AND PUBLIC—THE CARNE-
GIE FOUNDATION AND THE LAW

I T WAS several years before the Carnegie Foundation for the
Advancement of Teaching achieved a seal. The bylaws
adopted November 15, 1905, prescribed a seal, circular in form, to
bear the legend "The Carnegie Foundation, Seal, 1905," and placed
it in the official custody of the president. In 1913 Vanderlip asked
for a copy from which to have a carving made for the ceiling of his
drawing room at Scarborough; "There are to be a number of
panels," his secretary wrote, "and in each of them is to be carved
a seal of the organizations and institutions of exceptional character
with which he had been connected." Furst was obliged to reply that
"No seal has ever been made or used." But some weeks later the
executive committee, under instruction of the trustees, considered
several sketches and adopted the design of Charles S. Chapman,
N.A., then of Leonia, New Jersey, from which a zinc cut was made
and first used for Bulletin Number 7, *Education in Vermont*, and
the Ninth Annual Report, both published in 1914. One of the early
prints had gone in February to Vanderlip, but no die was actually
cut until 1931, when Suzzallo, who was something of a numismatist,
had one made and mounted for practical use. The bylaws of 1940
and thereafter placed the seal in the custody of the Foundation's
secretary.

TRUSTEES AND TRUSTEESHIP

The first directors or trustees were chosen by Mr. Carnegie, Pritchett being at his side, on the bases of geographical considerations, institutional prestige, and personal accomplishment and standing in education. These considerations, coupled with the desire to have both large and smaller colleges represented, have operated ever since. In the choice of candidates, while the president of the Foundation has always had influence, he has in the very large majority of cases never pressed for a particular name. Even after 1931 when, on Butler's initiative, to forestall the possibility of a hasty election, the board requested that the executive committee consider eligibles and suggest candidates, the president has had the responsibility of preparing and maintaining requisite lists. At the same time, for each election nominations have been invariably requested from the floor.

In one or two instances Pritchett sought and obtained before the annual meeting the consent of a possible candidate to the use of his name. Suzzallo and Jessup made the earlier approach invariable custom. Although this removed the element of pleasurable surprise for the trustee-elect, it did not lessen the honor he felt and it resulted in only one election being declined in the history of the Foundation —and even that was subsequently accepted. It is not to be denied that under these customs and usages certain younger men of promise have been passed over on one ground or another, but the fact remains that election to the Foundation board has come to indicate for American higher education that the men chosen have attained a certain standing in the field.

All told, up to November 15, 1950, the date of the forty-fifth annual meeting, eighty-eight men have served as trustees of the Foundation. Of these, eighty were college presidents when elected and eight were laymen. Currently the tendency appears to be to recruit younger men. Death has terminated trusteeship in only nineteen cases; resignation, generally at retirement, in forty-four. In only three instances have seats in the board been retained after retirement from academic presidencies without special request prompted by special conditions. The precedent set by Eliot in 1909, in spite of Mr. Carnegie's wishes, has been followed with considerable fidelity through the years. One trustee appointed by Mr. Carnegie still serves in 1950—and even more effectively than when he was selected as an awed youngster of thirty-five. Clearly from the beginning the Foundation has enjoyed in its Board of Trustees a noteworthy stability. As a member of the board once wrote: "There is comfort in the thought that the trustees are very carefully selected."

Officers of the Board

In theory at least the term of an officer of the Board of Trustees has always been one year, but exceptions to this general provision have been numerous. Indeed, Eliot, the first chairman, served 1905 to 1909; Peterson also for four years, Slocum for three, and Humphreys, Kirkland, and Vinson for two years each. For fifteen years after 1932 the chairman of the board by re-election served two terms, but after 1947, under a reconsidered policy, for one year only. Although Thwing and Aydelotte, respectively, served as secretary of the board for rather extended periods, it was somewhat usual for the vice-chairman to succeed the chairman in his turn, and later for the board's secretary to advance through vice-chairmanship to the position of chairman.

More recently resignations from the board have been accepted by the executive committee acting for it when not in session, but the executive committee has never exercised the full prerogative implied in the bylaws by electing a trustee.

During Pritchett's presidency the only nonmembers of the board admitted to trustee meetings were college presidents representing associations. Perhaps this fact is in part responsible for the board's having been termed "the most exclusive educational club in the world." In any event, strict observance of the custom has deprived the board of advantages that might have come from firsthand reports of staff members in charge of inquiries, and, in certain official relations, direct contact with officers of sister endowments such as Carnegie Corporation of New York.

Duties, Functions

"This seems to be essentially the business of the trustees—" wrote Pritchett to Plantz in 1909, "to legislate on the general principles which ought to govern us, lay these down for the guidance of the executive committee, and then leave the details . . . for the committee to carry out." When this principle has been followed all has invariably gone well. At the same time, with able presidents as guides the duties of no Foundation trustee have proved onerous, except regarding travel from distant points to attend meetings and even the service of attendance has frequently been combined with other business in New York City. Indications are few that any trustee has ever taken his comparatively nominal responsibilities otherwise than seriously.

In November 1941 it was proposed that Jessup, then president, constitute from among members of the Foundation board several groups to sponsor or conduct joint projects supported by Corporation grants. After long consideration Jessup reached a negative conclusion, which rested upon three grounds: First, the board membership had been selected for a different purpose and had grown accustomed to it. Secondly, it would be questionable policy to attempt to pin down trustees to so taxing a task. Thirdly, not all would be suited to it by age, experience, or interest, and selection— perhaps invidious—would be necessary; some would intuitively avoid adding to their responsibilities. The work of six trustees on the Pension Commission of 1916 under Slocum's chairmanship was the last really burdensome extra service exacted from any trustee, although not a few board members have acted as confidential advisers to each of the Foundation's presidents. In Pritchett's day this led to the practice of getting out each Annual Report and most of the Bulletins in confidential proof for prepublication comment, a device continued until 1948 with excellent suggestions resulting in many cases.

A custom initiated in 1907 has long endured. On the afternoon before the second annual meeting Mr. and Mrs. Carnegie received the trustees at 2 East 91st Street. Next day the Founder himself lunched with them at Delmonico's. Thus began a tradition which persists to this day in the trustee luncheon commemorating Andrew Carnegie, the president of the Foundation acting as host. Mrs. Pritchett recalls that Mr. Carnegie took great pleasure in these gatherings as long as he was active. His own after-luncheon remarks were memorable, particularly those of 1908, when he paid tribute to Charles W. Eliot's service to education, and also stressed his own view that the Foundation's retiring allowances were not charity but the teachers' "rightful heritage." After Mr. Carnegie ceased to attend, Pritchett for the remainder of his incumbency usually spoke of the Founder at these luncheons, and later Butler generally proposed the toast to the Founder's memory. More recently the pleasant duty has fallen to the chairman-elect of the board, with results that will be long remembered by those privileged to hear them.

THE EXECUTIVE COMMITTEE IN ACTION

The Foundation's bylaws have always designated the president as chairman ex officio of the executive committee. The other six members have been chosen for three-year, staggered terms by the Board of Trustees, on nomination of a committee constituted annually. The fact that the management of the Foundation has been centralized in the executive committee has necessitated more frequent meetings of that body than of the board. This at one time was regarded as placing a geographical limitation upon its composition and as requiring that its members reside within a distance of perhaps 350 miles from New York City. In the earlier days of the Foundation this situation led to a certain amount of question, which came down to an implied accusation of provincialism. A detailed review of the work of the committee has not substantiated that implication with any seriousness. The choice in 1950 of an executive committee member from the Middle West may have been in a measure prompted by a feeling that the composition of the committee might well be more widely representative, but personal qualities of character and capacity were probably more important in the selection than geographical considerations. At any rate, this departure from custom appears to be in nature experimental, to be appraised in the light of advantages gained and results achieved.

All versions of the bylaws have contained a provision to the effect that "during the intervals between meetings of the board of trustees, the executive committee shall exercise all the powers of the board of trustees in the management and direction of the business and conduct of the affairs of the corporation," a provision which has made the executive committee the most powerful single instrumentality in the Foundation's work. It might at any time have been viewed with alarm if an unfriendly critic had comprehended its implications, especially when coupled with the executive committee's putative control of the selection of trustees through nominating powers. Yet it has never been abused and it has expedited business in every particular.

During Pritchett's administration he, as president, customarily transmitted all reports and recommendations from the executive committee to the trustees. Jessup, with his strong feeling for the past and its precedents, would probably have followed this procedure, as had Suzzallo, except for his modesty and his respect for

individuals. Usually Jessup requested Butler to transmit to the
board the executive committee's nominations to fill vacant trustee-
ships. Each such transmittal Butler made an occasion through his
ability to transmute bare facts into brief biographical citations.
That and their structure and phrasing gave great pleasure to his
hearers. Although the bylaws are silent upon the matter, the tradition is that the president is the official channel of communication
between executive·committee and board and this tradition, which
embodies best academic practice, is not likely to be disregarded.

The only important routine document which passed regularly
from the executive committee to the Board of Trustees was the committee's formal annual report, which summarized the business of the
year. As a record its utility was high, but as a means of informing
board members upon the work of the committee its value was questionable, although its content was always indicative and available
to supplement the executive committee minutes distributed to board
members. It was abandoned in 1950.

MEETINGS AND PROCEEDINGS

Of the three administrative bodies that have held regular stated
meetings for the management of the Carnegie Foundation—the
Board of Trustees, the executive committee, and the investment or
finance committee—the most formal procedure has always attached
to the meetings of the trustees.

The Board

In Mr. Carnegie's day, and in Pritchett's as well, morning coats
at board meetings were almost *de rigueur*. By the time of Suzzallo's
brief administration this convention had begun to relax, and that
tendency has since continued as participation in the business of the
day has grown more general. Eliot's chairmanship set a standard
for presiding, traces of which still linger in spite of the practically
impossible order of business imposed by the bylaws. When in each
session the time came for the president to elaborate orally his annual
report, already in print and in the hands of the trustees, it became
customary for the chairman to "turn the meeting over" to the president, who conducted the rest of the proceedings until adjournment.
This has afforded each successive president opportunity to inform
the board fully of the Foundation's affairs and situation, but it is
said at one time to have stifled discussion even when invited.

FRUIT OF AN IMPULSE

After the pension agreement of 1929 had been ratified and Pritchett had become emeritus, matters tended to drag. The annual meeting of 1931 began in confusion, owing to the belated arrival of the chairman. Lamont endured it as long as he could, and then less in anger than in sorrow exclaimed: "This is terrible!" The next year each person who was to participate formally in the meeting received a set of "hand-notes" resembling the script of a play, which solved the problem and which with an adequate memorandum of business for each trustee made for some years Foundation board meetings models of dispatch and precision of action, enlivened in proportion to the skill of successive presidents in planning sessions and keeping them in interesting movement.

The Executive Committee

Before Suzzallo's presidency the executive committee at its meetings had in hand only lists of the allowances and pensions to be granted or approved, and occasionally notes or digests of cases to be decided. The rest of the business was brought up orally. Papers whatever their importance were seldom distributed in advance. Suzzallo introduced both preliminary and final agenda, with drafts of action indicated, which materially expedited business and cleared time for discussion. Thereafter it was seldom necessary to draft *extempore* votes, although upon occasion Lamont showed illuminating skill in this task. Suzzallo's schedule for executive committee meetings, discussed in Chapter 9, endured until 1950. On its abandonment the old difficulties of scheduling recurred. Nevertheless, over the years, many individual attendance records among this working group have been excellent.

The Investment Committee

For the finance subcommittee and its successors, the finance committee and the investment committee, a memorandum of business, lists of transactions, and such investment office materials as might be pertinent have been distributed in advance of each meeting since 1932. Without them and the presence of the investment officer it would have been impossible to reach the necessary decisions involving comparatively large amounts of data. Only successive organization meetings of this committee have ever approached the formal.

The minutes of the first incorporation, "The Carnegie Foundation," were colorless and stilted. Phrased in a lawyer-like fashion, they were characterized by directness and they emphasized action taken and ignored the reasoning that led to it. When the Carnegie Foundation for the Advancement of Teaching began to operate in 1906 the phrasing became less stereotyped. Thereafter, besides serving as a record of action the minutes, whatever the supposed dangers of the narrative type, usually sketched views expressed in discussion and other matters of background which lent them prime historical value. After 1932 all printed minutes had a format which considerably clarified their import and increased their utility.

From 1909 to 1929 minutes of the board were the responsibility of its secretary, although subsequently for a time they were drafted by the secretary of the Foundation or by his assistant, Miss Willie H. Chambliss. More recently they were taken by the secretary of the Foundation in the capacity of recording secretary *ad hoc*. Between 1906 and 1922 the executive committee minutes were signed and usually prepared by the secretary to or of (the phrasing is not fixed) the committee: T. Morrison Carnegie, Robert A. Franks, J. G. Bowman, or Alexander Humphreys, exceptionally by Pritchett. After 1922 the secretary of the Foundation prepared them, with a single exception when the committee was working in closed session and Pritchett signed them.

The bylaws of 1949-50 omit provision for a secretary of the board and assign the keeping of all records to the Foundation's secretary, except as provided by individual committees, approximately the arrangement used by Carnegie Corporation of New York since its inception. Minutes of the Board of Trustees have been sent to its members and to the president and secretary of Carnegie Corporation; of the executive committee, to board members and to the Corporation; and of the investment committee to members of the executive committee and officers of the Foundation board.

ADMINISTRATIVE PERSONNEL

The Foundation's administrative personnel has comprised its officers, staff members, and service assistants, all of whom were concerned with operations and none of whom, except the president, has invariably held membership in the Board of Trustees. The final choice and election of administrative officers has always rested with the board, but in no instance has the board overruled or even questioned a suggestion of the president in this field; apparently it has acted upon the principle that centralized responsibility implies the power necessary to support it. Even under the bylaws of 1949 this notion has held good.

Officers

Few agencies have been more closely identified in the public mind with their central figures than the Carnegie Foundation. From 1905 to 1930 this identity of man and works was inevitable, because the Foundation was passing through its formative period, and for Pritchett's purposes the problems solved by other philanthropies afforded small if any guidance. The president of the Foundation not only controlled and operated it but made his own precedents. During the Foundation's first quarter-century its policy and work perhaps reflected the Pritchett approach, method, and handling more closely than those of any other philanthropy mirrored the character of its presiding officer. Much the same may be said of the Suzzallo, Jessup, and Carmichael incumbencies.

When in 1933 the Board of Trustees were discussing what manner of man should succeed Suzzallo as president, members spoke their minds freely, possibly because none of them expected to be chosen: Fundamental and wide understanding of education is of much more importance than administrative ability. Although the presidency of the Foundation is less exacting than the presidency of a university, its influence is far greater and it equals in importance any other position in the field of education. The newcomer can do much in helping to shape American educational development. His post will have a threefold advantage: a national audience, opportunity to study any educational program, and complete freedom of expression. The Foundation's president should have "a passionate interest in education," ability to express himself effectively, impartial not extreme views, a judicial and open mind, practical wisdom, an adequate social point of view, philosophical insight; "he must rise above figures and statistics—he needs the wisdom to interpret figures . . . in far-reaching conclusions," "the ability to think clearly and soundly, . . . the qualities of educational statesmanship." The final action of the board implied that Jessup possessed these characteristics, which Pritchett had long displayed.

The Foundation has never had an administrative vice-president. When the president was unable to perform his duties they devolved upon the secretary of the Foundation, or merely waited for the president's return. During the periods when the presidency was vacant other provision was made, as indicated in foregoing pages.

The bylaws have formally provided for a secretary only since 1940. The duties implied in the title were previously performed by Derby, Bowman, Furst, and Savage, the first two under the cumbersome titles "secretary of the executive committee" and "assistant secretary." Later, when Learned felt the need of some sort of label while visiting German universities, he was made assistant secretary, a title formerly—and still—conferred upon the part-time custodian of the Foundation's Washington office of record.

If the choice of a first president reflected Mr. Carnegie's views, the election of two treasurers, T. Morrison Carnegie and his successor, Franks, undoubtedly was intended to symbolize the Foundation's relation to the Founder. The election, 1910, of Franks, who served also as treasurer of the Corporation and ultimately of T.I.A.A., has no traceable relation to a suggestion of 1914 from Major Henry L. Higginson, a trustee of Carnegie Institution of Washington, to Pritchett that there should be "a common treasurer for all the Carnegie institutions." The choosing of Vanderlip in 1935 was intended to honor him. A modicum of treasurer's duties has been performed by the assistant treasurers, who, in the persons of Hall, Josephs, and Monroe, have been primarily concerned with investment operations and policy. The treasurer's functions have always been in the main custodial. Accounting has been in the hands of the bursar, a position filled 1906-14 by Frank R. Cooper, 1915-17 by George L. Williams, 1917-18 by Ward Miller, and from 1918 onward by Harry C. Duryea, who among present employees has had the longest tenure.

Staff Members

Out of the experience of Pritchett and Bowman in handling the Foundation's earliest studies evolved a personnel pattern that obtained for many years. First use of its rudiments occurred in the spring of 1908, when for the proposed inquiry into medical education Pritchett engaged the young Abraham Flexner. The matter was handled with the fullest informality. Much of the same simplicity and directness marked the choice of Morris Llewellyn Cooke, for the study of the teaching of physics. Cooke's service closed in

1910 with the publication of his Bulletin Number 5, *Academic and Industrial Efficiency;* Flexner left the Foundation in 1912 for work with the General Education Board.

When, in 1913, Mr. Carnegie made the Division of Educational Enquiry a reality, Pritchett continued to appoint on the same informal basis as he had in the past. He offered Learned a position with the Vermont study on the sidewalk at the corner of Fifth Avenue and 91st Street. Apparently it was Sayre who brought Reed to Pritchett's notice, and Reed's actual appointment was almost as informal as Learned's.

Pritchett intended no extensive permanent group for studies and inquiries. In 1914 the executive committee reported to the trustees that it had "avoided the establishment of anything like a bureau, bringing in men from the outside, to take up under the direction of the president, the prosecution of particular studies." And yet in the same year Learned was appointed from March, to be "an assistant in the Foundation" in connection with "examination of records and in the study of educational questions." No duration was set for his appointment. Kandel succeeded Sayre in 1914. Whereas both Learned and Reed were recognizedly working in the Division of Educational Enquiry and were paid accordingly, Kandel's connection was apparently regarded as of a more inclusive nature. It was 1924 when, at Furst's suggestion, Learned, Reed, and Savage were formally voted the status and title of "staff member."

The seeming looseness which Pritchett used in these and other selections by no means implied lack of care. Each candidate was fully investigated and personally interviewed. His previous work and his capabilities were appraised at length. In at least one case Pritchett took pains to emphasize the facts that those in the employ of the Foundation were really only students of education and that there was no disposition to set up as an authority—a beneficial and clarifying point of view which, by one means or another, he impressed upon all newcomers to the staff. The result was that the men who, at least from 1923 to 1931 and thereafter, served as staff members had a uniform approach to their work and their relation to the Foundation, its officers, and the general public. The attitude was reinforced by weekly luncheon meetings of the group, at various clubs. For these occasions Furst was the moving spirit and each man acted as host in turn. Once in a while on invitation Pritchett made one of the party. Some of the officers of the Corporation were regular participants. Conversation was almost exclusively shop talk. Furst was also the author of the pleasant injunction upon traveling staff members never to take a meal alone if a teacher or an educational administrator could be recruited as a guest, a practice that made friends for the Foundation and often facilitated the gathering of information.

Gradually it became an understood thing that staff members were permanent appointees; men selected for particular studies were recognized as being on a different footing.

Staff Associates

It was Suzzallo who in 1931 invented the term "staff associate" to denote a person engaged by the Foundation on a temporary basis for a particular study. In point of time Cooke would probably have been the first on a considerable list of able men, among whose names would have stood those of Suzzallo himself, W. Carson Ryan, Harold W. Bentley, J. S. Noffsinger, John T. McGovern, David Spence Hill, Paul Webb, and others equally devoted and talented. (Flexner would probably have been a staff member even though his initial engagement was for his study of American medical education.) Although letters of appointment seem to have been first used in an instance or two about 1924, in 1931 they became the general rule. Signed by or for the president as appointing officer under the bylaws, they set forth the salary, arrangements for annuity contributions, if any, duration of the probationary period, vacations, probable length of service, and other pertinent details. There was no formal contract. The principal duties of staff associates were performed in the Foundation's own offices as distinguished from those of others engaged upon various studies who as a rule worked elsewhere.

The Service Staff

In 1906 the Carnegie Foundation for the Advancement of Teaching appears to have had a service staff of three: the personal secretaries of Pritchett and Bowman, and a file clerk. In 1931 it numbered twenty-three persons, according to the bursar's records. The first chart and table of organization were made by Suzzallo and Savage in the spring of that year. In 1950 the service staff comprised five persons, the services of two of whom were shared with Carnegie Corporation. Under Suzzallo the practice of starting newcomers at the telephone switchboard, a procedure sometimes used by Furst, became general policy. For a decade and a half it provided an effective means of "learning the floor."

Unfortunately, for a variety of reasons attempts to compile a complete list of service staff members have come to nothing. Such a list would assuredly include Miss Willie H. Chambliss, who came to the Foundation about 1906 and served it for some three decades, Misses Ruth Burns, Mildred Downs, Margaret Rabitte, private secretary to three of its presidents, Edythe W. Maslen, who worked first on the Missouri study, and Mrs. Anita W. Spear, all of whom were long-term appointees. Among this group there was a noteworthy *esprit* and solidarity, of which the informal celebrations of Christmas and birthdays in the tearoom were only one manifestation.

William Saunders has been the Foundation's loyal messenger for nearly thirty years.

The Rewards of Service

Although the Carnegie Foundation has never paid high salaries, compensation has as a rule reflected the purchasing power of the dollar. Pritchett's initial salary was at least comparable with what he received at M.I.T. Secretaries of the Foundation have had a decent salary. The pay of staff members has been comparable with the salaries attached to first-rate university professorships over the country. To be sure, there was little opportunity to earn on the side. A long-standing custom which became a rule was that an officer or staff member who wrote a piece or delivered an address for a nonprofit organization or institution accepted no honorarium, or else that if he could not escape it without giving offense he made it over to the support of some local activity or body related to the purposes he had tried to serve by his writing or speaking. For a time, service salaries approximated those paid the more competent workers in responsible positions in law firms and similar organizations. Since 1941 the burden of salaries has been considerably lightened through payments from Carnegie Corporation of New York for services rendered to it.

Four considerations suggest themselves as motives in seeking and holding positions with the Carnegie Foundation, whether as staff members or otherwise. First of all, there was the Foundation's prestige, which for many years was high, but any dreams of power or influence that a job-seeker had were soon dissipated before appointment, if any. He learned that the only influence or power the Foundation might possess resided in its publication of facts and justifiable inferences from them. Second, once appointment had come, both work and working conditions were agreeable. More than one person willingly sacrificed money for these advantages, which included a month's vacation. An officer, staff member, or associate who wished to work during the summer at a distance from the office has always had the privilege of taking his personal secretary with him at no expense to himself except her board and lodging. Third, for staff members there was a promise of a sabbatical year, even if only Learned got so far as starting one and his turned into a study of secondary education in Europe. Fourth, one was willing to keep a job with the Foundation because it afforded opportunity of independent thought for which Pritchett set the pace, and because there was about the office a good deal of gentle excitement, especially under Suzzallo. True, the load of work was at times undeniably heavy, and sometimes in individual cases approached a burden, but a task well done invariably won recognition. The educational inquiries of the Foundation were one-man studies; as Pritchett once wrote to Jessup: ". . . we have taken our man, given our criticism and co-operation, but allowed him to bring out a clearcut and consistent piece of work." Retirement provisions were first set up in the spring of 1906.

PRESS AND PUBLIC

One noteworthy aspect of the Foundation's experience has been its relations with the press. These were defined, for the early days, in a letter Pritchett sent to a solicitous publicity agent: "We have constantly pursued the policy of neither seeking to promote nor to avoid publicity. We print in a very complete form in our publications an account of the entire work of the Foundation and seek in this way to have the public know at first hand everything that is to be known concerning it. On the other hand we shall be slow, I think, to use any formal means to obtain a wider publicity than our regular publications tend to bring." This policy stood the test of more than forty years.

During the first decade it was Pritchett's practice to write to editors and publishers among his acquaintance concerning reports and other documents of the Foundation in advance of their appearance in print. In reply there frequently came deft and cordial invitations to prepare discussions of their material for periodicals.

Very early the Foundation became good newspaper copy; American dailies were not long in discovering its usefulness, pro and con, in educational matters. The first press summary issued in 1910 for the Fourth Annual Report. For many years a subscription to a press clipping agency, a long series of scrap books in which cuttings were pasted, and analysis of the geographical spread and the import of their contents yielded much information about the reception of prepared releases and the publications or events to which they pertained. After Bulletin Number 3, *Standard Forms for Financial Reports* of colleges and universities (1910) it was for nearly twenty years customary to submit proofs of Bulletins to institutions named in them. The first major departure from this advance notice, as it were, came with Bulletin Number 23 (1929) when digests of field reports were sent to college presidents instead of confidential proofs.

Furst once emphasized the principles which he had followed in talking with writers and journalists who wished to write about Foundation publications or business. No expenditure of his time was too great if he succeeded in making clear the facts involved; second, the most satisfactory source of quotable material was a printed document, which, of course, had been carefully prepared; and third, if the Foundation was not ready to discuss a topic or had no organized information about it, another subject might be substituted and the writer might get a story anyway. On one occasion a special writer preparing for an influential newspaper a hostile exposé of the Foundation called upon Furst with blood in his eye and a prepared series of questions for Furst to answer. Furst persuaded him that since the questions had all been treated in Foundation publications or correspondence he might prefer to inspect some of the documents involved. Accordingly the writer was provided with space in which to work on the pertinent materials, on which he spent three days. At noon of the fourth day he came to Furst's desk to tell him that he had the material for a story. "But," he added, with rather embarrassed frankness, "it won't be the story I was all set to write. I've changed my mind." The piece he turned out was among the most complimentary ever printed about the Carnegie Foundation. Pritchett early learned the futility of arguing with editors: "The criticisms of the editor," he once wrote to one of them who had dealt rather perversely with the Foundation and its president, "fall alike on the just and the unjust and one learns to accept them in a chastened spirit and not talk back."

Distribution of Bulletins, Annual Reports, and other documents has depended partly on individual requests by mail or in person for particular issues set down in the printed descriptive list of publications first issued in 1917, with a last printing thirty years later, but more upon carefully maintained mailing lists in two parts, the press list and the general list. To the press list went, in advance of issue, two copies of each Report or Bulletin, with a summary designed to assist writers in getting the gist of the document readily and quoting if desired. The general mailing list was subdivided for trustees of the Foundation, college presidents, other philanthropic agencies, libraries public and academic, teachers retirement systems, and a large group of school, college, and university officers and teachers who had expressed or demonstrated interest in the Foundation's work. Each study or inquiry as it progressed amassed its own special list of interested persons who received copies of published results. Pritchett stressed particularly the importance of reaching the college teacher: "The sole opportunity the Foundation has to influence the educational judgment of professors," he once wrote, "is through its publications, and these have weight only as they are sound and prove in the end to be wise." The general mailing list was subject to rather frequent revision downward, although requests to restore names thus removed were invariably met. The number of entries on both the press and the general mailing lists have varied widely under successive administrations. There has never been a charge for a Foundation publication, although since 1935 carriage on certain bulk shipments has been paid by recipients. No Foundation publication was ever copyright.

For many years, questions by mail, whether or not related to the Foundation's work, bulked large in correspondence. Many such inquiries could be answered through printed matter. Others could not by any conjecture be related to an item on the list of publications. The only reply possible would be either a guess or a confession of failure to identify what was being sought. Advisory or consultative conversations of officers and staff members with callers usually led to sending a publication or two, or even an addition to the general mailing list. It was all part of a long-term process of informing the public, and the friends it made were worth the trouble.

Except as trying to furnish concise and trustworthy information in a pleasant format may be one of the functions of the propagandist, no attempt has been made to "sell" the Foundation to anyone in any cause. The sympathetic treatment accorded the mass of matter published by the Foundation, some of it pretty technical in spite of its authors' intentions, has testified overwhelmingly to the friendly intelligence of American journalists and especially of editorial writers. Occasionally headlines and exigencies of makeup have left something to be desired, but on the whole even in days of greatest trial the Foundation has found no just cause for complaint over the treatment it has received on editorial and news pages, or the response of the public.

Since 1946 the Foundation's public relations have been in professional hands.

The Carnegie Foundation and the Law

The Foundation's legal business has never been sufficiently large or constant to justify retaining counsel on any protracted basis. Legal work connected with "The Carnegie Foundation" has received attention on early pages.

From the autumn of 1905 up to at least 1913, John L. Cadwalader acted as counselor. There is no record of his having charged a fee or presented a bill, even from law firms with which he corresponded in the Foundation's behalf. During 1908 and 1909 his opinions covered several matters, such as the location of offices, place of meetings, and the matter of vested rights in retiring allowances and pensions. On the trustees desiring "to know whether the individuals in any given institution acquire by the publication of [the Rules for the Granting of Retiring Allowances] rights [that] would prevent" changes in those Rules, Cadwalader, upon the premise that "it is of the essence of the power to administer the gift that there shall be changes," rendered an opinion in the negative, even as regards persons already in receipt of benefits. The same matter was re-examined when in 1915 changes in the Rules and their phrasing were under discussion, and the decision taken by the trustees after other advice coincided with Cadwalader's opinion.

Early in the work of the Foundation, Pritchett was able to state to the trustees that the grounds of objection to some of its activities concerned not its administration of benefits but the published results of its educational studies. These publications led to the instituting of several suits against the Foundation and individuals connected with it, the first of which grew out of Flexner's work in medical education. Gies's study in dental education produced another suit, but the offended university of medicine and dentistry in 1926 had its charter forfeited by the supreme court of the state in which it was doing business, and the suit came to nothing. Threats of libel suits over Bulletin Number 23, *American College Athletics* (1929), soon faded, thanks to the legal thoroughness with which the facts of the study had been handled. An action for libel brought in 1937 over passages in Eells's survey of surveys was discontinued in 1942 with a general release and without indemnifying expense. So far as known, the only action, not brought by the Foundation, which involved its benefits was dismissed in 1926. Of course, the Foundation itself sought court decisions in 1939 and 1945 upon its petitions, drawn by Root, Clark, Buckner & Ballantine, connected with the plan for completing payment of its allowances and pensions and the technical administration of the plan. No objection was encountered on either occasion.

⁓ 16 ⁓

Impulse and Fruits

IN THE BEGINNING · FOR BETTER FOR WORSE · SUNDRY DEFICIEN-
CIES—STRUCTURAL INADEQUACIES; OPERATIONAL SHORTCOMINGS ·
A PERPETUAL TRUST · VALUE RECEIVED—THE PENSIONING FUNC-
TION; PENSION STUDIES; PRINCIPLES AND PRACTICE; A MISAPPRE-
HENSION · EDUCATIONAL STUDIES—INQUIRIES AND INVESTIGATIONS;
OPERATIONS AND DEMONSTRATIONS; SERVICE EXTRAOFFICIAL · THE
PRINTED WORD—THE PURCHASE OF RESULTS · PAST AND FUTURE

FEW if any philanthropic endowments have sprung from kindlier motives than the Carnegie Foundation for the Advancement of Teaching. Mr. Carnegie's founding purpose was simple and heartwarming: to lighten the later years of the ill-paid college professor through a modest pension, an award which the Donor never regarded as a charity and indeed came later to think of as the teacher's "rightful heritage." He confined his benefaction to private and nondenominational institutions for reasons which seemed to him sufficient, and he selected for his trustees a board of honor whose aggregate personal achievements brought it immediate prestige in the educational world. For chief administrative officer he made one of the wisest choices in his long career of giving—a comparatively young man, of character, wisdom, scientific accomplishment, and proved administrative ability, not infallible but possessed of a patient integrity that no pressure, no calumny could swerve from the pursuit of right and truth as he saw them.

IN THE BEGINNING

It was allotted to Henry S. Pritchett to translate and develop the Founder's humanitarian impulse into a living organism. For

344

the first five or six years Pritchett adhered deliberately to the simplest of mechanisms, even after Mr. Carnegie, persuaded of the good that might flow from expansion, increased his original gift by half as much again. Then prompted by experience and results Pritchett sought and obtained from Mr. Carnegie, at first reluctant, funds for the study of educational problems. The need and worth of such inquiries had already been demonstrated by the new Foundation. Thus was provided the means of work in a cognate field, and the fundamental structure of the Carnegie Foundation was fixed, for good or for ill.

Meanwhile the public success of "Carnegie pensions" and the comfort and aid they brought to both individuals and institutions had begun to have their effects within the Board of Trustees and the executive committee. Mounting unexpended income, a growing liberality within the Rules that had been intended as safeguarding against log-rolling and favoritism, the inclusion of administrative officers, grants beyond the Rules, the institutional and administrative advantages of being able to transfuse new blood into many faculties with minimal pain or trouble, not to mention the quickening delight of distributing philanthropic largess, all had their effect upon policy and operation. This expansive process continued for almost a dozen years.

In the Foundation's early days there had risen occasional question whether its funds would suffice for its purposes as expanded and developed; even by 1911 when Mr. Carnegie "turned all over to the New York corporation," as he wrote his "Dear Frend," this possibility had acquired a considerable but not an alarming stature. The fact is that the Carnegie Foundation had been inaugurated and perforce conducted for several years without access to that full technical knowledge which by present standards should have surrounded even its inception. To be sure, it was learning fast through its own studies and experience, but the toils with which it had been forced to bind itself in order to operate at all were demonstrably tightening.

This was no case of conscious scientific demonstration, for the problems of the pension field scarcely lend themselves to short-term experiment. A goal had been set and endowed and the approach to it had to be surveyed, graded, paved, even widened and adorned, while the main end was being pursued. In the circumstances it is small wonder that the activation of Mr. Carnegie's benevolent impulse should have yielded in nearly half a century both bitter fruit and sweet.

FOR BETTER FOR WORSE

Among the shortcomings which have marked both the conception and the course of the Carnegie Foundation at least two or three have turned out to be basal to its nature and first purpose. They do not lend themselves to chronology or relative emphasis.

A sentence in a letter written in 1928 strikes deep: "The history of the Carnegie Foundation seems to illustrate the fact that however high-minded men may be, they enter upon doubtful ground in administering a trust in which they or their institutions are beneficiaries." This is a considerable extension of a position which Pritchett took when, in 1909, he acknowledged Charles W. Eliot's letter of resignation from the board: "It would be unfortunate," he wrote, "if this board came to be filled with men who were drawing pensions." The fact that most of the Foundation's trustees, at retirement, have heeded this principle does not dull the broader ultimate implication.

The Foundation's primary purpose has always been providing retiring allowances without cost to the recipients. This altruistic motive concealed perils which only experience on a comparatively large scale could uncover. There are evidences that Mr. Carnegie himself became conscious of the possibility that the "free" pensions he had brought into being might "corrupt" or "demoralize" recipients, not to mention those in whose hands he lodged responsibility for them. "The dangers of a non-contributory system lie mainly in those universal dangers which come from human weakness and human selfishness," says the Sixth Annual Report (1911). Not without justification did a famous economist call the Foundation "a temptation to institutions to retire men," and another critic, more hostile, to term its pension plan "a Stabilizer of Mentality." A passage in the Thirteenth Annual Report (1918) stands high among the classic discussions of the ill effects of "free" pensions in general and the Foundation's in particular: their corrupting of moral fiber in undertaking a responsibility that is partly the individual's, partly his employer's, the unintentional attractiveness of "something for nothing," the depression of salaries, discriminative restriction of payments to the few chosen beneficiaries, and other matters.

At one time the Foundation through the implications of its Rules bolstered the notion that there ought to be a more or less fixed relation between salary and pension—that half the active salary plus a little more should suffice in the retired status. This rule of thumb, an assumption still widely prevalent, is denied by a passage in the Twenty-third Annual Report (1928): "There is no definite ratio that can be assigned as between the teacher's active pay and his retired pay." The whole course of the Foundation's existence emphasizes the facts, first, that only "the unlimited taxing power of a government" can maintain a system of "free" pensions, with or without such a ratio; and, secondly, that probably the most dangerously unsound provision in any pension scheme is basing the retiring stipend upon the average salary over the final five or ten years of service, a provision by which the Foundation was grievously plagued until 1929, when most of its future allowances were to all intents pegged at $1,000 a year for age seventy. The Foundation through its offspring, the Teachers Insurance and Annuity Association, as well as its own simplified Rules, has sought to mitigate the ill effects that through lack of knowledge it once exemplified.

SUNDRY DEFICIENCIES

A number of other deficiencies, some of structure, others of operation, come into focus when the Foundation's experience is examined as a whole.

Structural Inadequacies

Except inferentially, no version of the Foundation's bylaws has provided for performance of the president's duties—or, for that matter, the duties of any other officer—during the incumbent's temporary absence or inability to serve, or in case of sudden vacancy. Preceding chapters have recounted how the gaps between administrations have been bridged or forded. A well-drawn provision for a vice-president, or for the performance of vice-presidential duties without adding another officer, could have sufficed administratively for any emergency in the presidency or its succession, or in connection with any other administrative office.

One means of approximating a degree of continuity in administration would have been a president's manual kept in long hand by each successive president for his own guidance, but especially for that of his successor. A notebook of this nature, containing jottings on operation, precedents, personnel, relationships internal and external, and similar matters, though at times irksome to maintain, would have become invaluable in the course of two or three presidencies. Not all new administrative officers are so fortunate as to have within call the wisdom of an emeritus predecessor for counsel in difficult situations.

The charge of provincialism in the necessary composition of the executive committee has been dismissed in Chapter 15 as "not proven." It is not so easy to dispose of the fact that some of the universities whose presidents held executive committee membership have had the longest lists of pensionables, and consequently highest total benefits. Much the same is true of certain institutions whose presiding officers have been influential or vociferous in the Board of Trustees. The stabilizing of the list of pensionables, 1929-31, ended this tendency.

In the development of the Division of Educational Enquiry from 1913 to 1946 certain contradictions are discernible between policy and action. The original intention was that the Division should not become a bureau with a long-term staff. And yet as the years passed it became precisely that, although in minuscule. While many men were employed temporarily on assignments *ad hoc*, a few remained until retirement. Adherence to the original policy would, it is true, have deprived the Foundation of some of Learned's imaginative vision and Reed's scholarship, but it would have brought new blood and energy in even greater measure than actually came to pass, and it would have contributed to the solution of a vexing problem.

That problem was how to terminate a study. Some inquiries certainly ran too long, and results showed it. Others could have been more precisely planned and promptly concluded, with consequent gain in timeliness and effect. This was indubitably true of the inquiries concerning engineering schools, the training of teachers, and legal education; it is possibly true of the pension studies. Cumulative results from extended inquiries are not to be disparaged, but arid, deep-frozen recommendations take a deal of moistening and warming before they nourish. The tendency to prolong inquiries leaves little to be gained from follow-up studies, and perhaps this accounts for the fact that formal attempts to appraise or audit their results have been undertaken in all too few cases: the Pennsylvania Study, the American Athletic Inquiry, and the Southern Program of Grants-in-Aid. The longer the time between the incep-

IMPULSE AND FRUITS 349

tion of an inquiry or an operating program and its appraisal, on
the one hand, the greater the difficulty in appraising the original
undertaking, on the other. In all too brief a period both merits
and defects become impossible to discern through the shadows of
the years.

Operational Shortcomings

The deficiencies just discussed had their origins in structural factors or in deviation from policies. Other shortcomings are traceable to measures adopted to meet conditions which were essentially
uncontrollable. In such instances judgment, even tentative, involves
hindsight and must always be provisional as of a moment in time.

One such deficiency may be summarized in the statement that
since 1918 the Foundation has had the full-time services of a minority of its senior appointees. For various overlapping periods the
working time and energy of all four presidents, two secretaries,
two treasurers, one staff member, three and more investment officers, and others as well, to a total of at least a dozen, have been
shared with one or more other agencies. During forty-five years
only four men have served the Foundation exclusively during their
tenure as officers or staff members. In some instances the loss to
the Foundation has been negligible—probably it has resulted in a
gain in service over the whole philanthropic field. In other instances
the Foundation has been the poorer for its generosity.

At the root of this imbalance, so to speak, have lain since 1918
the Foundation's growing poverty, its development of T.I.A.A.,
and its consequent relation to Carnegie Corporation. Sometimes
the challenge of dual service and the chance of obtaining wide results have been too strong to resist. Sometimes other circumstances
buttressed inclinations and influenced choice. In every instance this
sharing of services has appeared at its inception not only expedient
but wise. Each such step has had the deliberate consent of the
Foundation's Board of Trustees. The resulting economies in operating costs have been material. While some of the double duty has
occasioned misgivings about the load of work and responsibility,
none has brought protest or opposition, but when the advantages
and disadvantages are assessed over a term of years it becomes evident that the net gains, in reputation and in service, have in the
main accrued to the organizations with which the Foundation has
shared its personnel and not to the Foundation. The prime justification for this "doubling in brass" ought to lie not in personal

inclination but in the nominal or intermittent nature of the working loads attached to the posts affected.

A glance at the annual reports of the president of the Carnegie Corporation for the past five years reveals a change of program and emphasis under which the Corporation has been spending large annual sums in the field of higher education through direct grants to universities and colleges. The previous practice of routing such grants through the Foundation has been very considerably modified. The number if not the dollar aggregate of grants for joint projects has diminished, with a consequent reduction of red tape and an increase in the intimacy of contact between the Corporation and the recipient institutions. As a result, the Foundation's influence and standing in the college field as a whole has undoubtedly waned.

A PERPETUAL TRUST

In Chapter 1 reference was made to the Carnegie Foundation for the Advancement of Teaching as an endowment in perpetuity, and to some of the motives that led Mr. Carnegie to give it that status. Today perpetual trusts are somewhat out of fashion and there are doubts as to the wisdom of establishing or maintaining them. The matter engaged Pritchett's attention on various occasions. In two Annual Reports, the Twenty-second (1927) and Twenty-third (1928) he analyzed the question at length. His first discussion has already been quoted; his second runs in part:

> The *a priori* arguments made against the perpetual charitable trust seem to me to rest upon questionable assumptions. No human agency for the promotion of social advancement . . . will operate at its maximum efficiency at all times. Such agencies will have seasons of fruitful performance and at other periods may render but mediocre or commonplace service. But as times change, as new issues develop, as one group of trustees and executive officers gives place to other men, periods of fruitful service will again arise and new problems will be dealt with in the light of long experience. It may be true that an hundred million dollars can be distributed more wisely and can serve a larger purpose if completely distributed in a limited period of time rather than if it be constituted a perpetual endowment for the benefit of many generations, but there is no way of proving it. Mr. Carnegie . . . decided in favor of the perpetual trust, influenced in large measure by his faith in his fellow men. He believed that men would be found, from decade

to decade, and from generation to generation, who would administer such trusts wisely, unselfishly, . . .

In another connection Pritchett did not deny to terminable endowments their place in philanthropic giving, but he pointed out that a group of trustees faced with a necessity of increasing their rate of benefaction in order to expend capital within a fixed period are likely to find themselves approaching the terminus with very considerable sums still in their hands. They would then be forced to make extraordinarily large grants in order to meet their deadline. In such a process, Pritchett concluded, there can be no wisdom. For him solution of the controversy lay in the element of time—time for development of philanthropic intent, time to consider courses of action and select the best above the merely good, time to absorb the effects of lag or failure, time to discover the man for the emerging tasks. "Time," he once said in an address at the Carnegie Institute of Technology, Pittsburgh, "is the nurse and breeder of all good; but only those who have wisdom and imagination learn to work with time." Results in human progress, he saw, are cumulative.

VALUE RECEIVED

In spite of all that could be said about the Foundation's shortcomings and deficiencies—and preceding pages have only scratched the surface—American higher education, the teacher, and the public at large have greatly gained rather than lost through the work of the Carnegie Foundation for the Advancement of Teaching. Although no itemizing of these gains can be final while the nation or the Foundation endures, it will be well to pause in midstream and, having thrown overboard the less savory fruits, to take account of some of the more pleasant that remain. The Foundation's contributions to American life have grown in the two principal fields of its activities, pensions and educational studies. It would be useless to try to determine their relative values or absolute importance.

The Pensioning Function

In forty-five years the Carnegie Foundation has distributed more than $57,000,000 in retiring allowances for college teachers and administrators and in pensions for their widows, not an insignificant sum even in these days of billions. Its annual payments on this account still exceeded $1,800,000 in 1950, with more to come. By 1975 probably as many as 6,500 persons will have received these benefits in their later years. Through operation and demonstration in a field scantily known in 1905 it has in less than five decades brought into focus a problem of American higher education which, little appreciated at the Foundation's inception, has now been attacked and in a measure met for a whole nation. True, experience has demonstrated that the Foundation's own operations afforded few valid affirmative answers to the question involved, but its reports of these operations have maintained standards of frankness, of financial completeness, and of intelligibility that few other philanthropic agencies equal.

Pension Studies

Perhaps had present-day knowledge been available to Mr. Carnegie and his advisers when he was maturing his plans for his gift to the teachers it might have taken another form. Conceivably it would not have been made at all. Certainly its mode of operation and its development would have been very different. As matters stood, those to whom he entrusted the practical working out of his beneficence had to improvise procedures and devise principles as they went along, because "nobody knew any better." From these facts sprang the sharpest of the criticisms which were aimed at the Foundation and its first president.

The existence of the Carnegie Foundation has been bound round with promises which its own accumulating experience and knowledge have progressively proved to be erroneous. Much of the effort of its first quarter-century went into emphasizing this fact and in trying by a variety of means to save others from the pitfalls that its own shortcomings had digged. It made no bones about confessing its inadequacies and illustrating them out of its own experience and the social philosophy of retirement and pensions which it was helping to build. From these fetters the Foundation succeeded in ultimately freeing itself, but at the cost of decades of effort and only with the generous assistance of Carnegie Corporation of New York. The initial concepts would have proved equally faulty if the Foundation had had the wealth of the world to cushion their ill effects.

With no motives to serve but the Founder's honor the Carnegie Foundation was the first agency to emphasize the broad social bearings of pensions. In the writings and the spoken words of its officers it did not blink its own shortcomings; the hope was that its warnings might lead others to avoid them. It appreciated at full worth and sought to protect the individualism of the college teacher and to assist him in preserving his independence of thought and action within the bounds of loyalty and common sense. In face of temptations to become doctrinaire it has seldom pontificated, and it has endeavored to persuade by reason, never to coerce. Its own studies and its own experience furnished danger signals enough for its patient purposes.

There have been affirmations aplenty. Partly through the Foundation's influence, painful as it at times had to be for the hopes of individuals, the cause of teachers' retirement, and perhaps even of old age economic security itself, has been brought home to men's business and bosoms. As for the college professor, if he can indeed be singled out from among the generality of mankind, Mr. Carnegie's second gift in the sum of $5,000,000 and the "acceptance" of qualified state universities helped to open the doors of state retirement systems to professors in state universities. Even the scaling down of the benefits to be paid emphasized the employer responsibilities of American colleges for the old age of their professors, and pointed the need of supplementing the Foundation's own inadequate provisions. Under a variety of pressures it came formally to recognize some of the values of part-time work after retirement, and thus to facilitate for the older teacher a tapering off in academic duties as preferable to a complete discontinuance of the work of years. In a great volume of advisory consultation, before meetings of national and other bodies, in correspondence, and in discussions oral and written, the men in the Foundation's employ worked to guide pension development from day to day and from year to year in the direction of sound practice. Somewhat as the Founder lived up to his Gospel of Wealth, so the Foundation has aimed ultimately to effectuate sound theories of retirement. For industry as well as for education the Foundation's influence in the field of pensions had force, not alone in the United States and Canada, but in other countries. Its position of detachment from political, sectional, or commercial limitations and the thoroughness of its work enabled it for a quarter of a century to render a unique service to the profession it was designed to advance and to the society of which that profession is a component.

Principles and Practice

If the pension studies of the Carnegie Foundation had led only to devising and setting up the Teachers Insurance and Annuity Association of America its position still would have been unique.

Comment to the effect that T.I.A.A. was sired by the Foundation out of its own necessity, coupled with motives of self-preservation on the part of Carnegie Corporation of New York, is beside the point. The fact is that the successful founding and the progress of the Association have provided the college teacher with the means of independently, economically, soundly protecting himself and his family against the hazards not only of life after retirement but of the earning years as well. It has never been possible to provide this protection under any scheme of "free" pensions, because such an arrangement implies as a basis a contract legally enforceable. The setting up and development of T.I.A.A. to serve the profession in the United States and the Dominion of Canada has more than merely approximated a fulfillment of Mr. Carnegie's hope that in due time the college teacher should come to enjoy a retiring stipend as part of his compensation.

A Misapprehension

Mention has already been made of the error into which some have fallen by regarding the Foundation and its retiring allowances as "ended," "abandoned," "finished," or taken over by Carnegie Corporation. In the face of an annual load still heavy, although receding, which is expected to persist for another third of a century, such misapprehension approaches the absurd. The error is probably due to the fact that the Foundation has received and will continue to receive large sums from Carnegie Corporation to assist in meeting its pension needs. Even if the memory of the Foundation's pioneering service should fade altogether, its influence will still be traceable in American social economics.

EDUCATIONAL STUDIES

The educational studies of the Foundation, as distinguished from the publications embodying their results, have been mainly of two sorts: inquiries or, less aptly, investigations into particular problems, and operations or demonstrations. The two categories overlap at a number of points and some studies contain elements of both. With one exception, each study from its beginning was pointed towards publication. That exception was the Co-operative Graduate Testing Program, of which no full length account has ever been prepared.

Inquiries and Investigations

The Foundation's educational inquiries followed in general the pattern of Flexner's work on medical education in the United States and Canada, a fact hitherto insufficiently appreciated. In every major instance the Foundation undertook to investigate a phase of higher education, a state educational system, or some area or topic upon request from a representative or authorizing body, group, or officer. In practically no case did the Foundation inject itself into a situation without invitation, usually several times repeated. The advantages thus gained, both immediate and ultimate, in obtaining data and acquiring status for the work supplemented the leverage implicit in the invitation. But the invitation while important was only the first starting gun; a good deal of trouble and a considerable diplomacy were necessary to obtain the pledges of co-operation essential to even moderately clear sailing. The text of almost every Bulletin contains the statement that it was a report to a particular body or group. This was precisely true. It helped to define the target of the inquiry and took an audience for granted. The two outstanding exceptions were the British and American athletic studies. The work that led to Bulletin Number 18, *Games and Sports in British Schools and Universities*, was Pritchett's own proposal; Bulletin Number 23, *American College Athletics*, presented results of work urged over so many years and undertaken in response to so many pressures upon the Foundation that singling out one representative association to which the report could be addressed was impossible.

In none of the Foundation's studies has attempt been made to rate institutions on any basis whatever. The Accepted-Associated-Specified List is in no sense a rating of universities and colleges, although numerous attempts have been made to misuse it as such.

As noted in Chapter 15, the Foundation's investigations were generally one-man studies; in only a few instances were commissions involved, and in these cases the final reports were planned and drafted by individuals—for instance, the Vermont report in Bulletin Number 7, prepared principally by Learned, Dr. E. C. Elliott, and Dr. Hillegas, and the California report written and revised by Suzzallo but published by the State. Pritchett put his finger on the essentials:

> My experience . . . leads me to question somewhat the effectiveness of investigations pursued by groups having divergent points of view and possibly divergent interests. . . . So far as I have

been able to observe the single investigator working under supervision and taking up a definitely limited problem, is more likely to produce a clear, intelligible, fruitful study than can be had by the group method. . . . It rarely happens that the joint thinking of a group equals the clear and effective thinking of an intelligent and trained individual checked by some sort of supervisory group or groups.

In most instances the group in the Foundation's own offices provided the checking.

The chances are always against getting an incisive, operable result from a study conducted by a committee unless the person preparing the draft is strong and skillful enough to discard many comments and sharpen those accepted. In such matters majority rule is practicable only to a limited degree, for minority opinion tends to acquire a disproportionate emphasis that blurs the result. The one-man study, with or without consultants or advisers, remains easily the best implement in the field.

Operations and Demonstrations

The other type of educational study undertaken by the Foundation, the operation, experiment, or demonstration, comprises three notable enterprises: the Pennsylvania Study, the Co-operative Graduate Testing Program, and the Program of Grants-in-Aid in Southern Higher Institutions. Including in this classification the study of the relations of secondary and higher education in Pennsylvania may appear questionable. It is perhaps justifiable because although its main results were summarized in Bulletin Number 29, which Learned and Wood prepared jointly, its emphasis came progressively to fall on procedures and method, and the new-type comprehensive examination and the cumulative record card used initially as operational means to an end ultimately acquired, taken together, the status of an end in itself.

Projects involving the operational approach tend to cost immensely more than one-man studies, but if successful their results are more widely diffused and, as they spread, affect many more individuals. Enterprises of this type may bring more easily identifiable results, and those conducted by the Foundation which involved testing and examining appear to have had a curiously causal relationship in time; for example, the seeds of the Graduate Record Examination project would probably not have sprouted so soon if the soil had not been in a way prepared through the Pennsylvania

Study. These two ventures have no relation to the Southern Program of Grants-in-Aid, essentially a broad, co-operatively supported affair, which through careful planning, supervision both central and areal, and wide and catholic coverage, early acquired some of the aspects of a movement.

For the first of these three projects, the Pennsylvania Study, results were analyzed and published. From the second, the Co-operative Graduate Testing Program, developed Educational Testing Service, Inc. The Southern Program of Grants-in-Aid for scholarly or creative work will, it is to be hoped, lend itself to qualitative as well as to quantitative appraisal, and steps are being taken to that end. At any rate, none of the three, however important, could have been started by the Foundation, let alone concluded, without the generous support of Carnegie Corporation of New York.

Service Extraofficial

External services on the part of officers and staff members of the Foundation, made possible by the Foundation's position of detachment and the nature of its functions, should not go unmentioned. Unofficially these men participated in the work of a large number of committees, groups, and commissions, and in innumerable discussions and enterprises, all related to the field of higher education, without expectation of reward except the satisfaction of work well done. They have spent long hours in counseling those who requested help. Some have given much time and effort to the public good.

It has been as individuals rather than as Foundation employees that they have suggested, upon request, names of numbers of persons suitable to be considered for administrative posts ranging from federal commissionerships to teaching positions. If a few such suggestions could be enumerated it would be evident that success came mainly from two factors: the precision with which individual qualities of the man suggested sorted with the responsibilities which he was to discharge, and the usual practice of mentioning only one name for each position—the technique of the rifle rather than the shotgun.

THE PRINTED WORD

No one who reads consecutively the Bulletins and Annual Reports of the Foundation can fail to recognize the breadth and temperateness of the educational discussions they contain. They suggest or touch upon every development in the field that came to pass during the period in which they appeared. The pension Bulletins and Annual Report discussions bear a similar relation to retirement problems. The supplementary publications were timely in their day and many have enduring interest.

Although, as Pritchett once pointed out, the Carnegie Foundation may have had only a moderate function in educational discussion and criticism, its publications were the product of conditions that made for quality and for influence. In the first place, the subjects were usually selected with discernment. Secondly, the men and women who dealt with them were carefully chosen on the basis of both past performance and future promise. Their invariable assignment was to discover and tell the truth, no matter whom it touched. The Foundation's first president set the standard of independent thought and expression; even when his own convictions differed from those at which his colleagues arrived, he made no effort at suppression. But he did demand a clear and workmanlike product for the intelligent layman. This point of view his three successors have cherished and maintained. As one result, the Foundation's publications have been comparatively free from pedaguese and educational gobbledygook. The basis of the one hundred and more Bulletins and Annual Report discussions was scholarship in the best sense of the term.

The success of many of the supplementary publications was due in part to three factors: the care with which the officers or staff members or both together canvassed the ground before the person to undertake the work was chosen; the relations between these persons once selected and the Foundation's people during the task— the seeking and the give-and-take of advice, especially on peripheral matters; and the closeness with which the typescripts were read and brutally criticized in the office and the spirit in which suggestions were received. The result was a quality and pertinency which few of the regular publications surpassed. The only reason for assigning to these documents the supplementary status at all was the recognized temporary connections they involved and the conceivably ephemeral character of the subjects.

Publications that have resulted from special or joint Corporation-Foundation projects and have been issued by other agencies than the Foundation have equaled in quality, and sometimes surpassed in interest and utility, the Foundation's supplementary volumes. Those produced by specialists have been in general addressed to specialists; those whose authors were free-lance writers have found

their readers among both teachers and the general public. As in the
case of the Foundation's regular and supplementary publications
the effect which these documents have had upon American education
has probably exceeded any results ever claimed for them.

The Purchase of Results

It is perhaps worth suggesting that the studies or projects of the
Foundation which have had the promptest and most far-reaching
results have been those which have led to large investments of char-
itable and other funds to further the good works they proposed.
Flexner's medical inquiries were implemented by Rockefeller and
Carnegie millions and the other millions that these attracted. The
Teachers Insurance and Annuity Association was furthered by the
Corporation's gifts to the Foundation for the specific purpose. The
Co-operative Graduate Testing Program project developed into a
nationwide testing enterprise with the aid of Corporation grants
and considerable sums contributed by component bodies. The million and more of resources that went into the southern program of
college and university grants-in-aid was similarly and co-operatively
maintained. Conceivably, the Foundation's studies which have
brought the less immediate and the less direct results, such as the
Missouri teacher-training inquiry, the California study, the work
on college accounting, on the teaching of physics, on legal and on
dental education, and on education in Saskatchewan and the Maritimes, have not been followed by philanthropic or public investment.
The two enterprises that refuse classification in either group are
the study of education in Vermont, in part, and the American Athletic Inquiry, echoes of which still ring out after two decades. Perhaps it is not too much to say to the public and the philanthropoids
as well: "If you want educational change within a generation, you
have to buy it."

Some years ago Dr. Wriston, speaking "To the Memory of
Andrew Carnegie," pointed out that the Carnegie Foundation was
destined from its inception "to bring to teaching all the leverage
which sound principles of social insurance could provide. It touched
the weakest spot in the whole structure of higher education; it
directed attention to a problem until then virtually neglected; [that
problem] still grows in magnitude and has not yet reached its
zenith. . . . [Our] tribute is an expression of admiration for a

man, who, in unique degree, was able to identify critical issues and by imaginative foresight make provision for their support and for their reinforcement as time and circumstances might require."

For the Carnegie Foundation the next half-century is divided into two unequal periods: the period of obligation and the period of fruition. The period of obligation will see the discharge of the Foundation's pension load and considerable progress in repaying its borrowings. During that time, all things being equal, funds can be found to keep alive the Foundation's studies and other projects, on whatever basis administrative wisdom may reveal. Financial freedom once achieved, the Foundation will be ready to increase those broader activities which its charter contemplates. These activities would then become its primary rather than its ancillary concern.

In one respect the central problem of the Foundation's future is identical with that of its earliest days—it turns upon quality and aims of personnel. "Find the man" will merely become "Find the men"—for trustees and members of the executive committee, for administrative officers, and for those scholars who may become associated, briefly or for longer periods, in its work. Henry S. Pritchett insisted that for an educational philanthropy men are more important than money. Through them the fruits of Mr. Carnegie's magnificent impulse may be gathered in perpetuity.

Appendixes

Appendix A

THE CARNEGIE FOUNDATION FOR THE ADVANCEMENT OF TEACHING

A TABLE OF PENSIONING EXPERIENCE

Note: The data in this table are taken mainly from Annual Reports at five-year intervals and from other printed official documents as of the end of the fiscal years indicated. The single computed figure is in square brackets. During the period 1928-April 19, 1944, the sums needed to meet the pension load, over and above income, were drawn from principal of Reserve Fund Number One; in the period April 19, 1944-1950, the amounts so needed were borrowed equally from the principal of the General Endowment Fund and from Carnegie Corporation of New York.

	Cost of Allowances and Pensions in Force	Cost of Allowances and Pensions Becoming Operative (or Granted)	Income Available from Foundation's Own Securities	Number of Beneficiaries at End of Year	Number of Deaths of Beneficiaries	Estimated Pensionables
1906, Oct. 1	$ 122,130	$122,130	$ 292,763	90	1	2,042
1910	521,070	110,825	543,881	346	23	3,512
1915	690,668	66,773	712,852	445	28	6,626
1920	870,670	97,180	706,383	555	32	4,552
1925	1,184,673	108,318	749,239	736	45	[3,743]
1930	1,524,975	154,040	1,557,991	918	54	3,190
1935	1,808,871	174,712	1,367,860	1,185	69	2,674
1940	1,895,267	129,445	854,362	1,542	113	1,905
1945	1,868,898	130,363	546,176	1,876	105	1,203
1950	1,836,107	117,055	479,498	2,061	122	485

Appendix B

FIFTY-NINTH CONGRESS OF THE UNITED STATES OF AMERICA;

At the First Session,

Begun and held at the City of Washington on Monday, the fourth day of December, one thousand nine hundred and five.

AN ACT

*To incorporate The Carnegie Foundation
for the Advancement of Teaching.*

Be it enacted by the Senate and House of Representatives of the United States of America in Congress assembled, That the persons following, namely, ARTHUR T. HADLEY, CHARLES WILLIAM ELIOT, NICHOLAS MURRAY BUTLER, JACOB G. SCHURMAN, WOODROW WILSON, L. CLARK SEELYE, CHARLES C. HARRISON, ALEXANDER C. HUMPHREYS, S. B. McCORMICK, EDWIN B. CRAIGHEAD, HENRY C. KING, CHARLES F. THWING, THOMAS McCLELLAND, EDWIN H. HUGHES, H. McCLELLAND BELL, GEORGE H. DENNY, WILLIAM PETERSON, SAMUEL PLANTZ, DAVID S. JORDAN, WILLIAM H. CRAWFORD, HENRY S. PRITCHETT, FRANK A. VANDERLIP, T. MORRIS CARNEGIE, ROBERT A. FRANKS, their associates and successors duly chosen, are hereby incorporated and declared to be a body corporate in the District of Columbia by the name of The Carnegie Foundation for the Advancement of Teaching, and by that name shall be known and have perpetual succession, with the powers, limitations and restrictions herein contained.

SEC. 2. That the objects for which said corporation is incorporated shall be—

(*a*) To receive and maintain a fund or funds and apply the income thereof as follows:

To provide retiring pensions, without regard to race, sex, creed, or color, for the teachers of universities, colleges and technical schools in the United States, the Dominion of Canada, and Newfoundland, who, by reason of long and meritorious service, or by reason of old age, dis-

ability, or other sufficient reason, shall be deemed entitled to the assistance and aid of this corporation, on such terms and conditions, however, as such corporation may from time to time approve and adopt;
Provided, however, That the said retiring pensions shall be paid to such
teachers only as are or have been connected with institutions not under
control of a sect or which do not require their trustees, their officers,
faculties, or students (or a majority thereof) to belong to any specified
sect, and which do not impose any theological test as a condition of
entrance therein or of connection therewith.

(*b*) In general, to do and perform all things necessary to encourage,
uphold, and dignify the profession of the teacher and the cause of
higher education within the United States, the Dominion of Canada,
and Newfoundland aforesaid, and to promote the objects of the foundation, with full power, however, to the trustees hereinafter appointed
and their successors from time to time to modify the conditions and
regulations under which the work shall be carried on, so as to secure the
application of the funds in the manner best adapted to the conditions
of the time: *And provided,* That such corporation may by a vote of
two-thirds of the entire number of trustees enlarge or vary the purposes
herein set forth, provided that the objects of the corporation shall at
all times be among the foregoing or kindred thereto.

(*c*) To receive and hold by gift, bequest, devise, grant, or purchase,
any real or personal property, and to use and dispose of the same for
the purposes of the corporation.

SEC. 3. That the direction and management of the affairs of the cor-
poration, and the control and disposition of its property and funds,
shall be vested in a board of trustees, twenty-five in number, to be
composed of the following individuals: ARTHUR T. HADLEY, CHARLES
WILLIAM ELIOT, NICHOLAS MURRAY BUTLER, JACOB G. SCHURMAN,
WOODROW WILSON, L. CLARK SEELYE, CHARLES C. HARRISON, ALEXAN-
DER C. HUMPHREYS, S. B. McCORMICK, EDWIN B. CRAIGHEAD, HENRY
C. KING, CHARLES F. THWING, THOMAS McCLELLAND, EDWIN H.
HUGHES, H. McCLELLAND BELL, GEORGE H. DENNY, WILLIAM PETER-
SON, SAMUEL PLANTZ, DAVID S. JORDAN, WILLIAM H. CRAWFORD,
HENRY S. PRITCHETT, FRANK A. VANDERLIP, T. MORRIS CARNEGIE, and
ROBERT A. FRANKS, being twenty-four in number with power to said
board to increase the same to twenty-five in all, who shall constitute the
first board of trustees and constitute the members of the corporation.
Vacancies occurring by death, resignation, or otherwise shall be filled
by the remaining trustees in such manner as the by-laws shall prescribe,
and the persons so elected shall thereupon become trustees and also
members of the corporation.

Sec. 4. The principal office of the corporation shall be located in the District of Columbia, but offices may be maintained and meetings of the corporation or the trustees and committees may be held in other places such as the by-laws may from time to time fix.

Sec. 5. That the said trustees shall be entitled to take, hold, and administer any securities, funds, or property which may be transferred to them for the purposes and objects hereinbefore enumerated, and such other funds or property as may at any time be given, devised, or bequeathed to them, or to such corporation, for the purposes of the trust; with full power from time to time to adopt a common seal, to appoint officers, whether members of the board of trustees or otherwise, and such employees as may be deemed necessary in carrying on the business of the corporation and at such salaries or with such remuneration, as they may think proper; and full power to adopt by-laws and such rules or regulations as may be necessary to secure the safe and convenient transaction of the business of the corporation; and full power and discretion to invest any principal and deal with and expend the income of the corporation in such manner as in their judgment will best promote the objects hereinbefore set forth; and in general to have and use all the powers and authority necessary to promote such objects and carry out the purposes of the donor.

The said trustees shall have further power from time to time to hold as investments any securities transferred or which may be transferred to them or to such corporation by any person, persons, or corporation, and to invest the same or any part thereof from time to time in such securities and in such form and manner as is or may be permitted to trustees or to savings banks or to charitable or literary corporations for investment, according to the laws of the District of Columbia or in such securities as may be transferred to them or authorized for investment by any deed of trust or gift or by any deed of gift or last will and testament to be hereafter made or executed.

Sec. 6. That the said corporation may take and hold any additional donations, grants, devises, or bequests which may be made in the further support of the purposes of the said corporation.

Sec. 7. That the services of the trustees of the said corporation, acting as such trustees, shall be gratuitous, but such corporation may provide for the reasonable expenses incurred by trustees in the performance of their duties.

Sec. 8. That as soon as may be possible after the passage of this Act, a meeting of the trustees hereinbefore named shall be called by HENRY S. PRITCHETT, CHARLES WILLIAM ELIOT, ARTHUR T. HADLEY, NICHOLAS MURRAY BUTLER, WOODROW WILSON, JACOB G. SCHURMAN, CHARLES C. HARRISON, ALEXANDER C. HUMPHREYS, and GEORGE H.

DENNY, or any six of them, at the Borough of Manhattan, in the city and State of New York, by notice served in person or by mail addressed to each trustee at his place of residence; and the said trustees named herein, or a majority thereof, being assembled, shall organize and proceed to adopt by-laws, to elect officers, fix their compensation, and generally to organize the said corporation.

The corporation hereby incorporated may accept a transfer of all the real and personal property of any other corporation created for similar objects, notwithstanding the fact that both said corporations may have common trustees, upon such terms as may be agreed upon, and may receive, take over, and enter into possession, custody, and management of all such property, real and personal: *Provided, however,* That such property shall be applied to the purposes of the corporation hereby incorporated as hereinbefore set forth.

SEC. 9. That such corporation hereby incorporated upon accepting a transfer of all the real and personal property of such other corporation shall succeed to the obligations and liabilities and be held liable to pay and discharge all the debts, liabilities, and contracts of such corporation so existing to the same effect as if such corporation hereby incorporated had itself incurred the obligation or liability to pay such debt or damages.

SEC. 10. That Congress may from time to time alter, repeal, or modify this Act of incorporation, but no contract or individual right made or acquired shall thereby be divested or impaired.

SEC. 11. That this Act shall take effect immediately on its passage.

Approved March 10, 1906

Appendix C

TRUSTEES OF THE
CARNEGIE FOUNDATION FOR THE ADVANCEMENT OF TEACHING
With institutions over which they presided when
chosen and dates of their service.

Note: In some instances, the careers of individual trustees have included
service at other institutions than those from which they were chosen.
Names of trustees who have served as members of the Executive Committee are marked with an (E).

Raymond B. Allen, University of Washington	1948-
Frank Aydelotte, Swarthmore College	1921-
Hill McClelland Bell, Drake University	1905-1918
William Lowe Bryan, Indiana University	1910-1938
Marion LeRoy Burton, Smith College	1915-1925
Nicholas Murray Butler, Columbia University (E)	1905-1947
Samuel Paul Capen, University of Buffalo	1935-1950
Oliver Cromwell Carmichael, Vanderbilt University	1937-
T. Morrison Carnegie	1905-1924
Lotus Delta Coffman, University of Minnesota	1930-1938
Arthur Holly Compton, Washington University	1946-
James Bryant Conant, Harvard University (E)	1934-
Edwin Boone Craighead, The Tulane University of Louisiana	1905-1917
William Henry Crawford, Allegheny College	1905-1920
Sir Arthur William Currie, McGill University	1927-1933
Carter Davidson, Union College (E)	1946-
Arthur Hobson Dean	1950-
George Hutcheson Denny, Washington and Lee University	1905-
Albert Bledsoe Dinwiddie, The Tulane University of Louisiana	1923-1935
Harold Willis Dodds, Princeton University (E)	1935-
Dwight David Eisenhower, Columbia University	1950-
Charles William Eliot, Harvard University	1905-1909
Edward Charles Elliott, Purdue University	1934-1946
Sir Robert Alexander Falconer, University of Toronto (E)	1917-1932

Livingston Farrand, Cornell University	1929-1939
Frederick Carlos Ferry, Hamilton College (E)	1920-1939
Dixon Ryan Fox, Union College	1939-1945
Robert Augustus Franks (E)	1905-1935
Edwin Broun Fred, University of Wisconsin	1946-
Eugene Allen Gilmore, State University of Iowa	1938-1948
Frank Porter Graham, University of North Carolina	1932-
Alfred Whitney Griswold, Yale University	1950-
Reuben Gilbert Gustavson, University of Nebraska	1949-
Arthur Twining Hadley, Yale University (E)	1905-1921
William Rainey Harper, University of Chicago	1905-1906
Rufus Carrollton Harris, The Tulane University of Louisiana	1945-
Charles Custis Harrison, University of Pennsylvania (E)	1905-1910
John Grier Hibben, Princeton University	1920-1932
Albert Ross Hill, University of Missouri	1918-1936
Edwin Holt Hughes, DePauw University	1905-1908
Alexander Crombie Humphreys, Stevens Institute of Technology (E)	1905-1927
Walter Albert Jessup, State University of Iowa	1932-1944
David Starr Jordan, Stanford University	1905-1916
Devereux Colt Josephs, Carnegie Corporation of New York	1947-1949
Henry Churchill King, Oberlin College	1905-1927
James Hampton Kirkland, Vanderbilt University	1917-1937
Thomas Stilwell Lamont (E)	1949-
Thomas William Lamont (E)	1917-1948
Ernest Hiram Lindley, University of Kansas	1934-1940
Clarence Cook Little, University of Michigan	1927-1929
Robert Abercrombie Lovett (E)	1937-
Abbott Lawrence Lowell, Harvard University	1910-1933
Howard Foster Lowry, College of Wooster	1948-
John Hanson Thomas Main, Grinnell College	1924-1931
Thomas McClelland, Knox College	1905-1917
Samuel Black McCormick, Western University of Pennsylvania	1905-1923
Frederick Arnold Middlebush, University of Missouri (E)	1937-
John Schoff Millis, Western Reserve University	1949-
Walter Charles Murray, University of Saskatchewan	1918-1938
William Allan Neilson, Smith College (E)	1920-1946
John Lloyd Newcomb, University of Virginia	1936-1947
George Norlin, University of Colorado	1925-1939

Josiah Harmar Penniman, University of
Pennsylvania (E)   1924-1941
Sir William Peterson, McGill University   1905-1918
Samuel Plantz, Lawrence College   1905-1924
Henry Smith Pritchett, Massachusetts Institute of
Technology   1905-1930
Ira Remsen, The Johns Hopkins University   1909-1913
Rush Rhees, University of Rochester   1922-1935
Jacob Gould Schurman, Cornell University (E)   1905-1920
L. Clark Seelye, Smith College   1905-1910
Charles Seymour, Yale University (E)   1939-1950
Kenneth Charles Morton Sills, Bowdoin College (E)   1933-
William Frederick Slocum, Colorado College   1906-1917
Edgar Fahs Smith, University of Pennsylvania   1913-1920
Franklyn Bliss Snyder, Northwestern University   1940-1949
Robert Gordon Sproul, University of California   1939-
Henry Suzzallo, University of Washington   1918-1933
James Monroe Taylor, Vassar College   1910-1914
Charles Franklin Thwing, Western Reserve University   1905-1922
Alan Valentine, University of Rochester (E)   1945-1950
Frank Arthur Vanderlip (E)   1905-1937
Charles Richard Van Hise, University of Wisconsin   1909-1918
Robert Ernest Vinson, University of Texas   1920-1934
Robert Charles Wallace, Queen's University   1938-
Herman B. Wells, Indiana University   1941-
Clement Clarence Williams, Lehigh University (E)   1939-1946
Woodrow Wilson, Princeton University (E)   1905-1910
Henry Merritt Wriston, Lawrence College (E)   1932-

Appendix D

Presidents

Henry S. Pritchett	1905-30
Henry Suzzallo	1930-33
Walter A. Jessup	1934-44
Oliver C. Carmichael	1945-

Secretaries

Albert LeForest Derby, Assistant Secretary	1905-06
Walter M. Gilbert, Assistant Secretary	1905-47
John G. Bowman	1906-11
Clyde Furst	1911-31
William S. Learned, Assistant Secretary	1920-31
Howard J. Savage	1931-49
Paul Scherer, Assistant Secretary	1947-
Robert M. Lester (Associate Secretary 1947-49)	1949-

Treasurers

T. Morrison Carnegie	1906-10
Robert A. Franks	1910-35
Frank A. Vanderlip	1935-37
Howard J. Savage	1937-49
C. Herbert Lee	1949-

Assistant Treasurers

Note: The letter (I) indicates that these assistant treasurers served also as Investment Officers.

John G. Bowman	1910-11
Clyde Furst	1911-21
Samuel S. Hall, Jr. (I)	1921-39
Devereux C. Josephs (I)	1939-45
Parker Monroe (I)	1945-48
C. Herbert Lee (I)	1948-49

Staff Members

Note: The title "Staff Member" was first formally conferred in 1924.

A. Monell Sayre	1905-13
Abraham Flexner	1908-12
William S. Learned	1913-46
Alfred Z. Reed	1913-40
I. L. Kandel	1914-23
Howard J. Savage	1923-31;
	1949-51

Actuarial Consultant

Note: The title "Actuarial Consultant" was first conferred in 1931.

Charles E. Brooks, "Actuary to the Foundation"	1918-20
Raymond L. Mattocks	1922-

Staff Associates

Note: The title "Staff Associate" was first conferred in 1931.

Harold W. Bentley	1926-29
Paul Webb	1931-32
David Spence Hill	1931-34
W. Carson Ryan	1936-40
Charles R. Langmuir	1936-42
Kenneth W. Vaughn	1942-47

Appendix E

ANNUAL REPORTS

First Annual Report of the President and of the Treasurer, *84 pages.* 1906.

An historical sketch of the Foundation, a study of army and professorial pensions, and a statement of the general policy, the educational standards, and the administrative Rules of the Foundation.

Second Annual Report of the President and of the Treasurer, *124 pages.* 1907.

Discussions of the place of the college and the university in the United States, the function of college entrance requirements, the forms of denominational control, the relation of the Foundation to denominational and state institutions, and the ratio between institutional cost and efficiency.

Third Annual Report of the President and of the Treasurer, *211 pages.* 1908.

Academic and financial data concerning institutions on the accepted list; and discussions of the problems of financial reports, pensions, and life insurance; of the governmental and political aspects of tax-supported institutions; of entrance requirements, instruction, higher and professional education; and of the influence of denominational boards of education.

Fourth Annual Report of the President and of the Treasurer, *201 pages.* 1909.

Discussions of the Rules for retirement, of agricultural education, of college administration and advertising, and complete records of the practice of the institutions on the associated list of the Foundation in admitting regular, conditioned, and special students.

Fifth Annual Report of the President and of the Treasurer, *113 pages*. 1910.

Discussions of the relation of colleges to professional, technical, and industrial education, to secondary schools, to the training of teachers, and to state supervision; together with the comments of Oxford tutors on American education as represented by Rhodes scholars.

Sixth Annual Report of the President and of the Treasurer, *154 pages*. 1911.

Discussions of the application of the Rules for retirement, and the obligations and influences of pension systems; together with a critical and constructive survey of education from a national point of view, as this is reflected in legislation, state systems, regional conditions, the relations of school, college, and university; in professional and graduate study and religious education; and in the problems of political and alumni influence.

Seventh Annual Report of the President and of the Treasurer, *194 pages*. 1912.

Discussions of actual and possible systems of college pensions; state, district, and local pensions for public school teachers; industrial and civil service pensions; contributory and non-contributory, subsistence and stipendiary pensions in general; and a review of the administrative, financial, and educational experience of the Foundation; together with comments upon admission to college and to advanced standing, medical progress, college financial reporting, advertising in education, education and politics, and sham universities.

Eighth Annual Report of the President and of the Treasurer, *158 pages*. 1913.

Discussions of recent pension developments, of Carnegie Corporation of New York, of the establishment of the Division of Educational Enquiry and its studies of medical education, education in Vermont, and legal education; together with comments on college entrance requirements, the state regulation of higher education, politics and education in Iowa, the improved financial status of college teachers, and college catalogues.

Ninth Annual Report of the President and of the Treasurer, *154 pages*. 1914.

Discussions of pension principles and of recent developments in the fields of teachers, industrial, and federal pensions; records of the progress of the Foundation's studies of legal education, engineering education, and the training of teachers; comments upon the results of its study of education in Vermont and upon recent developments in medical education; and discussions concerning educational standards, state educational reports, and educational surveys.

Tenth Annual Report of the President and of the Treasurer, *142 pages*. 1915.

Discussions of pensions for public school and for university teachers, clergy pension funds, and industrial pensions, with tabular statements of 65 teachers and 58 industrial and institutional pension systems; together with reports of the progress of the Foundation's studies of legal education, engineering education, and the training of teachers in Missouri, the results of its study of education in Vermont; and a discussion of college charges for tuition.

Eleventh Annual Report of the President and of the Treasurer, *172 pages*. 1916.

Discussions of a comprehensive plan of insurance and annuities for college teachers with the comments of the associated institutions, and discussions of teachers, industrial, and clergy pension funds in general; together with reports of progress in the Foundation's studies of legal education, engineering education, agricultural education, and the training of teachers; and a study of college entrance certificates, with suggestions for a uniform blank.

Twelfth Annual Report of the President and of the Treasurer, *154 pages*. 1917.

Discussions of insurance and annuities for college teachers, with the report of a Commission on Insurance and Annuities and the charter of the Teachers Insurance and Annuity Association of America; descriptions of current developments in the general field of pensions; and reports of progress in the Foundation's educational inquiries.

Thirteenth Annual Report of the President and of the Treasurer, *162 pages.* 1918.

A description of the inauguration of the contributory system of annuities, reports concerning the plan by two actuarial committees, the new Rules of the Foundation, discussion of the present-day pension problems, and reports of educational inquiry.

Fourteenth Annual Report of the President and of the Treasurer, *148 pages.* 1919.

A tribute to Mr. Carnegie's service to teachers, a record of the adoption by universities and colleges of the contributory system of annuities, discussion of recent developments in the field of pensions, college government and current tendencies in education, and reports of educational inquiry.

Fifteenth Annual Report of the President and of the Treasurer, *171 pages.* 1920.

Statements concerning the exemption of retiring allowances from income tax, the longevity and the salaries of college teachers; records of the admission of institutions to association with the Foundation, of the increasing adoption of contractual annuities for college teachers, and of pension systems and pension legislation for public school teachers; together with discussions of legal education, with a descriptive list of law schools, and current developments in medical education and in the training of teachers.

Sixteenth Annual Report of the President and of the Treasurer, *205 pages.* 1921.

Records of the admission of institutions to association with the Foundation, the development of contractual annuities for college teachers, and of pension systems for other teachers, clergymen, civil servants, and industrial workers; together with a comprehensive study of the relation of medical education to medical progress, and briefer discussions of college entrance requirements, the training of teachers, and legal education.

Seventeenth Annual Report of the President and of the Treasurer, *211 pages.* 1922.

Records of the admission of institutions to association with the Foundation, the modification of the Rules for retirement, the development of contractual annuities for college teachers, a survey of the theory of pensions and the progress of pension legislation;

together with reports of studies of dental education, the training of teachers, and legal education, and a comprehensive discussion of the rising cost of education.

Eighteenth Annual Report of the President and of the Treasurer, *166 pages*. 1923.

Records of the activities of the Foundation for the year, the progress of the system of contractual annuities for college teachers, the development of retirement plans for public school teachers in several states, federal pensions, and industrial pensions; studies in the life expectation of college teachers, and the abuse of intercollegiate athletics; and discussions of legal education, dental education, and, continuing the consideration of the rising cost of education, the teacher's responsibility for our educational integrity.

Nineteenth Annual Report of the President and of the Treasurer, *236 pages*. 1924. (Also Condensed Edition, *56 pages*.)

A comprehensive discussion of the direction of educational progress, records of the admission of institutions to association with the Foundation, and a statement of some of the results of the Foundation's system of retiring allowances; typical forms for the use of universities and colleges in establishing contractual old-age annuities for their faculties; and evaluation of the first three volumes of the Educational Finance Inquiry Commission report; current developments in legal education and in dental education; and a survey of results of the year's activities affecting teachers retirement in the United States and England, governmental pensions in other countries, pensions in industry, and old-age pensions.

Twentieth Annual Report of the President and of the Treasurer, *241 pages*. 1925.

A discussion of national and international education—the quality of the educational process in the United States and in Europe, the study of English, with comments of Oxford teachers and former Rhodes scholars on recent examinations in English set by the College Entrance Examination Board, and a preliminary statement concerning American college athletics; thrift for teachers; records of the work of the Foundation during the year; some contrasts between American and Canadian legal education; current developments in dental education; and consideration of various phases of the problems of old-age retirement in the United States, Canada, England, France, and the Netherlands.

Twenty-first Annual Report of the President and of the Treasurer, *250 pages.* 1926.

Records of the activities of the Foundation, the progress of contractual annuities for college teachers, the rise in college salaries; of retirement systems for teachers, the members of other professions, and for government and industrial workers; together with discussions of legal education, dental education, athletics at Oxford and Cambridge, and the conclusion of the discussion of the quality of the educational process in the United States and Europe, which was begun in the Twentieth Report.

Twenty-second Annual Report of the President and of the Treasurer, *168 pages.* 1927.

A review of the history of the Foundation and of the work of the year; discussions of college athletics and scholarship, dental education, and legal education; and comments on recent pension plans for teachers, clergymen, nurses, industrial workers.

Twenty-third Annual Report of the President and of the Treasurer, *166 pages.* 1928.

Discussions of the perpetual trust, the rise of endowed foundations in the United States, the future of the Carnegie Foundation; longevity, teaching, and research, the relations of secondary and higher education in Pennsylvania, legal education, dental education, and recent developments and studies in the field of pensions and retiring annuities in the United States, Great Britain, and Australia.

Twenty-fourth Annual Report of the President and of the Treasurer, *204 pages.* 1929.

A statement concerning a definitive revision of the Foundation's Rules for retirement; discussions of the social philosophy of pensions, the relations of secondary and higher education in Pennsylvania, legal education, dental education, and the Foundation's study of American college athletics; and reviews of developments in teachers retirement in the United States and Switzerland.

Twenty-fifth Annual Report of the President and of the Treasurer, *206 pages*. 1930.

A summary of the first quarter-century of the Foundation's activities and a brief statement concerning a new administration; discussions of the college budget and taxation, pensions and politics, secondary and higher education in Pennsylvania, legislation affecting admission to the practice of the law, dental education, and the study of American college athletics; and comments on paternalistic pensions and contractual retiring annuities, teachers retirement in the United States and Canada, pensions for ministers, and two Australian actuarial valuations.

Twenty-sixth Annual Report of the President and of the Treasurer, *129 pages*. 1931.

A statement concerning the relation of the Foundation to American education, past and future; report of progress of the study of secondary and higher education in Pennsylvania; discussions of co-operation for the study of legal education, certain aspects of American college athletics, and the work of the Foundation during the year.

Twenty-seventh Annual Report of the President and of the Treasurer, *174 pages*. 1932.

Records of the activities of the Foundation; discussions from various points of view of education and the economic situation; statements concerning the study of state higher education in California, admission to college as reflected in the study of the relations of secondary and higher education in Pennsylvania, local provision for higher education in Saskatchewan, educational finance and student selection, and American college athletics.

Twenty-eighth Annual Report of the President and of the Treasurer, *189 pages*. 1933.

Discussions of our tradition of institutional individualism, the "unit" in admission to college, the study of the relation of secondary and higher education in Pennsylvania, learned professions and their organization; means employed to supplement the retiring allowances of the Foundation, and a proposal to give a national secretary of education a seat in the cabinet.

Twenty-ninth Annual Report of the Foundation, *167 pages*. 1934.
Records of the administration of the funds during the year, and discussions of the current situation in American higher education, the social conscience in relation to government, the junior college and its relation to the community, the salaried professor in the learned professions, and educational grants of Carnegie Corporation of New York and the Foundation.

Thirtieth Annual Report of the Foundation, *208 pages*. 1935.
Discussions of spiritual resources of the American college, the old-age pension as related to American life, the beginnings of the Carnegie Foundation, variability in education, and the problem of tax exemption, and records of the administration of the trust.

Thirty-first Annual Report of the Foundation, *193 pages*. 1936.
Sections on youth and educational abstractions, the Carnegie centenary and related matters, tested achievement of prospective teachers in Pennsylvania, the contribution of the medieval university to American higher education, and the administration of the Foundation during the fiscal year.

Thirty-second Annual Report of the Foundation, *202 pages*. 1937.
Discussions of college competition and the student; maladjustment in college; professional recognition, accrediting, and licensure; and certain notes on pioneer efforts in graduate education in the United States, together with records of administration and a historical sketch of the Foundation.

Thirty-third Annual Report of the Foundation, *239 pages*. 1938.
Discussions of our itinerant students, life insurance for college teachers, completed lives of Foundation beneficiaries, misplacement in college, the measurement of student knowledge as a basis for graduate study, origins of licensing in the learned professions, further notes on early graduate education in the United States, and administration of the Foundation, together with statements on the new corporation, Trustees of T.I.A.A. Stock, by the president of the Teachers Insurance and Annuity Association, and on Rules for the Granting of Retiring Allowances of the Foundation 1938.

Thirty-fourth Annual Report of the Foundation, *207 pages*. 1939.
Materials on the college, the public and philanthropic endowments, Foundation impostors, accrediting agencies, certain procedures in testing for the Pennsylvania study, and records of administration.

Thirty-fifth Annual Report of the Foundation, *170 pages*. 1939-40.
Commentary upon American and European higher education during a time of storm and stress, the plan adopted for supplementing payment of the Foundation's retiring allowances and widows'
pensions, tribute by Dr. Nicholas Murray Butler to the Foundation's first president Henry Smith Pritchett 1857-1939, a description of the Graduate Record Examination project, materials
from the Pennsylvania Study on the unexpectedly long persistence
of acquired knowledge, and records of administration.

Thirty-sixth Annual Report of the Foundation, *183 pages*. 1940-41.
The American college in a land on the verge of war, a Foundation
impostor, some account of a symposium on student appraisal, success in college and financial success in later life, data on the administration of the Foundation during its fiscal year 1940-41.

Thirty-seventh Annual Report of the Foundation, *179 pages*. 1941-42.
Discussion of American colleges in total war, financial data on institutional supplementing of the Foundation's retiring allowances
and widows' pensions, results of a study of the relation between
Graduate Record Examination scores and college "grades," a
summary of the history of the Graduate Record Examination to
1942, and information about the operation of the Foundation
during the year.

Thirty-eighth Annual Report of the Foundation, *175 pages*. 1942-43.
The American college at war, use and abuse of the term "Approved by the Carnegie Foundation," the first twenty-five years
of the Teachers Insurance and Annuity Association, conclusions
drawn from the Foundation's twenty-year testing study of American higher education, a statement of co-operating graduate deans
about the Graduate Record Examination, and administrative summaries for the year.

Thirty-ninth Annual Report of the Foundation, *167 pages*. 1943-44.

A future for American graduate education, work after retirement among Foundation beneficiaries, the operation of the Teachers Insurance and Annuity Association, the Graduate Record Examination and returning service personnel, the Engineering Measurement-Guidance Project, data on the year's administration of the Foundation.

Fortieth Annual Report of the Foundation, *140 pages*. 1944-45.

An account of the management ad interim of the Foundation prepared by Edward C. Elliott, chairman of the Board of Trustees, planning a college retirement system, the work of the Graduate Record Examination 1944-45, measuring the outcomes of higher education, and statistical, administrative, and financial summaries.

Forty-first Annual Report of the Foundation, *160 pages*. 1945-46.

The teacher and educational results, a record of experience with the Closed List of pensionables, extended consideration of examinations and education, information concerning administration of the Foundation during the fiscal year.

Forty-second Annual Report of the Foundation, *136 pages*. 1946-47.

International studies and their place in higher education, senior beneficiaries of the Foundation, the beginning of the experimental co-operative program of grants-in-aid for college professors in the southern area, work of the Graduate Record Office, and negotiations looking to establishment of a national testing service, data on the operation of the Foundation during the year.

Forty-third Annual Report of the Foundation, *155 pages*. 1947-48.

The improvement of college teaching, the Carnegie Foundation and the rise of the unit, progress of the experimental college grants-in-aid program, the founding of Educational Testing Service, Inc., records of the year's operations.

Forty-fourth Annual Report of the Foundation, *61 pages*. 1948-49.

The president's report treats of education in values; the secretary's, of the third year of the southern grants-in-aid experiment, the year's work, and the Foundation's retiring allowances and widows' pensions; the treasurer's, of financial procedures.

Forty-fifth Annual Report of the Foundation, *67 pages*. 1949-50.

The president reviews a century of higher education; the secretary summarizes the fourth year of the southern grants-in-aid program and the Foundation's operations in respect of retiring allowances and pensions; the treasurer presents financial data for the year.

BULLETINS

Number One. Papers Relating to the Admission of State Institutions to the System of Retiring Allowances of the Carnegie Foundation, *45 pages*. 1907.

Including arguments in favor of the admission of state and provincial universities to the benefits of the Foundation, and a statement by the president of the administrative and financial problems involved.

Number Two. The Financial Status of the Professor in America and in Germany, *101 pages*. 1908.

A study of the expenditure for instruction in one hundred and fifty-six American institutions, with comparisons of the maximum and average salaries, the average age, the amount of teaching, the appointment, tenure, and retirement privileges of professors in the United States and Canada and in Germany.

Number Three. Standard Forms for Financial Reports of Colleges, Universities, and Technical Schools, *37 pages*. 1910. Second edition, 1921.

Containing twenty-five typical blank forms for the public reporting of the financial receipts and expenditures of universities and colleges, with an introduction recommending the modification of current practice in directions commended by educators, financiers, and accountants.

Number Four. Medical Education in the United States and Canada, *346 pages*. 1910.

A comprehensive report to the Foundation, by Abraham Flexner, on medical education in the United States and Canada, with regard to the course of study, financial aspects, medical sects, state boards, post-graduate schools, and other special forms of medical education; with descriptive and tabular accounts of all of the medical schools throughout the United States and Canada; and a general plan for reconstruction, with an introduction by the President of the Foundation.

Number Five. Academic and Industrial Efficiency, *134 pages.* 1910.

A report to the Foundation, by Morris Llewellyn Cooke, on the teaching and research in physics in eight American universities, colleges, and technical schools, with an endeavor to estimate efficiency in organization, teaching, research, the use of buildings, and in financial, departmental, and student administration.

Number Six. Medical Education in Europe, *357 pages.* 1912.

A report, by Abraham Flexner, concerning the contemporary condition in Germany, Great Britain, and France, of the basis of medical education, the preliminary and the medical sciences, clinical instruction, curricula and examinations, post-graduate education, the medical education of women, the number and distribution of physicians, the financial aspects of medical education, and the problem of sects and quacks; together with an introduction by the President of the Foundation, contrasting these European conditions with those in the United States and Canada.

Number Seven. Education in Vermont, *241 pages.* 1914.

A study prepared at the request of the Vermont Educational Commission, giving the reason for and the method of the inquiry, description and discussion of the entire educational system of the state, with certain conclusions and recommendations, and a brief statistical appendix.

Number Eight. The Common Law and the Case Method in American University Law Schools, *84 pages.* 1914.

A report to the Foundation, by Josef Redlich, of the University of Vienna, dealing with law as a science and a profession, early methods of legal instruction, the development and success of the case method, its weaknesses, and suggestions for improvement in legal instruction, scholarship, and research.

Number Nine. A Comprehensive Plan of Insurance and Annuities for College Teachers, *68 pages.* 1915 and 1916.

A discussion, by the President of the Foundation, of pensions, annuities, and life insurance in general and for teachers in particular, with indications of the limitations of the Foundation's present system and suggestions for the development of a comprehensive and permanent plan. (Confidential edition for officers and professors in the institutions associated with the Foundation, October, 1915. Reprinted, with a preliminary statement, for general distribution, April, 1916.)

Number Ten. Federal Aid for Vocational Education, *127 pages*. 1917.
A study, by I. L. Kandel, dealing with the legislative history of the various acts for the establishment and support of land grant colleges, the political and educational policies underlying this form of legislation, the development of the land-grant colleges and their relation to social demand, and the influence of the precedents established by these acts on the movement for Federal aid for vocational education.

Number Eleven. Engineering Education, *135 pages*. 1918.
A study, by Charles Riborg Mann, at the request of a joint committee of the national engineering societies, of the development of engineering schools in the United States—their aims, resources, administration, curricula, instruction, and student progress; the chief problems of engineering education—admission, curricula, courses, testing, and grading; with suggestions concerning the curriculum, specialization, teaching, and the professional spirit.

Number Twelve. Pensions for Public School Teachers, *90 pages*. 1918.
A report, by Clyde Furst and I. L. Kandel, for the Committee on Salaries, Pensions, and Tenure of the National Education Association, describing all existing systems of pensions for teachers, discussing their limitations in the light of experience and the fundamental principles of pensions, and presenting an illustration of a financially and socially sound state system of pensions for teachers, based upon a complete census of the teachers in the State of Vermont.

Number Thirteen. Justice and the Poor, *252 pages*. 1919. Second edition, 1921. Third edition, 1924.
A study, by Reginald Heber Smith, of the present administration of justice in the United States to determine how far it actually secures equality before the law to poor and immigrant citizens; analysis of the defects which cause denial of justice; and a complete outline of all agencies, both legal and extra-legal, which are

being employed or may be employed to remedy the present situation; with particular attention to small claims courts, industrial accident commissions, domestic relations courts, public defenders, and legal aid organizations. With a foreword by Elihu Root.

Number Fourteen. The Professional Preparation of Teachers for American Public Schools, *456 pages*. 1920.

By William S. Learned, William C. Bagley, and others. A study, made at the request of the Governor and State Superintendent of Public Schools in Missouri, of the tax-supported normal schools of that state, together with an examination of the general principles of organization, administration, and curriculum construction in teacher-training agencies in the United States.

Number Fifteen. Training for the Public Profession of the Law, *498 pages*. 1921.

A study, by Alfred Z. Reed, of the historical development and principal contemporary problems of legal education in the United States, with some account of conditions in England and Canada; including a description of the organization and recruiting of the American legal profession as affected by bar admission rules, by law schools, and by bar associations.

Number Sixteen. Education in the Maritime Provinces of Canada, *50 pages*. 1922.

A report to Carnegie Corporation of New York by William S. Learned of the Foundation staff, and Kenneth C. M. Sills, President of Bowdoin College, including a brief survey of elementary and secondary education in these provinces, a detailed analysis of the institutions for higher education, and proposals for the reorganization and concentration of the leading colleges at one institution.

Number Seventeen. Retiring Allowances for Officers and Teachers in Virginia Public Schools, *70 pages*, with chart. 1926.

A study made at the request of the Virginia State Teachers Association and the State Board of Education, by Clyde Furst, Raymond L. Mattocks, and Howard J. Savage, with a preface by Henry S. Pritchett, including a plan of retiring allowances, a discussion of the principles and details of operation, and complete actuarial and financial data with tables. The chart presents the plan in tabular form.

Number Eighteen. Games and Sports in British Schools and Universities, *252 pages.* 1927.

An exposition, by Howard J. Savage, with a preface by the President of the Foundation, of the place, functions, and conduct of athletics at English public and day schools, Oxford and Cambridge, the newer English universities, and the universities of Scotland and Ireland, with discussions of the British sports tradition and the amateur tradition in British sports; and an appendix setting forth rules and accounts of various college and university sports bodies.

Number Nineteen. Dental Education in the United States and Canada, *692 pages.* 1926. (Issued in 1927.)

A report, by William J. Gies, with a preface by the President of the Foundation, presenting a general history of dental education in North America, a discussion of the conditions in the practice of dentistry that determine its educational requirements, with statistical statements and descriptive accounts of all the dental schools in the United States and Canada in 1925-26, and a general plan for the reorganization of dental education to promote the development of dental practice as a division of health service.

Number Twenty. The Quality of the Educational Process in the United States and Europe, *133 pages,* with chart. 1927.

A discussion, by William S. Learned, first published in the Twentieth and Twenty-first Annual Reports of the Foundation, dealing with the aims of the student and the treatment of gifted pupils in American, English, French, and German schools, colleges, and universities; with the lack of adjustment between school and college, and the elective and course-credit systems in the United States; together with emphasis on the tutorial system and comprehensive final examinations as means for developing intellectual abilities and attainment.

Number Twenty-one. Present-Day Law Schools in the United States and Canada, *598 pages.* 1928.

A study, by Alfred Z. Reed, of the organization and curriculum of law schools, with special emphasis upon the time element in legal education. Among the topics discussed are the relation between law and politics, the supervision and improvement of law schools by professional associations and bar admission authorities, the academic affiliations and financial resources of law schools, their entrance requirements, the length of their course, summer sessions, the elective system, and the problem of the night or "part-time" law school.

Number Twenty-two. A Retirement Plan for Colorado Public Schools, *72 pages*. 1928.

A study made by Howard J. Savage and Edmund S. Cogswell, at the request of the Colorado Education Association and the State Department of Public Instruction, presenting a plan of retiring allowances, a discussion of principles and details of operation, and complete actuarial and financial data with tables. The introduction, by the Secretary of the Foundation, sets forth the considerations underlying any sound system of retiring annuities for teachers.

Number Twenty-three. American College Athletics, *383 pages*. 1929.

A study, undertaken at the request of the Association of American Colleges, the Association of Colleges and Secondary Schools of the Southern States, the National Collegiate Athletic Association, and other representative bodies, by Howard J. Savage, Harold W. Bentley, John T. McGovern, and Dean F. Smiley, M.D., of the history, conduct, and values of sports and games in American universities, colleges, and schools, the development of the modern amateur status, the administrative control of college athletics, athletic participation and its results, the hygiene of athletic training, the coach in college athletics, athletic conferences and associations, the recruiting and subsidizing of athletes, and the relation of the press to college sport; with an appendix setting forth statistical materials and also excerpts from correspondence to recruit college athletes, and a preface by the President of the Foundation concerning "Athletics, an Element in the Evolution of the American University."

Number Twenty-four. The Literature of American School and College Athletics, *305 pages*. 1929. (Issued in 1930.)

A digest, by W. Carson Ryan, Jr., with a foreword by the President of the Foundation, of more than a thousand books, pamphlets, articles in magazines and periodicals, and certain hitherto unpublished materials, on athletics as education, their history, administration, organization, and financing, the health of athletes, coaches and coaching, school sports and games, athletics for girls and women, sportsmanship, professionalism and amateurism, tests and measurements, with bibliographies and lists of sources, a statement of findings, and a brief summary of tendencies.

Number Twenty-five. The Social Philosophy of Pensions with a Review of Existing Pension Systems for Professional Groups, *85 pages.* 1930.

A discussion, by Henry S. Pritchett, of the economic and social considerations underlying a sound pension system, retired pay for college and public school teachers, pensions for ministers, and the problem of retirement protection for members of the classified civil service of the United States.

Number Twenty-six. Current Developments in American College Sport, *58 pages.* 1931.

A summary and evaluation, by Howard J. Savage, John T. McGovern, and Harold W. Bentley, with a preface by Henry Suzzallo, of significant changes in the relation of sport to the educational process from the autumn of 1929 to the beginning of 1931; including administrative changes; financial arrangements; facilities; coaching; relationships with alumni, other colleges, athletic conferences, the press, and the public; the attack upon recruiting and subsidizing; and the changing character of college sport, including the undergraduate attitude.

Number Twenty-seven. Local Provision for Higher Education in Saskatchewan, *30 pages.* 1932.

An advisory memorandum on university policy proposed at the request of the University of Saskatchewan, by W. S. Learned and E. W. Wallace, with a foreword by Henry Suzzallo. The memorandum includes discussions of the provincial university, the principle of affiliation, the junior college, the division of provincial funds for higher education, a fair method of equalizing opportunity, a new type of institute, the effect on the university of the coming realignment in education, and the evidence of coming change in American and Canadian institutions.

Number Twenty-eight. Examinations and their Substitutes in the United States, *183 pages.* 1936.

A report, by I. L. Kandel, professor of education and associate in the International Institute, Teachers College, Columbia University, with a preface by Walter A. Jessup, resulting from the international examinations inquiry instituted by Carnegie Corporation of New York, presenting at the request of the Corporation a unified account of the experience of the United States with examinations and their substitutes, and containing chapters on the problem of examinations and its social setting, the traditional examination, the scientific attack on examinations, and education, examination, and the individual, together with an appendix describing the international examinations inquiry.

Number Twenty-nine. The Student and his Knowledge, *406 pages.* 1938. (Second and third editions 1939.)

A report by William S. Learned and Ben D. Wood, director of Collegiate Educational Research, Columbia College, with a foreword by the President of the Foundation, on the results of the high-school and college examinations given in the study of the relations of secondary and higher education in Pennsylvania, 1928, 1930, and 1932, including a summary of results and conclusions drawn from the high-school and college examinations, an academic inventory of the baccalaureate mind based upon the college-senior examination of 1928, and a discussion of the academic growth of the baccalaureate mind embracing secondary-school backgrounds, the college sophomore and senior examinations 1930 and 1932, progress and learning in high school and college, the achievement of contemporary college classes and of prospective teachers in the Commonwealth of Pennsylvania, together with an appendix on the tests and their results, treatment of data, institutional studies, explanation of the sigma scale, and a list of participating universities, arts colleges, and technical schools.

Number Thirty. Studies in Early Graduate Education, *167 pages.* 1939.

A historical discussion by W. Carson Ryan, staff associate, of the founding and ensuing development of The Johns Hopkins University, Clark University, and the University of Chicago, and of other initial efforts respecting American graduate education, with a preface by Walter A. Jessup, President of the Foundation, and a bibliography.

Number Thirty-one. An Experiment in Responsible Learning, *61 pages.* 1940.

A report by William S. Learned and Anna L. Rose Hawkes, staff assistant, with a foreword by the President of the Foundation, on the introduction and use for 135 Pennsylvania high-school pupils of a cumulative record of school achievement in four Pennsylvania school systems, together with views of administrative officers, verdicts of teachers, and transcriptions of student records.

OTHER PUBLICATIONS

Act of Incorporation, By-Laws, and Rules for the Admission of Institutions and for the Granting of Retiring Allowances, *16 pages.* 1906. Revised, *12 pages.* 1908; *12 pages.* 1910; *10 pages.* 1913; *15 pages.* 1918; *25 pages.* 1920; *28 pages.* 1922; *35 pages.* 1929; *38 pages.* 1938; *41 pages.* 1940.

A Plan for an Exchange of Teachers between Prussia and the United States, *7 pages.* 1908.

An American Teacher's Year in a Prussian Gymnasium, *37 pages.* 1911.

Curricula designed for the Professional Preparation of Teachers for American Public Schools, *60 pages.* 1917.

Some Misapprehensions Touching Life Insurance, *76 pages.* 1919.

Review of Legal Education in the United States and Canada for the years 1926 and 1927, *43 pages.* 1928.
    Standards recommended by associations, bar admission requirements, list of law schools and statistics.

Review of Legal Education in the United States and Canada for the year 1928, *51 pages.* 1929.
    "Present-Day Law Schools" (Bulletin Number Twenty-one), essentials of a sound bar admission system, registration of law students.

Review of Legal Education in the United States and Canada for the year 1929, *72 pages.* 1930.
    The missing element in legal education, practical training and ethical standards.

Review of Legal Education in the United States and Canada for the year 1930, *67 pages.* 1931.
    Bar admission statutes, progressive differentiation of law schools.

Review of Legal Education in the United States and Canada for the year 1931, *51 pages*. 1932.
Co-operation for improvement, the National Conference of Bar Examiners.

Review of Legal Education in the United States and Canada for the year 1932, *67 pages*. 1933.
Educational finance and student selection, major problems of professional education.

Review of Legal Education in the United States and Canada for the year 1933, *67 pages*. 1934.
Learned professions and their organization.

Review of Legal Education in the United States and Canada for the year 1934, *75 pages*. 1935.
The salaried professor in the learned professions.

A Study of the Relations of Secondary and Higher Education in Pennsylvania: Program, *17 pages*. 1928.
Progress Report I, *12 pages*. 1929.
Progress Report II, The College and the Freshman, *48 pages*. 1930.
Progress Report III, Memorandum of Proposals for the Treament of the Secondary Enquiry Group in the Senior High School, 1931-1934, *20 pages*. 1931.
Progress Report IV, Case Studies and Special Curricula Proposed for Secondary Pupils Expecting to Enter College, *34 pages*. 1931.

The Carnegie Foundation for the Advancement of Teaching, *10 pages*. 1937, 1943.
A revision from the Thirty-second Annual Report of the Foundation (1937) setting forth the Foundation's development, activities, and resources.

Life Insurance for College Teachers, by R. L. Mattocks, actuarial consultant, *8 pages*. 1938.
A reprint of an informative discussion in the Thirty-third Annual Report of the Foundation (1938).

The Student and his Knowledge, *71 pages*. 1938.

A reprint summarizing results and conclusions of the study of the relations of secondary and higher education in Pennsylvania, from Bulletin Number Twenty-nine of the Foundation.

What's in a "Mark"? by William S. Learned, staff member, *36 pages*. [1942]. (Reprinted from the Thirty-seventh Annual Report of the Foundation, 1941-42, pages 27-62.)

Control of Tax-supported Higher Education in the United States, by David Spence Hill, staff associate, Carnegie Foundation for the Advancement of Teaching, with a preface by Howard J. Savage, *385 pages*. 1934.

Surveys of American Higher Education, by Walter Crosby Eells, professor of education, Stanford University, with a foreword by Howard J. Savage, *538 pages*. 1937.

In co-operation with the United States Office of Education:

The State and Higher Education—Phases of Their Relationship, by Fred J. Kelly, chief, and John H. McNeeley, research assistant, Division of Colleges and Professional Schools, United States Office of Education, with an introduction by Howard J. Savage, *282 pages*. 1933.

Economy in Higher Education, by David Spence Hill, staff associate, Carnegie Foundation for the Advancement of Teaching, and Fred J. Kelly, chief, Division of Colleges and Professional Schools, United States Office of Education, with a preface by Howard J. Savage, *124 pages*. 1933.

In co-operation with Purdue University:

Charters and Basic Laws of Selected American Universities and Colleges, by Edward C. Elliott, president, Purdue University, and M. M. Chambers, honorary fellow, Ohio State University, *640 pages*. 1934.

The Colleges and the Courts, by Edward C. Elliott, president, Purdue University, and M. M. Chambers, member of staff, American Youth Commission of the American Council on Education, *563 pages*. 1936. (Second edition 1942.)

The Colleges and the Courts 1936-40, by M. M. Chambers, chief, Student Project Planning Section, Division of Student Work, National Youth Administration, with a foreword by Edward C. Elliott, president, Purdue University, *126 pages*. 1941.

The Colleges and the Courts 1941-45, by M. M. Chambers, assistant director, Commission on Implications of the Armed Services Educational Program, American Council on Education, with a foreword by Edward C. Elliott, president-emeritus, Purdue University, *156 pages*. 1946.

Charters of Philanthropies, by Edward C. Elliott, president, Purdue University, and M. M. Chambers, American Youth Commission of the American Council on Education, *744 pages*. 1939.

Charters of Philanthropies, a study of selected trust instruments, charters, bylaws, and court decisions, by M. M. Chambers, director, foreign universities project of the American Council on Education, with a foreword by Edward C. Elliott, president-emeritus, Purdue University, *247 pages*. 1948.

Studies in American Graduate Education, a report to the Carnegie Foundation by Marcia Edwards, with introduction by Walter A. Jessup, president of the Foundation, *71 pages*. 1944.

The Graduate Record Examination:

A Memorandum on the General Character and Purpose of the Examination, *38 pages*. 1941.

An Historical Minute, by Charles R. Langmuir, *5 pages*. [1942]. Reprinted from the Thirty-seventh Annual Report (1941-42) of the Foundation.

A Statement by the University Deans who have co-operated in the Graduate Record Examination 1937-1942, *3 pages*. 1942. Reprinted from the Thirty-eighth Annual Report (1942-43) of the Foundation.

A Descriptive Prospectus [of the Examination] for College Students, *16 pages*. [1942].

Occasional Circular Number 1, a Progress Report on the Sopho-
more-Senior Achievement of 383 Twice-Tested College Students
of Liberal Arts, *8 pages.* 1943.

Occasional Circular Number 2, a Progress Report of the Committee
on Basic Concepts in Biology, *7 pages.* 1943.

Occasional Circular Number 3, Test Scores of Honors Students,
7 pages. 1944.

Occasional Circular Number 4, Interpreting Scores in the Verbal
Factor Test, *12 pages.* 1945.

The Graduate Record Examination and Returning Service Personnel, containing a descriptive prospectus for men and women in the
Armed Services who desire advanced collegiate and graduate study
after the war, *13 pages.* [1944]. Reprinted from the Thirty-ninth
Annual Report (1943-44) of the Foundation.

A General Examination for Advanced College Students—a plan to
make the Graduate Record Examination available to individual
students anywhere within the continental United States or Canada,
6 pages. 1944.

Cases Illustrating [the Use of the Examination] for the Admission
and Adjustment of Returning Service Men and Women, *15 pages.*
1944.

A Descriptive Statement for Men and Women in the Armed Services,
8 pages. [1944].

A Measurement and Guidance Project in Engineering Education,
7 pages. 1944. Reprinted from the Thirty-ninth Annual Report
(1943-44) of the Foundation.

A Descriptive Prospectus for Men and Women in the Armed Services
who Desire Advanced Collegiate and Graduate Study after the
War, *13 pages.* [1944].

Measuring the Outcomes of Higher Education, including a Summary
of the Activities of the Graduate Record Office for 1944-45, *30*

pages. [1945]. Reprinted from the Fortieth Annual Report of the Foundation (1944-45).

The Graduate Record Examination: Cases Illustrating its Use for the Appraisal of Applicants to Medical Schools, *7 pages.* 1945. Prepared for the fifty-sixth annual meeting of the Association of American Medical Colleges.

An Inquiry into Postwar Conditions in American Colleges, *8 pages.* 1946.

Appendix F

Costs of Carnegie Foundation Educational Studies

Note: Each entry below sets forth, at the left, the approximate duration of the study; the field or subject of investigation or experiment; the person in charge or principal participants; the author, title, and date of final or other reports; and the computed costs. In calculating costs a study was regarded as comprising (a) an investigation or experimental program and (b) publication of terminal results. Cost figures are based upon printed documents, published or otherwise, including the Foundation's Twenty-fifth Annual Report (1930). From the figures cents are omitted. Except as indicated, all studies were financed from Foundation income: for those within the dates 1913 and 1931 funds came principally from the Division of Educational Enquiry.

1908-10   The Teaching of Physics. M. L. Cooke, *Academic and Industrial Efficiency*, Bulletin Number 5. (Compensation not included) $ 4,805

1908-12   Medical Education. Abraham Flexner, *Medical Education in the United States and Canada*, Bulletin Number 4, 1910; *Medical Education in Europe*, Bulletin Number 6, 1912   60,457

1912-14   Education in the State of Vermont. E. C. Elliott, M. B. Hillegas, W. S. Learned, and others, *Education in Vermont*, Bulletin Number 7, 1914   16,702

1912-17   Vocational Education and the United States Government. M. Sayre to 1913, I. L. Kandel after 1914. Kandel, *Federal Aid for Vocational Education*, Bulletin Number 10, 1917. (Compensation not included)   4,250

1913-19   Engineering Education. C. R. Mann, *Engineering Education*, Bulletin Number 11, 1918   41,801

1913-35   Legal Education. J. Redlich, *The Common Law and the Case Method*, Bulletin Number 8, 1914; R. H. Smith, *Justice and the Poor*, Bulletin Number 13, 1919. (Study requested and supported by Carnegie Corporation of New York in amount of $3,600.) A. Z. Reed, *Training for the Public Profession of the Law*, Bulletin Number 15, 1921; *Present-Day Law Schools in the United States and Canada*, Bulletin Number 21, 1928; *Annual Review of Legal Education*, 1928-35. (All except Bulletin Number 13 from Carnegie Foundation funds.) $246,450

1913-20   Teacher Training in Missouri and elsewhere. W. S. Learned and others. W. C. Bagley, *Curricula . . . for Preparation of Teachers*, 1917. Learned, Bagley and others, *The Professional Preparation of Teachers for American Public Schools*, Bulletin Number 14, 1920   184,350

1921-31   Dental Education. W. J. Gies, *Dental Education in the United States and Canada*, Bulletin Number 19, 1926 [1927]   64,524

1921-22   Education in the Canadian Maritimes. W. S. Learned and K. C. M. Sills, *Education in the Maritime Provinces of Canada*, Bulletin Number 16, 1922. (Study requested and supported by Carnegie Corporation of New York, which expended directly $3,131 in addition to $12,443 reimbursed to the Foundation.)   15,574

1925-27   British Athletic Inquiry. Howard J. Savage, *Games and Sports in British Schools and Universities*, Bulletin Number 18, 1927   3,900

1926-31   American Athletic Inquiry. Howard J. Savage, Harold W. Bentley, John T. McGovern, and others, *American College Athletics*,

Bulletin Number 23, 1929; W. C. Ryan, Jr., *The Literature of American School and College Athletics*, Bulletin Number 24, 1929 [1930]; Savage and others, *Current Developments in American College Sport*, Bulletin Number 26, 1931 $111,140

1926-27   Comparative Education. W. S. Learned, *The Quality of the Educational Process in the United States and Europe*, Bulletin Number 20, 1927   5,000

1926-40   The Pennsylvania Studies. W. S. Learned, Ben D. Wood, C. R. Langmuir, and others. Learned and Wood, *The Student and his Knowledge*, Bulletin Number 29, 1938, 1939. Learned and Anna L. Rose Hawkes, *An Experiment in Responsible Learning*, Bulletin Number 31, 1940. (Carnegie Corporation support $227,950; Carnegie Foundation support $105,237.)   333,187

1927-44   Graduate Education. Henry Suzzallo, W. A. Jessup, W. C. Ryan, Jr., D. S. Hill, others. Ryan, *Studies in Early Graduate Education*, Bulletin Number 30, 1939; Marcia Edwards, *Studies in American Graduate Education*, 1944. (Supported by Carnegie Corporation of New York.)   53,100

1931-32   Education in Saskatchewan. W. S. Learned and E. W. Wallace, *Local Provision for Higher Education in Saskatchewan*, Bulletin Number 27, 1932. (Carnegie Corporation funds, $1,200; Carnegie Foundation, $250.)   1,450

1931-32   State Higher Education in California. Henry Suzzallo, Commission of Seven, and others. Report published by the State. (Supported jointly by State appropriation for "compensation," $25,000, and Carnegie Corporation grant, $25,000.)   48,100

1933-36   American Examinations. I. L. Kandel, *Exami-*
          nations and their Substitutes in the United
          States, Bulletin Number 28, 1936. (Re-
          quested and supported by Carnegie Corpo-
          ration.) $ 9,500

1937-48   Co-operative Graduate Testing Program and
          related projects in engineering education,
          etc. W. S. Learned and C. R. Langmuir
          until 1946; K. W. Vaughn thereafter.
          (E.C.P.D. contributed $6,000, and exami-
          nation fees partially reimbursed certain
          costs. Carnegie Corporation granted addi-
          tionally $750,000 towards endowment of
          Educational Testing Service, Inc.). Carne-
          gie Corporation support.   774,800

1946-[51] Southern Experimental Co-operative Pro-
          gram of Grants-in-Aid. O. C. Carmichael,
          R. M. Lester, areal and local committees.
          Participating colleges contributing about
          $300,000; Carnegie Corporation granting,
          all told, 1946-51, $980,000.   1,280,000

Index

Academic and Industrial Efficiency, 101, 108, 222, 336

Actuarial Society of America, 118

Ailes, M. E., 8

Alabama, University of, 229, 272

Allegheny College, 18, 21, 55

Allen, Raymond B., 282

American Association of University Professors, 138-140, 210, 232, 257; and life insurance plan, 116-118, 138-140, 256

American College Athletics, 157-158, 343, 355

American Conference of Pharmaceutical Faculties, 164

American Council on Education: Co-operative Test Service of, 136, 286-288, 293, 297, 299, 301; and Foundation, 135, 141, 149, 209, 232, 257, 279-280

American Experience Table, 168, 175

American Field Service Fellowships, 141

American Institute of Actuaries, 118

American Medical Association, *see* Council on Medical Education

American Mortality Tables, 85

American Society of Civil Engineers, 148

American Teacher's Year in a Prussian Gymnasium, An, 94

Analytical Bibliography of Modern Language Teaching, An, 232

Angell, James Burrill, 74, 76

Angell, James Rowland, 75, 131, 155

Aniseikonia as Related to Disability in Reading, 232

Annual Review of Legal Education, 208, 233

Arbuthnot, Dr. Thomas S., 247

Arnett, Trevor, 135

Art a Way of Life, 229

Art, Artist and Layman, 255

Association of American Colleges, 117, 134-135

Association of American Medical Colleges, 294, 295

Association of American Universities, 72, 99, 116-117, 134, 235, 273, 290

Association of College Presidents of Pa., 217

Association of Colleges and Preparatory Schools of the Middle States and Maryland, 141

Association of Colleges and Secondary Schools of Southern States, 141, 156, 279, 281, 292

Association of State Universities, *see* National Association of State Universities

Aydelotte, Frank, 178, 255, 285, 328

Ayres, Leonard, 153-154

Bagley, W. C., 144, 152-154

Balfour, Arthur J., 26

Baltimore and Ohio Relief Association and Pension System, 113

Barnett, George E., 113

Baron de Hirsch Fund, 26

Barrow, David C., 76

Bell, Hill McClelland, 21, 49-50

Bentley, Harold W., 157, 337

Berea College, 18

Bernard, L. L., 230

Bertram, James, 68, 109

Bevan, Dr. Arthur D., 105

Bianchi, John, 276

Binet, Alfred, 284

Bowditch, Henry P., 66

Bowdoin College, 67

Bowman, John Gabbert: as secretary, 31, 73, 91, 95-97, 147, 163, 333, 335; studies by, 99, 104, 112, 204

Brackett, Edgar T., 60

Brigham, Carl C., 286, 288

Brooks, Charles S., 114, 120

Brown, Herbert D., 113

Brown University, 14, 112, 223, 290

Bryan, William Jennings, 76

Bryan, William Lowe, 189

Bryn Mawr College, 17, 86

Buffalo, University of, 216, 285

Buhl Foundation, 29

Burgess, W. Randolph, 8

Burns, Ruth, 338

Burton, Marion LeRoy, 117

Butler, Nicholas Murray, 18, 51-52, 69, 133, 210, 240, 257, 282, 300; member board and executive committee, 11, 14, 21, 44-46, 50, 52, 57, 75, 81-82, 96, 98, 124, 175-176, 181, 184, 197, 210, 327, 329, 331; and Pritchett, 126, 187, 189, 239

Buttrick, Wallace, 133

Cadwalader, John L., 6, 51, 52, 57-62, 65, 67, 115, 200, 342

California Study, 209, 214-217, 355, 359

California, University of, 75, 76, 114, 293

Cannon, Joseph Gurney, 58

Capen, Samuel P., 216, 265, 285

Carmichael, Oliver C.: and board and executive committee, 272-273, 279-281; and Corporation, 272, 276, 279; and finances, 317, 321, 324; as president, v, 31, 271-325, 334; and testing project, 299, 300, 302-304

Carnegie, Andrew, 3-4, 6, 24, 25, 30, 123, 133, 141, 166, 257, 284, 306, 312, 318; and board and executive committee, 12, 18, 45-46, 95, 327, 329, 331, 344; and Corporation, 118, 123, 213; and educational inquiry, 95, 98, 104, 108, 109, 336; endowments of, 4-5, 23-28, 30, 99, 240, 256-257; and Foundation, 4, 6-22, 28, 30, 41-48, 50-123, 124, 168, 172, 181, 189, 305, 307, 308, 310, 335, 344-346, 352, 354; *Gospel of Wealth,* 23-24, 353; and Letter of Gift, 10, 15-17, 18-21, 76; and life insurance, 4, 114-118, 123; and perpetuity, 28-30, 248, 350; and Pritchett, 6-8, 24, 42, 43, 53-55, 64, 68-69, 96, 108-109, 115, 123, 126, 189-190

Carnegie Corporation of N. Y., 27-28, 31, 35-36, 160, 164, 189, 239, 256, 257, 259, 276, 282, 311, 333; and Carnegie centenary, 256-257; celebration of founding of, 24; choice of president by, 265, 269, 270, 271; direct grants of, 114, 205-206, 350; and educational inquiry, 35, 155, 156, 165-166, 207-209, 213, 215, 217, 221-235, 252-255, 259, 271, 273, 274, 276, 279-281, 290, 296, 298, 302, 308, 312, 318, 329, 350, 357, 358, 359; finance committee, finances, and investments of, 132-133, 213, 250-251, 316, 321, 324 (*see also* Co-operative Investment Office); formation of, 95; and Foundation, 32, 34-39, 118, 127, 129-133, 165-166, 176-189, 196, 198, 200, 205, 208, 209, 211-214, 223-235, 238, 247-252, 255-256, 263-266, 268-274, 306-307, 324, 328, 333, 335-338, 349; grants of, to Foundation, for benefits, 33, 119, 130, 172, 180, 184, 198, 202, 213, 309, 310, 313, 319, 320, 352, 354, 359; grants of, to Foundation, for joint projects, 35, 149-150, 155, 156, 165-166, 207-209, 213, 215, 217, 221-235, 253-255, 259, 279-281, 290, 294, 296, 298, 302, 329, 357-359; headquarters of, 125, 274-275; loans of, to Foundation, 180, 246-249, 268, 322, 361; and Suzzallo memorial service, 210; and testing project, 283, 290, 300-302, 357, 359; *see also* Carnegie, Andrew; Carnegie Foundation; *and* TIAA

Carnegie Dunfermline Trust, 25

Carnegie Endowment for International Peace, 28, 132-133, 240, 251, 256, 311

Carnegie Foundation: academic requirements of, 46, 48-50, 52, 61, 64, 66-67, 73-74, 84, 90-92, 100-103; Accepted-Associated-Specified List, 46, 65, 73, 77, 79, 80, 84, 103, 113, 134, 170, 173, 199, 200, 229, 240, 243, 244, 246, 253, 278, 348, 355 (*see also* and pensions); and actuarial studies, *see names of actuaries;* administrative budget of, 195, 198, 242; allowances of, outside Accepted List, 78-82, 84, 170; annual meetings of, 45-47, 123, 124, 179, 188, 195-197, 239-240, 244, 258, 266, 267, 272, 273, 277, 280, 301, 322, 327, 329, 332 (*see also* board of); Annual Reports of (*for complete list of, with descriptions, see* Appendix, 371-381), 19, 29-30, 36, 68, 71-72, 78, 83, 85, 86, 92, 95, 96, 99-102, 111-113, 115, 116, 120, 129, 130, 134, 136, 137, 141, 144, 146, 147, 156, 161, 162-164, 168, 174, 175, 177, 189, 190, 197, 204, 214, 217, 218, 221, 222, 224, 231, 233, 235, 237, 244, 245, 252-253, 256, 260, 267, 271, 276-279, 284, 285, 288, 291, 308, 326, 329, 331, 340, 341, 346, 347, 350-351, 357-359; arranges for exchange of teachers, 93-94; benefits and rules of, 32-33, 73-74, 76-77, 79-82, 86-93, 102, 114, 117, 119, 120, 130, 138-139, 167-169, 171-175, 177-179, 182, 185-188, 197-199, 203, 204, 229, 239-241, 243-246, 258, 267, 278, 306, 310, 320, 342, 345, 347; board and executive committee of (*for complete list of members, see* Appendix, 366-368), 14, 19-22, 45-50, 62-67, 69-70, 78-79, 123-124, 197-200, 202, 204, 206, 207, 240-241, 247, 265-267, 269, 270, 272, 275, 278, 282, 300, 314, 316, 322, 326-334, 345, 346, 348, 349, 360 (*see also* annual meetings of); Bulletins of, *see* publications of; bylaws, charter, and incorporation of (*for complete text of charter, see* Appendix, 362-365), 10-11, 43-46, 51, 56, 204, 241-242, 251, 266, 270, 271, 277, 314, 325, 326, 328, 330, 331, 333, 334, 335, 337, 347 (*see also* Carnegie Foundation for Advancement of Teaching, District of Columbia charter of); and college athletics, 155-160, 205, 207, 208, 213, 222, 240, 245, 254, 348, 355, 359; Committee on the Presidency of, 265-267, 270-271; consultative functions of, 32, 37, 73, 196, 208, 209, 341, 357; criticisms of, 14, 55, 89-93, 100-103, 129, 136-140, 158, 172, 188, 229-230, 330, 342-343, 347, 348; deficiencies of, 346-351; and denominational institutions, 11, 18, 20, 48-50, 54-55, 64, 73, 77-79, 82, 90, 141-142, 344; and educational inquiry, 32, 98, 99, 101, 109-110, 125, 143, 144, 146-155, 160-162, 164-167, 196-198, 208-209, 213-235, 252-255, 271, 273, 276, 279-281, 284, 308, 336, 339, 341, 342-343, 345, 348-349, 351, 354-357, 359 (*see also* publications of, studies of, *and* Division of Educational Enquiry); and examination techniques, 136, 283-304 (*see also* Graduate Record Examination); finance committee, finances, and investments of, 38-39, 63, 65, 67, 132-133, 168, 175, 185, 198, 207, 246-252, 258, 266, 268-270, 275, 277, 305-325, 331, 332, 335 (*see also* Co-operative Investment Office); first announcement and inception of, 4, 6-7, 13, 30; Funds of, *see names of Funds;* headquarters of, 11, 44, 125, 126, 274-275; Letter of Gift for, 10, 15-17, 18-21, 30-31, 71, 76, 109, 284, 306, 325; minutes of, 333; name for, 18, 55-57; as operating organization, 35-36; and pensions (*for* Table of Pensioning Experience, *see* Appendix, 361), 9, 32, 39-40, 42-44, 49, 62, 63, 78, 79, 81, 82, 84-89, 98, 99, 108, 112-113, 137-138, 143-146, 167-188, 196, 199-200, 204-206, 213, 240-241, 243-247, 258, 267, 268, 277-278, 280, 308, 310, 317, 323, 324, 329, 332, 342-348, 351-354, 358, 360 (*see also* special Pension Committee of); personnel of (*for complete list of officers and staff members, see* Appendix, 369-370), 31-32, 95-96, 125-127, 195, 242-243, 273-275, 333-339, 360; and press and public relations, 13-14, 47, 76, 89-90, 94, 96, 154, 157-158, 163, 249-250, 276, 339-342; publications of (*for complete list of Bulletins and supplementary publications, see* Appendix, 381-394), 34-37, 73, 94, 99, 101, 104-113, 116, 130, 136-138, 141, 143-167, 199, 203, 204, 207-210, 214-222, 225, 233-235, 253-254, 267, 276-277, 283-285, 290, 295, 326, 329, 336, 339-343, 354, 355, 357-359 (*see also* Annual Reports of, and educational inquiry, *and* studies by); relations of, with other organizations, 127-142, 257, 357; and Sayre, 127-129; service retirement rule of, 84-89, 92-93; special Pension Committee of, 178-183, 329; and state universities, 18, 20, 54, 61, 64-66, 73-77, 79, 90, 100, 353; studies by (*for costs of, see* Appendix, 395-398), 32-34, 60-61, 71-73, 91, 95-96, 98, 99, 104-113, 133, 136-138, 144-167, 196, 205, 207-209, 213-233, 252-255, 267, 278-281, 335, 336, 341-343, 345, 348-349, 351, 354-357, 359, 360 (*see also* and college athletics, and educational inquiry, and pensions, *and* publications of); taxation exemption for, 10, 249, 323; and World War I, 100, 120; and

World War II, 257-259; *see also* Carnegie, Andrew; Carnegie Corporation; *and* TIAA

Carnegie Foundation for Advancement of Teaching, 19, 57, 59-65, 256; District of Columbia charter for, 19, 59, 60, 72, 115, 249, 308; *see also* Carnegie Foundation

Carnegie Hero Fund Commission, 5, 26, 28, 131, 256

Carnegie Institute, of Pittsburgh, 4, 24, 256

Carnegie Institute of Technology, Pittsburgh, 30, 351

Carnegie Institution of Washington, 5-7, 26, 27, 51, 57, 58, 61, 65, 240, 256, 307, 311, 335; co-operative investing by, 132-133, 251

Carnegie, Margaret, 3

Carnegie Pensions, 139

Carnegie Relief Fund, 30

Carnegie Steel Company, 25

Carnegie, T. Morrison, 21, 22, 31, 46, 47, 55, 64, 65, 124, 307-308, 333, 335

Carnegie United Kingdom Trust, 28

Catholic Education Association, 90

Cattell, James McKeen, 92, 118, 139, 140, 283

Chambers, M. M., 234, 279

Chambliss, Miss Willie H., 333, 338

Chapman, Charles S., 326

Charters and Basic Laws of Selected American Universities and Colleges, 234

Charters of Philanthropies, 234

Chase, George H., 287

Chicago, University of, 14, 21, 45, 75, 82, 147, 153, 216, 223, 230, 285, 298

Church Pension Fund, 114, 128, 205-206

Citadel, The, 18

City That Art Built, A, 229

Clark University, 223

Claxton, P. P., 73

Coffman, Lotus D., 216, 228, 238

Cogswell, Edmund S., 145

Coleman, Algernon, 232

College Art Association, 164

College Entrance Examination Board, 91, 102, 135-136, 254, 285, 286, 300; and testing project, 136, 287-288, 294, 299, 301

College of William and Mary, 17

Colleges and the Courts, The, 234, 279

Collins, Judge William T., 33, 249

Colorado College, 18

Colorado Education Association, 145

Columbia University, 14, 17, 21, 92, 93, 99, 110, 147, 149, 156, 157, 184, 217, 232, 282, 285, 287; graduate education at, 223; and testing project, 285, 288, 290, 298

Colwell, Dr. N. P., 105, 136

Committee on Standards of the American Council, *see* National Conference Committee

Common Law and the Case Method in American Law Schools, 34, 111, 149

Comprehensive Plan of Insurance and Annuities for College Teachers, A, 112, 116

Compton, Arthur H., 282

Conant, James B., 257, 300

Conference of Bar Association Delegates, 151

Contingency Fund, *see* Reserve Fund No. 2

Control of Tax-Supported Higher Education in the United States, 234

Cook, W. W., 92, 118, 138, 140

Cooke, M. Llewellyn, 34, 96, 101, 108, 222, 335-337

Cooper, Frank R., 335

Co-operative Graduate Testing Program, *see* Graduate Record Examination

Co-operative Investment Office, 133, 251, 258, 268, 275, 314, 315, 324

Cornell University, 14, 17, 21, 30, 47, 49, 66, 85, 91, 157, 232, 247

Corson, Hiram, 66

Council on Engineering Education, 147-148

Council on Medical Education, 105-106, 136, 257

Cox, Robert L., 60

Crabtree, J. W., 137

Craighead, Edwin B., 21

Crawford, William Henry, 18, 21, 46, 55, 124

Croswell, James G., 94

Culberson, Charles A., 59

Current Developments in American College Sport, 159

Cyclopedia of Education, 111

Davidson, Carter, 282

Dean, Arthur S., 282

Dearborn, Walter F., 153, 232, 284

Democracy Enters College, 102

Dental Faculties Association of American Universities, 160

Depression, Recovery and Higher Education, 232

Denny, George H., v, 21, 47, 109, 282

Dental Education in the United States and Canada, 34

Derby, Albert L., 31, 62, 65, 73, 335

Devine, Peter C., v

Dewey, John, 116

Dewey, Melvil, 52

Dillingham, William P., 58-59

Dinwiddie, Albert Bledsoe, 238

Division of Educational Enquiry: endowment of, 34, 37-38, 109-110, 148, 149, 250, 252, 275, 308, 309, 312, 313, 316, 318-319, 321, 322, 324, 336; work of,

35, 125, 146-150, 165, 198, 202, 203, 207, 208, 213, 252, 279, 290, 336, 348; *see also* Carnegie Foundation, and educational inquiry

Downs, Mildred, 338

Drinker, Henry S., 76

Driscoll, Alfred E., 165

Duffus, R. L., 102

Duggan, Stephen, 259

Duryea, H. C., 296, 335

Economy in Higher Education, 234

Education in the Maritime Provinces of Canada, 36, 155

Education in Vermont, 35, 326

Educational Finance Inquiry Commission, 163, 171

Educational Records Bureau, 298-300

Educational Testing Service, Inc., 136, 215, 220, 232, 273, 301-304, 357

Edwards, Marcia, 222, 235, 290

Eells, Walter C., 235, 343

Effective and Ineffective College Teacher, The, 232

Eisenhart, L. P., 287

Eisenhower, Dwight D., 282

Eliot, Charles W., 12, 14, 21, 22, 45-48, 51, 57, 62, 69, 75, 80, 81, 98, 105, 115, 240, 327, 328, 331, 346; and Carnegie, 18, 95, 329

Elliott, Edward C.: studies by, 110, 234, 284, 355; trustee, 165, 260, 265-267, 271

Emergency Reserve Fund, 37, 39, 119, 202-204, 207, 275, 309, 313, 315, 318, 320-322

Engineering Education, 34

Engineers' Council for Professional Development, 149, 292-293

English and Everyday Life, 232

Enrichment of the Common Life, 229

European Examinations Inquiry, 225-226, 253, 290

Examinations and Their Substitutes in the United States, 34, 225, 253, 283

Experiment in Responsible Learning, 220

Fackenthal, F. D., 156

Falconer, Sir Robert, 178

Fansler, Thomas, 216

Farrand, Dr. Livingston, 210, 238, 247, 265

Farrand, Wilson, 102, 285

Farrington, Edward H., 110

Faunce, William H. P., 14

Federal Aid for Vocational Education, 35, 111-112, 141

Fellows, George N., 74, 75

Ferry, Frederick C., 102, 124, 178, 197, 240

Field Foundation, 29

Fife, Robert H., 232

Financial Status of the Professor in America and in Germany, The, 104

Fine, Henry B., 87, 88

Fisk University, 229
Flexner, Abraham, 109, 133, 141, 148-149, 222, 280; medical studies by, 34, 96, 101, 104-108, 136, 150, 158, 162, 335-337, 343, 355, 359
Flexner, Dr. Simon, 105
Flint, Charles Wesley, 120
Ford Foundation, 29
Forty Years of Carnegie Giving, 28
Fox, Dixon Ryan, 282
Franks, Robert A., 10, 12, 18, 119, 238, 256, 335; on board and executive committee, 11, 21, 44-46, 57, 67, 197, 333; on finance committee and as treasurer, 31, 65, 124, 198, 239, 251, 308, 313, 314, 335
Fred, Edwin B., 282
Freeman, Joseph E., 10, 42
Frew, W. N., 7
Furniss, Edgar S., 287
Furst, Clyde: and Annual Reports, 168, 175, 285; death of, 194, 196; pension studies by, 99, 100, 112, 113, 116, 137-138, 144, 145, 199; relations of, with other organizations, 102, 120, 129-142; and Sayre, 128-129; as secretary, 31, 91, 96, 117, 118, 125-127, 130, 144, 148, 149, 154, 156, 157, 162, 164, 170, 171, 176-178, 180, 181, 184, 186-189, 193-196, 201, 203, 242, 247, 285, 311, 326, 335-338, 340

Games and Sports in British Schools and Universities, 157, 355
Gary, Elbert H., 311
Gates, Frederick T., 133
Galton, Sir Francis, 283
Gee, Wilson, 230-231, 280
General Education Board, 26, 133, 135, 148, 227, 285, 336
General Education in Action, 280
General Endowment Fund, 33, 34, 37-38, 202, 248, 250, 251, 268-270, 275, 309, 311-316, 318-324, 361
Gennadius, Johannes, 132
George Peabody College for Teachers, 5, 153, 229
Gies, William J., 34, 144, 160-161, 343
Gilbert, Walter M., 31, 65, 189
Gildersleeve, H. A., 11, 44
Gilman, Daniel Coit, 5-6, 27, 223
Gladstone, W. E., 23, 24
Glover, James W., 201, 205, 256
Goddard, H. H., 283
Gospel of Wealth, 23-24, 353
Government of Higher Education, The, 165
Graduate Record Examination, 215, 222, 235, 253, 259, 260, 267, 273, 286-304, 354, 356-357, 359
Gregory, G. E., 8, 11, 42
Griswold, Alfred W., 282
Guggenheim, John Simon, 29
Gustavson, Reuben G., 282

Hadley, Arthur T., 14, 18, 21, 45, 48-51, 54, 69, 93, 115, 117
Haggerty, M. E., 228, 229
Hall, Arnold Bennett, 210
Hall, Samuel S., Jr., 132-133, 198, 238, 247, 250, 311-316, 335
Hall, Samuel S., Sr., 83-85, 114, 115, 120, 168, 308
Hamilton College, 73, 178, 197, 290
Handbook for American Students in France, 208
Harper, William R., 14, 21, 45, 46, 50, 223
Harrington, Thomas H., 147
Harris, A. W., 82
Harris, M. Anstice, 82
Harris, Rufus C., 282
Harris, William T., 8-9, 65, 66
Harrison, Charles C., 14, 21, 45, 46, 80, 81
Hart, John G., 92
Harvard University, 14, 17, 18, 21, 22, 48, 51, 66, 73, 92, 99, 103, 110, 153, 176, 232, 257, 284, 287, 300; GRE at, 288, 290; graduate education at, 223; grant to, 232
Haverford College, 113
Hawkes, Anna Rose, 220
Hawkes, Herbert E., 232
Hayden, Charles, 29
Heller, Otto, 92, 138
Hendrick, B. J., 24, 25, 82-83; *Life of Andrew Carnegie,* 25
Henry S. Pritchett, 105
Herter, Albert, 126
Hibben, John G., 124
Higginson, Henry L., 6, 335
Hill, David Spence, 165, 216, 234, 337
Hillegas, Milo B., 110, 355
Hoffman, Frederick L., 176, 177
Home Trust Co., 10, 12, 21, 65
Hughes, Edwin H., 21, 49-50
Humphreys, Alexander C., 11, 18, 21, 44-47, 50, 98, 148, 328, 333
Humphreys, Walter, 8, 11
Hunter, Arthur, 118

I Remember, 105
Inquiries into Human Faculty, 283
Institute of Governmental Research, 210
Institute of International Education, 208, 234, 259
International Business Machines Corp., v, 297-298
International Institute, Teachers College, 36, 141, 225
Iowa, State University of, 31, 96, 136, 211, 236, 290

James, Henry, 76, 247, 256, 257
Jastrow, Joseph: criticism by, 55, 92, 93, 118, 139, 140, 188; and liberalization of rules, 82, 113; and life insurance

Jastrow, Joseph (Cont.)
plan, 138, 139; and state universities, 75, 76
Jessup, Walter A.: and annual meetings, board, and executive committee, 239-241, 273, 281, 327, 329, 330; and Corporation, 237, 255-256, 263-265, 271; death of, 235, 238, 259-260, 264, 265, 275; and educational inquiry, 222, 223, 235, 240, 254, 255; as president, 31, 134, 136, 197, 206, 211, 227, 235, 236-260, 263-268, 271, 316, 331, 334; and Pritchett, 189, 240, 284; and Suzzallo, 211, 236-237, 240; and testing project, 287, 291, 293, 296, 297
John Edgar Thompson Foundation, 26
Johns Hopkins University, The, 5-6, 14, 17, 92, 105, 113, 140, 223
Johnson, B. Lamar, 280
Joint Committee on Engineering Education, 147, 149
Jordan, David Starr, 18, 21, 47, 55, 69, 73, 82, 93, 117
Josephs, Devereux C.: as Corporation president, 256, 269, 271, 282, 300, 301; as investment officer and treasurer, 238, 251, 266, 268, 269, 319, 335; as TIAA president, 256, 271
Josselyn, Homer, 152, 153
Journal of Education, 137
Judd, Charles H., 153, 216
Judson, Harry Pratt, 82
Justice and the Poor, 34-35, 149, 150

Kandel, I. L.: as staff member, 31, 127, 141, 144, 148, 149, 163, 242, 336; studies by, 34, 35, 111-113, 116, 137-138, 141, 144, 154, 163, 204, 218, 225, 226, 253, 254, 283, 290
Karpinski, Louis Charles, 120
Kelley, Truman L., 285
Kelly, Fred J., 234, 284
Kendrick, B. B., 230-231
Keniston, R. Hayward, 232
Keppel, Frederick P., 42, 134; as Corporation president, 132, 140, 156, 162, 165, 166, 201, 207, 210, 246, 247, 287, 296; and educational inquiry, 165, 213, 215, 218, 222, 223, 225, 228, 230, 255; and Foundation finances, 176-189, 202, 247, 313; retirement of, 255, 263; and Suzzallo, 165, 166, 210
King, Henry C., 18, 21, 45, 49-50, 117
Kirkland, James H., 103, 156, 272, 328
Knox College, 21, 101
Krey, August C., 229

Lamont, Thomas S., 282, 314
Lamont, Thomas W., 124, 189, 190, 265, 282, 314, 316, 332
Langmuir, Charles R., 288, 291, 297, 302
Latham, O. R., 216
Lawrence, Bishop William, 128
Lawrence University, 14, 21, 49

Learned, William S.: and Annual Reports, 163, 217, 221, 288; Co-operative Graduate Testing enterprise of, 220, 222, 223, 235, 253, 259, 267, 286-288, 290, 291, 293, 295-297, 299, 300, 303; as staff member, 31, 94, 109, 126, 127, 135-136, 141, 144, 160, 162, 193, 194, 199, 211, 227, 238, 242, 257, 264, 274, 300, 335, 348; studies by, 35-36, 94, 101, 104, 110, 127, 136-137, 152-155, 161-162, 196, 207-209, 217-222, 225, 253, 254, 284, 285, 298, 336, 339, 355, 356
Lee, C. Herbert, vi, 31, 274
Leffingwell, R. C., 132
Leland Stanford Jr. University, 17, 21, 73, 93
Leslie, William, 110
Lester, Robert M., 28, 30, 31, 274, 280
Life of Andrew Carnegie, 25
Lindley, Ernest H., 238
Literature of American School and College Athletics, 34, 159-160
Lloyd, R. McAllister, 256
Local Provision for Higher Education in Saskatchewan, 208-209
London *Times,* 96
Lovejoy, A. O., 92, 118, 138, 139
Lovett, R. A., 258, 267, 275, 314, 317
Lowell, A. Lawrence, 82, 110
Lowry, Howard F., 282

McCleary, James T., 58, 59
McClelland, Thomas, 21, 49-50, 76
McClintock Tables, 84, 85, 115, 116, 118, 174, 175
McCormick, Samuel B., 14, 21, 117, 139
McGovern, John T., 157, 337
Mackenzie Committee, 176-179, 246-247
Mackenzie, Michael A., 176, 177, 180, 182-185, 187
McMurry, Charles A., 153
McNeely, John H., 234
Maddox, Dorothy A., vi
Major, Gov. Elliott W., 152
Mann, Charles R., 34, 144, 147-149, 217, 285
March, Francis A., 66
Maslen, Edythe W., v, 244-245, 278, 338
Massachusetts Institute of Technology, 6, 14, 17, 21, 60, 245, 285, 309, 338
Mattocks, R. L., 31-32, 145, 168, 169, 174, 175, 177, 178, 180, 184, 185, 187, 199-200, 203, 204, 206, 243-248, 251, 268, 269, 278, 320
Maurice and Laura Falk Foundation, 29
Medical Education in Europe, 107
Medical Education in the United States and Canada, 105
Mental and Social Measurements, 284
Meredith, A. B., 216
Merrymount Press, 210, 276-277
Michigan, University of, 74, 76, 77, 120, 201, 223, 290

Miller, Ward, 335
Millis, John S., 282
Minnesota State Board of Education, 229
Minnesota, University of, 77, 216, 222, 228, 229, 232, 235, 290
Missouri, University of, 42, 279, 284
Monroe, Parker, 269, 335
Monroe, Paul, 36, 111, 225
Montana, University of, 73
Mora, Louis, 257
Morgan, J. Pierpont, 5, 25
Morgan, J. P., & Co., Incorporated, 275, 324-325
Munro, William B., 232

Nation, The (London), 96
National Association of State Universities, 65-66, 74-77, 116, 117, 136, 141, 209, 254, 257
National Collegiate Athletic Association, 156, 158
National Conference Committee on Standards of Colleges and Secondary Schools, 91, 102, 135
National Conference on Uniform Entrance Requirements, 285
National Education Association, 102, 112, 136-138, 166, 209-210, 233, 257, 259
Neilson, William A., 124, 240, 247
New England Association of Colleges and Secondary (Preparatory) Schools, 99, 141
Newlands, Frank G., 59
New York Public Library, 206, 257, 285
New York Times, 4, 13, 14, 163
New York *Tribune*, 5, 13
New York University, 216, 232
New York, University of the State of, 166
Nicolson, Frank W., 156
Noffsinger, J. S., 156, 157, 337
Norton, John K., 138

Oberlin College, 17, 21
Odum, H. W., 230-231
Ogburn, W. F., 230-231
Olshausen, G. R., 110
Omaha *Herald*, 76
O'Rourke, L. J., 232
Owatonna, the Social Development of a Minnesota Community, 229

Parkin, George R., 96
Peck, Judge David W., 270
Pegram, George B., 287, 291
Peik, W. E., 229
Penniman, Josiah H., 178, 181, 182, 189, 197, 238, 240, 242
Pennsylvania Study, 207-209, 214, 217-221, 223, 227, 228, 253, 254, 260, 284, 286, 288, 290, 296, 298, 302, 348, 356-357
Pennsylvania, University of, 14, 21, 81, 140, 178

Pensions for Public School Teachers, 112, 137, 144
Peterson, Sir William, 21, 43, 45, 49-50, 54, 81, 82, 124, 328
Philbin, Beekman and Menken, 10, 44
Pittsburgh, 247
Plan for the Exchange of Teachers with Prussia, 233
Plantz, Samuel, 14, 21, 49, 328
Plumley, Gardner Ladd, 83-84
Pope, Arthur, 255
Potter, N. B., 110
Present Day Law Schools in the United States and Canada, 151
Princeton University, 14, 17, 22, 86, 87, 223, 287, 288, 290
Pritchett, Mrs. Eva McAllister, v, 329
Pritchett, Henry S.: and academic requirements, 91-92, 100-103; as acting president, 210-211; and actuaries, 83-85, 113-114; and annual meetings, executive committee, and board, 48-51, 67, 123-124, 196-197, 327-331, 342, 346; and Annual Reports, 72, 95, 100, 101, 111, 115, 116, 130, 134, 136, 137, 156, 163, 164, 175, 189, 190, 222, 284, 350-351; articles by, 69-70, 74, 101, 113; and Carnegie, 6-9, 18, 24, 29-30, 42, 43, 52-55, 64, 68-69, 96, 99, 108-109, 115, 123, 124, 126, 189-190, 306, 327, 344-345; comments on, 47, 189-190; and Corporation, 95, 114, 118, 125, 131-133, 160, 189, 210, 238, 246; criticism of, 93, 100-103, 136-140, 172; and educational inquiry, 42, 53-54, 61, 72, 83, 91, 98-100, 104, 106-107, 109, 143, 144, 146-155, 160-162, 164-166, 209, 215, 222, 274, 284-286, 336, 339, 345, 355-356, 358; and finances, 50, 132-133, 181-183, 307-309, 311-314, 316, 322-323; and Foundation, 6-14, 17-18, 21, 30, 31, 41-48, 50-70, 72-190, 212-213, 242, 328, 329, 333-335, 338, 339, 350-351, 360; illness and death of, 89, 96, 126-127, 238, 239; introductions to Bulletins by, 107, 108, 111, 112, 144-145, 149, 151, 158, 233, 284, 285; and pensions, 62, 112, 113, 116, 117, 143-146, 169, 170-173, 175, 176, 178-179, 184-185, 196, 200, 204-206; as president emeritus, 188-189, 194, 199, 237, 265, 332; and press, 96, 339-341; relations of, with other organizations, 102, 127, 129-142; resignation of, 145, 188-189; and Sayre, 128-129; and Suzzallo, 166, 193-194, 199, 200, 205, 208; and TIAA, 119, 120, 189, 201, 203, 256; and Wilson, 75, 87-89
Professional Preparation of Teachers for American Public Schools, The, 136, 152, 154
Progressive Education Association, 226-228

Psychological Corporation, 232
Purdue University, 37, 165, 234

Quality of the Educational Process in the United States and in Europe, The, 161, 217

Rabitte, Margaret, 338
Ramsay, Sir William, 7
Rappard, Wilhelm, 222
Rebuilding the English-Usage Curriculum to Insure Greater Mastery of Essentials, 232
Redlich, Josef, 34, 111, 149, 222
Reed, Alfred Z.: retirement of, 242, 264, 274; as staff member, 31, 109, 125, 127, 135, 141, 144, 162-164, 166, 193, 194, 211, 238, 253, 287, 336, 348; studies by, 35, 111, 150-152, 163, 196, 208, 233, 253
Reed, Anna Y., 232
Remsen, Ira L., 14
Report of the Committee on College and University Teaching, 232
Research Barriers in the South, 230-231, 280
Reserve Fund, *see* Emergency Reserve Fund
Reserve Fund No. 1, 37-38, 119, 175, 180, 202, 247, 248, 250, 252, 268, 309, 312, 313, 315-320, 361
Reserve Fund No. 2, 37-39, 130, 171, 202, 206, 242, 251, 275, 309, 313, 318, 320-322
Retirement Plan for Colorado Public Schools, A, 145
Retiring Allowances for Officers and Teachers in Virginia Public Schools, 145
Rhees, Rush, 178
Rice, J. M., 283
Richards, Robert Hallowell, 245
Richtmyer, F. K., 232
Robbins, R. B., 205, 280
Rochester, University of, 178, 282, 290
Rockefeller Foundation, 29, 105, 108, 133, 137, 222, 359
Rockefeller, John D., Jr., 95
Rockefeller, John D., Sr., 26, 223
Rolph, Gov. James, Jr., 215
Roosevelt, Theodore, 5, 6, 59
Root, Elihu, Jr., 117, 248, 249; law firm of, 117, 120, 248, 343
Root, Elihu, Sr.: and Carnegie, 26-28, 118; and Corporation, 131, 133, 177-178; foreword by, 150; and Foundation, 58, 59, 61, 181
Russell, James E., 216
Russell, William F., 210
Ryan, W. Carson, Jr., 34, 137, 144, 154, 157, 159, 222-223, 235, 238, 253, 290, 337

Sachs, Julius, 93
Saunders, William, 338

Savage, E. Graham, 161
Savage, Howard J.: and Annual Reports, 163, 244, 278; begins study of Foundation, 274; college athletic studies by, 127, 135, 156-159, 162, 205; pension studies by, 144, 145, 163, 199, 200, 204, 205, 243-245, 267, 278; as secretary, staff member, and treasurer, 31, 144, 162, 165, 193-196, 203, 205, 211, 215, 222, 238, 241-243, 251, 264, 266, 269, 287, 297, 335-337
Sayre, Monell: pension and other studies by, 83, 85, 99, 104, 111-113, 144, 204; relations of, with Foundation, 127-129; resignation of, 111; as staff member, 31, 95, 109-110, 336
Scherer, Paul A., 31
School and Society, 139
Schurman, Jacob Gould, 14, 21, 45, 47, 49, 52, 54, 69, 82, 91, 118, 124
Scotland, Carnegie Fund for the Universities of, 5, 25, 26
Seager, Henry R., 184
Seelye, L. Clark, 14, 21
Sills, K. C. M., 155, 265
Simplified Spelling Board, 141
Slater Fund, 26
Sledd, William A., 103
Slocum, William F., 328, 329
Smiley, Dr. Dean F., 157
Smith College, 14, 21, 247
Smith, Edgar Fahs, 124, 140
Smith, Reginald Heber, 34, 144, 149, 150
Snyder, Franklyn B., 265
Social Philosophy of Pensions, The, 145-146
Social Science Research Council, 230-231, 280
Society for the Promotion of Engineering Education, 148, 149, 292-293
Some Misapprehensions Touching Life Insurance, 130
South Carolina, University of, 103
South Dakota, University of, 293
Spanish Syntax List, 232
Spear, Anita W., 338
Spectator, The (London), 96
Standard Forms for Financial Reports, 340
Starch, Daniel, 284
State and Higher Education, Phases of Their Relationship, The, 234
Stead, W. T., 23
Stearns, L. E., 110
Stevens Institute, 17, 21, 67, 99, 148
Stone, Harlan F., 138, 139
Strayer, George D., 153
Student and His College, The, 218
Student and His Knowledge, The, 218-220
Studies in American Graduate Education, 235
Studies in Early Graduate Education, 223

Study of Engineering Education, A, 149

Surveys of American Higher Education, 235

Suzzallo, Henry: and annual meetings, board, and executive committee, 195-200, 202, 206, 278, 327, 330-332; and Corporation, 194, 196, 207, 210; death of, 197, 210, 265; and educational inquiry, 196, 197, 207, 212-213, 215, 217, 225-227, 230, 233-235; and finances, 195, 198, 206, 207, 312-314; and Jessup, 211, 236-237; and pensions, 196, 199-200, 205, 206; as president, 31, 137, 166, 188-189, 193-210, 212, 213, 226, 230, 233, 234, 236-237, 238, 247, 326, 334, 337, 339; and Pritchett, 193-194, 199, 200, 205, 208; relations of, with other organizations, 209-210, 257; studies by, 144, 165, 193, 209, 214-216, 222, 223, 337, 355; and TIAA, 196, 201, 203

Swain, Joseph, 137-138

Swarthmore College, 137, 157, 178, 285

Taylor, Charles R., 131

Teachers College, Columbia University, 93-94, 96, 99, 100, 110, 111, 127, 153, 160, 193, 210, 216, 225, 253

Teachers Insurance and Annuity Association of America, 9-10, 31-33, 38, 112, 123, 138-140, 145, 146, 162, 170-171, 173, 174, 182, 184-186, 189, 239, 243, 247, 251, 256, 257, 271, 280, 309-311, 313, 320, 347; autonomy of, 256; co-operative investing by, 132-133, 251; and Corporation, 32, 119, 129-130, 185-186, 198, 201-203, 243, 246, 256, 354, 359; establishment of, 115-120; and Foundation, 114-120, 125, 127, 129-132, 196, 198, 201-202, 204, 205, 242-243, 335, 349, 353-354; Handbook of, 120; headquarters of, 125; takes over pension studies, 205

Terman, Lewis M., 284

Thomas, Calvin, 93

Thomas, Charles R., 58

Thompson Fund, 26

Thorndike, Edward L., 100, 149, 283-285

Thurstone, L. L., 298

Thwing, Charles F., 18, 22, 45, 46, 62, 64, 117, 328

Toronto, University of, 77, 176, 178

Training for the Public Profession of the Law, 151

Tulane University, 17, 21, 66, 229, 282

U.S. Bureau of Education (Office of Education), 37, 73, 99, 137, 233, 234, 259

U.S. Steel Corporation, 25, 58, 95, 168, 185, 246, 307, 309-311

Updike, D. B., 276-277

Utah, University of, 293

Valentine, Alan, 282

Vanderbilt University, 31, 103, 156, 171, 229, 271, 272, 321

Vanderlip, Frank A.: and Carnegie, 8-9, 11-12, 18; death of, 238, 239, 251, 317; on finance committee and as treasurer, 31, 65, 198, 250, 307, 313, 314, 316, 335; and Foundation, 8-14, 18, 22, 31, 41-47, 50, 53-54, 61, 67, 72, 83, 89, 91, 96, 100, 109, 197, 326; survey of education by, 42, 53-54, 61, 72, 83, 91, 98-100

Van Hise, Charles R., 74, 75, 82, 117

Vaughn, K. W., 293, 294, 298, 300, 302

Vinson, Robert E., 124, 178, 328

Virginia State Board of Education, 145

Virginia, University of, 229, 230

Wainwright, J. M., 60

Wallace, E. W., 208

Washington, University of, State, 31, 165, 193, 236, 282, 293

Washington University (St. Louis), 66, 92, 138, 140, 230, 282

Washington and Lee University, 17, 21, 229

Watson, Thomas J., 297-298

Webb, Paul E., 216, 337

Welch, Dr. William H., 105

Wesley, Edgar Bruce, 229

West, C. J., 113

Western Reserve University, 17, 22, 178, 282

Western University of Pa., 14, 18, 21

What Is Religion?, 6

Wheeler, Benjamin Ide, 75, 76

White, H. C., 54, 74, 75

Wigmore, John H., 116, 138

Wiley, Francis J., 97

Willcox, W. F., 85, 113, 115

Willey, M. M., 232

Williams College, 17, 102

Williams, George L., 335

Williams, John Sharp, 59

Wilson, E. B., 176, 177, 309

Wilson, Woodrow, trustee, member executive committee, 14, 18, 22, 45-47, 69, 75, 82; and service retirement rule, 85-89

Wisconsin Free Library, 110

Wisconsin, University of, 55, 74, 75, 77, 82, 92, 110, 140, 188, 282, 290

Wood, Ben D., v; studies by, 217-219, 227, 286, 298, 356; and testing project, 286-288, 296, 299, 303

Wriston, Henry M., 242, 314, 359-360

Wyoming, University of, 293

Yale University, 14, 18, 21, 48, 51, 92, 131, 281, 282, 287; graduate education at, 223; GRE at, 288, 290

Zook, George F., 216, 287

The text of this book is set in Linotype Scotch, a style of type which came into use after 1833, when fonts were cast at the foundry of Alex. Wilson & Son at Glasgow. The book was composed, printed and bound by Quinn & Boden Company, Inc., Rahway, New Jersey.